Andrew Fletcher
and
The Treaty of Union

For Laura

Other Books by P. H. Scott
1707: The Union of Scotland and England (1979)
Walter Scott and Scotland (1981)
John Galt (1985)
In Bed with an Elephant (1985)
The Thinking Nation (1989)
Cultural Independence (1989)
Towards Independence: Essays on Scotland (1991)

Edited
(With A. C. Davis) *The Age of MacDiarmid* (1980)
Sir Walter Scott's The Letters of Malachi Malagrowther (1981)
Andrew Fletcher's United and Separate Parliaments (1982)
(With George Bruce) *A Scottish Postbag* (1986)

Contributions to joint volumes in
(Ed. J. H. Alexander and David Hewitt) *Scott and his Influence* (1983)
(Ed. M. Anderson and L. Dominguez) *Cultural Policy in Europe* (1984)
(Ed. Douglas Gifford) *The History of Scottish Literature*, Vol. 3 (1988)
(Ed. Angus Calder) *Byron and Scotland* (1989)
(Ed. C. J. M. MacLachlan and D. S. Robb) *Edwin Muir: Centenary Assessments* (1990)

Andrew Fletcher
and
The Treaty of Union

PAUL H. SCOTT

JOHN DONALD PUBLISHERS LTD
EDINBURGH

© Paul H. Scott 1992

The publisher acknowledges subsidy from
the Scottish Arts Council towards the
publication of this volume.

ISBN 0 85976 363 3

British Library Cataloguing in Publication Data

A catalogue record for this
book is available from the
British Library

Phototypeset by The Midlands Book Typesetting Co., Loughborough
Printed and bound in Great Britain by Hartnolls Ltd, Bodmin, Cornwall

Introduction

The origin of this book lies in a request from John Hulbert of the Andrew Fletcher Society that I should write a biography of the man after whom the society is named. He added, and he was entirely right, that he thought that it would be necessary to give a sufficient account of the historical background to make the events of Fletcher's life intelligible. This was a task which I undertook with enthusiasm because I have been interested in Fletcher ever since I first read W. C. Mackenzie's biography while I was still at school. That was published in 1935 and, as many people have remarked, there has long been a need for a new book on the subject. Some new sources have come to light and Fletcher's own writing has been reinterpreted since Mackenzie's time.

When I began what I originally thought would be a fairly short book, I soon realised that I would have to undertake an account of part of the history in much more detail than I had expected. For the 17th Century background, a fairly brief and general account would be sufficient to show where Fletcher stood in the Scotland of his day. The Parliamentary sessions of 1703, 1704, 1705 and 1706–7, however, required as particular an account as the surviving evidence permits.

There are several reasons for this. It is the most important part of Fletcher's life, the part on which his reputation as the Patriot depends. He was a key figure as a member of the Scottish Parliament in these tense and crucial debates, in which he consistantly sought to preserve the Parliament and to transfer real power to it from the Monarchy and English ministers. Because in these years he was such a prominent and public figure, it is also the period for which most evidence has survived.

There is a further reason. These debates, which led to the Union of 1707, determined the course of the next 300 years of Scottish history. They are full of passion, drama and intellectual interest. Many of the issues discussed still perplex us and have not yet been solved. Fletcher and many of the other men involved were articulate and intelligent. It is possible to piece together a fairly complete picture of the course of events from their letters, memoirs and official records. Yet, in spite of all of this, these events with such far reaching and continuing consequences are obscure and are generally misunderstood and misrepresented.

When he gave the Ford Lectures in Oxford in 1914 the historian, Hume Brown, addressed himself to this question. 'How are we to explain', he asks, 'this ignorance on the part of Scotsmen generally of one of the most fateful periods in their national history?' As a tentative explanation he suggests that it might be that there was no writer at the time with 'the devouring eyes and the portraying hand' to write an account that 'would permanently stamp its characters and its events on the mind of posterity'. He then largely undermines this explanation be/ referring to Lockhart of Carnwath, whom he describes as 'both a keen observer and a caustic writer.'[1] I should have thought that Lockhart's *Memoirs* was precisely a book with the capacity to imprint the events on the memory. Lord Byron knew about the book. When he was in Pisa in 1822 looking for a country to liberate, and before he decided on Greece, he wrote to John Murray to ask for a copy.[2] I do not know if it reached him. If it had, he might have decided on Scotland instead of Greece and our history might have taken a different course.

Hume Brown then offers an alternative explanation. 'It is a period when human nature does not appear at its best.' He meant that many members of the Scottish Parliament, after years of resistance, eventually sucumbed to intimidation and bribery. 'A people does not gladly turn its eyes to a period when its representative men, whether from their own natural failings or as the result of temporary circumstances, compromise the national character in the eyes of the world. So it is, perhaps, that by a kind of unconscious instinct Scotsmen have averted their gaze from a reign so mementous in their country's destinies, and abounding, moreover, in men of striking gifts and individuality.'[3] Whether or not an unconscious instinct was at work, there can be little doubt that historians added to the mystification by deliberately playing down, ignoring or suppressing the evidence. From about the middle of the 18th Century, after the bloody suppression of the '45, Scots realised that they had no choice but to accept the Union and that they had better make the best of it. It was less wounding to national self-esteem to try to believe that the Union was a wise act of statesmanship than to look the sordid facts in the face. This, by and large, is what the historians did. Almost the only honest account of the transaction of the Union is the whole of the 19th Century in a Chapter LX of Sir Walter Scott's *Tales of a Grandfather*, where he speaks with passion and in some detail of the 'total surrender of their independence, by their false and corrupted statesmen . . . . . . despised by the English and detested by their own country.'[4]

Hume Brown himself must have been aware of the facts, because he was clearly familiar with the sources and indeed edited one of them, the Letters of Seafield. He does his best to tone down the harsh realities. For example, as an appendix to the book from which I have been quoting, he prints a letter from the Earl of Glasgow of 22 November 1711. This confirms that he was involved in the secret disbursement of £20,000 which, if it had been discovered at the time, 'the Union had certainly broken'. This is damning enough, but Hume Brown, without any indication that anything has been left out, omits the phrase 'our mob and generality of Scotland being so incensed against the Union'.[5]

This is, of course, no longer such a painful subject as it once was. With the dissolution or drastic modification of the Union now very much on the political agenda, there is no longer the same compulsion to join the conspiracy to pretend that it was an admirable and enlightened transaction. Scottish historians such as William Ferguson and Bruce Lenman have done admirable work. Even a distinguished English historian, Christopher Hill, recently wrote quite bluntly: 'Scotland was bribed and swindled into Union with England in 1707'.[6] Even so, the old orthodoxy is still strong.

There are other forms of misunderstanding as well. It seems to me that some modern writers have been misled by assuming that such words as treaty, union and federal have always been used in the sense which we now usually attach to them.[7] They therefore think that they have detected Fletcher in an inconsistency when they find him speaking favourably of Union. In fact, he always did so but in the sense of an agreement for co-operation which would not detract from the independence of the Scottish Parliament.

For all these reasons, I have found it necessary to write a history of the Union debates as well as a life of Fletcher. In any case, Fletcher was so closely involved in the debates that the two are inextricable. This has meant going over much of the ground which I covered briefly in my *1707: The Union of Scotland and England*, published in 1979; but I have now had the benefit of some additional years of research and the present account is much fuller.

As so often, I am grateful to the ever-helpful staff of the National Library of Scotland and Edinburgh University Library, to A. C. Davis and Bruce Lenman who read the typescript and made very helpful comments, to my daughter, Catharine Howard, for the index and to Caroline Miller who helped with the typing. I am, of course, myself responsible for any imperfections.

Edinburgh, 1992   P.H.S.

Contents

1

The Reputation of Andrew Fletcher

'One of the brightest of our gentry'
— Robert Wodrow

When Nigel Tranter in 1982 published a novel about Andrew Fletcher of Saltoun it was natural and inevitable that he should call it quite simply, *The Patriot.* This particular Andrew Fletcher of Saltoun, for there is a long line of them, was born in 1653 and died in 1716. He has long been known as 'the Patriot', a title awarded to him by popular consent and usage because of his resistance to the absorption of Scotland by the Treaty of Union of 1707.

This is a very remarkable distinction because it has been given to no one else in the whole history of Scotland, not even Wallace or Bruce. A country which defended its independence for hundreds of years against the repeated attacks of a much larger neighbour has had no shortage of patriots, as well as others of a different kind who succumbed to the blandishments of money or office from south of the Border. Both types are with us still. Perhaps the distinction of Fletcher as a patriot has lived in popular reputation because he was a conspicuous exception in an unheroic age. The independence of Scotland was under attack by means more subtle than armed invasion. In the highly unrepresentative Parliament of the time, in Scotland as elsewhere, power lay in the hands of the nobility, the gentry and the merchants, very much in that order of importance. Scotland had been disastrously weakened in defence as well as in foreign policy, trade and the patronage of the arts, by the succession of James VI of Scotland to the English throne in 1603. At the end of that century, the Darien Scheme was a great patriotic endeavour to restore the fortunes of Scotland. Virtually everyone who could raise any money at all invested it in the Company. When it failed, partly because of English intrigue and hostility, the investors were ruined. Most of them were from the classes represented in Parliament and they were therefore now particularly vulnerable to bribery. In the words of Robert Burns:

> We're bought and sold for English gold,
> Such a parcel of rogues in a nation![1]

Perhaps not so much rogues as men confused, impoverished and tempted. It was against this background that Fletcher's patriotism and integrity were outstanding.

1

I do not know when Fletcher was first described as 'The Patriot'. Contemporary references to him stress his devotion to the interest of Scotland without actually using the word. The title was evidently established by the middle of the eighteenth century. A document of that time in Edinburgh University Library[2] uses the term as a matter of course. So does Andrew Johnson in his description of Saltoun parish in the first *Statistical Account of 1792*: 'The parish was the birth place of Andrew Fletcher of Saltoun, the famous patriot'.[3] The entry on Fletcher in the 3rd edition of the *Encyclopaedia Britannica* (published in Edinburgh in 1797) describes him as 'a celebrated Scots patriot and political writer . . . the ornament of his country and the champion of its freedom'. In 1827, when Sir Walter Scott wrote his *Tales of a Grandfather*, he referred to Fletcher as 'one of the most accomplished men, and best patriots, whom Scotland has produced in any age'.[4] Robert Chambers in *A Biographical Dictionary of Eminent Scotsmen* (1835) said that he was 'so much celebrated for his patriotism and political knowledge . . . an ardent lover of liberty, and of his country'. In 1863, William Anderson in *The Scottish Nation* described him as 'a celebrated political writer and patriot'.[5]

If Fletcher is unique as pre-eminently 'the Patriot', in a country of many patriots, he is also unique in attracting the nearly unanimous admiration of politicians and historians both in his own day and since. In the words of Robert Chambers, he was, and still is, 'the subject of almost universal and unlimited panegyric'.[6] David Hume said that he was 'a man of signal probity and fine genius',[7] and Tobias Smollett: 'a man of undaunted courage and inflexible integrity, who professed republican principles, and seemed designed by nature as a member of some Grecian Commonwealth'.[8] Sir John Dalrymple wrote of him as one 'whose mind was inflamed by love of public good, and all of whose ideas to procure it had a sublimity in them. Fletcher disliked England, merely because he loved Scotland to excess'.[9] In 1955 the Saltire Society placed a plaque to Fletcher on the Kirk of East Saltoun where he is buried. Since then, on the first Saturday of September each year, the Society has organised a meeting in the kirk at which a distinguished historian, lawyer, economist, writer or whatever gives his views on Fletcher. All of them have spoken of him in terms of high admiration.

All of this is the more remarkable because Fletcher was not a man who sought easy popularity or cultivated the arts of winning friends. He did not suffer fools gladly. He had a quick temper, which at least once made him shoot a colleague. Many people at his own time and since have found some of his ideas fanciful and visionary. He was strongly individual and not by any means a natural party man or collaborator. The people who praise him are usually aware of these defects and admit them. They evidently feel that the negative qualities are heavily outweighed by the positive.

I have left to this point the evidence of his own contemporaries, the people who knew Fletcher, worked with him in Parliament or elsewhere, and were able to judge the man directly and not only from his writings. We are fortunate in having extended comments from a number of them and from political opponents as well as friends. They agree to a remarkable extent about both the good and the bad points. I think that they are worth quoting at length, because they are the nearest that we can now get to a first hand impression of the man himself.

The first is from the man who was for several years responsible for his education. This was Gilbert Burnet, a Scotsman who became Bishop of Salisbury and who wrote one of the liveliest of historical memoirs, *The History of My Own Time*. I shall have more to say about him in the next chapter but in the meantime, this is his description of Fletcher: 'A Scotch gentleman of great parts, and many virtues, but a most violent republican, and extravagantly passionate'.[10]

The Sir John Clerk of Penicuick of the day yielded to the pressure of his patron, the Duke of Queensberry, to support the Union in Parliament and was rewarded with a sinecure as a Baron of Exchequer which gave him a secure income for the rest of his life. He was therefore an opponent politically, but I think a grudging admiration comes through from this description of Fletcher in his *Memoirs*:

> Amongst their Gentlemen was one Mr. Fletcher of Saltoun, a Man of Republican principles, who had spent his youth in Holand, had been forfeited under the late King James, but afterwards restored under King William by Act of Parliament. He was a man a little untoward in his temper, and much inclined to Eloquence. He made many speeches in Parliament, which are all printed, but was not very dexterous in making extemporary replies. He was, however, a very Honest Man, and meant well in every thing he said and did, except in cases where his humure, passion, or prejudices were suffered to get the better of his reason.[11]

The next witness is a Hanoverian secret agent, John Macky, who was employed at various times to spy on the Jacobites in England, Scotland and France. The work by which he is best known is a series of character sketches of the members of the Scottish and English Parliament written in about 1703 for the Electress Sophia of Hanover. The English Act of Settlement of 1701 had conferred the succession to the English throne (but not necessarily the Scottish) on Sophia and her heirs and she evidently wanted to know something about the sort of people she might have to deal with. These *Characters* are admirable brief sketches, summing up a man in a few memorable phrases. They are frank and fair. Because they are often the most vivid description that we have of the men of the time, they have been quoted by innumerable historians ever since, with or without acknowledgement. This is the entry on Andrew Fletcher, which, I think, has an unmistakable quality of direct observation about it:

Andrew Fletcher, of *Salton*,

Is a Gentleman of a fair Estate in *Scotland*, attended with the Improvement of a good Education. He was Knight of the Shire for *Lothian*, in that Parliament wherein the Duke of *York* was Commissioner, in the Reign of King *Charles* the Second; and openly opposed the arbitrary Designs of that Prince, and the fatal Bill of Accession, which obliged him wisely to retire first to *England*, and then to *Holland*.

The Duke of *York* could not forgive his Behaviour in that Parliament: They summoned him to appear at *Edenburgh*, which he not daring to do, he was declared a Traytor, and his Estate confiscated. He retired to *Hungary*, and served several Campaigns under the Duke of *Lorrain*; returned to *Holland* after the Death of King *Charles* the Second, and came over to *England* with the Duke of *Monmouth*; had the Misfortune to shoot the Mayor of *Lime*, after his Landing; on which Accident he returned again to *Holland*, and came over at the *Revolution* with the Prince of *Orange*.

He is so zealous an Assertor of the Liberties of the People, that he is too jealous of the growing Power of all Princes, in whom he thinks Ambition so natural, yet he is not for trusting the *best* of Princes with a Power which *ill* ones may make use of against the People; believing all Princes are made *by* and *for* the good of the People; and thinks Princes should have no Power but that of *doing Good*. This made him oppose King *Charles*, and King *James*, and withstand the giving so much Power to King *William*, whom he never would serve: Nor does he ever come into the Administration of *this Queen*; but stands up as a stout Pillar for the Constitution in the Parliament of *Scotland*.

He is a Gentleman steady in his Principles, of nice Honour, with abundance of Learning; brave as the Sword he wears, and bold as a Lion. A sure Friend, but an irreconcileable Enemy; would *lose his* Life *readily*, to *serve his Country*; and would not do a *base Thing* to *save it*. His Thoughts are large, as to Religion, and could never be brought within the Bounds of any particular *Sect*; nor will he be under the Distinction of *Whig* or *Tory*; saying, these Names are only used to cloak the Knavery of both Parties.

His *Notions* of *Government* are too fine spun, and can hardly be lived up to by Men subject to the common Frailties of Nature; neither will he give Allowance for extraordinary Emergencies, witness the Duke of *Shrewsberry*, with whom he had always been very intimate; yet the Duke being made Secretary of State, a *Second Time*, purely to save his Country, this Gentleman would never be in common Charity with him afterwards: And my Lord *Spenser*, now Lord *Sunderland*, on Voting for the Army, was used by him much after the same Manner.

He hath written some excellent Tracts, but not published in his Name; and hath a very fine Genius; is a low, thin Man, brown Complexion, full of Fire, with a stern, sour, Look, and fifty Years old.[12]

John Macky's *Characters* were published posthumously in 1733 by his son in a book called *Memoirs of the Secret Services of John Macky*. Jonathan Swift had a copy of this book in which he added his own marginal comments. They were usually ill-natured, especially about the Scots. Of Andrew Fletcher, he wrote: 'A most arrogant, concited Pedant in Politics; cannot indure the least Contradiction in any of his opinions or Paradoxes'.[13]

There is, incidentally, some mysterious connection between John Macky and Gilbert Burnet. The volume of 1733 among other miscellaneous material prints a copy of Burnet's will. It complains about the delay in the publication of the second and third volumes of Burnet's *History of My Own Time*, (the first volume was published in 1724 but the second and final one not until 1734) and it alleges that Burnet had inserted most of Macky's *Characters* in these volumes. Precisely how Macky and Burnet were involved with one another is obscure.[14]

If John Macky, the Hanoverian agent, was lyrical in his praise of Andrew Fletcher, so also was a man who was at the opposite end of the political spectrum. This is the George Lockhart of Carnwath who, like Fletcher, was a member of the Scottish Parliament of 1703 to 1707. He was an ardent Jacobite and devoted most of his life at great personal risk to working for the restoration of the Stuarts to the throne. Fletcher was unenthusiastic about hereditary monarchy of any kind, but he and Lockhart were allies in Parliament, because they both opposed the Treaty of Union.

The most vivid and comprehensive account of the events which led to the ratification of the Treaty was written by Lockhart himself. This is his *Memoirs Concerning the Affairs of Scotland* first published in a pirated edition in 1714 and then along with other material in the two volumes of *The Lockhart Papers* in 1817. It is a magnificent piece of memoir writing, vivid, lively and passionate, one of the best things of its kind in our literature. Lockhart is frankly partisan and makes no secret of his Jacobitism or of his detestation of the Union. This does not mean that he distorts the facts. As far as I know, he has never been shown as inaccurate on any point of substance. Like Macky, Lockhart has a particular gift for brief character sketches. The following is the frequently quoted passage in which he introduces Fletcher:

Andrew Fletcher of Salton, in the first part of his life, did improve himself to a great degree by reading and travelling; he was always a great admirer of both ancient and modern republicks, and therefore the more displeas'd at some steps which he thought wrong in King Charles the Second's reign, whereby he drew upon himself the enmity of the ministers of that Government, to avoid the evil consequences of which, he went abroad; during which time, his enemies malice still continuing, he was upon slight frivolous pretences summon'd to appear before the Privy Council and their designs to ruin him being too apparent, he was so enrag'd that he concurred; and came over with the Duke of Monmouth, when he invaded England; upon which he was forfeited. Thereafter he came over with the Prince of Orange: but that prince was not many months in England, till he saw his designs, and left him, and ever thereafter hated and appeared as much against him as any in the kingdom. Being elected a Parliament man in the year 1703, he shew'd a sincere and honest inclination towards the honour and interest of his country. The thoughts of England's domineering over Scotland, was what his generous soul could not away with. The indignities and oppression Scotland lay under, gaul'd him to the heart; so that in his learned and elaborate discourses he exposed them with undaunted courage and pathetick eloquence. He was bless'd with a soul that hated and despised whatever was mean and unbecoming a gentleman, and was so stedfast to what he thought right, that no hazard nor advantage, no not the universal empire, nor the gold of America, could tempt him to yield or desert it. And I may affirm, that in all his life he never once pursued a measure with the prospect of any by-end to himself, nor furder than he judg'd it for the common benefit and advantage of his country.

He was master of the English, Latin, Greek, French, and Italian languages, and well versed in history, the civil law, and all kinds of learning; and as he was universally accomplished, he employ'd his talents for the good of mankind. He was a strict and nice observer of all the points of honour, and his word, sacred; as brave as his sword, and had some experience in the art of war, having in his younger years been some time a volunteer in both the land and sea service. In his travels he had studied, and came to understand, the respective interests of the several princes and states of Europe. In his private conversation affable to his friends (but could not endure to converse with those he thought enemies to their country), and free of all manner of vice. He had a penetrating, clear and lively apprehension, but so extreamly wedded to his own opinions, that there were few (and those too must be his beloved friends, and of whom he had a good opinion) he could endure to reason against him, and did for the most part so closely and unalterably adhere to what he advanc'd (which was frequently very singular) that he'd break with his party before he'd alter the least jot of his scheme and maxims; and therefore it was impossible for any set of men, that did not give up themselves to be absolutely directed by him, to please him, so as to carry him along in all points. And thence it came to pass, that he often in Parliament acted a part by himself, tho' in the main he stuck close to the Country party, and was their Cicero.

He was, no doubt, an enemy to all monarchical governments, at least thought they wanted to be much reformed: but I do very well believe, his aversion to the English and the Union was so great, in revenge to them, he'd have sided with the Royal Family: but as that was a subject not fit to be enter'd upon with him, this is only a conjecture from some innuendo's I have heard him make: but so far is certain, he liked, commended, and conversed with high-flying Tories more than any other set of men, acknowledging them to be the best Country men, and of most honour, integrity, and ingenuity. To sum up all, he was a learned, gallant, honest, and every other way well accomplish'd gentleman; and if ever a man proposes to serve and merit well of his country, let him place his courage, zeal, and constancy as a pattern before him, and think himself sufficiently applauded and rewarded, by obtaining the character of being like Andrew Fletcher of Salton.[15]

The Parliament of 1703 was Fletcher's finest hour. He took the initiative by the sheer force of reasoning and won wide support in spite of the boldness and originality of his ideas. It was only in the years that followed that the Ministers, appointed in London in the name of the Queen, were gradually able to win a majority by various means. In 1704 George Ridpath published *An Account of the Proceedings of the Parliament of Scotland which met at Edinburgh May 6 1703*. He included the text of most of Fletcher's speeches and commented on them in his Preface. In their 'good sense, good Language and strong Argument' they were 'equal to the best pieces of the sort, that either Antiquity or Latter Ages have produc'd . . . The Memory of this Parliament will be precious to the Nation, so long as it has a being'.[16]

Robert Wodrow (1679–1734) published his *History of the Sufferings of the Church of Scotland* in 1721. It is a book which is both painstaking in its detail and deeply felt because Wodrow strongly sympathised with the Covenanters.

His view of Fletcher agrees essentially with his other contemporaries, but also reflects his own standards of value:

> Mr Fletcher of Salton is likewise well known to the world, as one who endeavoured to make a stand against every thing he reckoned against liberty and property, and his appearances in our Scots parliaments since the revolution, are generally known. He is lately deceased, and was one of the brightest of our gentry, remarkable for his fine taste in all manner of polite learning, and his curious library, his indefatigable diligence in every thing he thought might benefit and improve his country, his bold and brisk appearances against what he reckoned encroachments upon the privileges of the subject, as well as his sobriety, temperance, and good management.[17]

R. A. Scott Macfie, who wrote a Bibliography of Fletcher in 1901, quotes some anonymous verses about him published in 1705. They sum up the impression of Fletcher which lingered in the Scottish memory:

> A Genius past the reach of English Gold,
> Great and refin'd cast in no common mould.
> Were all thy Peers, O Scotland, such as he,
> It were impossible to Conquer Thee[18]

Fletcher's reputation even reached a man who spent most of his life immersed among the books of the Bodleian in Oxford. This was the antiquary, Thomas Hearne, who lived from 1678 to 1735 and was therefore a contemporary of Fletcher. He was a Tory of Jacobite sympathies and far removed from Fletcher politically, but his diary of 17 August 1731 refers to 'that Famed Republican Fletcher of Saltoun, the only man of his age that ever faithfully adhered to his principles, bad as they were, and acted accordingly.[19]

James Boswell, the biographer of Dr Samuel Johnson and the author of the most sustained and self-revealing series of journals in the English language, had an insatiable desire to meet the great and the famous. As he said in a letter to Frederick the Great: 'It is certain that I am not a great man, but I have an enthusiastic love of great men and I derive a kind of glory from it'.[20] This attempt to persuade Frederick to receive him, an unknown young man of 23, failed. He had more luck when he wrote a few months later, on 3 December 1764, to Jean Jacques Rousseau. As part of his effort to sell himself, he invoked Fletcher's name: 'Believe me, you will be glad to have seen me. You know what Scots pride is. Sir, I am coming to see you in order to make myself more worthy of a nation that has produced a Fletcher of Saltoun and a Lord Marischal'.[20]

Boswell's use of these two names was a ploy to catch Rousseau's attention. George Keith, 10th Earl Marischal, with whom Boswell had travelled from Utrecht to Berlin, was one of two remarkable brothers. They were both exiled from Scotland because of their Jacobitism and both distinguished themselves working for other governments in Europe. The younger brother, James, after service in Russia, became a Field Marshall of Frederick the Great and a Prussian military hero. The older brother, George, Lord Marischall, was Frederick's Ambassador in France and then Spain and Governor of Neufchâtel. It was there that Rousseau met him. He says in his *Confessions*, 'this illustrious and virtuous Scotchman made a powerful impression upon my heart'.22

Boswell, of course, knew of Rousseau's admiration and affection for George Keith. He also knew that Keith had persuaded Rousseau to write Fletcher's life. As he recorded the conversation in his *Journal*, Boswell steered the subject towards Fletcher:

ROUSSEAU. 'Yes, you will find great souls in Spain.' BOSWELL. 'And in the mountains of Scotland. But since our cursed Union, ah —' ROUSSEAU. 'You undid yourselves.' BOSWELL. 'Truly, yes. But I must tell you a great satisfaction given me by my Lord. He calls you Jean Jacques out of affection. One day he said to me, "Jean Jacques is the most grateful man in the world. He wanted to write my brother's life; but I begged him rather to write the life of Mr. Fletcher of Saltoun, and he promised me he would do so." ' ROUSSEAU. 'Yes, Sir; I will write it with the greatest care and pleasure. I shall offend the English, I know. But that is no matter. Will you furnish me with some anecdotes on the characters of those who made your Treaty of Union, and details that cannot be found in the historians?' BOSWELL. 'Yes, Sir; but with the warmth of an ancient Scot.' ROUSSEAU. 'By all means.'23

I have discussed this episode with Rousseau at some length because it provides evidence of Fletcher's reputation about fifty years after his death and also because it may help to explain the virtual disappearance of his private papers and correspondence. Rousseau, unfortunately, never wrote his life of Fletcher, but there is evidence that the papers were sent to him. No one seems to have heard of them since then.

In the Library of Edinburgh University there is a manuscript history of the Fletcher family which concentrates on Andrew Fletcher, the Patriot.24 A note on the cover says that it was presented to the Earl of Buchan by Madame Lally, Daughter of Sir L. Halkett of Pitferran Bart, 1785. We are also told that Elisabeth Halkett was a daughter of Elisabeth Fletcher who was in turn a daughter of Lord Milton. This Lord Milton, another Andrew Fletcher (1691–1766), who was a great power in the Scotland of his day as Lord Advocate and confidential agent of the Duke of Argyle. As such he became strongly Unionist. He was the nephew of the Patriot and was with him when he died in London in 1726. The manuscript is initialled E H and is evidently the work of this Elisabeth Halkett herself. She had clearly taken a close interest in the history of her Fletcher ancestors, drawing presumably both on the written archives and on oral tradition. Her memoir is an important piece of evidence, because it is the original, and often only, source of many points about Fletcher, including several of the anecdotes which are virtually all we know about some of the years which he spent abroad. It has been quoted directly or indirectly in almost everything that has been written about Fletcher's life, in the biographies by G. W. T. Omond or W. C. Mackenzie, in the essay by the Earl of Buchan or in works of reference such as the *Encyclopaedia Brittanica* or the *Dictionary of*

National Biography. Oddly enough, it is usually attributed, quite incorrectly, to Sir David Dalrymple, later Lord Hailes. There is a letter from him to Buchan about Fletcher,[25] but it is quite separate, and quite different in tone.

Unfortunately it cannot be said that Elisabeth Halkett can be accepted as an entirely reliable source. In the first place, she fails to understand, or has been seriously misled, perhaps by her grandfather, Lord Milton, about Fletcher's position politically. She gives him the 'merit' of both the Test Act of 1681 (see Chapter 4) and of the Union of 1707. To both of these he was, of course, strenuously opposed. Also she tells some picturesque, but highly improbable, tales about Fletcher's adventures in Spain. Ramsay MacDonald rightly says of these that they are 'rather valuable as an indication of the veneration in which his memory was long held than for the truth'.[26] Elisabeth Halkett leaves no doubt that she did venerate Fletcher's memory. This leads her sometimes into rather extravagant praise. But with all these limitations, most of her narrative is consistent with other evidence and is probably generally very close to the truth.

The immediate point of interest about Elisabeth Halkett's memoir is that she is quite definite about the removal of papers to help Rousseau with his biography:

> Lord Marishall who held Mr Fletcher's character in high admiration — when Governor of Neufchâtel where Rousseau resided about the year 1766 — prevail'd with this very extraordinary genius to write the life of a man whose character and actions he wished to have transmitted with advantage to Posterity. For this purpose his Lordship applied to an honourable relation of Mr Fletcher's for materials which were by him transmitted to Lord Marishall'.[27]

This is a very convincing story for two reasons. Elisabeth Halkett wrote her memoir some time before 1785. She was therefore talking about something which had happened only about 20 years before, probably in her own lifetime and certainly in the recollection of her mother. Secondly, Boswell's account, which confirms that Rousseau agreed to write the life, was published for the first time in 1953. There is therefore no possibility of one account simply repeating the other.

Another confirmation that Fletcher's papers were sent to Rousseau is the sad fact that very few of them have survived. This is surprising because he belonged to a family with a large country house and a great library, who carefully preserved their letters, accounts, legal documents and other papers. They are now deposited in the National Library of Scotland where they make up a collection of well over 1,000 items and most of these items are files of some hundreds of documents.[28]

It is true that there are comparatively few papers before the late seventeenth Century, but this is probably because the lands of Saltoun were forfeited in January 1686 when Andrew Fletcher was condemned for treason. The estate was then granted to the Earl of Dumbarton who held it until it was restored to

Fletcher in June 1690. Scott Macfie says in his Bibliography that Dumbarton destroyed many of the papers while he was in occupation and that is certainly consistent with the scarcity of early documents. From about the end of the 17th Century, however, the collection is very full indeed. You have the impression that the Fletchers kept almost every paper that passed through their hands including quite short and trivial notes. The conspicuous exception are the papers of Andrew Fletcher, the Patriot.

You would not, of course, expect to find Fletcher's own letters for the periods when he was living at Saltoun, unless he kept copies. But you would expect many letters addressed to him. There are hardly any. His mother, who survived until 1713, might have been expected to preserve letters from Fletcher when he was a student abroad or while he was in political exile from 1682 to 1688 and to take them back to Saltoun with her when the house was restored to the family. There are no such letters. Fletcher was abroad again for much of the time between the end of the Union debate in January 1707 and his own death on 15 September 1716. In the National Library collection there are a number of letters exchanged between Fletcher and other members of his family from October 1715 to September 1716. Of these, seventeen were written by Fletcher himself. That he wrote so many letters in the last year of his life, when his health was in final decline, suggests that he was a diligent correspondent. Indeed, Elisabeth Halkett is her memoir says that 'he maintained a useful and extensive correspondence with the friends of liberty'.[29] If so, almost all of these letters have been lost. There are also no diaries, no manuscripts of his works published or unpublished, and no notes for his speeches. The only extensive body of writing in Fletcher's own hand are two catalogues of his library at Saltoun.[30] These are useful as an indication of the range of his intellectual interests and I shall discuss them in the next chapter. They also suggest that a man who took such trouble to catalogue his books would be sufficiently active with his pen to write far more than we can now find. When one compares the great quantity of papers that have survived from other members of his family with the pitiful handful which is all that remains connected with the Patriot himself, it is impossible to avoid the conclusion that his papers have been systematically removed.

Other people have been blamed for the loss of Fletcher's papers. One of them is David Erskine, the 11th Earl of Buchan, who founded the Society of Antiquaries in 1780. He was an energetic, if somewhat eccentric, enthusiast for Scottish literature and history. In 1792 he published an *Essay on the Life and Writings of Fletcher of Saltoun*, and it is for this that he asked Elisabeth Halkett and Lord Hailes to supply material. It is very doubtful if he had other sources, because most of the very thin substance of his *Essay* comes from the Halkett memoir. Unfortunately, the *Essay* is strong on enthusiasm but weak on fact. Scott Macfie is not unfair in describing it as a 'quasi-biographical rhapsody'. It would have been more useful if Buchan had simply reprinted Elisabeth Halkett's memoir. He does add some of Fletcher's own writings but they had all been in print more than once before.

Lord Hailes's letter to Buchan is brief, caustic and amusing. He says of Fletcher: 'It may well be supposed that considering the people from whom I come, he is no saint in my calendar'.[31] Hailes was a judge of formidable scholarship who published an astounding number of works on Scottish literary and historical subjects. They included his *Annals of Scotland* which set new standards for the scrupulous examination of historical evidence. As Walter Scott said, he had 'habits of accuracy pushed almost to the point of prudery'.[32] Perhaps then the brief anecdotes which he passed on to Buchan had a more solid basis in fact than such things usually have. One is about a servant of Fletcher who wanted to leave because he could not stand his temper:

'To be sure, I am passionate, but my passion is no sooner on than it is off.' 'Yes', replied the footman, 'but then it is no sooner off, than it is on.' In the other, Fletcher makes fun of the idea of hereditary kingship by pretending to have heard of a hereditary Professor of Divinity at Hamburg. If you think that absurd, what about a hereditary king? It was said of Fletcher, Hailes adds, that he wished for a republic in which he himself might be king.

Because of the gaps in the records, however they may have occurred, there are parts of Fletcher's life about which we know very little. This is particularly true of the three periods which he spent abroad. We have some glimpses of him as a political exile in Holland and the account by his nephew of his last days in Paris and London. Apart from these, there are only a few anecdotes about strange escapes in Spain and references to military service in Hungary. Fortunately, we have a fairly complete picture of the most important phase of his life, the sessions of Parliament from 1703 to 1707. All before that can be seen as preparation and all after as anti-climax. We have the text of several of his speeches, but only those of 1703, which were published as pamphlets, reproduced by Ridpath and much later by Buchan. They were also included in the only book attributed to Fletcher by name, *The Political Works of Andrew Fletcher, Esq. of Saltoun*. This was first published in 1732, sixteen years after Fletcher's death, with subsequent editions in 1737, 1749 and 1798. We also have accounts of the sessions of Parliament in the official Proceedings and in books by Lockhart, Hume and Ridpath. Fletcher makes frequent appearances in the correspondence of other people, especially, for different years, in the letters of the Earls of Mar and Seafield. They show Fletcher fighting tirelessly for the cause of Scottish independence. The longest book on the subject, Daniel Defoe's *History of the Union*, is so biased in the unionist cause that it makes no reference to Fletcher at all; but Defoe was a paid agent and propagandist of the English government. He was not the last man in his trade to believe that silence is the best response to a formidable opponent.

Fletcher's reputation as a political thinker rests on this one posthumous volume, *The Political Works*, which contains four essays, one dialogue and eighteen speeches. Other short essays have been attributed to him, but a good case can be made for only two or three of them. It seems little enough for a man with such a fluent pen, originality of thought and strength of conviction. If he wrote any more, especially after he left Scotland in 1708, it has disappeared without trace.

Our estimate of the thought and significance of Andrew Fletcher must depend on this small volume of his own writing, on his record in the Scottish Parliament and on the views and reactions recorded by his contemporaries. As we have seen, there is no doubt that he made an overwhelming impact in his own time. This impact was so strong that it has continued to echo ever since in popular memory as well as in the work of historians. His reputation and the reason for it are well summarised in a passage in Hume Brown's *History of Scotland*;

Among the throng of party leaders who were confounding the councils of the nation there was one heroic figure who has retained an abiding place in the memories of his countrymen — Andrew Fletcher of Saltoun. Fletcher was an idealist and a doctrinaire, unique among the men that surrounded him. At a period when civic virtue seemed a chimaera, he had a reputation for singleness of purpose to which his bitterest opponents paid ungrudging homage. In religion his ideal was a church without dogma; in politics, a republic, in which a nation should have its destinies in its own hands. Ideals more incongruous with the spirit of the time it would be hard to conceive; and in the eyes of all parties Fletcher was a visionary who yet extorted esteem because his words were a voice of the human conscience. As the nearest approach to a republic, he desired a monarchy restricted by a constitution which should make the prince the guardian and not the author of the law. It was in the history of Scotland since the Union of the Crowns that he found practical reasons for his hardy proposal. Since that date Scotland had been a dependency of England controlled by English statesmen doing the bidding of an English King. For such a state of things there was but one remedy: the prerogative of the Crown must be subordinated to the will of the people.[33]

2

Education

Andrew Fletcher was born in 1653 as the eldest son of a prosperous laird, Sir Robert Fletcher of Saltoun, in East Lothian. The family was of Norman origin and had come to Scotland from England five generations before. In the past, they had been merchants in Dundee and lairds in Angus. It was from the family property there that his grandfather, a senator of the College of Justice, had taken his title of Lord Innerpeffer, but he bought Saltoun in 1643. Andrew Fletcher's mother, Katherine Bruce, claimed descent from the grandfather of Robert the Bruce. She had connections with many other distinguished families, both Highland and Lowland, including the Haldanes of Gleneagles.

Fletcher's family background was therefore comfortable and privileged. Lairds were Barons, although they were not peers, because they held land by charter *in liberam baroniam* with the right to preside over the court of the barony. This heritable baronial jurisdiction was much more significant than the office of justice of the peace, an English institution introduced by James VI and I, and to which many lairds were appointed. Since the time of the Reformation, the lairds had been playing an increasingly important part in the political life of the country. They had become one of the estates of Parliament under an Act of 1567 which provided for the lairds in each shire to elect two of their members to attend Parliament as Commissioners of the shires. Lairds were often lay members of the General Assembly of the Kirk, at a time when the Church and its Assemblies were of central importance. Except for the years when patronage was abolished, they had the right to present ministers. Many of the ministers were themselves younger sons of lairds. The lairds had financial responsibilities for the upkeep of the local church, manse and school, for poor relief and the upkeep of roads. Advocates and judges, who were then the backbone of intellectual life, were almost always from the landowning class. In every sense, by Fletcher's time and for the next century at least, the lairds were 'the most powerful social and political class in the country'.[1] They were born not necessarily to great wealth, but to a sense of influence, importance and responsibility.

Although Andrew Fletcher ridiculed the institution of hereditary monarchy, he never seems to have questioned the justice of hereditary property in land. Much of his writing reflects an unconscious assumption that it was inevitable and right that the landowners should act as a social and political élite. In this, he was, of course, accepting one of the established ideas of his time. Few people then questioned the idea that political rights derived from the responsibility of property especially in land. Fletcher's consciousness of an assured and privileged place in society probably contributed to his sensitive pride which could thole no insult. This went along with his temper which was liable to explode whenever he suspected a slight and which involved him in trouble more than once. In his *Essay* the Earl of Buchan quotes a family manuscript which says that Fletcher 'was from his infancy of a very fiery and uncontrollable temper; but his dispositions were noble and generous'. In this respect he did not change as he grew older.

Fletcher was fortunate in his parents who, by all accounts, seem to have been admirable people. Of his mother, Andrew once said: 'if there is anything in my education and acquirements during the early part of my life, I owe them entirely to that woman'.[2] His father, Sir Robert Fletcher, shared this concern for education. In 1664 he succeeded in persuading Gilbert Burnet to come to Saltoun in the dual capacity as minister of the parish and to help with the education of his sons. In the original draft of his Memoirs, Burnet describes his first meeting with Sir Robert:

As I was one day standing . . . on the streets of Edinburgh, a gentleman of pale countenance and in a very plain garb came to us and made me a great compliment in acknowledgement of the kindness he had received from my father at Paris. I thought he was some ordinary man, and did not much mind his compliment, but we went on in our discourse, and he happened to say some things that discovered both great learning and much sense. So I asked who it was, and found it was Sir Robert Fletcher; thus did I stumble on my first patron. We had a great deal of discourse, and I had the luck to please him; at which I wonder much, for he was one of the humblest and modestest men in the world, and I was then one of the vainest and insolentest. His genius lay to mathematics and philosophy, and he wanted a friend and companion in study, so he began to resolve on having me about him.[3]

Burnet was then only 21 and a recent graduate from Marischal College, Aberdeen, but it was already clear that he was a man to be reckoned with. He was thorough and painstaking in everything he did, and he was of deep and wide scholarship. But he was no dull pedant. Even as a young country minister, he was soon on terms of confidence with many of the leading men of church and state. When he was only 23 he drew up a paper to denounce the abuses of the Bishops and defended it to their face. Dryden described him in his *Hind and Panther* as 'Broad-backed and brawny, built for lover's delight', an unusual description of a bishop. This may explain why he married three times, one of them to a woman celebrated for her beauty.

Burnet afterwards recorded in his 'Rough draft of my own life' his feelings about Robert Fletcher and about his first appointment in Saltoun:

The parsonage house [by the time he wrote this Burnet had become accustomed to English terms] was not only convenient but noble; it was near all my friends; but the gentleman's own conversation was more than all these. He was an humble, good, and worthy man; he had a great love of learning and had made considerable progress in it; and his two eldest sons were then under a very exact education and in the years most capable of it, so he intended that I should live in the house with him, and assist both himself in his own studies and his sons' tutor in instructing them.[4]

Burnet evidently had an enormous capacity for work. When he was a Professor in Glasgow after he left Saltoun in 1669, he is said to have worked from 4 in the morning until 10 at his own study and to have taught from that time until late at night. Such a man might easily be a tyrant as a teacher, but we get a very different impression from an essay, *Thoughts on Education*, which he wrote at Saltoun in 1668. (It was first published in 1761 with a later edition in Aberdeen in 1914). This must be one of the most enlightened works on education of its time and for long afterwards. Certainly he sets his sights high and proposes that the pupil by the age of 14 or 15 (the age of Andrew Fletcher at the time the essay was written) should have a good grounding in Latin, History and Geography, some Greek, French, Italian and Spanish. After that, he suggests such studies as agriculture, anatomy, botany and mathematics, but not politics or philosophy 'which requires maturity of spirit'. Throughout he stresses a gentle approach quite different from the harsh discipline which was normal for more than 200 years afterwards. 'Praise and kindness are the best encouragement of children . . . The philosopher's stone, and master-piece of education, is so to ply a child as to gain his heart, and retain his affection.' Burnet was celebrated for his liberal views and wide tolerance on questions of church policy; he was no less tolerant in his views on education. He recognised the important place which Latin had to take at a time which it was still the common currency of men of learning. But he accepted that some pupils could not learn Latin or had an 'unconquerable aversion' to it. He continues: 'I would not for that judge him lost, nor drive him to it as to alienate his mind from study; since he may be a knowing man without a word of it.' Wise words. If schoolmasters in general had agreed with him, an incalculable amount of youthful misery might have been avoided during the next two or three hundred years. Burnet was equally tolerant and enlightened about recreations. The pupil should be left to 'his own choice and inclination' and encouraged, if he wished, in such pursuits as gardening, music and painting.[5]

In 1665 Sir Robert Fletcher died. Andrew, who was 12, became laird of Saltoun and Burnet took over full responsibility for his education. In his essay, Burnet said that 'the best and greatest Princes have been those whom philosophers bred'. Perhaps he thought of himself and Fletcher in that light. A laird was a kind of minor prince and as a probable future member of the Scottish Parliament he was potentially a legislator. At all events, Burnet's scholarship and the good sense of his Essay suggest that Fletcher's education as a man of affairs was in very good hands.

An early record of Fletcher's exercising his responsibilities as laird appears in the Acts and Proceedings of the Presbytery of Haddington.[6] On 9 August 1666 the young Laird, accompanied by two others, inspected the library mortified (ie bequeathed) to the parish by Norran Leslie, one of Burnet's predecessors as a tutor in the Fletcher family. They found the library 'intire'. When Burnet was persuaded with difficulty and hesitation to leave Saltoun in 1669 to take the Chair of Divinity at Glasgow, he gave some books to the library. He had not forgotten it when, as Bishop of Salisbury, he came to write his will long afterwards. He left 20,000 marks to the lairds of Saltoun and Hirdmonton to be used for the education and clothing of 30 poor children in the parish, a new school house, an increase in the schoolmaster's salary and the increase of the library. To Aberdeen, the other setting of his youth, he left the same amount.[7]

Burnet seems to have been happy at Saltoun and to have kept fond memories of it. He must have known Fletcher very well from the five years he spent at Saltoun in a close relationship and from the years that they spent together as political exiles in Holland. It is a pity that he did not record more about Fletcher, especially as he had a gift for gossipy and vivid memoirs. In chapter one I quote his brief description of Fletcher in his *History of My Own Times*. The tone of that suggested that he admired Fletcher but did not entirely approve of him or even like him very much. This final version was a watering down of the original draft which was even more disapproving: 'A Scotch gentleman of great parts, but very hot and violent, and a most passionate and indiscreet assertor of public liberty'.[8]

There is a hint from another source that Fletcher and Burnet were not on very good terms. An edition of Burnet's *History* published in 1823 reprinted marginal comments by a few of Burnet's contemporaries. They include the Earl of Dartmouth who was Secretary of State and afterward Lord Privy Seal during the reign of Queen Anne. His comments have to be treated with some reserve because as a Tory he was opposed to both Fletcher and Burnet politically, and, in the words of the editor, 'entertained a great personal dislike to the bishop'. At all events, this is what he has to say about Fletcher:

> He was very brave, and a man of great integrity, he had strange chimerical notions of government, which were so unsettled, that he would be very angry next day for any body's being of an opinion that he was of himself the night before, but very constant in his dislikes of bishop Burnet, whom he always spoke of with the utmost contempt'.[9]

It is quite likely that Fletcher and Burnet had incompatible personalities, although each had qualities of mental energy, integrity and essential decency that the other would be likely to respect. Macaulay, not unfairly, speaks of Burnet's 'high animal spirits, his boastfulness, his undissembled vanity, his propensity to blunder, his provoking indiscretion, his unabashed audacity'.[10] (It is ironic that a man noted for his indiscretion should have complained that

Burnet was indiscreet). By nature, Fletcher was more reserved and austere than the bustling and, in many ways, childlike Burnet. They might easily have got on one another's nerves.

Darmouth does not tell us what period he is speaking about, although he implies that he was on familiar terms with Fletcher. This is only one among several indications that Fletcher at some periods of his life had friends, or at least acquaintances, in influential circles in London. His own pamphlet, *An Account of A Conversation* of 1704 suggests that this was so. There is similar evidence in some of his few surviving letters. Another marginal comment to the same passage in Burnet's *History*, but this time by Speaker Onslaw, says of Fletcher. 'He of Saltoun, so well known afterwards in Scotland and England'. In the context, 'afterwards' means later than 1685 which is the year with which the passage is concerned. For all we know, Burnet and Fletcher may have fallen out when they were together in Holland. There is nothing to suggest that there was any difficulty or tension between them when Burnet was acting as the tutor in Saltoun. Andrew Johnston, the Minister of Saltoun in his description of the Parish in the first *Statistical Account* followed, or perhaps established, the traditional opinion on the matter. It was from Burnet, he wrote, that Fletcher 'seems to have imbibed much of that liberal and independent character, which he displayed through life'.[11]

At least by the time when he was writing his *History of My Own Times*, which he was working on up to his death in 1715, Burnet's attitudes and opinions were very different from Fletcher's. He says of the session of the Scottish Parliament in 1703, in which Fletcher largely set the tone: 'A national humour of rendering themselves a free and independent Kingdom did so inflame them, that . . . they seemed capable of the most extravagant things that could be suggested to them'. Of the 'limitations' which Fletcher proposed in that Parliament, he says that they would have set up a 'commonwealth with the empty name of a King . . . by which no shadow of power was left with the crown and it was merely a nominal thing.'[12] This sort of language, although what he says about the limitations is accurate enough, is consistent with his description of Fletcher as a 'violent republican' and as a 'most passionate and indiscrete assertor of public liberty'. Burnet, after all, was an Episcopalian who became a Bishop in England and therefore upheld hierarchy with the monarchy at its head. He remained a close associate and advisor of King William with whom Fletcher was soon disillusioned after 1688. It was inevitable that Burnet should come to think of Fletcher as a dangerous extremist and that Fletcher should lose all patience with him.

We do not know with certainty how Fletcher continued his education after Burnet left Saltoun in 1669. Both Buchan and Omond say that he went to the Continent. He was then 16, old enough by the habits of the time to go to university in Scotland but perhaps a little too young to go abroad alone. The usual course for a young man in his position would have been to go first to a Scottish university. G. W. T. Omond in his biography of Fletcher says that the name, Andrew Fletcher, occurs in the Register of Edinburgh University for the year 1668, but W. C. Mackenzie says that a more recent examination has failed to find it.[13] Fletcher's Library catalogue includes a copy of the Statutes of the University of St. Andrews and he may therefore have gone there as a student. The Earl of Buchan in his *Essay* says that Fletcher 'was sent to travel on the Continent'.[14] This probably means not so much a Grand Tour, in the usual 18th Century sense, as a period of study at a University, probably in Holland, combined with some travel. We know that Andrew Fletcher's nephew, also called Andrew Fletcher, matriculated in Leyden in 1714. For several centuries study in a continental university was normal for young Scotsmen who could afford it and who had ambitions, especially in the law, but also in medicine or the church. Writing in the early 19th century Dugald Stewart attributed the 'sudden burst of genius' after 1745, the Scottish Enlightenment, partly at least to the 'continued intercourse "between Scotland and the Continent" from time immemorial'. It applied particularly to the lairds. 'Of our smaller country gentlemen, resident on their own estates, (an order of men which, from various causes, has now, alas totally vanished) there was scarcely one who had not enjoyed the benefit of a university education; and very few of those who could afford the expense of foreign travel, who had not visited France and Italy'.[14] With their fertile estates in East Lothian, the Fletchers of Saltoun were among the more prosperous of lairds. It was natural that Andrew Fletcher, a young man who was his own master, with strong curiosity and appetite for learning, should follow the time-honoured route.

Fletcher had a life-long enthusiasm for books. He built up a notable library, long preserved at Saltoun, but sadly dispersed in this century. Now only the empty shelves are there, along with a marble tablet in which one of his descendants commemorates Andrew Fletcher of 'illustrious memory' and his 'excellent collection of books'. It goes on to remind their successors that 'the love of letters or of arms has always distinguished the family of Saltoun'. The catalogues at least are in the National Library of Scotland.[16] It is obvious from everything that he wrote that Fletcher was of trained intelligence, widely read, especially in the classics, and wide-ranging in his interests. His appreciation of literature is best expressed in the famous remark in his *An Account of a Conversation*, 'if a man were permitted to make all the ballads, he need not care who should make the laws of a nation'.[17] Gilbert Burnet should have been proud of him.

Several members of the Fletcher family made manuscript catalogues of their books. One of the files of the Saltoun papers in the National Library has a number of them from 1529 onwards.[18] Among them is 'The Inventer of My Bookes' signed on each page by Fletcher's mother, K. Bruce. You can tell a lot about a man or woman from their collection of books. Katherine Bruce lists about 200 volumes. Almost all of them are religious, mainly sermons. There is some history, but that usually has a religious flavour as well, Bishop Spottiswoode's *History of the Church of Scotland* and Bishop Burnet's *Abridgement of the History of the Reformation* and his *Travels*. One of the very few purely secular books is one which reflects her pride in her ancestry. It is described as *The Life of King Robert Bruce* and is presumably Barbour's epic poem. Katherine Bruce was evidently a very pious woman. It is no surprise to discover from a letter about her death on 2 February 1713[19] that her last thought were with the poor of the parish of Saltoun and the widows of the Episcopalian ministers.

Andrew Fletcher's two library catalogues are also very revealing of his character and interests. The older one in a vellum cover[20] has obviously been built up over many years with books being inserted in the appropriate section as they are acquired. The result, of course, is that the pages are very crowded and that the order of books within a section is largely haphazard. Section headings are in Latin: Historici, Poetae, Oratores, Theologi, Legislatores, Physici, Matematici and Juridici. There are sections at the end for Libri Omissi (presumably because there was no space in the appropriate section) and Libri Manuscripti. Books are not separated by language. There are more in Latin, Italian, French or Spanish than English, and other languages are represented, including, of course, the Greek classics. The two largest sections are Historici and Legislatores, the latter term including what would now be called political science, Aristotle, Machiavelli, Buchanan, Moore, Hobbes and so on. Physici includes a wide range of sciences, especially medicine, chemistry, botany and agriculture. Matematici includes military studies such as fortification and artillery. I have not made an exact count, but since the catalogue has 192 pages and an average of about 30 items per page, the whole library amounts to nearly 6,000 items. Many of the items are works in several volumes, so that the total number of books must have been about 10,000. Elisabeth Halkett says in her Memoir that it was the best private library in Scotland.[21] The first *Statistical Account*[22] goes further. The library, it says, 'for variety, elegance and selection of volumes is perhaps the best private collection in Britain'.

The theology section is one of the largest, although there is nothing to suggest that Andrew Fletcher (unlike his mother and his brother) was particularly religious. In the 17th Century, religion was of primary importance to most people and it was the main issue in politics. No one concerned with the life of the time could afford to ignore theology. It has its proper place, therefore, in Fletcher's library, which shows every sign of deliberate planning to provide the basis for a sound understanding of the problems of the age.

There are some notes towards the end of the catalogue which Fletcher seems to have made when he was preparing to leave Saltoun in 1708. Since they include lists of Fletcher's own writings, they are a useful check on the works attributed to him. I shall return to this in a later chapter. Inside the back cover, there are additions which include some books published in 1713 and one in 1715. This does not necessarily mean that he was back in Saltoun for a time before he left on the journey in which he died in 1716. A reference to his catalogue in a letter from Paris of 8 May 1716 suggests that he carried it with him.[23]

The other catalogue[24] is obviously the beginning of an attempt to rewrite the first one in a neater, more detailed and systematic manner. It begins with the same first subject, history, perhaps implying that it was his favourite study. This time it is subdivided by geography and to some extent by period leaving space for subsequent additions. The thoroughness and comprehensiveness of the collection are striking. Fletcher begins with Greek and Roman history and then Italian history from 1300. There follows headings for the Italian States, Sicily, Naples, Venice, Florence, the Papal States, Milan, Piedmont, Genoa and Liguria, Sardinia and Corsica. Spain and France follow in a similar manner. The rest of Europe is treated systematically country by country, and the rest of the world is not forgotten. There are headings for Persia, the Tartars, India, China, Japan, Africa and America. Inevitably the number of books under each heading varies greatly. No other country is covered with anything like the thoroughness of Italy. Sometimes, as with Ireland and Japan, there are headings but no books.

The next main subject, again following the order of the first catalogue, is Literae Humaniores, by which he evidently meant languages and literature. It begins with grammars and dictionaries for Greek, Latin, Italian, French, Spanish, English and Dutch. For Hebrew, there is a dictionary but no entry under the heading for grammars of Hebrew and other Middle-Eastern languages. Perhaps he intended to learn Hebrew, but had not made a serious start. Greek and Latin literature then follow, but there the catalogue comes to a premature end with plenty of blank pages waiting to be filled. Probably, Fletcher started work on this catalogue between 1708 and his death in 1716, during the times when he was in Saltoun between journies abroad. We know from the group of letters from the last year of his life[25] that he was still collecting books systematically and eagerly only a few months before his death.

Lord Hailes's letter to the Earl of Buchan says of Fletcher that 'like the elder Cato and the elder Scaliger, he went late to the study of Greek'.[26] On the evidence of the catalogue, it looks as if he was at least thinking of taking up other languages in the last years of his life. Three of his brother's letters shortly before he died are replies to questions he had sent about the design of the Highland targe and matters of Scottish history. Perhaps he was working on a book on a Scottish theme. All the evidence is that Fletcher was one of those fortunate people with unflagging curiosity for whom education is a life-long process. I think that Fletcher might have said of his library what Edward Gibbon said of his own: 'a numerous and select library, the foundation of my works, and the best comfort of my life'.[27] It may often indeed have been his only comfort and solace. On the surviving evidence, Fletcher seems to have had many acquaintances but few close friends. He never married. Some brief 'recollections' of Fletcher family history published in 1803[28] may throw some light on this. It refers to Catherine Carnegie of Pittarow (although her name was in fact Margaret). She was the wife of Andrew's younger brother, Henry, and first brought the barley mill to Scotland. Then it adds: 'Andrew, observing the many domestic virtues of this Lady, when they spoke of marriage, said, "My brother has got the woman that should have been my wife." ' Perhaps then Andrew was disappointed in love, but we know no more about it than this. The general impression from the evidence is that he led a rather lonely life.

Any man who takes the trouble to draw up such long library catalogues in his own hand is clearly a man devoted to books and learning. Since he systematically collected books about every country in the known world, there seems to have been no limit to his intellectual curiosity about politics and history. His earlier catalogue suggests there was virtually no branch of learning in which he was not prepared to take an interest, everything from gardening to philosophy, as in Voltaire's famous remark about the literati of the Scottish Enlightenment. Indeed many years before the period usually ascribed to the Enlightenment, Fletcher's library catalogue suggests many of its fundamental characteristics, the historical approach, the receptiveness to ideas from abroad, the unbounded curiosity and the refusal to divide enquiry into water-tight compartments.

3

Scotland in the 17th Century

'The darkest and sublimest passages of the national history'
— P. Hume Brown

I now digress into some brief comments on the history of Scotland in the 17th Century up to the time when Andrew Fletcher began to take an active part politically in the 1680s. This digression back about 50 years before he was born is necessary because the situation that faced him cannot be understood without some idea of the way in which it had evolved.

The troubles of Scotland in the 17th Century, and the problems which Fletcher confronted, were largely the consequence of a dynastic accident, the accession of James VI to the throne of England in 1603. This had been foreseen as a possibility three generations before when the marriage of James IV to Margaret, the daughter of Henry VII of England, was under negotiation. Some of Henry's advisers realised that it might one day bring England under the rule of a Scottish King. Henry told them not to worry. 'It would be an accession, not of England to Scotland, but of Scotland to England, since the greater would always draw the less, as England had drawn Normandy under her sway'.[1]

Henry was right. When James flitted to London in 1603, nothing had changed in constitutional theory except that the two separate and independent countries of Scotland and England now shared the same king. In fact, the consequences were disastrous for Scotland. On the credit side, the wastage and destruction of border warfare was brought to an end, although the invasion and military occupation of Scotland still recurred later in the century. On the other hand, Scotland ceased at a stroke to have an independent foreign and trade policy. Foreign policy was a royal prerogative and the king of Scotland was now living in London and necessarily concerned mainly with the interests of his larger kingdom. The trade of Scotland was impaired and destroyed by England's wars with her main trading partners, France and Holland. 'From the Union of the Crowns the sole business of Scotland with foreign countries was to contribute men and money towards whatever policy her predominant partner might choose to adopt'.[2]

In addition, the absentee king in his dealings with Scotland could draw on the wealth and power of England. All state appointments, all patronage (which meant the power of bribery) rested in the hands of the king. This was not a mere fiction, as it later became, but a serious reality. 'From the end of the sixteenth century until the Revolution, except during the covenanting rebellion

22

and the Cromwellian conquest; authority pertained to the King in person and his immediate advisors'.[3] These advisors were in London and for the most part English. James VI and his successors became much more authoritarian and despotic than the king of an independent Scotland had ever been. In Hume Brown's words, James transformed the Scottish constitution: 'He found it a monarchy strictly limited, and left it all but a pure despotism'. Or, as James put it himself: 'This I must say for Scotland, and may truly vaunt it: Here I sit and govern it with my pen: I write and it is done; and by a Clerk of the Council I govern Scotland now, which others could not do by the sword'.[4] It was still worse that it was despotism from a distance, using the demoralising instruments of intimidation and bribery.

The removal of the royal court from Edinburgh was a devastating blow to the cultural identity and self-confidence of Scotland, to the languages and literature and indeed to all the arts. Royal patronage, in the more favourable sense of the term, was then almost indispendable for the survival of many of the arts, the theatre and the more elaborate forms of music. It was not only a question of money, but of royal protection and encouragement of the performers against the disapproval of some circles in the church. In the 16th century, even after the Reformation, the court had been the centre of music, drama and poetry.[5] All this came to an end in 1603. Sir David Lindsay, whose *Satire of the Thrie Estates* had given a resounding opening to the drama in Scotland, had no successors. One of the richest tradition of folk music, poetry and dance in Europe survived, but it was survival in defiance of discouragement. The language of the royal court was now English, not Scots. Increasingly anyone with social or political ambitions felt obliged to form his speech and behaviour on the English model. The bible, in the English translation authorised by James, became for about 300 years the most widely read and influential of all books in Scotland. God spoke in English with the implication that this was the appropriate language for matters of importance. This not only frustrated the development of Scots prose, but introduced a damaging division in the Scottish consciousness, between writing and speech, between thought and emotion.

James's doctrine of the divine right of kings was difficult to reconcile with divergencies between two independent countries. As soon as he succeeded to the English throne he set about trying to assimilate the two into one. 'What God hath conjoined let no man separate', he said in his first address to the English Parliament in March 1603. 'I am the husband and the whole isle is my lawful wife; I am the head and it is my body; I am the shepherd and it is my flock. I hope therefore that no man will think that I, a Christian King under the Gospel, should be a polygamist and husband to two wives; that I being the head should have a divided or monstrous body as that being the shepherd to so fair a flock should have my flock parted in two'.[6] By the exercise of his prerogative alone, and without parliamentary agreement in either kingdom, he adopted the title of King of Great Britain and introduced the Union Flag and a unified coinage. As the Crown Law Officers confirmed in 1604, shared monarchy implied shared citizenship, at least for those born after 1603.[7] All of

James's efforts to push assimilation further broke down because of the passive resistance and opposition of the great majority of people in both countries.

This resistance was inevitable. For three hundred years England had made repeated attempts to subjugate Scotland by force. In Bruce Galloway's words: 'England and Scotland before 1560 were two of the most hostile nations in Christendom. Centuries of warfare and prejudice had isolated them from each other. Scotland's natural ally was France — natural, because both faced English aggression. England claimed material, moral, spiritual, judicial and feudal superiority over Scotland — the last being a formal assertion of suzerainty, resisted steadfastly by successive Scots kings, rebutted by generations of her scholars'.[8] The consequences of this were summarised by the English historian, J. A. Froude: 'The English hated Scotland because Scotland had successfully defied them: the Scots hated England as an enemy on the watch to make them slaves. The hereditary hostility strengthened with time, and each generation added fresh injuries to the accumulation of bitterness'.[9]

The two nations were divided not only by this legacy of hostility but by differences in their historical experience which had produced very different institutions, habits of thought and standards of value. Scotland as a small country subject to constant aggression by a larger neighbour, had sought friends, allies and trading partners all over Europe. Scotland was international in outlook, England was insular and self-sufficient. Scotland was not subject to the same drive towards centralised power which in England was stimulated by the need to finance foreign wars. Although Scotland was more peaceful internally than most European countries,[10] power was dispersed. Scottish constitutional theory believed neither in an omnipotent king nor an omnipotent parliament, but in a balance between a number of institutions with sovereignty resting ultimately in the hands of the whole community. Scotland was marked by an egalitarian spirit and the absence of rigid class divisions. England was much more hierarchical. In nothing was this difference more apparent than in education. Scotland since 1562 had sought to establish a school in every parish and the Church of Scotland laid great stress on the importance of education. The Scottish people as a whole became the best educated in Europe, the foundation of what George Davie has called the Democratic Intellect.[11] In England, education was largely confined to the prosperous until late in the 19th century. Scotland was less prosperous than England because of the harsher climate and more mountainous terrain and because a large part of the fertile south was frequently laid waste by English invasions.

For all these reasons, James's attempt to impose uniformity on his two kingdoms failed to overcome their mutual suspicions and hostility and the difference of laws, institutions and attitudes. The English had a deep-rooted conviction that they were vastly superior to the Scots and to everyone else and could not conceive of a union as anything but the subordination of Scotland to England which they had sought for centuries. If there was to be a union, the Scots wanted equal treatment or some form of federation in which the autonomy of each country would be combined with co-operation for common purposes.

James's successors on the throne maintained the same policy and some show of negotiation was made from time to time by the two Parliaments without very much conviction or sense of purpose. A form of Union was imposed under Cromwell by military force from 1651 to 1660, but this collapsed on Cromwell's death without regret on either side of the Border. About 100 years after the accession of James to the English throne, a combination of circumstances made it clear that the Scots might reassert their independence and chose their own monarch to succeed the last Stuart ruler Queen Anne. It was only then that the English government made a determined bid to secure the union of the parliaments. Queen Anne then had the satisfaction of seeing at last the achievement of what we might call her family policy. Even then, it did not go as far as James VI would have wished. Scotland lost her parliament and any vestige of political independence, but she retained her own church and legal, educational and administrative systems. Scotland was weakened but not destroyed.

Another family policy of James VI and his successors was their attitude to the church in Scotland. In James's view the 'divine right of kings' made him absolute master of his kingdom. This was in flat contradiction to the predominant opinion of Presbyterian Scotland. As James himself said 'Presbyterianism agreeth as well with monarchy as God and the devil'.[12] To the absolute claims of the king, the Presbyterians opposed an equally unyielding demand. In Falkland Palace in September 1596, Andrew Melville, a leading spokesman of Scottish presbyterianism, told James to his face that he was 'God's sillie vassall'. His nephew, James Melville, made the same point in slightly more tactful, but equal forceful, language: 'Ther is twa kings and twa kingdomes in Scotland; Thair is Christ Jesus and his kingdome the Kirk, whose subiect King James the Saxt is, and of whuse kingdome nocht a King, nor a lord nor a heid, bot a member'.[13] Both James and the Kirk in fact claimed divine right. The Kirk recognised that the king had powers to 'govern civilly', but 'spirituall government' was exclusively in the hands of the kirk because of 'a certane power grantit by God'.[14] Since religion was then a matter of the utmost importance to most people, and affected their lives more than any other institution, James was bound to see the pretensions of the Kirk as an intolerable challenge to his authority.

Even before James left Scotland, he had made progress in curbing the power and independence of the Kirk and in bringing it under control through bishops appointed by himself. This had a double-edged effect in strengthening royal authority because of the role of the bishops in Parliament. The Scottish Parliament sat as a single chamber, consisting in the 16th Century of four estates: the nobles, the bishops, the commissioners (or barons) of the shires and the commissioners of the burghs. The Committee of Articles had a central role in its procedure because it alone had the power to propose legislation and consider it in detail for subsequent ratification by the whole House. In 1621, James was able to achieve an ingenious arrangement. 'The bishops selected eight nobles, who in turn chose eight bishops and those sixteen then chose the barons and burgesses. This represented a triumph for the crown, because, since the bishops were the King's creatures, they necessarily chose the nobles whom he recommended, and those nobles, in choosing bishops, had only royal nominees to choose from'.[15]

There was an overall consistency about James's policy. Remote in England and supported by English wealth and power he had been able to impose a new autocracy on Scotland. It was no longer true as Sir John Fortescue wrote of the King of Scots in the 15th century, 'he may not rule his people by other laws than such as they assent unto'.[16] This new power enabled James to impose his will on the Kirk. This, in turn, was in line with his desire to unify his two kingdoms since what he set to do was to bring the Scottish church into line with the English, subject to royal authority through the bishops. His preference for the more docile and controllable system of the Church in England may generally have disposed him towards the imitation of English practice in other matters, and be part of the motive behind his general policy of union and assimilation. By the end of his reign in 1625 he seemed almost to have achieved his will over the Kirk, but it was an unstable achievement because it did not rest on the consent of the people. Events were to show that there was still a sense in which Sir John Fortescue was right.

James's son, who succeeded to the throne as Charles I in 1625, continued the same policies in Church and State as his father but without the same understanding of his Scottish subjects. James was born and educated in Scotland and he had ruled as King of Scots for more than 30 years before he left for London. Charles was less than 3 years old when he left Scotland and did not visit the country again until he was 33. James could boast that 'he knew the stomach' of the Scots; Charles had been educated entirely in England and had no understanding of the national character and national aspirations of his Scottish subjects.[17] Charles followed the same policy of asserting royal power but with an arrogance, tactlessness and ineptitude that provoked open rebellion in each of his three kingdoms, Scotland, England and Ireland.

The Scots took the initiative and, in H. A. L. Fisher's words, 'precipitated the Great Rebellion'.[18] The signature of the National Covenant in 1638, 'signed with an enthusiasm such as had never before swept over the Scottish people',[19] was the first act of defiance. Never was a revolutionary manifesto so studiously moderate in its terms. It avoided a specific attack on the powers of the king or his bishops, but by calling for the need for all innovations to 'be tryed and allowed in free assemblies and in Parliament',[20] it effectively repudiated all that James and Charles had been trying to achieve.

Charles's attempts to subdue his Scottish subjects by force by invading Scotland in the two Bishops' Wars ended in humiliation for him and the triumph of the Covenant. The Scottish estates met in 1640 in defiance of the king and not only approved the National Covenant but adopted several measures which transferred real power from the king to Parliament itself. The bishops were abolished and with them the arrangement which had enabled the king to control Parliament through the Committee of the Articles. A full and free parliament was in future to meet at least once every three years and all matters and grievances were to be raised and debated in the full parliament. In future, parliament was to have the power to approve or veto nominations to the Privy Council and judiciary.[21] These arrangements for government by parliament and not by royal prerogative were very similar in effect to those which Andrew Fletcher afterwards sought to recover through his proposal for limitations on the royal power.

It was necessary for Fletcher to fight this battle over again in 1703 for the achievements of the Scottish Revolution of 1637–1644[22] did not survive in the complicated events which followed. When the English in turn rebelled against the king, they sought Scottish help. 'All their last hope seemed to be in their blessed brethern the Scots'.[23]. This the Scots granted through the alliance of the Solemn League and Covenant in 1643, but the outcome was disastrous for Scotland. When the English executed Charles in 1649, the Scots, who had not been consulted, proclaimed Charles II in his place. This gave a pretext to Cromwell to invade Scotland and impose a union of the two kingdoms. The union did not long survive Cromwell who died in September 1658. Hardly anyone in either country was in favour of retaining it. The experience of the Cromwellian union, wrote H. A. L. Fisher, left a 'bitter taste' in Scotland.[24]

Not surprisingly, therefore, the restoration of Charles II in 1660 was greeted in Scotland with enthusiasm; but the satisfaction was short lived. The new king wasted no time in showing that he meant to follow the same policies in Church and State as his father and grandfather. He proposed to reassert the direct personal authority of a king claiming divine right which was incompatible with the Presbyterianism of the majority of his Scottish subjects. It was as though the Scottish Revolution and the English Civil War had never happened. Charles appointed his Privy Council before calling Parliament. When he did call Parliament in January 1661, it had been carefully selected to ensure a docile majority. They proceeded in no fewer than 393 Acts to put the clock back to the time when the absolute monarchy of James VI had been unchallenged. A general Recissory Act declared the proceedings of every Parliament since 1637 null and void. To the king was given 'the sole choice and appointment' of all the great officers of State, the right of summoning and dissolving Parliaments at his pleasure, of making war and peace and concluding leagues and treaties.[25] Next year, Parliament readmitted bishops and restored lay patronage (ie the appointment of ministers by the landowners). Parliament completed the process in 1663 by restoring the method of electing the Lords of the Articles which gave effective control to the king through his bishops. The king who had now assumed such arbitrary and complete power was, of course, now a king resident in London, knowing little about Scotland and subject to predominantly English influence through his advisors and courtiers. Charles never visited Scotland after his accession to the throne.

It was the legislation of 1662 on lay patronage and episcopacy which began the sorry process of persecution which filled the reigns of Charles II and James VII, in Hume Brown's words, with 'the darkest and sublimest passages of the national history'.[26] Since episcopacy had been abolished in 1638 and lay patronage in 1649, most ministers by 1662 held their churches by direct appointment from their congregations and presbyteries. An Act of 11 June 1662, required all such ministers to receive presentation from the landowner holding the right of patronage and approval by the appropriate bishop by 20 September. Since few responded, the time limit was twice extended and the pressure increased. Even so, between 200 and 300 ministers, about a third of the total, preferred to sacrifice their livings and abandon their home and stipends, rather than compromise with their conscience.

This impressive demonstration of the probity of the Scottish ministry was to be repeated in the Disruption of 1843 and over one of the same issues, lay patronage. This had once again been imposed on the Church of Scotland by the British Parliament shortly after the Union of 1707 and in violation of its terms. Lord Cockburn said that the sacrifice of all their worldly interests for the sake of conscience by hundreds of ministers was 'one of the rarest occurrences in moral history. I know no parallel to it'.[27] He was right that such unselfish devotion to principle by so many was unusual, but he evidently did not know of the very close parallel of 1662, under conditions which involved much greater personal risk.

From 1662 onwards, and indeed for the next 26 years, government was carried on through the Privy Council appointed by the King. For much of the period, from 1667 to 1678, the Secretary, the Duke of Lauderdale, although acting in the King's name, became a virtual dictator. The main business of Government was to try to enforce on a reluctant people a form of Church and State which they had already resisted for more than fifty years. It was a struggle which aroused the strongest of feelings because it was a matter not only of politics but of deeply held religious convictions. Religion to many people was more important than life itself; they were prepared to die rather than yield on any essential point of their belief. Many of them did in fact give up their lives as the Privy Council devised more and more drastic means to suppress opposition. Torture, execution, transportation to slavery in the English colonies, imprisonment in intolerable conditions were all used, as well as arbitrary fines and the quartering of troops on families to exact compliance. It was the blackest time in Scottish history because it was the only period in which the State used such methods to try to impose its will, a totalitarianism of the worst kind. It was also, to use Hume Brown's word, the sublimest, because it revealed the endurance, courage and dignity of ordinary people under intense pressure, even if the sufferings of some drove them to fanaticism and excess.

Of course not all men have the endurance to survive more than 25 years of persecution. Eventually, by a policy of alternating concession and repression, the Privy Council broke the solid force of Scottish Presbyterianism. Through three successive Acts of Indulgence they succeeded in making many Presbyterians compromise with the essential principles of their belief, the equality of all men before God and government of the Kirk, not by a king and bishops, but through free General Assemblies. Those who resisted to the end, the

Covenanters or Cameronians, the men and women forced to practice their religion in conventicles in the fields, became a remnant hunted like wild animals by men like Claverhouse and Dalziel. Even the Presbyterians who compromised or escaped persecution, and that included the majority of the population, suffered agonies from the damage inflicted on their kirk. Robert Wodrow, the historian of these events, has a memorable passage about this. Although 'public and barbarous violences, tortures, public executions and murders in cold blood', comprise the 'frightful impressions of the blackness of the time', we should not forget the sufferings of the other Presbyterians who avoided these worst excesses. They suffered 'daily distress and terror . . . . together with the lamentable prospect they had of their posterity's being brought up in ignorance and profanity, and under the want of the gospel purely dispensed'.[28]

This period of oppression, the 'Killing Times', was unlike anything else in Scottish history. Apart from the trials for sedition of a few people when Government panicked after the French Revolution, there is no other instance of a deliberate and sustained policy to use violence to suppress opinion. It was a direct consequence of the Union of the Crowns of 1603. The form of Church government, and of the relations between Church and State, which successive kings tried to impose from London was an English view of these matters, although it was one that happened to suit the personal aspirations of a Scottish king, James VI. More than that, a king and his advisors and officers could not have attempted to impose any policy so repugnant to the majority of the Scottish people, if he had not been remote from the scene and backed by English power.

Since Andrew Fletcher was born in 1653 and therefore reached maturity in the 1670s, he grew up in the middle of this period of oppression imposed by an absentee king. People who have written about him have often attributed his radical and republican views to the influence of Gilbert Burnet or to his reading of the Greek and Latin classics. These influences no doubt played a part, but it seems likely to me that the most important influence of all was what Fletcher saw happening around him in the Scotland of the Restoration.

4

Protest and Exile; 1678–1682

'Salton was always observed to be turbulent and factious'
— Sir John Lauder of Fountainhall

We really do not know where Fletcher was or what he was doing in the years immediately after Gilbert Burnet left Saltoun in 1669. It is very probable that he studied in one or more universities and travelled in Europe. Even if Lord Buchan had not reported the family tradition, everything that Fletcher wrote suggests such a background. He may also have served in some European army, because only a few years later he seems already to have the reputation of an experienced cavalry officer. We can only speculate, because no written records survive, or at least none which have so far come to light. There is, however, no doubt that Fletcher was back in Scotland by 1678. That is the year when his political career begins and references to him start to appear both in the official record of the Scottish Parliament and in the memoirs and letters of the time.

A Convention of the Estates was called to meet in Edinburgh on 26 June 1678 with John, Duke of Lauderdale as High Commissioner. According to the official record,[1] two commissioners were returned for the shire of Haddington, Adam Cockburn of Ormeston and James Fletcher of Saltoun. The name James was clearly a mistake, because there was no doubt that Andrew was laird of Saltoun. A Convention had the same membership as a Parliament, but it was generally expected to sit for a shorter period and to be more restricted in its activities. It could vote funds for the government but was not expected to indulge in important legislation. The absentee King, Charles II, and his agent in Scotland, Lauderdale, made it very clear to this particular Convention that their business was to vote the supply of money and nothing else.

Since 1667 the administration of Scotland had been in the hands of Lauderdale. He said that his great aim was to make Charles master 'in all causes and over all persons'.[2] John Hill Burton wrote of them: 'never was Eastern despot blessed with a minister of his will more obedient, docile, and sedulous'.[3] In practice, Charles left Lauderdale a free hand to run Scotland as he pleased, provided it was done in the royal name to serve royal purposes. Parliament was rarely summoned or allowed to interfere. It was fitting, Lauderdale believed, 'that this Kingdoms return to the good old form of government by his Majesty's Privy Council'.[4] It was despotism, even if, as it used to be said of the Austrian Empire, despotism softened by muddle and incompetence. There was little resistance, apart from the 'poor, suffering, bleeding remnant' of the Covenanters, mainly in the south west. The country had hardly recovered from the trauma and humiliation of the Cromwellian occupation. The bulk of the people conformed, no doubt often reluctantly and with resentment. Lauderdale, even if he alternated between repression and indulgence, could be ruthless and he represented the unassailable King in London backed by English power. The traditional leaders of the community, the lords and lairds, were poor in money if not in land and depended heavily on royal favour. It was a highly demoralising form of government. 'Possibly the worst aspect of the Restoration regime in Scotland was the way in which exaltation of the royal prerogative and venality combined to rot away nearly every vestige of public morality'.[5]

Not the least unfortunate consequence of an absentee King with the wealth and power of England at his disposal was its effect on the Scottish Parliament. We have, of course, to remember that during the whole of the period under discussion Parliament, in both Scotland and England, was representative of only a very small proportion of the population. In Scotland all estates of Parliament sat together in the same House. The Lords were there by hereditary right. In periods of Episcopacy, the Bishops were appointed by the King and one of their functions was to help in the management of the Parliament in the royal interest. The Commissioners of the Burghs were selected by the Town Councils, which were themselves self-perpetuating oligarchies. Those of the Shires were chosen out of their own number by the lairds. That was all. There was no representation of the mass of the people and nothing at all equivalent to general elections in the modern sense.

This meant that the King and his administration could manage and control Parliament without having to worry about an electorate. It was sufficient to manipulate the 200 or so members. For this purpose, the royal control of patronage was a powerful instrument. All government posts, pensions and sinecures, all jobs in the state service from the highest to the lowest were in the gift of the King personally or of the officials acting on his behalf. The members of Parliament came precisely from the classes who relied on patronage for themselves and their relations; very few other ways of making a living were open to them. In these circumstances, it is not surprising that Parliament tended to be under the control of the Administration. What is more surprising is that they did at times assert themselves, as in 1641 when they obliged Charles I to accept parliamentary control and again, as we shall see, in 1703, largely under the influence of Andrew Fletcher. The habit of managing Parliaments by patronage, which is a polite word for bribery, survived long after the Union. It was at its height between the Restoration of 1660 and the first Reform Act of 1832, not by any means that it has now disappeared as an instrument of government. One of the reasons why Andrew Fletcher made such an impression on his contemporaries was that he exposed this system and refused to accept it at a time when it was at its height and was widely regarded as the norm of parliamentary behaviour.

1678, the year of Fletcher's parliamentary debut, was a year of crisis. Lauderdale's clumsy attempts to deal with religious dissent were only increasing the problem. Feeling against him was hardening both in Scotland and England. His actions suggest that he was becoming desperate. In 1674, all heritors and masters, that is landowners and employers, had been made responsible for the conduct of their tenants and servants. Lauderdale went further by an Act of Council in 1677 which required the heritors and masters to sign a bond for the loyal behaviour of all persons residing on their lands. Not unnaturally many of the landowners, especially in the south west, refused to accept an obligation which they had no power to fulfill. This refusal was taken as conclusive proof that the country was ripe for rebellion, and to counter it Lauderdale took an extraordinary step. In February 1678, a force of 6,000 Highlanders and 3,000 of the Lowland militia, the so-called Highland Host, were sent to Ayrshire with instructions to take up free quarters wherever they wished, disarm the country and exact signatures to the bond. This course was so misguided as a means of winning support for an unpopular government that Burnet thought that it was a deliberate attempt to provoke an uprising which would justify arrests for treason and the confiscation of estates. People saw through it, and 'bore the present oppression more quietly than otherwise they would have done', but Lauderdale's party was so sanguine in their hopes of fomenting a rebellion that they began to reckon upon confiscated lands, and 'on Valentine's day, instead of drawing mistresses, they drew estates'.[6]

It was against this background of arbitrary government and intimidation that the Convocation of Estates of 1678 met in June. The proceedings began with Lauderdale informing the members that the King wished them to be reminded of the Act of 1661 which prohibited assemblies 'for treating or consulting in any matter of state . . . without his Majesty's consent and approvation'.[7] Thus chastened, the Convocation for the next four days considered several cases of disputed membership. Fletcher took an early opportunity to demonstrate that he was not to be intimidated and would not hesitate to challenge Lauderdale himself. The episode was trivial enough, but it showed the pride, courage and determination to defend the right which marked the whole of Fletcher's parliamentary life.

The incident was recorded by Sir John Lauder of Fountainhall (1646–1722) who for more than 40 years as a lawyer and member of parliament kept voluminous notes of decisions in the courts and of political events. They are of such accuracy that, as 'Fountainhall's Decisions', they can be cited as precedents in the Scottish courts. Like Fletcher he was a laird from the Shire of Haddington. Indeed he was a close neighbour because his seat near Ormiston is only about five miles west of Saltoun. From 1685 to the Union, he was one of the Commissioners from Haddington in ten Parliaments. Although he was not in the Convention of 1678, he shared the representation of Haddington with Fletcher in the Parliaments of 1703 to 1706 and joined with him in opposing the proposals for the Union. He clearly took a close interest in the activities of his neighbour from Saltoun who appears frequently in his *Historical Observes* and *Historical Notices*.

The first of these references is this apparently trivial episode in 1678, which served notice that Fletcher was not to be counted on as docile respecter of authority. Fountainhall tells us that an order had been given that only members were to be allowed to 'adventure in' to Parliament Hall during the meetings. He continues:— 'Yet, on the 2nd of July (which was the 4th meeting), Henry Fletcher, brother to Salton on of the Commissioners, having got in, was observed, and sent to the Tolboth, and fined in 20 dollars; whiron Salton, the meeting theireafter, pitched on little William Talmush as no member, so that the Commissioner was forced to oune him as on of his servants, whom he had priviledge to bring in'.[8] Lauderdale's second wife, Lady Dysart, was the widow of Sir Lionel Talmash. She was a domineering and ostentatious woman, of whom it was said that if Lauderdale ruled Scotland, his wife ruled him.[9] This 'little William Talmush' was presumably a member of her family; Fletcher was deliberately baiting Lauderdale at a sensitive point.

When the Convention finally got down to business on the 4 July, Lauderdale presented a letter from the King demanding the supply of money to pay for defence against 'foreign invasions and intestine comotions especially at a tyme when these dangerous field conventicles (so justly termed in our Lawes, the Rendezvouz of Rebellion) doe still grow in their numbers and insolencies'. To this the King's letter added bluntly, 'This is the only business youw are to doe in this Convention', the Convention duly did as it was told. 'Chearfully and unanimouslie', according to the official record, they voted a supply of eighteen hundred thousand pounds Scots to be raised from the shires and burghs over five years.[10]

The business ended on 11 July with the approval of a letter to the King which is a curious document in several respects. The Scots were evidently still ready to claim Charles II as a fellow countryman, although he had been brought up under English influence and had become entirely English in his attitudes. The letter began by speaking of 'the great happiness of living under a King of our own Nation and religion, whose predecessors have for so many ages kept us from being conquered by strangers'. It is tactfully silent on the point that these 'strangers' were the same people who had now made the King one of their own. It goes on to refer to the Covenanters who were resisting the régime. 'These errors do in most proceed rather from a misrepresentation of your Majesties' inclinations than from any formal resolution of apposing your authority'. (An excuse with which we are still familiar from contemporary governments; it is not that their policy is wrong, but that they have failed to explain it properly). The letter ends with flattering allusions to Lauderdale and then expresses the hope that 'wee may continue to bliss God for a King who like God (From whom alone our Kings deryve their power) never uses his power but to do good'.[11] A far cry from 'God's sillie vassall'.

Burnet said that the praise of Lauderdale was 'so base and abject a thing that it brought the whole nation under great contempt'.[12] Fountainhall has some robust comments about the comparison of the King with God. Some thought, he wrote, that it 'wanted not much of blasphemy'. As for the claim that his power derived from God, some denied it. Even if it were true, it would apply equally to all princes and 'hinders not but the people are God's instrument in conveying the said power'.[13] Of course, Burnet and Fountainhall were right. It was abject that the Convention should so tamely give the government what it wanted, apparently without criticism of their flagrant abuse of power, and endorse the divine right of kings without asserting the traditional Scottish view that sovereignity depended on the will of the people. Apart from the usual effects of patronage, there were some other factors. In the first place, Lauderdale had called the Convocation while many of the Scottish nobility had gone to London to complain to the King about the mismanagement of the government. Then, the government was ruthless. Their willingness to quarter troops with a licence to loot in the houses of dissidents was a powerful means of persuasion. Also, we have only the official record of the proceedings and Fountainhall was unfortunately not a member and therefore not in a position to give us a fuller account of what went on in the debates. The official record gives the impression that all decisions were unanimous, but gives no voting figures. Fountainhall, on the other hand, does tell us that about 39 generally voted with the opposition led by the Duke of Hamilton and about 100 with Lauderdale. He mentions Fletcher as one of the opposition.[14] In the circumstances of the time even to vote against the government took courage. We have no record of the speeches.

Lauderdale's attempts to suppress dissent by raising troops and quartering them on dissidents did not succeed. In 1679 Archbishop Sharp, regarded by the Covenanters as a traitor to the cause, was murdered. In the open civil war which followed, the royal forces were commanded by the King's bastard son, the Duke of Monmouth. He won the day at the Battle of Bothwell Brig, but showed by his conduct that he was in favour of a more moderate and conciliatory policy. Lauderdale's twelve years of power were at an end. For the next Parliament, which met on 28 July 1681, after a gap of nine years, the King's brother, James, Duke of Albany and York, appeared as Commissioner. He was the heir to the throne and a declared Catholic, facts which caused great unease in both Scotland and England.

Fletcher of Saltoun and Cockburn of Ormeston were again elected by the lairds of the shire of Haddington, but this time their elections was disputed by the Government. The Chairman of the Committee on disputed elections was Bishop Paterson of Edinburgh, naturally enough since one of the roles of the King's bishops was to act as his agents in the control of Parliament. He proposed that, 'for the sake of serving the King', some of the votes cast for Fletcher and Cockburn should be disregarded.[15] Evidently the Government was doing its best to silence them. In fact the Committee upheld the election of both and they took the oath, and presumably their seats, on 18 August.

This meant that Fletcher was not in the House on 11 August for the important debate on the Act 'acknowledging and asserting the right of succession to the Imperial Crown of Scotland'. This was clearly intended to ensure the succession of James in spite of his Catholicism. It asserted that 'no difference in

Religion nor law nor act of Parliament made or to be made can alter or direct the Right of Succession and Lineal descent of the Crown', and that it was treason to oppose this.[16] Parliament was sufficiently docile to pass the Act, although once again no voting figures were recorded. Although Fletcher was not there to resist or protest, Fountainhall tells us that he was 'always observed to be turbulent and factious' and that he sent letters to members urging them to oppose the Succession Act.[17] Fletcher was no religious bigot or enthusiast, but he shared the general view that James was likely to be even more tyrannical than his predecessors.

Fletcher was present for the next important debate on 31 August on the Test Act, an 'Oath to be taken by all Persons in publick Trust'.[18] According to Burnet, this originated in a promise by the Government that the Succession Act would be balanced by every imaginable guarantee for Prostestantism. When it came to the drafting, the government could not resist the temptation to insert clauses condemning the Covenants, and banning all resistance to the will of the King or any attempt to make any change or alteration either in Church or State. The difficulty of defining Protestantism was solved by a proposal of James Dalrymple, designed deliberately to confuse the issue, to adopt the Confession of Faith of 1559. 'That was a book', Burnet says, 'so worn out of use that scarce any in the whole Parliament had ever read it'.[19] It was also quite inconsistent with the current régime in the Church, especially as it endorsed resistance to tyranny as a duty. The result was 'a medly of popery, prelacy, erastianism and self-contradiction', but it passed, according to Burnet by a majority of ten votes. It was also resolved that the electors of the Commissioners of the Shires should be required to take this strange hotch-potch of an oath. At this point, the official record makes the only admission of dissent: 'The Laird of Saltoun and the Laird of Grant having voted in the Negative desired their dissent might be marked'.[20] Once again, Fletcher had stood up to be counted.

James Dalrymple, who confused the Test Act so ingeniously, was at that time Lord President of the Court of Session. In the same year as this Parliament, he published his great work, the *Institutions of the Law of Scotland*, which codified Scots law into a coherent philosophical system. Like Fletcher he fled to Holland to escape persecution and both men were later cited together for treason. Again like Fletcher, he returned with William of Orange. He was reappointed as Lord President and made a Viscount as Lord Stair. He died in 1695.

The Test Act was so objectionable in its demands for the royal prerogative, and so unintelligible in its contradictions, that Dalrymple and about 80 of the clergy chose to resign rather than comply. When the Earl of Argyll was asked to take the oath he did so 'as far as it was consistent with itself'.[21] This was not good enough for James who was determined 'either to gain him or ruin him'. On a very slender pretext, Argyll was tried for treason and condemned. 'No sentence was more universally cried out on as this', says Burnet. 'All people spoke of it, and of the Duke that drove it on, with horror'.[22] Argyll in fact escaped from Edinburgh Castle in disguise and made his way to Holland. Even so, the whole episode shows the very real danger that Fletcher was facing in confronting the Duke of York.

Fletcher's opposition was not confined to Parliament. From 1680 onwards, he was conducting a campaign of obstruction and resistance to the Government's militia. On 29 July 1680 he and two other lairds were summoned before the Privy Council to answer charges of 'seditiously and factiously opposing, at least obstructing his Majesty's service'. In their defence, they argued practical difficulties and, contrary to expectations, escaped with a rebuke.[23] Next January, Fletcher along with Lord Yester and 'ten other gentlemen of East Lothian' petitioned the Privy Council against the quartering of troops on them. This act, says Fountainhall, was 'extremely resented, because it called Quartering contrare to law; and seemed to derogate from the King's prerogative, and reflected on the Government'.[24] No doubt, a challenge to royal power and a reflection on the Government was exactly what Fletcher intended.

Fletcher and some other unnamed lairds of East Lothian were in trouble with the Privy Council again in April 1682 for their refusal to co-operate in the sale of corn, straw, grass and hay for the horses of the militia. The irritation of the authorities is very obvious in the terms of the complaint by the Lord Advocate. He accused them of pretending to cooperate by setting prices but failing to make any arrangements for the sale. It was, he said, a 'designe and snare to his Majesty's forces and as an engine to put the forces and country people by the eares rather than ane act of obedience to his Majesties authority'.[25] Fountainhall says that 'after much travill and paynes' on the part of the Council, the lairds agreed to name storehouses where the soldiers could come for their supplies.

No government likes to have its authority mocked and flouted like this, and one resting on arbitrary royal power least of all. The trial of Argyll in 1681 had shown how harsh and intolerant the Government was prepared to be. It is therefore not surprising that, shortly after the complaint by the Lord Advocate, Fletcher decided to join Argyll and other opponents of the régime who were gathering in Holland around William of Orange. He was obliged to flee to Holland, says Elisabeth Halkett in her memoir, 'to avoid persecution which would have proved fatal.' No doubt she is right about this, but we do not know the exact timing or circumstances of Fletcher's flight to political exile. He may have had some warning that he was about to be arrested or he may have decided that he could be more useful if he joined the other dissidents who were preparing an attempt at liberation from the outside. He was certainly abroad in 1683. Elisabeth Halkett says that he went in that year from Holland to England with Baillie of Jerviswood 'in order to concoct measures with the friends of liberty in that country'.[26] He was also in France on a similar mission. On 5 October 1683, the English Ambassador, Lord Preston, wrote from Paris to Lord Halifax: 'Here is one Fletcher, Laird of Saltoun, lately come from Scotland. He is an ingenious but a violent fanatic, and doubtless hath some commission, for I hear he is very busy and very virulent'.[27]

5

Monmouth's Rebellion; Exile Again. 1683–1688.

'A person of character and worth in a decisive engagement'.
— *Robert Ferguson*

In the 1680s men who wanted to curb the arbitrary power of Charles and prevent the accession to the throne of his brother, James, were planning secretly in both Scotland and England and gathering together in exile in Europe, especially in Holland. In London the Rye House Plot of 1683 was an ill-conceived and confused attempt to assassinate both Charles and James. Quite separate from that was the more serious and realistic opposition of the Council of Six, led by Lord Russell, and involving the Duke of Monmouth.

According to Elisabeth Halkett, Fletcher and Robert Baillie of Jerviswood when they went to London from Holland were 'the only persons who were entrusted so far as to be admitted into the secrets of Lord Russell's Council of Six, and these two were the only two persons whom the Earl of Argyll consulted in Holland concerning the common measures which were then conducted with so much danger for the preservation of the constitution & liberties of both Kingdoms'.[1]

There is some confusion in this account. Burnet, who met Baillie in London, does not mention Fletcher in this connection. He says that Baillie, whom he knew well and was cousin german to him, came from Scotland and was accompanied by 'two other gentlemen of Scotland, both Campbells'.[2] Also, certainly far more people than two were involved in Argyll's preparations in Holland. The same Robert Baillie was not one of them (although his son was there) because he was arrested in London in 1683, treated with extreme brutality, and taken to Edinburgh for trial and execution. He died without incriminating any of his associates despite repeated torture. To suggestions that his life might be spared if he gave information about others, he made the memorable reply: 'They who make such a proposal, neither know me nor my country'.[3]

On the other hand, there is some confirmation in Fountainhall that Fletcher did visit London at about this time for talks with the people close to Monmouth. 'They say', Fountainhall wrote in 1685, 'what irritated him, was, that the present King hearing he was at Brussels, sent over privily to the Marquis de Grana to cause apprehend him; whereon Saltoun getting account, it forced him to flee in to London, wher he met Monmouth's unfortunate Company'.[4] Fleeing to London may seem a strange way to avoid arrest at the request of the King, but it is typical of Fletcher to respond to an assault by direct counter-attack.

37

Also, since he shortly became closely involved with Monmouth's rebellion, it is quite likely that he had established contact at an earlier stage.

The fact that Burnet does not mention a visit by Fletcher to London does not necessarily mean that it did not happen. Burnet tells us himself that he prudently refused an offer by Hampden, one of the Council of Six, of a full account of its affairs. With the experience of people like Robert Baillie in mind, he did not want to know secrets which he 'might be obliged to reveal, or to lie and deny my knowledge of them'.[5] With equal prudence, he went to France at about this time, 'chiefly to be out of the way'.[6] As I mentioned at the end of the previous chapter, we know that Fletcher was also in Paris in October 1683. Possibly he and Burnet travelled from London together. They were certainly soon afterwards together in Holland. No doubt, Burnet could have told us much more about Fletcher than he does. Unfortunately, as I have said, the sad fact is that they did not like each other very much. It is perhaps for this reason alone that the normally garrulous Burnet has so little to say about Fletcher.

If the Government had been able to find Fletcher in London in 1683, he would no doubt have suffered the same treatment as Robert Baillie. Whether he was there or not, the Government seems to have been trying to keep track of his movements and activities. The request to de Grana and the report from the Embassy in Paris suggests as much. The Government went further in November 1684. Fountainhall records that criminal letters were posted at the Mercat Cross of Edinburgh and the Pier and Shore of Leith requiring him to appear within 60 days on a charge of 'conversing with Argyle, and other rebells abroad'.[7] This amounts to a formal accusation of treason. It was a clear warning to Fletcher of what he might expect if he fell into the hands of the Government.

Fountainhall adds a comment: 'His converse with Monmouth cannot be criminell, he having got a remission from his Majesty in December 1683, unlesse he has committed some crime since that tyme'. Monmouth was the son of Charles II and his mistress, Lucy Walter. He was born in Holland in 1649 but came to England in 1662 and was received with every mark of approval by the King. In 1663 he was created a duke and married to the wealthiest of Scottish heiresses, Ann Scott, countess of Buccleuch in her own right. He was a handsome, dashing figure with every quality likely to attract popularity. Rivalry with the King's brother, James, Duke of York, was inevitable. Monmouth began to appear as a possible successor to the throne, especially because of the wide-spread distrust in both kingdoms of James's Catholicism. In the event, the King refused to desert his brother. Monmouth defied an order to go abroad and made a series of progresses through parts of England where he was enthusiastically received. He seems to have been involved in the Rye House Plot. For all of this he was pardoned by the King and he took refuge in Holland early in 1684. The death of Charles II in February 1685 and the succession of York as James VII or II destroyed Monmouth's hopes of succession.

Fountainhall's point was that any association with Monmouth could not be regarded as criminal at that time because of the royal pardon, but Argyll as a condemned and escaped traitor was a different matter. By the time of the posting of the summons to Fletcher in November 1684, Monmouth, Argyll, Fletcher and many other opponents of the regime were all in Holland and mostly in Amsterdam. 'It soon appeared' Macaulay wrote, that they 'had scarcely anything in common except hatred of James and impatience to return from banishment. The Scots were jealous of the English, the English of the Scots. Monmouth's high pretensions were offensive to Argyll, who, proud of ancient nobility and of a legitimate descent from kings, was by no means inclined to do homage to the offspring of a vagrant and ignoble love'. He goes on to say that some of the Scots had been so much influenced by long opposition to tyranny that they were not prepared to tolerate any restraint and were therefore unwilling to submit themselves to the leadership of Argyll.[8]

Fletcher, in fact, in spite of the proclamation at the Mercat Cross of Edinburgh, seems to have had very little to do with Argyll. According to Fountainhall, Argyle complained that Fletcher was so 'ill-mannered' that he sent no reply to several letters which Argyle had sent to him.[9] Argyle and Monmouth eventually made up their disagreements when Argyll was preparing to make a landing in Scotland. Instead of offering Monmouth the command, Argyll suggested that he should take a separate expedition to England. Burnet, who was in a position to know, says that 'Fletcher, a Scotch gentleman of great parts, and many virtues, but a most violent republican, and extravagantly passionate, did not like Argyll's scheme: so he resolved to run fortunes with the duke of Monmouth'.[10]

Fletcher, although vehemently anxious to see the overthrow of James, did not like Monmouth's scheme much better. He saw no prospect of success in his expedition and argued strongly against it. To Lord Grey who said that Henry VII had landed with a smaller number and succeeded, Fletcher replied that Henry 'was sure of several of the nobility, who were little princes in those days'. Even Monmouth thought that it was 'a mad and desperate undertaking . . . It was throwing away all his hopes in one day'. Fletcher told Burnet that 'Monmouth was pushed on to it against his own sense and reason; but he could not refuse to hazard his own person, when other were so forward'. Fletcher, with his high ideals of honourable behaviour, evidently also felt obliged to go ahead, against his better judgement. The Earl of Dartmouth adds the comment that Fletcher had told him that he had good grounds to suspect that William of Orange (who of course had his own designs on the British throne) had encouraged the expedition with the deliberate purpose of ruining Monmouth. Sir John Dalrymple said of this: 'the authority is high, because Fletcher was in a situation to know and was incapable of lying'.[11]

Both expeditions were disastrous failures. In Scotland, Argyll's small force was soon broken up and he was captured and executed without further trial. Monmouth too was defeated at Sedgemoor and executed along with many of his followers. Fletcher escaped this fate only because he was obliged to abandon the expedition almost as soon as it landed in June 1685. Burnet gives an account of what happened:

> Soon after their landing, lord Grey was sent out with a small party. He saw a few of the militia, and he ran for it: but his men stood, and the militia ran from them. Lord Grey brought a false alarm, that was soon found to be so: for the men whom their leader had abandoned came back in good order. The duke of Monmouth was struck with this, when he found that the person on whom he depended most, and for whom he designed the command of the horse, had already made himself infamous by his cowardice. He intended to join Fletcher with him in that command. But an unhappy accident made it not convenient to keep him longer about him. He sent him out on another party: and he, not being yet furnished with a horse, took the horse of one who had brought in a great body of men from Taunton. He was not in the way: so Fletcher, not seeing him to ask his leave, thought that all things were to be in common among them, that could advance the service. After Fletcher had rid about as he was ordered, as he returned, the owner of the horse he rode on, who was a rough and ill bred man, reproached him in very injurious terms, for taking out his horse without his leave. Fletcher bore this longer than could have been expected from one of his impetuous temper. But the other persisted in giving him foul language, and offered a switch or a cane: upon which he discharged his pistol at him, and fatally shot him dead. He went and gave the duke of Monmouth an account of this, who saw it was impossible to keep him longer about him, without disgusting and losing the country people, who were coming in a body to demand justice. So he advised him to go abroad the ship, and to sail on to Spain, whither she was bound. By this means he was preserved for that time.[12]

Elisabeth Halkett has a different story.[13] She says that Fletcher himself told the Earl Marischall that he abandoned the rebellion only when Monmouth had himself proclaimed as King 'several weeks' after the shooting. In fact the proclamation was in Taunton on June 20, only nine days after the landing. It is very unlikely that there was such a conversation between Fletcher and Marischall, who was less than twenty at the time of Fletcher's death. All contemporary accounts, in fact, agree that Fletcher had to leave immediately after the incident. The man involved, a goldsmith from Taunton named Dare, was well-known and influential locally. Monmouth would have lost all hope of raising support if he had kept Fletcher with him.

Robert Ferguson, known as 'the Plotter' because of his involvement in many of the intrigues of the age, was one of those who landed with Monmouth. He says that Fletcher drew his pistol only to ward off Dare's assault with a cane. The shooting was accidental, 'contrary to his thoughts and inclinations, and to his unconceivable grief'. Ferguson speaks highly of Fletcher. 'He was a person who by his courage, military skill, civil prudence, application to business, and the interest he had in the Duke, would have contributed much to the conduct of our whole affairs, and have promoted the embracing all opportunities for action, attended with any probable success, so he would have done everything that could have been expected from a person of character and worth in a decisive engagement'. He was, Ferguson adds, one of Monmouth's 'two best officers'.[14] We do not know where or how Fletcher acquired this reputation for military skill. It was presumably during his first absence abroad from about 1669 to 1678, when he was between 16 and 25 years old.

From the time when Fletcher sailed to Spain in June 1685 until he returned to Scotland in 1688, he disappears again from any surviving contemporary record. Elisabeth Halkett has a brief account, with two picturesque if unlikely episodes. She says that he was thrown into prison when he arrived in Spain, but was rescued by a 'venerable personage'. The doors of the prison were found to be open and the three guards were all fast asleep. On another occasion, he was warned by an unknown lady to avoid a road through a wood. He learned later that travellers on it had been robbed and murdered by bandits. More credibly, she tells us that Fletcher used the time of his 'long and painful exile' to add to his 'curious collection of Books which comprise the best private library in Scotland'. Also, that 'he maintained a useful and extensive correspondence with the friends of liberty at home'. If this is so, and it is entirely probable, all trace of it has unfortunately vanished. From Spain Elisabeth Halkett says, Fletcher went to Hungary to join the army as a volunteer against the Turks.[15]

Fletcher was not, however, forgotten by the courts in Edinburgh. We have seen that he was cited in November 1684 to appear on a charge of associating with Argyll and other rebels abroad. In January 1685, he was summoned again as one of 22 'fugitive rebels' to appear before Parliament on the 26 of March.[16] His Brother, Henry Fletcher, (who had stayed in Scotland) was arrested on 17 May. He was presumably released shortly afterwards because he was not brought to trial. Fountainhall comments that at this time, before Monmouth's expedition to England, Fletcher was 'in a fair way of being absolved, for Argyle purged him'.[17] This seems to refer to Argyll's complaint that Fletcher had never replied to his letters. How the authorities knew this, and why they should attach such weight to the evidence of a man already condemned as a traitor, is obscure.

Fletcher's brief participation in Monmouth's landing meant that he was clearly a traitor in the eyes of the law. Fountainhall mentions the shooting of Dare, 'which accident tends to the preservation of his life at this tyme'. By his flight to Spain he had escaped the hazards of the Battle of Sedgemoor and the executions which followed. On the other hand, his clear association with Monmouth had, Fountainhall adds, put his guilt beyond all contradiction.[18]

The law proceeded to take its course, even in the absence of the accused. On 15 August 1685 two witnesses against Monmouth and Fletcher arrived in one of the King's yachts at Leith.[19] On 24 September, in a special warrant from the king, the heirs of the late Duke of Monmouth (for he had already been executed by then), Sir James Dalrymple of Stair and Andrew Fletcher of Saltoun were cited to appear in the criminal court within 60 days on a charge of treason.[20] The inclusion of Monmouth's heirs, who were in no way involved in the rising, may seem odd; but the penalty for treason included the forfeiture of the estate, which, of course, concerned the heirs. No one either in Scotland or

England ever seems to have contemplated charging Fletcher with the murder of Dare. There are three possible explanations: the shooting was accepted as an accident, the killing of one traitor by another was thought to be of no account, or the charge of treason was so serious and all-embracing that isolated acts merely became part of it.

The trial began in the Criminal Court on 21 December 1685, with no less a person than the Earl of Lauderdale as foreman of the jury. The charges against Fletcher of complicity in the plots of 1683 against the life of the king were dropped for lack of evidence, and he was accused only of taking part in Monmouth's invasion. Even on this charge, the prosecution had some difficulty in proving to the satisfaction of the whole jury that Fletcher had been identified as a participant beyond all doubt. He was at length found guilty on 16 January 1686 and the sentence for treason was pronounced against him 'with all the formalities of sound of trumpet, tearing his arms and reversing them on the crosse' as Fountainhall put it.[21] This meant that he had been sentenced to death wherever he could be found. He was attainted as a traitor, his name and memory declared extinct, his blood tainted, his descendants incapable of holding any place or honours, and all his estates forfeited to the Crown. A week later, on 23 January, the estate was formally gifted to the Earl of Dumbarton, a brother of the Duke of Hamilton. In October 1688, shortly before his flight from the country which brought his reign to an end, James VII declared a general pardon. This was a desperate, last-minute attempt to restore his fortunes by appeasing his opponents. Even so, some people were excluded from the pardon. Among them were both Fletcher and Burnet.

By this time, Fletcher was in Holland preparing for the attempt on the throne by William of Orange. The circumstances were very different from Monmouth's premature gamble three years before. Not only was William a man of more solid qualities than Monmouth, but his wife, Mary, was a Stuart in the legitimate line. Discontent with James in both England and Scotland had reached the point where his position was becoming untenable. Recognising this, he lost his nerve and created the vacuum which William and Mary were ready to fill.

To pass from serious matters to a strange and improbable story, we might at this stage bring in one of the few anecdotes that have survived of Fletcher's various periods of residence in Holland. It was recorded many years later by Mrs Calderwood of Polton, who wrote a very lively account of a journey to Holland in 1756. Fletcher undoubtedly had a quick temper and was not a man to stomack an insult, but we have no reason to suppose that he was capable of deliberate and calculated murder. In any case, the method alleged is not very convincing. This is what Mrs Calderwood tells us:—

They tell a story of old Fletcher of Salton and a skipper: Salton could not endure the smoak of toback, and as he was in a night-scoot, the skipper and he fell out about his forbidding him to smoak; Salton, finding he could not hinder him, went up and sat on the ridge of the boat, which bows like an arch. The skipper was so contentious that he followed him, and, on whatever side Salton sat, he put his pipe in the cheek next him, and whifed it in his face; Salton went down severall times, and brought up stones in his pocket from the ballast, and slipt them into the skipper's pocket that was next the water, and when he found he had loadened him as much as would sink him, he gives him a shove, so that over he hirsled. The boat went on, and Salton came down amongst the rest of the passengers, who probably were asleep, and fell asleep amongst the rest. In a little time bump came the scoot against the side, on which they all damned the skipper; but, behold, when they called, there was no skipper; which would breed no great amasement in a Dutch company.[22]

6

Return to Scotland. The Claim of Right. 1689–1692

'No man . . . . busier than Saltoun'
— Sir William Lockhart

On 5 November 1688, William landed at Torbay with the sea and land forces
of Holland at his command. He had sufficient strength to avoid a repetition
of the Monmouth fiasco, but there was no need for him to risk a battle. On
18 December William took possession of Whitehall and on the twenty-third
James fled the country. In England at least, a bloodless transfer of power,
the so-called Glorious Revolution, had been accomplished. The nature of the
new settlement remained to be established with the Parliaments of the two
kingdoms if they were to continue under the same king.

Both Andrew Fletcher and Gilbert Burnet were in the party which accompanied William. They were joined in London by a considerable group of Scots
who had rushed south to discuss the future government of the country. A letter
from Fletcher survives from this time. He wrote to a friend in Rotterdam on
8 January 1689: 'For my own part I think we can never come to any true
settlement but by uniting with England in Parliaments and Trade, for as for
our worship and particular laws we certainly can never be united in these'.[1]

In recent years there has been some controversy about the interpretation
of this letter. T. C. Smout, who seems to have been the first historian to
come across it, thought it meant that Fletcher in 1689 was in favour of an
incorporating union between Scotland and England. He even suggests that the
letter is evidence that there was in Scotland at the time a strong sentiment in
favour of such a Union.[2] William Ferguson argues that the letter is 'too cryptic'
to support these conclusions.[3] It seems to me that Smout was assuming that the
words 'uniting in Parliaments' must mean the type of Union which was in fact
established by the Treaty of 1707. I have pointed out elsewhere[4] that 'union',
and its derivatives, has been used with a variety of meanings at different
periods. The examples in the Oxford English Dictionary show that before 1707
it was generally used in a rather vague sense to mean an association or alliance
for any common purpose or the mere absence of dissention or discord. When
the Treaty was under discussion the adjective 'incorporating' had to be inserted
to indicate the type of union on which the English were insisting. Without that
qualification union could easily mean an agreement on trade or other matters
between the two countries without any effect on their constitutional status.

Since 1603 there had been many proposals for Union between the two
countries.[5] They came usually from the monarch who was looking for a

solution to the problem of trying to rule simultaneously two very different kingdoms with conflicting interests and attitudes. Since the proposals found very little support in either country they were never worked out in any detail, but many variations were possible. James VI would have preferred to unify everything, including religion and the law. Other proposals related mainly to trade. The arrangement actually made in 1707 'incorporated' the two Parliaments and provided for free trade, but it left almost everything else unaffected. In the first flush of the 'Glorious Revolution', Fletcher may have gone through a phase of optimism about a new era in Scottish-English relations. He may have been thinking about a federal arrangement between Parliaments, as his use of the plural suggests. Fletcher was bitterly opposed to the abolition of the Scottish Parliament and to the loss of Scottish control over Scottish affairs, but he was never opposed to 'union' in the sense of amicable cooperation over such matters as trade and defence. The fullest statement of his political philosophy, *Notes of a Conversation* of 1706, proposes the extension over the whole of Europe of a system which would combine highly decentralised autonomy with international cooperation of this kind. As we shall see, Fletcher and others constantly argued simultaneously for union, meaning international co-operation, and for the maintenance and strengthening of the power of a separate Scottish Parliament. They saw no conflict between these two objectives.

There is therefore nothing surprising, or inconsistent with his later position, in Fletcher's reference to 'uniting' in his letter of 8 January 1689. There is a short anonymous pamphlet of about the same time which refers to 'Union' in even more approving terms. The title is *A letter to a Member of the Convention of States in Scotland by a Lover of His Religion and Country* and it is dated 1689. From the text it was evidently written after William and Mary had accepted the English throne but before the issue had been settled in Scotland, or in other words in the early months of 1689 before 11 April. It refers to James as the King and to William, who has not yet succeeded to the throne of Scotland, as 'the Prince of Orange'. The pamphlet has been attributed to Fletcher and Scott Macfie in his Bibliography agrees that this is possible. If so, it is Fletcher's first published work.

Certainly the style and general approach of the pamphlet suggests Fletcher's hand. It is a strong argument in favour of the rejection of James and the acceptance of William. Very much in line with Fletcher's consistent attitude, it rejects arbitrary royal power and approves of resistance to it:

> The *Speculative Doctrine* of passive obedience has done too much Mischief among us, and what had befallen the King may be justly imputed to it, for the believing that without Opposition he might do what he pleased, encouraged him to take such Measures as have drawn all these Misfortunes on him.

That is the authentic voice of the liberal, 'republican' Fletcher, or of a kindred spirit, but what are we to make of this other passage:

If the King returns we will burst into a Flame, and *England* which has already declared will quickly be on our Top, an Enemy too Potent and too numerous for us, tho we were all united, besides the Danger to which such a Procedure will expose us, we cut off all Hopes of an Union with that *Nation,* and thereby Deprive ourselves of an unspeakable Advantage, which would redound to all sorts of People, and would be the only means to support an Impoverish'd and sinking Nation.[6]

If Scotland had opted for a return of James in 1689 it may well have provoked an English invasion. Scotland disarmed and impoverished by the events since 1603 was in no position to resist. As Hume Brown expressed it: 'Ecclesiastically and politically the Union of the Crowns in 1603 had brought little good to Scotland, and commercially it had been disastrous. Again and again the foreign relations of England had played havoc with the trading interests of the lesser country'.[7] Fletcher in his later speeches and writings repeatedly analysed and deplored the serious disadvantages which Scotland had suffered from absentee Kings under English influence and the consequent loss of an independent foreign and trading policy. If he did, in fact, write this pamphlet, there is again no necessary contradiction to find him speaking about the unspeakable advantage of a union. In 1689 it was reasonable to assume that under William the Scottish Parliament would be able to loosen royal control and reach a satisfactory alliance, or union in that sense, with England to encourage trade and avoid war. This presupposes a degree of confidence in the good intentions of William, but that was the general feeling in the first flush of enthusiasm for the Revolution.

Gilbert Burnet begins his account of the reign of William and Mary by saying that he had before him a reign 'that drew upon it an universal expectation of great things to follow, from such auspicious beginnings; and from so general a joy as was spread over these nations'.[8] James had been widely seen as a threat to both political liberty and to Protestantism. His sudden disappearance from the scene must have seemed like a miraculous liberation. Fletcher had a strong personal reason for satisfaction and optimism. Under James he had been condemned as a traitor and forced into exile. Now he could return to Scotland and his estate and he was free to work for the ideals in which he believed. It would be natural for him to look forward with confidence and to expect a better relationship with England with William as king. Both the letter and the pamphlet of 1689 may reflect such an optimism; but if Fletcher had high hopes of William's reign, he (like Scotland generally) was to be very quickly disillusioned.

The Convention of the Estates to which the pamphlet of 1689 was addressed met in Edinburgh on 14 March. Fletcher was not a member and indeed he was not eligible because the forfeiture of his estate had not yet been rescinded. This must have been frustrating to him because the issues which fell to this Convention were important and very closely involved with some of the main objectives of his political thought, the wish to curb, if not abolish, the royal prerogatives and to transfer real power to Parliament. The most pressing matter was to settle the position of the king in the new situation, a problem which was simplified by the withdrawal of the Jacobites into armed opposition under Viscount Dundee.

On 11 April the Convention adopted a Declaration which embodied a Claim of Right and an offer of the throne to William and Mary as part of an implied contract.[9] The Claim was modelled on the English Bill of Rights, but it was very different in spirit and in its conclusions. The English document was based on the convenient evasion that James had abdicated. The Scottish Claim went much further. After listing abuses of power by James, it concluded that he had 'invaded the fundamental constitution of the Kingdom, and altered it from a legal limited Monarchy to an arbitrary despotick Power'. For this reason, it declared that James had 'forefaulted the right to the Crown'. The document went on to call for the abolition of Prelacy (ie Episcopacy which was the form of the Established Church of England) on the grounds that it 'is and hath been a great and insupportable grievance and trouble to this Nation'. Next the rights of Parliament which 'ought to be frequently called, and allowed to sit, and the freedom of speech and debate secured to the members'. All these things, the Convention 'do claim, demand and insist upon'.

The Claim of Right was therefore a fundamental repudiation of the doctrine of the divine right of kings; it was a reassertion of the traditional Scottish belief, expressed in the Declaration of Arbroath as early as 1320, that sovereignty rested not with the King but with the people. The thought of the Claim, and even the forcefulness of much of its language, is so close to the attitudes and ideas which Fletcher was about to express in his speeches and pamphlets that it is quite likely that he was active in the background and had a hand in the drafting. Those, like Fletcher, who had been sentenced to forfeiture under James were not forgotten in the Claim. One of the charges against James was that he had caused the forfeiture of 'several persons upon stretches of old and obsolete laws, upon frivolous and weak pretences, upon lame and defective probations'. The reconsideration of such cases and the redressing of the parties injured by them was among the demands. When the Scottish Parliament passed an Act on 30 June 1690 restoring Saltoun to Fletcher, the preamble referred to these passages in the Claim of Right and used much of the same language.

The Convention which had passed the Claim of Right and offered the Crown to William and Mary met as Parliament on 5 June 1689. William showed that he meant to hold on to as much of his prerogative power as he could by appointing his Scottish Privy Council even before Parliament had assembled. He made Lord Melville Secretary, but retained him in London, a disturbing repetition of the device used by James to exercise remote control through Lauderdale. On 11 July Sir William Lockhart wrote from Edinburgh to Melville in London about the state of play in the Scottish Parliament: 'the nobility and gentrie ar almost all of our syd, except the Club . . . and no man, tho not a member, busier than Saltoun'.[10] Fletcher's activities had evidently already attracted the attention of the Government.

The Club mentioned by Lockhart was an organised opposition party. It consisted partly of men, like its leader Sir James Montgomery, who were disappointed because they had been refused office, and of others who shared Fletcher's aspirations for constitutional reform. They were aiming at a return to the Act of 1641 which during the ascendancy of the National Covenant had established parliamentary control over appointments to offices of state, Privy Council and judicature. Sir James Dalrymple wrote to Melville on 9 April 1689 to warn him 'that was to leave nothing to the king but an empty name'.[11] This was exactly what Fletcher wanted, not only because he thought it illogical that power should be exercised by a hereditary monarchy (and, in any case, the claim to hereditary right had now become very tenuous), but also because it was the royal control over appointments which enabled England to exercise a potent and destructive influence over Scottish affairs. William, with his autocratic instincts, resisted. The result was a compromise in which the Scots secured the re-establishment of Presbyterianism but only moderate constitutional reform which left appointments in the hands of the King.

The Club did however win a notable victory over the Committee of Articles which had been another instrument of royal control by means of denying to Parliament as a whole the right to take initiatives or decide on subjects for debate. On 13 April 1689, two days after the adoption of the Claim of Right, the Convention had approved a further list of grievances. The first of these described the Committee as 'a great grievance to the nation', and continued: 'there ought to be no committees of parliament but such as are freely chosen by the estates to prepare motions and overtures that are first made in the house'.[12] Just over a year later, on 8 May 1690, Parliament passed an Act which abolished the Articles 'in all tyme comeing'. It also restricted the rights of officers of state (who were equivalent to what we now call ministers). They were to be allowed to attend committees of Parliament, to propose and debate, but not to vote.[13]

This was a major reform. Parliament had been reduced to a body with the power to say yes or no to the proposals put to it by the Articles. The whole House was now free to initiate, debate and pass or reject whatever legislation it pleased. Legislation was still subject to royal veto; the officers of state, although no longer entitled to vote, were still appointed by the king. Even so, there had been a very real transfer of freedom and power to Parliament. Without this, the great debates in the Parliaments of 1703 to 1707, in which Fletcher paid a leading role, would not have been possible.

The hopes which many people in Scotland, including Fletcher, had placed in William were quickly tarnished by the struggles over constitutional reform and the Church. He had made it only too obvious that he wanted to retain personal control and to establish Episcopalianism. John Macky, in his character sketch of Fletcher, says that his principles made him 'withstand the giving so much power to King William, whom he would never serve'.[14] Lockhart's comment is even stronger. He tells us that before William had been many months in England, Fletcher 'saw his designs, and left him, and ever thereafter hated and appeared as much against him as any in the kingdom'.[15] Perhaps Lockhart exaggerates a little, but not much. Robert Wodrow reports a story which he had heard from Fletcher himself. Fletcher and the others involved were naturally impatient for the return of their confiscated estates after the Revolution. After more than a year had passed without action, Fletcher, as the most effective spokesman, was asked to put the case to the Duke of Hamilton, then Commissioner. 'You can tell King William from me', Fletcher said, 'that he has not soe good a right to his croun as I have to my estate'. 'Devil take me', Hamilton replied, 'if it be not treu'.[16]

In spite of Fletcher's reservations about William, he still thought that he was the lesser of two evils when there was a prospect of a Jacobite restoration. In 1692 there was a threat of a French invasion in the Jacobite interest. At that time Hamilton had been replaced as Commissioner by Melville and had retired in disgust. Fletcher appealed to him to come back and add the weight of his influence and advice. As Buchan describes the episode: 'Fletcher's ruling principle (though dissatisfied with King William) was the good of his country. He used all his influence with the Duke of Hamilton to forget the causes of his disgust, and to co-operate with his friends of a free constitution'.[17] Fletcher's letter to Hamilton on 29 April 1692 has survived:

> I know you will be surprised to receive a letter from me; but my writing to you in such an exigence shows the high esteem I must have of you; and of the true love you bear your religion and country. If, laying aside all other considerations, you do not come in presently, and assist in council, all things will go into confusion, and your presence there will easily retrieve all. The castle has been very near surprised, and an advertisement which secretary Johnston had from France, and wrote hither, has saved it. When things are any ways composed, you may return to your former measures, for I do approve of them. I do advise your Grace to the most honourable thing you can do; and without which your country must perish.[18]

The tone of this letter suggests that Fletcher, presumably with the standing of a man who had come from Holland in the immediate circle around William, spoke with distinct authority. His appeal seems to have been effective. At all events, Hamilton stopped sulking and returned to an active role in affairs. Next year he was again presiding over the debates of Parliament.

William's reputation in Scotland was further damaged by the Massacre of Glencoe, authorised by 'letters of fire and sword' which he signed on 11 January 1692. The massacre gave an extra edge to Fletcher's criticism of the royal Court and of the harmful influence in Scotland of the officials appointed by the King. The Earl of Stair, in particular, was believed to be largely responsible for the policy of intimidation which led to the Massacre. Stair afterwards became one of the most able and determined advocates of Union, but he was not allowed to forget Glencoe. In at least one of his speeches Fletcher said that he deserved to be hanged for his part in the affair. (see page 133)

The Darien tragedy in the following years was to put even more strain on the relations between William and his Scottish subjects.

7

Darien. 1692–1702

'The door of the seas and the key of the universe'
— William Paterson

In the course of the 17th century, while other European countries were developing trade with Asia, Africa and America, the trade of Scotland was in decline partly as a consequence of the Union of the Crowns. Because of that Scotland had lost its ancient privileges in France. The wars of Charles II with Holland had damaged the most important branch of Scottish overseas trade. Scotland was obliged to supply men and money for Wars fought in the name of the shared monarch, but received no benefit from the peace settlements. The Navigation Act and the Act for the Encouragement of Trade, passed by the English Parliament in 1660 and 1663, were intended to exclude Scotland from the valuable trade with the Plantations. It is not surprising that towards the end of the Century, Scotland turned its attention to international trade as a means of escape from national decline and impoverishment.[1]

This new preoccupation with trade was one which Andrew Fletcher shared and which he encouraged through his pamphleteering and personal influence. In one of three pamphlets published in 1698, *The First Discourse Concerning the Affairs of Scotland,* he explained the difference which the new mercantile age had made to the relative standing and security of Scotland. In the past, when military power had depended on unpaid feudal levies, Scotland had been able to put a force in the field which was adequate for her own defence. Now every country was obliged to defend itself by 'force of money', that is by professional mercenary troops. 'But such a vast expense the riches of no country is able to support without a great trade. In this great alteration our case has been singularly bad and unfortunate: for partly through our own fault, and partly by the removal of our kings into another country, this nation, of all those who possess good ports, and lie conveniently for trade and fishing, has been the only part of Europe which did not apply itself to commerce; and possessing a barren country, in less than an age we are sunk so low as to be despised by all our neighbours and made incapable to repel an injury'.

Fletcher goes on to notice the change of national attitude: 'by no contrivance of any man, but by an unforeseen and unexpected change of the genius of this nation, all their thoughts and inclinations, as if united and directed by a higher power, seem to be turned upon trade, and to conspire together for its advancement, which is the only means to recover us from our present miserable and despicable condition'.[2] (We might notice in passing, this anticipation of the ideas of Ferguson and Adam Smith about the way in which human affairs often take a turn which nobody had foreseen or intended. This is by no means the only respect in which Fletcher was one of the precursors of the Scottish Enlightenment).

The damage inflicted on overseas trade was not the only reason for the impoverishment of Scotland during the 17th century. Religious and political conflict and the Cromwellian occupation impeded economic development. To make matters much worse, a succession of bad harvests due to wet summers and early frosts caused a serious famine between 1695 and 1699. Thousands died from starvation and disease in 'these Seven Ill Years', or 'King William's Years' as the Jacobites called them.[3] It was a drastic situation to which Fletcher proposed a drastic solution in his *Second Discourse* (to which I shall return later).

The Acts of the English Parliament of 1660 and 1663 were not entirely successful in excluding Scottish trade with the American plantations. For one thing, there were colonies of Scots along the eastern seaboard of the American states, even if many of them had originally been sent there against their will. Cromwell had deported 5,000 Scots to New England after his victory at Dunbar. Others had been deported either as religious recusants or as criminals during the reigns of Charles II and James VII. Towards the end of the century Scottish traders in the American colonies became so active that the English merchant companies complained that their trade was being ruined by ships trading directly from Scotland and Ulster.[4]

If Scotland was to join in the trade with America, Africa and Asia on an equal footing with other European countries, it required the support, like the others, of companies authorised by the Government. In 1693 the Scottish Parliament passed an Act declaring that Scottish merchants could form companies for trading in all kind of commodities in all parts of the world with which the King was not at war. This was likely to be seen by the English companies as a challenge to their monopolies, but the Act was nevertheless approved by William, who was anxious at the time to distract attention from the agitation for an enquiry into the Massacre of Glencoe. It was, of course, only an enabling Act and the King, his ministers and the English trading companies probably intended that no more should come of it. There were, however, other forces in play, and among them was Andrew Fletcher.

The initiative for further action seems to have been taken by James Chiesly, a Scottish merchant living in London. He realised the potential of the Act of 1693 and he brought it to the attention of another Scotsman then living in London, William Paterson. He could not have found anyone more responsive. Paterson, a native of Dumfriesshire, was a man of wide experience and very fertile in ideas. He had made something of a fortune in the West Indies, where he was variously said to have been a buccaneer and a missionary. On his return to Europe, he urged a number of European governments to adopt various trading and financial projects which he had devised. One of them led to the foundation of the Bank of England, of which he was one of the original directors. Another was a proposal for a trading colony in the Isthmus of Panama. He saw it as 'this door of the seas, and the key of the universe', a great entrepôt where the goods from the Atlantic could be exchanged for goods from the Pacific, anticipating the Panama Canal by 200 years.[5]

What happened next is described by Sir John Dalrymple:

> Ingenious men draw to each other like iron and the loadstone: Paterson, on his return to London, formed a friendship with Mr. Fletcher of Saltoun, whose mind was inflamed with the love of public good, and all of whose ideas to procure it had a sublimity in them. Fletcher disliked England, merely because he loved Scotland to excess; and therefore the report common in Scotland is probably a true one, that he was the person who persuaded Paterson to trust the fate of his project to his own countrymen alone, and to let them have the sole benefit, glory, and danger of it; for in its danger Fletcher deemed some of its glory to consist.
>
> Although Fletcher, who had nothing to hope for and nothing to fear, because he had a good estate and no children, was of the country party; yet, in all his schemes for the public good, he was accustomed to go as readily to the King's ministers as to his own friends, being indifferent who had the honour of doing good, provided it was done. His house in East Lothian was near to that of the Marquis of Tweddale, then minister for Scotland, and therefore they were often together. Fletcher brought Paterson down to Scotland with him, presented him to the Marquis, and then, with that power which a vehement spirit always possesses over a diffident one, persuaded the Marquis, by arguments of public good, and of the honour which would redound to his administration, to adopt the project.[6]

Accordingly, the Scottish Parliament on 26 May 1695 passed the 'Act for a Company trading to Africa and the Indies'. The Company was to have a monopoly of trade with Asia and Africa for all time coming, and in America for 31 years. During 21 years, all goods imported by the Company, except sugar and tobacco, were to be free of duty. With the consent of the inhabitants, colonies might be planted in any part of Asia, Africa and America, provided it was not already in the possession of any European sovereign. At this stage, there was no decision to settle a colony at Darien. Nor was it proposed to restrict participation in share holding to Scottish residents, although 50 per cent was reserved to them. The other 50 per cent, assigned to England, was oversubscribed within a few days.

The reaction of English trading interests and the English Parliament was swift because the Scottish Company was seen as a potential rival to the English East India Company. On 17 December the Lords and Commons presented an address to the King representing 'the great prejudice, inconvenience, and mischiefs' that would result to English trade from the Scottish Act. 'I have been ill-served in Scotland', William replied, 'but I hope some remedies may be found to prevent the inconveniences which may arise from the Act'.[7] As King of Scots, William did not withdraw royal approval from the Act; but, as King of England, he proceeded to do all he could to sabotage and frustrate the Scottish Company. The English subscribers withdrew. English diplomatic pressure prevented subscriptions in Amsterdam and Hamburg. A circular letter was sent to the Governors of the Plantations instructing them to prohibit all assistance to the Scottish Company.

Thus thrown on their own resources, the Scottish population responded with an outburst of patriotic fervour which reminded people of the response to the National Covenant in 1638. The full £400,000 called for was subscribed although it amounted to half of the total money in circulation in the country. Many people invested their entire fortune. Fletcher himself subscribed £1,000.

English hostility had another and more unfortunate effect. The original scheme of trade with Asia, Africa and America now became much more problematical. For one thing, even the benevolent neutrality of the English Navy and their colonies could not be assumed. The fatal decision was therefore taken on 23 July 1696 to commit the entire venture to Paterson's dream, the establishment of a trading colony on the Isthmus of Panama at Darien. It seemed at the time a very promising venture. The site was a potential artery of trade between east and west. Reports by men who had visited the area reported rich resources of timber and gold. The natives were friendly and ready to cooperate in exchange for protection against the Spaniards. Spain had not so far established a foothold in the area, even if they made a general claim to the entire region. The Scots were not to know that they would be repudiated by William whose Ambassador would virtually encourage Spain to attack.

It is significant of Fletcher's involvement in the venture that when Lionel Wafer, a traveller with personal knowledge of Darien, was summoned to Edinburgh to brief the manager of the Company, the meeting was at Fletcher's house of Saltoun.[8] His *First Discourse Concerning the Affairs of Scotland* was published in 1698, evidently some time after the expedition set sail from Leith on the 17 July. 'Scotland has now a greater venture at sea', he wrote, 'than at any time since we have been a nation . . . Especially since the nation has so great a concern in this enterprise, that I may well say our hopes of ever being any other than a poor and inconsiderable people are embarked with them'. But he had a clear sighted view of the risks. It could easily be ruined by the loss of ships, 'by the sickness of the men, who for the most part are neither accustomed to such long voyages, nor to climates so different from their own', by lack of fresh provisions, by being attacked, or a 'thousand other accidents'.[9]

Fletcher was, of course, right. All of these things did happen to the expedition. Mismanagement, compounded by English hostility and Spanish attack, led by the 30 March 1700 to the complete abandonment of the Colony and the loss of most of the men and their ships, although the first expedition of 1698 had been reinforced by a second and third. Disaster could not have been more complete and more humiliating. It was more than a failure of a commercial venture; it was a national reverse which led directly to the Union which followed seven years later. It had long been obvious that there were serious disadvantages for Scotland in sharing with England a King who was bound to put English interests first. 'Contemporary writers are unanimous in charging the political system established in 1603, as the main cause of the national depression, that culminated in the poverty and misery of the last decade of the seventeenth, and the opening years of the eighteenth centuries'.[10] Darien exposed the problem so blatantly that it could no longer be ignored. Constitutional change was now inescapable. Scotland must either return to complete independence with a separate King or find some more equitable relationship with England.

At the same time Darien impoverished the whole country. It ruined the people who invested in it and that meant a large proportion of the members of Parliament. In his *First Discourse*, Fletcher had denounced the corruption of Parliament by 'the constant bribes of places and pensions',[11] a natural consequence of administration by an absentee Court supported by English wealth. These legislators were now much more vulnerable to bribery than ever and it is significant that one of the clauses of the Treaty of Union provided for the compensation of the shareholders in the Scottish Company, with money that was simultaneously described as compensation for Scotland's acceptance of a share of the English national debt.

The cynical self-interest of the English Parliament and establishment generally over Darien inevitably increased the dislike and distrust with which they were regarded in Scotland. G. W. T. Omond speculates how Fletcher himself was probably affected by the experience:

Fletcher was a rich man, and the disaster at Darien did not mean ruin to him, as it did to so many of his countrymen. But the sight of their sufferings, the callous indifference of the English Government, and the knowledge that there was not one London merchant in a hundred who did not, in his heart, rejoice in the ruin which had befallen the Scottish traders made him, as it made most Scotsmen, distrust England, and devote himself, heart and soul, for the rest of his life, to the cause of Scottish independence.[12]

Omond may well be right. Fletcher may at first have hoped that Scotland could establish a reasonable working relationship with William. His writings and speeches after the failure of the Darien expedition reflect an increased distrust of the English government and a more explicit commitment to Scottish independence.

From the English side also, the Darien experience gave a strong impulse towards a policy of 'incorporating' Union in a form which would eliminate the Scottish Parliament and enable England to exercise effective control. William needed no persuasion. Like his predecessors since James VI he had always been in favour of such a union to avoid the difficulties of exercising royal control over two separate kingdoms with different, and often conflicting, interests. These difficulties had been blatantly exposed by Darien. William as King of England had acted in complete contradiction to himself as King of Scots. Not only that, but the activities of the Scottish Company had made problems for his foreign policy which involved the conciliation of Spain in the interests of containing the ambitions of France. Also as King of England, William was anxious to keep control of Scotland which had contributed a disproportionate share of money and men to fight wars, although they were conducted in the interest of England alone. This was another point to which Fletcher drew attention. 'I am credibly informed', he wrote in his *First Discourse*, 'that every fifth man in the English forces was either of this nation, or Scots-Irish, who are people of the same blood with us'.[13]

The decisive change in England was in the attitude of the English merchant classes and of Parliament. Since James VI first raised the idea in 1603, they had invariably opposed any suggestion of Union because they were afraid that it would enable the Scots to compete in trade which they wanted to keep to themselves. They were, of course, also influenced by the deeply ingrained habits of hostility between the two peoples. Never, Defoe wrote, had two nations 'such inveteracy and aversion to one another in their blood'.[14] The establishment of the Company of Scotland by the Scottish Parliament changed the attitude of English trading interests. They would be less exposed to the risks of Scottish competition if there was no longer a Scottish Parliament capable of taking independent initiatives. It is surprising that it took them so long to see that free trade between the two countries would be more in the interest of England than of Scotland. Manufacturing was more highly developed in England which was richer and had a larger population. Inevitably, therefore, Scotland would import more from England than it was capable of exporting. William's last message to the English House of Commons before his death in 1702 was to urge them to work for a closer union between the two kingdoms.

8

Fletcher as Pamphleteer: the Militia Question and the Affairs of Scotland. 1697–1701

'His flashes are sometimes as quick as lightning'
— Sir John Dalrymple

While Fletcher was watching the tragedy of Darien and influencing events from the side-lines, he was still not back in Parliament and was therefore deprived of a forum where he could advance his ideas. He took the only course available to him and wrote a series of pamphlets, published anonymously as was the usual practice of the time. From references to them in the letters of his contemporaries it seems to have been generally known that he was the author, although, to this day, there are some doubtful cases. We have no reason to doubt that the seven items attributed to him in *The Political Works* of 1732 are genuine, although that was the first publication under his name and it was 16 years after his death. The seven items are:

1. *A Discourse of Government with relation to Militias*, 1697
2. *The First Discourse Concerning the Affairs of Scotland*, 1698
3. *The Second Discourse Concerning the Affairs of Scotland*, 1698
4. *A Discourse concerning the Affairs of Spain*, 1698
5. *A Speech upon the State of the Nation*, 1701
6. *Speeches by a Member of the Parliament*, 1703
7. *An Account of a Conversation*, 1703

I propose to consider now the first five of these, which were written in or just before the year in which the first expedition sailed to Darien. I shall leave the last two for a later chapter which deals with the events of 1703.

Caroline Robbins in a book first published in 1959, *The Eighteenth-Century Commonwealthman*, drew attention to Fletcher's affinities with a school of English and Irish political writing, the Commonwealthmen or Real Whigs. They went back to the ideas of Harrington, Nedham and Milton at the time of Cromwell and of Sidney, Neville and Locke after the Restoration. In Fletcher's own time, men like Molyneux, Molesworth and Trenchard (who were all graduates of Trinity College, Dublin) Moyle and Pownall shared views very similar to his own. They were, in the words of Caroline Robbins 'much interested in the relations of the different parts of Great Britain, and the degree to which a government centered in London fulfilled the demands for natural rights.' She adds that 'Fletcher, like Archbishop William King in

Ireland, feared a government centered in London. Other parts of the island would suffer. All interest and wealth would crowd there. Fletcher would only have consented to a Union on "equal terms", by which he meant federal terms, and he insisted on certain limitations on prerogative as an essential part of the settlement.' Trenchard and Moyle, like Fletcher, were also opposed to a standing army in peace time.[1]

On the strength of one reference in a pamphlet attributed to Daniel Defoe, *A Brief Reply to the History of Standing Armies in England* (London, 1698), Caroline Robbins suggests that Fletcher was a member of a group, which included Moyle and Trenchard, who met regularly in the Grecian Tavern in London. They were described in the pamphlet as a 'club of mistaken politicians' who 'set themselves up as champions of people's liberties and Sydney's Maxims'. Apart from this single reference, there is no evidence that I know of which confirms that Fletcher was in direct touch with the other members of the group. On the other hand, as Robbins says, the appearance of pamphlets on broadly similar lines by several of these men and the publication of works of the 'sacred canon' of Sidney, Milton, Harrington and others between 1697 and 1701 'powerfully supports the description of concerted effort'.[2] Fletcher may well have known Molyneux, and he certainly had his work in his library. Both of them were in Holland at the same period when Molyneux studied medicine at Leyden. He became a physician in Dublin and a life-long enthusiast for John Locke, with whom Fletcher was probably on friendly terms. An inscribed copy of one of Locke's books for the Saltoun library still exists and his work is well represented in Fletcher's catalogues. There Locke is referred to only by his initials, which is presumably a mark of special familiarity.

Much of what Robbins says about the views of the group certainly applies to Fletcher. 'They fully recognised that ministerial power could be as dangerous as monarchical. They, therefore, wished to separate legislative and executive branches more completely, and roundly condemned placemen and cabals.' At the same time, they were 'not egalitarian . . . A ruling class and an uneducated and unrepresented majority . . . were taken for granted.' Fletcher, however, unlike the others, 'was also immensely interested in the poor and the hungry'. Robbins recognises this as a Scottish characteristic. Fletcher's successors of the Scottish Enlightenment, such as Hutcheson, Wallace, Smith and Adam Ferguson, 'all were sympathetic with the "dregs of society" at a time when none of the English devoted a page to their plight.'[3]

This is fair comment. Fletcher was a democrat in wishing to curb the arbitrary power of Kings, nobility and ministers and in his concern for the poor and hungry. He was not a democrat, as probably no one was at that time, in wishing to extend the franchise to the people at large. He would have been perfectly content to see power exercised benevolently by the men, like himself, whose property in land gave them independence. He was in advance of his time in many of his ideas, but not in this.

The first published work attributed with confidence to Fletcher was *A Discourse concerning Militias and Standing Armies; with relation to the Past and*

Present Governments of Europe and of England in particular, published in London in 1697. In the following year, a new edition, with additions which made the pamphlet applicable to Scotland as well, was published in Edinburgh as *A Discourse of Government with relation to Militias*. It was presumably published first in London, and directed at an English audience, because Fletcher intended it as a contribution to the controversy in the English Parliament in 1697 to 1698 whether William should maintain a standing army after the Peace of Ryswick. Nearly always Fletcher's pamphlets are aimed at a current situation with the practical objective of influencing the decision.

In this case, Fletcher was also joining in a long political debate which went back through Machiavelli and other writers of the Florentine renaissance to classical antiquity and ultimately to Aristotle. It is a subject which in the present century has been the special province of J. G. A. Pocock, who first drew attention to the importance of Fletcher's pamphlet in this context.[4] In England in the 17th century, Aristotle's *Politics* had been reinterpreted and adapted to local conditions by James Harrington (1611–1677). He was a man of somewhat similar disposition to Fletcher with republican views for which he suffered imprisonment after the Restoration. His principal work, *Oceana*, published in 1656, was a prescription for the creation of an ideal state in Cromwell's England. He believed that Tudor land legislation and the dissolution of the monasteries had emancipated tenants from feudal dependence on their lords. This gave the opportunity for a republic of freeholders with the right 'to bear arms in his own or the Commonalty's Quarrel . . . . The right to bear arms, and the propertied independence enabling one to provide one's own, became the test of citizenship in Harrington's England as they had been in Athens or Rome'. It was the possession of land that gave a man independence, which in the last analysis meant the ability to bear arms and use them in his own quarrels.[5] Fletcher's library was very strong in all the main works of this tradition and in political philosophy generally. Under the heading, 'legislatores', it occupies 29 pages of the first catalogue, and, of course, includes Aristotle, Machiavelli and Harrington.

There is an obvious affinity between Harrington's views and the argument of Fletcher's *Militia* pamphlet; but, as Pocock says, 'his interpretation of European political history — for all its preconceptions and naiveties — represents an advance in terms of historical explanation, over anything of which Harrington was capable'.[6] Fletcher in fact approached the problem at issue very much in the spirit of the Scottish Enlightenment. This was what Dugald Stewart called 'Theoretical or Conjectural History' in the work of such men as Lord Kames, Adam Smith and John Millar.[7] Their instinct in approaching any problem was to consider the way in which it had probably evolved from the earliest times. They sought to establish, in Lord Kames's words, 'A chain of causes and effects'[8] and they invariably attached importance to economic factors. This evolution they saw as very often more a matter of accident than intention, 'the result of human action, but not the execution of human design'.[9] They were concerned with all aspects of the life of man in society and with ways in which human happiness might be increased and morality sustained. They drew many of the examples from classical Greece and Rome and they admired, in particular (to quote Adam Ferguson again) 'the devoted patriotism of an early Roman'.[10]

From the renaissance until well into the 19th century it was entirely natural for men to look to classical antiquity for ideas and inspiration. The education was almost entirely centered on ancient Greece and Rome. They had read far more deeply in Latin, and to a lesser extent Greek, literature than in any other and knew more about the history of Greece and Rome than of their own country. Fletcher's own library was well stocked with Greek and Latin texts and he was very much part of this tradition. His contemporaries realised that he was deeply involved with the ideals of Republican Rome. There is plenty of evidence of this in the Militia pamphlet (as in almost everything that he wrote). He describes the Roman Republic as 'the greatest that ever was amongst men' and their militia as 'the best that ever was'.[11]

In the course of only a few pages, Fletcher displays many of the characteristics of the Scottish Enlightenment, more than fifty years before the time generally attributed to it. His purpose is to argue that standing mercenary armies were 'calculated to enslave a nation' and that it is therefore better to rely on a voluntary militia. (This is a cause which was later to be taken up with enthusiasm, but under different circumstances, by Adam Ferguson and others of the Enlightenment literati). Fletcher begins his historical analysis 'about the year 400' after the dissolution of the Roman Empire. Feudalism which was then established 'put the sword into the hands of the subject, because the vassals depended more immediately on the barons than on the king, which effectually secured the freedom of those governments.' This system began to break up 'in most countries of Europe about the year 1500', as a consequence of historical changes, but not 'by the contrivance of ill-designing men'.[12]

Fletcher accepts that what he regards as the underlying reasons for these changes may 'seem very strange' since they are the renaissance of learning and the invention of printing, the compass and gunpowder. 'Such odd consequences . . . accompany extraordinary inventions of any kind'. He argues that the ultimate effects of these inventions was to persuade first of all the Italians and later other Europeans to abandon 'their frugal and military way of living' and to sink 'into an abyss of pleasures'. Barons accepted rents instead of military service from their tenants and kings levied taxes on 'people grown rich by trade' to pay for mercenary armies. 'The power of the sword was transferred from the subject to the king', with the consequent loss of political liberty.[13]

Pocock recognised that at this point Fletcher had introduced a new element into the debate on this so-called civic tradition, the importance of money or, in other words, of economic factors. 'Fletcher really is talking about the rise of the modern state and the effect of money upon society; but he is not doing so out of a bourgeois consciousness, or out of an increasing awareness of the "market" or "entrepreneurial" element in social relationships. What moves him is an increasing — and hostile — awareness of the importance of money in government: of public finance, of the professionalization of army and bureaucracy, of the inducements which a well-financed court bureaucracy can offer its subjects to co-operate. And this awareness grows out of an ultimately mythical idealization of the role in politics of propertied independence, a kind of radical Aristotelianism which is Harringtonian.'[14]

Pocock recognised that Fletcher understood the significance of economic cause and effect and distrusted the use of money by governments to influence and control their subjects. But Fletcher's reaction to the problem is not as simple and one-sided as Pocock suggests in this passage, and as he recognised in a later book, *The Machiavellian Moment*. Here he says that Fletcher 'developed the neo-Harringtonian version of history further than anyone had yet carried it, and significantly revealed its latent ambivalences.'[15]

Pocock sees these ambivalences as an apparent incompatibility between liberty and virtue on one hand and 'luxury' on the other.[16] In Fletcher's view, the increased knowledge and refinement which the renaissance had introduced had led also to loss of liberty, but they 'might have proved of infinite advantage to the world, if their remote influence upon government had been obviated by suitable remedies'.[17] The question then resolved itself into finding those remedies and one of them was to replace professional standing armies with a citizen's militia.

Two other writers who have followed Pocock's lead, Nicholas Phillipson and John Robertson, have seen the ambivalence more specifically in terms of trade and economic development.[18] On one side of Fletcher's argument he saw the loss of political liberty as a result of the rise of trade and well financed governments. On the other, he recognised that Scotland had been left behind in trade, partly as a consequence of the Union of the Crowns, and there was now a desperate need to improve both trade and agriculture, if the country was to escape from its miserable condition.[19] From this point of view, the ambivalence resolved itself into the question of how the economy could be developed without loss of liberty. Fletcher saw this in Scotland's case, as requiring the transfer of power from the king, the manipulator of corruption, to the Scottish Parliament.

Pocock was, in fact, mistaken when he implied in his earlier work that Fletcher regarded trade only with distaste. Perhaps at that stage he had read only the Militia pamphlet and not the two *Discourses Concerning the Affairs of Scotland* in which Fletcher passionately urges measures for economic development. John Robertson sees this as another of Fletcher's original contributions to the debate. 'Neither the Florentine humanists nor even Harrington had sought as Fletcher now did to make a civic social order the framework for the active pursuit of economic growth'. Robertson points out that Fletcher insists on regarding economic development as a public responsibility, not only to eliminate poverty but to create public wealth in works and buildings.[20]

I agree with David Daiches when he says, in his edition of Fletcher's writings, that Fletcher was a man of passionate moral, but not religious, beliefs.[21] His moral sense was strong and sometimes austere. Throughout his speeches and pamphlets, he is as concerned with morality as with liberty. The Militia *Discourse* is no exception. He objects to mercenary armies not only because they undermine political liberty but because of the moral consequences for officers and soldiers. The officers he says (and he had been one himself) 'become insensibly engaged in numberless frauds, oppressions and cruelties'; the soldiers turn 'to all manner of debauchery and wickedness, committing all kind of injustice and barbarity against poor and defenceless people'. In complete contradiction to this, the militia which Fletcher proposed was to be 'as great a school of virtue as of military discipline'. The young men were to be exorted by some of their own number 'to all Christian and moral duties, chiefly to humility, modesty, charity, and the pardoning of private injuries'. Fletcher's austerity, or puritanism one might call it, appears in another provision: 'No woman should be suffered to come within the camp, and the crimes of abusing their own bodies any manner of way, punished with death'.[22]

It is an essential part of Fletcher's morality that he was strongly opposed to corruption. This is a word which has a special technical sense in the Florentine and subsequent literature which we have been discussing. It is explained by Pocock as follows. In Machiavelli's view only a mixed or balanced constitution combining the qualities of monarchy, aristocracy and democracy 'could hope to escape the doom of degeneration through excess . . . . The technical term for this sort of degeneration is corruption'. Pocock goes on to warn us that 'it is important to realize that the word "corruption" in the eighteenth century is very often being used in its Machiavellian sense, as well as in the vulgar sense of bribery'.[23]

As far as Fletcher is concerned this warning is unnecessary. Fletcher hardly ever uses the word in any sense other than bribery by money, appointments (or places, as he calls them) or pensions. He is quite specific about this in the beginning of his *First Discourse*. Corruption, he says, is the 'blackest of crimes' and anyone guilty of it is 'a very odious criminal'. He then goes on to give examples which leave no doubt what he means. The worst instance of all is the legislator (by which he means member of Parliament) who is bribed. He is astonished that people should tolerate the system which allows 'great numbers of those who have the legislative authority to receive the constant bribes of places and pensions to betray them'.[24] Fletcher's indictment of the system of rule by absentee kings was precisely that it was corrupt in this crude and direct, if 'vulgar', sense.

Two final points about the *Militia* discourse. Modern commentators seem to have jumped to the conclusion that Fletcher would have confined membership of his militia to landowners or freeholders on Harringtonian principles.[25] This is not what he says and indeed it would obviously make no military sense. He says that the militia would take into its training camps 'men of quality and estate, or men of any rank'. Those who have fortune to maintain themselves would stay in the militia for two years (a questionable privilege, perhaps), but those who could not pay for their maintenance would stay one year only at the expense of the public. The only other distinction for 'persons of quality or estate' is that they would be trained in fortification, gunnery and engineering. All would wear the same 'plain, coarse' clothes and eat the same simple food.[26] The proposal is in fact conspicuously egalitarian. Here, as elsewhere, Fletcher saw property as conferring responsibility as well as privilege.

Nicholas Phillipson describes Fletcher as irascible and anglophobic.[27] Irascible he certainly was, but the Militia *Discourse* ends with one of the most laudatory passages about England and the English which has ever been written by anyone other than one of themselves. Much as he distrusted the swollen power of London, he described it as 'the pride and glory, not only of our island, but of the world'. Fletcher was utterly opposed to English interference in Scottish affairs. That did not mean that he disliked the English as individuals, however much he disapproved of their governments. He visited London quite frequently and had friends and acquaintances there, not all of whom were Scottish.

I have already mentioned Fletcher's next work, *Two Discourses Concerning the Affairs of Scotland Written in the Year 1698*, published in the same year in Edinburgh. They were concerned essentially with the problems of the economic development of Scotland. As we have seen this was an innovation in the tradition in which he was writing because none of his predecessors had considered the active pursuit of economic growth. There is, however, a continuity in thought between all three of these pamphlets. In the Militia *Discourse* he had argued that Scotland before 1603 had escaped the risk of mercenary forces, partly because of the shortage of funds available to the King and partly because the Scots understood their disadvantages and dangers. In the *First Discourse* he argued that Scotland had fallen behind other countries by neglecting trade, but attitudes had changed and the Darien venture had been launched. Fletcher welcomed this, not, of course, as a means of raising funds to support mercenary forces, but for the sake of reducing poverty and of avoiding the emigration of families because they could not find work at home. Not the least misfortune of Scotland had been the pressure on younger sons of the nobility and gentry to become soldiers of fortune abroad, 'an idle, for the most part criminal, and almost always unprofitable sort of life'. They would be much 'better employed in trade and husbandry to the improvement of their country'.[28]

In any case, he argues in the *First Discourse*, Scotland did not need mercenary forces. 'There is no pretence for them, except only to keep a few wretched Highlanders in order'. One of the complaints made against James in the Claim of Right was that he had kept a standing army in time of peace, without the consent of Parliament. Under William, Scotland had been paying disproportionately in blood and taxes to support the English and Dutch forces, without receiving any benefit from the peace. 'This is to load a poor nation with taxes, and to oppress them with soldiers in order to procure plenty and riches to other countries, of which they are not to have the least share'. Instead of a land-tax in Scotland 'for maintaining forces to defend the English and Dutch trade, we should raise one for the carrying on of our own'. Since Scotland and England are 'separate kingdoms and have separate ministers at home, we ought to have separate ministers abroad', especially where 'we may have a separate interest from England, which must always be in matters of trade'.[29]

That last point did not mean that Fletcher shared the mercantilist views, generally held at the time, according to which one state could only get rich at the expense of another. He anticipated Adam Smith in believing in the interdependence of countries and that the prosperity of one tended to benefit others. Fletcher gave a hint of this idea in the *First Discourse*: 'I shall not say, that when the English nation shall come to a perfect knowledge of their interest, they will be convinced that riches in Scotland will be beneficial to England, since the seat of the monarchy is there'. He expanded the idea in his final and most polished pamphlet, *An Account of a Conversation* which he wrote about 5 years later: 'I am of opinion . . . that the true interest and good of any nation is the same with that of any other. I do not say that one society ought not to repel the injuries of another; but that no people ever did any injustice to a neighbouring nation, except by mistaking their own interest'.[30]

In the *Second Discourse* Fletcher asked Parliament to consider the most critical problem in the 1690s, the famine following the bad harvests of the 'Ill Years', the 'many thousands of our people who are at this day dying for want of bread'. He made a direct appeal to compassion in more eloquent terms, perhaps because it was closer to his real feelings than the harsh disciplinarianism which he sometimes professed. Any unnecessary expense, or 'the least finery in our houses, clothes, or equipage' would be barbarous 'so long as people born with natural endowments, perhaps not inferior to our own, and fellow citizens, perish for want of things absolutely necessary to life'.[31]

Fletcher proposed a drastic remedy to the problem of the unemployed poor who were wandering over the country as beggars. Once again he went back to classical antiquity and concluded that this problem was unknown at that time because of the institution of slavery. Christianity had created the mischief by liberating the slaves. Fletcher says that he does not doubt that this argument will produce an outcry, but the fact is that slaves in antiquity, when 'no man might want the necessity of life' were better off than the starving poor in the contemporary world. He distinguishes between a slave in the proper sense 'who is absolutely subjected to the will of another man without any remedy' and others, who ought to be called servants, who are 'subjected under certain limitations'.[32]

The limitations which Fletcher goes on to propose are very far-reaching indeed. The servants, and their wives and children, should be provided with clothes, food and lodging. They should be educated and provision made for sickness and old age. 'In everything, except their duty as servants, they should not be under the will of their masters but the protection of the law'. On these conditions, every man of a certain estate would be obliged to take a proportion number of the 'vagabonds' (or as we should say homeless and unemployed poor) and put them to useful work.[33]

There are some harsh aspects in what Fletcher proposed. He suggests (perhaps not too seriously) that some notorious villains might be sent to Venice to serve in the galleys, and that the 'handful of people' in the Highlands who disturb the peace should be transplanted to the Lowlands.[34] Generally, however, the whole essay, although it might be regarded as visionary (as he concedes), is marked by compassion and a desire to benefit the poor and society as a whole. It is visionary because it proposes that the lairds should take on themselves the responsibility and the burden of feeding and caring for the poor. It makes excessive demands on good nature and benevolence, not the opposite.

Even so, the essay led about 150 years later to the first serious break in the almost unanimous approval of Fletcher. Hugh Miller (1802–1856), the astonishing self-taught genius from Cromarty, seems to have been the first writer to make the point. It appears in his *First Impressions of England and its People*, published in 1846. Scotland, he says, has a remarkable record in maintaining its independence intact against formidable enemies for hundreds of years. On the other hand it has had no 'true patriots' in his sense of the term. By this he means those whose object is 'to elevate the mass of the people and give to them the standing, in relation to the privileged classes, which it is their right to occupy'. For Miller, Fletcher fails by this standard because 'while he would have made good the claims of his country against the world, would, as shown by his scheme of domestic slavery, have subjected one-half his countrymen to the unrestrained despotism of the other half'.[35] This, of course, overlooks the care which Fletcher took to insist that the servants under his system would be protected from such a despotism: 'the condition of such a servant is to be esteemed free; because in the most essential things he is only subject to the laws, and not to the will of his master'.[36] Either Miller was properly sceptical about the effect that these safeguards would have in practice or he had not read the pamphlet and had accepted a distorted view of Fletcher's proposals.

Miller's criticism was carried further a few years later by the distinguished historian, T. B. Macaulay, in his *History of England from the Accession of James II* (first published between 1849 and 1861):

A far higher character belonged to Andrew Fletcher of Saltoun, a man distinguished by learning and eloquence, distinguished also by courage, disinterestedness, and public spirit, but of an irritable and impracticable temper. Like many of his most illustrious contemporaries, Milton for example, Harrington, Marvel, and Sidney, Fletcher had, from the misgovernment of several successive princes, conceived a strong aversion to hereditary monarchy. Yet he was no democrat. He was the head of an ancient Norman house, and was proud of his descent. He was a fine speaker and a fine writer, and was proud of his intellectual superiority. Both in his character of gentleman, and in his character of scholar, he looked down with disdain on the common people, and was so little disposed to entrust them with political power that he thought them unfit even to enjoy personal freedom. It is a curious circumstance that this man, the most honest, fearless, and uncompromising republican of his time, should have been the author of a plan for reducing a large part of the working classes of Scotland to slavery. He bore, in truth, a lively resemblance to those Roman Senators who, while they hated the name of King, guarded the privileges of their order with inflexible pride against the encroachments of the multitude, and governed their bondmen and bondwomen by means of the stocks and the scourge.[37]

Macaulay has been followed gratefully by some writers of the present century anxious to destroy Fletcher's reputation for their own political motives.[38] Fletcher was certainly irritable and proud, although he showed much more concern for the ordinary man than Macaulay suggests, not least in the pamphlet which is the basis for his attack. There is also some truth in the charge that Fletcher guarded the privileges of his own order, or rather that he accepted on this point the social conventions of his age which were so far largely unquestioned. He constantly argued for a reduction in the powers and privileges of the monarchy and nobility but never those of his own class, the lairds who had the sole right to elect one or two of their number to represent their Shire in Parliament. In this respect, Fletcher was reflecting the prevailing attitude of his time. Apart from the Harringtonian theory about the relationship between property and political independence, there was a general assumption, still almost unquestioned, that only men of property had the right to influence political decisions. Proposals for parliamentary reform only began to appear, then only on a basis which still accepted property qualifications, about a century later. Macaulay is therefore criticising Fletcher for not being well ahead of the accepted wisdom of his time in this as he was in many other respects.

The same is also true of the attacks on Fletcher by both Miller and Macaulay for his 'plan for reducing a large part of the working classes of Scotland to slavery'. Fletcher was saying nothing new in suggesting that 'vagabonds and sturdy beggars' should be compelled to work. A whole series of Acts of the Scottish Parliament from 1579 to the end of the 17th century had made provisions precisely for that, even if they remained ineffective, except in coal-mining and salt-panning. An article in the *Edinburgh Review* in January 1899, which went into the whole question in some detail, describes it as 'the favourite solution during the whole of the 17th century of our still pressing problem of the unemployed'.[39] This was not a survival of mediaeval serfdom, which disappeared in Scotland earlier than in most countries, but a logical extension of the Calvinist work ethic. John Knox's *First Book of Discipline* said that 'stout and sturdy beggars must be compelled to work'. The work of Francis Hutcheson (1694–1747) was one of the foundations of the Scottish school of philosophy and of the Scottish Enlightenment. He is described in the *Edinburgh Review* article as 'a most ardent and enlightened advocate of freedom', but in his *System of Moral Philosophy* he also proposed the 'perpetual slavery' of 'idle vagabonds'.[40]

To a point, therefore, Fletcher was again following the accepted attitude of his time in proposing a desperate remedy for a desperate problem, long before unemployment insurance and the welfare state were within the remote realms of possibility or imagination. What was new about his approach was his compassion and his concern for the well being, education, health and provision for the old age of the workers. He was anticipating, in a very rudimentary way, the idea of the welfare state. The young Ramsay MacDonald, the future Prime Minister, showed an understanding of this point in an essay of 1893 about Fletcher when he wrote (perhaps with the attacks of Miller and Macaulay in mind): 'No one who knows the scheme in its entirety, or who is aware of the conditions of labour in Scotland at this time, will regard the proposal as anything but humane — we might almost say enlightened'.[41] In any case, the proposal for compulsory labour was not one of Fletcher's favourite themes. It occurs only in this one pamphlet, and some passages may have been written in a spirit of Swiftian irony.

In the same *Discourse* Fletcher went on to propose a radical reform of agriculture. 'The principal and original source of our poverty', he argued, was 'the letting of our lands at so excessive a rate as makes the tenant poorer even than his servants whose wages he cannot pay'. This abuse of 'racking the lands' had reduced the country to such an extremity that a completely new system of land ownership and management was needed. He proposed that interest on money should be prohibited and no man should be allowed to own more land than he could cultivate with his servants. By this means, he believed, all the money and all the people would soon be employed either in cultivation or in trade and manufacture. Again this might be called 'visionary', but Fletcher had led the way in proposing the drastic overhaul of land tenure and agricultural method, which was desperately needed.[42]

The next two items in the *Political Works* differ from all the others in dealing not with Scotland but with international relationships in Europe. Both were concerned with the question of the Spanish succession, the inheritance of the Spanish Empire on the death of the imbecile King of Spain, Charles II. The first of the two pamphlets is an able account of the nature of the problem, and an analysis of the possible solutions and their effects. Curiously enough it was written in Italian with the title *Discorso delle cose di Spagna, scritto nel mese di luglio 1698*. According to the title page, it was published in Naples in the same year, although from the type and the paper it seems in fact to have been printed in Edinburgh.[43]

No one has offered a satisfactory explanation for this mystification. David Dalrymple, Lord Hailes, refers to it in the letter to the Earl of Buchan from which I quoted in chapter one: 'He had acquired', he says of Fletcher, 'such knowledge of Italian as to be able to compose a treatise in that language. Prince Eugene spoke to him in Italian, but Fletcher was not able to answer Yes or No!'.[44] Of course, it is not unusual for someone who has learnt a language mainly from books to be at a loss when suddenly addressed in the spoken tongue. Perhaps Hailes means to imply that Fletcher was merely being ostentatious in displaying his written Italian, although the pamphlet, like the others, was anonymous. Certainly, there was a fashion among the wits of Edinburgh of the day to air their Italian, as proof perhaps that they had made the Grand Tour. The name of one of the parties in the Scottish Parliament, the *Squadrone Volante*, is another instance of the same affectation.

On the other hand, Naples was at the time one of the Spanish territories involved. Fletcher may have thought that the pamphlet would have more weight and influence if it seemed to be expressing a Neapolitan opinion. John Robertson has suggested that the reason for the Neapolitan pose was that Fletcher was reacting to Tommaso Campanella's *De Monarchia Hispanica* of which he had a copy in his library of the Latin edition of 1640.[45] In this book, Campanella, who was for many years imprisoned in Naples, advocated a universal empire under the King of Spain. Certainly it was exactly this threat that Fletcher was concerned to oppose. Perhaps the whole mystification was a device to make it plain that the pamphlet was intended for Italian readers as a reply to Campanella. There is, however, no evidence that Fletcher's pamphlet was circulated to any extent in Italy itself. According to Scott Macfie, the Naples Library acquired a copy only in 1898. There should, he adds, be a copy in the Biblioteca Angelica at Rome, but it is 'successfully concealed by a wrong entry in the catalogue'. He failed to trace any copy in the Italian second-hand book trade.[46]

A Speech upon the State of the Nation: In April 1701 is in the form of an imaginary speech not to the Scottish Parliament but to the English. Fletcher was trying to influence William's foreign policy and the English Parliament would be a much more effective forum for the purpose. By this time Charles II of Spain had died and the question was whether the Second Partition Treaty would be carried out. As in the *Discourse* on Spanish affairs, Fletcher was concerned that a combination of Spain and France would lead to their domination of the world. He was opposed to arbitrary power internationally as well as internally. There are many signs in the speech of Fletcher's utter disillusion by this time with William and his government: 'The English nation have now nothing remaining but the outward appearance and carcase, as I may call it, of their antient constitution. The spirit and soul is fled. Jealousy for Public liberty is vanished'.[47]

I think that I have quoted enough from these pamphlets to give the flavour of Fletcher's writing. He has a gift for the pungent and memorable phrase which often has an ironic twist. 'A cunning and able prince, who by the world is called a wise one', he writes, for instance, in the *Discourse* on Militias.[48] His prose style has often been praised. For example, Francis Espinasse in his article on Fletcher in *The Dictionary of National Biography* says: 'As a writer he is superior to any Scotsman of his age, and his oratory, nervous and incisive, is made eloquent by his sincerity and earnestness'. There is a more extended comment in Sir John Dalrymple's *Memoirs of Great Britain and Ireland* (1788):

Mr Fletcher's style is easily known, because every word has a precise meaning, and distinct from any other in the sentence; the structure of the sentence is as simple, but as varied as that which is used in private conversation; the method in his composition is perfectly regular, but artfully concealed; and one singularity in his reasoning is, that the arguments are placed in an order to derive force from what went before, and to give force to what comes after, so as to seem to grow out of each other. But, above all, when he is animated with passion, his flashes are sometimes as quick as lightning, and sometimes followed by a thunder of period: All which mark an original genius, but made chaste by the reading of the ancients. The volume of his works is unequally collected, and his discourse on the affairs of Spain is a poor translation from the Italian, in which he wrote it.

The lightning flashes are more distinctive of Fletcher's style than the thunder of period, but Dalrymple is right in saying that it is simple and conversational. Fletcher's writing is lively and clear and always a pleasure to read. There is an idiomatic ease and verbal dexterity about the writing which conceals the labour which Fletcher probably spent on it, because, as John Clerk tells us, he was not 'very dexterous' in extempore speaking.[50] Such a fluent and apparently natural command of English is also very remarkable in a Scotsman at a time when it was not the spoken language of any class in Scotland.

Later in the 18th century the *literati* of the *Scottish Enlightenment* still spoke Scots but for writing they had developed an effective, but Latinate and sometimes ponderous, English prose. The English officer, Edward Topham, who spent six months in Edinburgh between 1774 and 1775 said of them, 'I shall only say, that they appear to me, from their conversation, to write English as a foreign tongue; their mode of talking, phrase and expression, but little resembling the language of their works.'[51] Their prose style owned more to the influence of Latin in which they were steeped in school than to the rhythms of English speech which they seldom heard. Lord Mansfield told Alexander Carlyle, that the histories of Hume and Robertson did not sound to him as though they were in English.[52]

How then is it that we find Fletcher, born about 60 years before David Hume, writing English with such conversational familiarity and confidence? Even making allowances for a quick ear and gift for languages, Fletcher must have been well exposed to native English conversation as well as books. He was in English as well as Scottish company during his time as a political exile in Holland. As I have mentioned before, he was in London more than once and had experience of London society. His *Account of a Conversation* shows him talking at ease with members of the English House of Commons. We may regret, that a Scotsman, renowned for his patriotism, and addressing his own countrymen on Scottish issues, should even before the Union write an English prose which has no hint of a Scottish flavour. Under the Influence of the Authorised Version of the Bible and the practice of the Kirk, the tradition had already been established that English was the appropriate language for the written discussion of serious issues. At all events, Fletcher managed English prose with a dexterity well in advance of his time. Fletcher anticipated the men of the Scottish Enlightenment in his historical approach, the boldness and originality of his thought and his concern for social and economic issues; but in his handling of written English he easily excelled them.

Many people have been reluctant to believe that a man so fertile in ideas and so agile with his pen would have written no more than the seven short items collected in the *Political Works*. In Fletcher's time pamphlets were usually published anonymously, and several of these have been attributed to him. Some of the attributions are clearly absurd and need not be taken seriously. About others, there is an element of doubt. (I have already discussed one of these in Chapter Six, *A Letter to a Member of the Convention*). Fletcher's bibliographer, Scott Macfie, takes issue with the statement of John Dalrymple that his style is 'easily known'. 'Those who are bold enough,' he writes, 'to attempt the task will find that the difficulty of identifying Fletcher's style is much under-rated by Dalrymple'.[53] It is certainly impossible to be certain on stylistic grounds alone.

John Robertson has suggested[54] that there may be some evidence about the extent of Fletcher's writing in notes in the first of his two manuscript catalogues of his library. There are, in fact, two separate notes.[55] The first is headed, 'Books put in a box to be sent to London Aug 1708.' There follows a list, spread over two pages, of just over 100 books, grouped by format: folio, 8vo, 12vo, and 16vo or smaller. They include the minutes of the Parliamentary Sessions of 1704 and 1705 and a separate volume for 1706; the Acts of the last Session of the Scottish Parliament; and 'some Treatises on the Union'. There are many volumes of political philosophy, including Aristotle, Plato, Thucydides, Machiavelli, Pascal, Moore's *Utopia*, Locke *On Government* and Molyneaux on *The Government of Ireland*. Some are religious: Buchanan's translations of the Psalms in Latin and another version in English metre, a book on *The Rights of the Church* and another on *The Power of the Magistrates in the Matter of Religion*. Others are geographical: maps of Germany and accounts of Sweden and Denmark. There are a number of military textbooks. As far as Fletcher's own writing is concerned, there are two entries. Under 8vo, he notes, '3 copies of my books being 6 vol'. At the bottom of the same page (the second of the two) there is the following list:

    12 Speeches in 4vo
     3 Dialogues
     1 Discorsi Ital.
     2 Disc of the Militia
     1 of the 2 Discourses of Scotl.
     2 Speeches of the first Session in Parlm.

The second note, which is on the following page of the catalogue, is headed, 'Left in the great drawer of my cabinet Sept 1708.' Another list follows:

    Bound   14 Discourses etc
             14 Speeches & Dialogues
              2 Speeches

Stitched	42 Discorsi di cose di Spanga
	33 Discourses of the affairs of S.
	26 Dis of the Militia
	30 Speeches of the partition Treaty
In quares	66 of these speeches
	3 of those in Par.
	12 Letters.

What can we conclude from all of this? '3 copies of my books being 6 vol' presumably means that he had some copies of his publications bound together in two volume sets, but it tells us no more than that. The lists are more informative. If we assume that 'Dialogues' refers to *An Account of a Conversation* and note that the two *Discourses Concerning the Affairs of Scotland* were published together as one item, then both lists are seen to consist, in an abbreviated but perfectly recognisable form, of the seven titles which were published after Fletcher's death as the *Political Works,* with one addition. That is *Letters,* which could refer to copies of *A Letter to a Member of the Convention,* which I discussed on pages 45 and 46. The items in the drawer of Fletcher's cabinet are presumably his remaining stock in various states of the same publications. These lists therefore strongly suggest that he had published nothing else before September 1708. Of course, this is not absolutely conclusive. There could have been other pamphlets that he did not particularly wish to preserve or of which he had disposed of all the copies. 'Some Treatises on the Union' in the box for London could include others, such as *Separate or United Parliaments,* which I shall discuss in Chapter 14. This is separate from the obvious lists of his own publications, but it is conceivable that something of his own might be included under this general heading.

We do not know why Fletcher intended to send such a substantial collection of books to London or why he felt it necessary to record the items left in a drawer. The most obvious explanation is that he was preparing for a long absence abroad and was sending ahead books that he would want for pleasure or study. The large number of political works suggests that he may have had in mind some further work of his own in the field. Although he was now 55, the inclusion of geographical and military texts could mean that he was thinking of returning to his military career, perhaps in Germany or Scandinavia. That was, after all, a common enough resource for Scots, especially when they were out of sympathy with the political situation at home. In any case, he may have changed his mind. Whether he left Scotland in 1708 or not, he was certainly back two or three years later. (See page 214.)

Robert Wodrow records a conversation with Fletcher in May 1712 which is also discouraging to anyone hoping to find other unidentified work: 'I enquired at him if he had writt the History of the Union. He lamented that he had not kept a daily account of their proceedings, and tells me he had writt nothing but his speeches, and it's impossible nou for him to doe any thing. He compleans extremely of his memory'.[56] It is possible to read this in more than one way, but the most likely interpretation is that the reference is only to a history of the Union, not to an inability to write anything else.

In the same conversation, Fletcher goes to speak about his speeches in Parliament, confirming Clerk's opinion that he was not strong in extempore speaking. He told Wodrow that he had written everything that he said in Parliament and went to 'incredible fatigue' in learning them by heart. 'He did it evry day as ever a schoolboy did his gramer, and directly repeated some of them ten or twenty times; and being uncertain what matters wer to come before them, he was oblidged sometimes to have six or ten speeches, upon distinct heads in readiness at once'.

In spite of the evidence to the contrary, there are two or three other pamphlets which echo the voice of Fletcher so powerfully in thought and language that it is difficult to believe that he did not write them, at least in part. One of these is *United and Separate Parliaments*, which I have already mentioned. Another is *A Defence of the Scots Settlement at Darien*, published under the pseudonym, 'Philo-Caledon', at Edinburgh in 1699. Fletcher had a copy in his library.[57] It is a robust statement of the Scottish case which reads, as is quite probable, like the joint effort of several collaborators. But the voice of Fletcher seems unmistakable in such remarks as these: 'The City of London, which being the Seat of the Government, will as certainly draw money from Scotland, as the Sun draws Vapours after it'. Or, of the consequences for Scotland of participation in English wars, 'We are forc'd to be sharers in their Troubles, tho they will not allow us to partake of their Profits'. Or, 'We never believ'd that Doctrine in Scotland, that it is unlawful to resist a King, or any that have a Commission under him, upon any pretence whatsoever'.[58]

The pamphlet is also consistent with the attitudes of Fletcher in simultaneously asserting the distinctiveness and independence of Scotland and advocating a 'stricter union' with England. In the context, union could only mean a military alliance between two independent countries to 'render us less liable to Convulsions and intestine Commotions at home, and put us out of danger of being attack'd by Enemies from abroad'.[59]

Another pamphlet which Scott Macfie accepts as 'possibly by Fletcher'[60] has the title: *Proposals for the Reformation of Schools and Universities In Order to the Better Education of Youth. Humbly Offer'd to the Serious Consideration of the High Court of Parliament*. It is, as usual, anonymous and it is dated 1704. Macfie offers two fairly convincing arguments in support of this attribution. The first is a remark which he quotes from Cobbett's *Parliamentary History of England*, but of which the original source (as so often) is Elizabeth Halkett's manuscript family history in Edinburgh University Library. She quotes Fletcher as saying: 'The education of youth is one of the noblest objects of government', and she comments: 'on this subject he wrote a treatise, still extant, most characteristic of himself'.[61] The other argument for accepting the 1704 publication as this 'treatise' is simply that its style and content do indeed seem characteristic of Fletcher. Macfie writes:

The style is very like Fletcher's, and the radical changes proposed, as well as the commonsense and completeness of the scheme are quite in his manner. In addition, the author's desire to keep the common people to their mechanical employments, the allusion to classical writers, and the dating of the decline of learning from the Union of the Crowns are exactly like Fletcher's way of handling such topics.' (The pamphlet does not, in fact, mention the Union of the Crowns specifically, but that is implicit in its dating of the decline: 'Where we have now one who can write one single sheet, a hundred years ago we had twenty who could have written volumes in good sense and good Latine.')

The pamphlet is a brief work of only 8½ pages. It begins by deploring the decay of learning and argues that its encouragement and improvement are much in the interest of the nation. He offers an unexpected explanation for its present low estate: it is 'too easily and cheaply purchas'd', and by this he evidently means that the available resources are spread too widely and too thinly. It would be better for the 'poorer sort of People' to send their sons to the plough and other trades. (There is, of course, no mention of daughters.) 'People who are daily pinch'd for the Back and the Belly, cannot spend much time on the Improvement of their minds'. There is a need to 'reconcile the Gentleman with the Scholar'. Present methods tend to 'unfit a scholar for a Gentleman, and to render a Gentleman asham'd of being a scholar'.

This deplorable display of class prejudice is particularly incongruous in Scotland, where so many of the most brilliant and learned have come from the humblest of backgrounds. After this, however, the author makes some perfectly sensible proposals for the curricula in grammar schools, of which there should be one in each Shire, and in the universities, of which he thinks two would be sufficient. He calls on Parliament to vote funds for schools of law and physic so that Scottish students would not have to go abroad, and suggests that no one should be allowed to practise the professions of the law, medicine and the Church without certificates of qualification.

This certainly sounds like Fletcher in its curious combination of the complacent assumption of class privilege along with bold ideas for social improvement, as these were at that time, and constant concern for the well-being of Scotland.

9

The Parliament of 1703

'The Memory of this Parliament will be precious to the Nation, so long as it has a being'
— *George Ridpath*

Not only Fletcher but the majority of Scots had become thoroughly disillusioned with King William long before he died on 20 February 1702. To the Jacobites he was always a usurper, but he had also alienated many of those who looked to him as a liberator from the tyranny under James VII. His behaviour over Darien had shown beyond all doubt that he was ready to sacrifice Scottish interests to England. Blame for the Massacre of Glencoe in 1692 clung to his reputation. His dying wish was that Scotland and England should be joined in an incorporating union as soon as possible. Like his royal predecessors he wanted to ride one horse and not two that were liable to go off in different directions.

This constant policy of all monarchs, since James VI went to London in 1603, was immediately endorsed by his successor, Queen Anne, the sister of Queen Mary and the last of the Stuarts. According to Gilbert Burnet, many of her closest advisers 'opposed it with much heat, and not without indecent reflections on the Scotch nation'. Yet it was, he says, so visibly the interest of England, and of the present government, to shut that back-door against the practices of France', that the Queen had her way and Parliament agreed to her appointing commissioners for the negotiation of a Treaty.[1] Commissioners from both countries began negotiations in November 1702. Their talks proceeded with little enthusiasm and never resumed after they adjourned in February 1703. English parliamentarians had never shared the enthusiasm of their monarchs for the idea of union; they disliked the Scots as traditional enemies and had no wish for a closer association with them. Events, however, were soon to persuade the English that their interests required a firm and continuing means of controlling Scotland.

The long war of the Spanish Succession helped to bring home to English statesmen their need of Scotland. England declared war on France on 4 May 1702 without consulting Scotland. Since the Union of the Crowns, Scotland had no share in deciding on questions of war and peace. War was conducted in the name of England and for English interests and usually against Scotland's traditional allies and trading partners. Scotland was expected to contribute men and money, but was forgotten again in the distribution of any benefits that might flow from the peace. All of this was a consequence of the Union of the Crowns. Foreign policy was made, and was carried on, by the monarch. When

Scotland lost her own king in 1603, she also lost her own foreign policy and any influence over these matters which might vitally affect her interests. The disastrous consequences of this was a constant theme of Fletcher's pamphlets and speeches.

From the English point of view, of course, the situation seemed quite different. It was convenient to be able to draw on Scottish resources to serve the interests of England. It was even more important to be able to deny the use of Scottish territory to an enemy. In the course of the war against Louis XIV, the English began to realize how serious the loss of Scotland could be to them. An independent Scotland might, as in the past, make common cause with France or another enemy of England and open the northern border to attack. England could never become a European or world power without first securing that border. As it happened, the outcome of the war, with Marlborough's victories over France, enabled England to bargain with Scotland from a position of overwhelming strength.

It was the question of the Succession to the throne which brought the relationship between the two countries to a critical point which had to be resolved one way or another. On 30 July 1700, William, Duke of Gloucester, the last survivor of Queen Anne's eighteen children, died. She was already too old to have more children. There was no longer any obvious and automatic heir to the throne. The legitimate line of descent from James VII and II, the Jacobite Pretender, could not be re-established without overthrowing the Protestant settlement of the 'Glorious Revolution'. The English Parliament, again with no consultation with Scotland, decided the matter to its own satisfaction in the Act of Succession of 1701. This offered the throne to the Protestant Sophia, Electress of Hanover, and her descendants. Sophia had a claim to the Succession because of her descent from a daughter of James VI and I; but this was only one possible solution and it was not in any way binding on Scotland. The English Parliament seems to have assumed that Scotland would meekly accept their decision. In fact, their high-handed action called in question the survival of the fusion of the two monarchies which had come about by dynastic accident in 1603. For all these reasons, the relationship with England reached a critical point in the early years of Anne's reign. 'All thinking Scots, indeed, by the end of William's troubled reign agreed that the existing bond between the two kingdoms was unsatisfactory and that it was slowly strangling the weaker nation. The unionists believed this no less than the anti-unionists'.[2] There was general agreement, in other words, that constitutional change was urgently needed, but no clear idea or agreement about the form which it should take.

It was in this atmosphere that a new Parliament was elected in Scotland in 1703, to the limited extent that parliaments were then subject to election (see page 31). This was the first such election since 1689 and therefore the first for which Fletcher was eligible as a Commissioner of a Shire after Saltoun was restored to him in 1690. He was duly elected as one of four Commissioners for the Shire of Haddington. This Parliament met for the first time on 6 May

1703. It remained in being, with meetings usually spread over a few months each summer, until it adjourned on 25 March 1707 after the ratification of the Treaty of Union. For reasons which I shall discuss later, the atmosphere and balance of opinion changed from year to year, but the composition of the Parliament remained the same with no new election after 1703.

This Parliament was the climax of Fletcher's political life. His historical reputation largely depends on his speeches and activities during these three and half years. It is also the part of his life for which we have by far the most detailed record and from several points of view. The official record, *The Acts of the Parliament of Scotland*, is mainly a record of decisions, with the full texts of Acts but no speeches (except a few formal ones) and no voting figures, except for the final debate on the Treaty. Fortunately, however, two members of the Parliament wrote an account of its proceedings. Sir David Hume of Crossing kept an inelegant but informative diary and George Lockhart of Carnwath wrote a vivid and passionate account in his *Memoirs*. Lockhart was a Jacobite and his account is frankly partisan; but his bias coloured his opinions more than his facts which are consistent with other evidence and are probably reliable. Several other members wrote letters about the proceedings which have been published in the papers of Carstares, Baillie of Jerviswood, Mar and Kellie, Seafield and Portland. Of these, the letters of Mar and Seafield are particularly useful, for different years, because they are long and detailed reports to their masters in London. Sir John Clerk of Penicuik was also a member of this Parliament who wrote *Memoirs*. He has some illuminating asides but no sustained account of the proceedings. For the session of 1703 we have the additional advantage of a book, *An Account of the Proceedings of the Parliament of Scotland which met at Edinburgh, May 6, 1703*, by George Ridpath, a very active pamphleteer of the time in the Scottish interest. Andrew Fletcher's speeches to this session were printed both in this book and as a separate pamphlet. Daniel Defoe's *History of the Union* throws no light on Fletcher for two reasons. In the first place, Defoe arrived in Edinburgh only in October 1706. Secondly, he was a paid agent of the English government with instructions both to spy on the Scots and to do all he could to bring about the acceptance of the Union. He could hardly change his attitudes and arguments when he wrote his *History* after the event. He dealt with Andrew Fletcher by simply pretending that he did not exist.

The Officers of State, which we might now call the ministerial team responsible for conducting government business in Parliament, were appointed for each session by the Queen, acting on the advice of her English ministers. Since the abolition of the Committee of Articles in 1690, the Scottish Parliament was free to discuss and to introduce proposals as it wished, but all executive power, and the disposal of all appointments, rested in London, nominally in the hands of the Queen. Acts passed by the Scottish Parliament required the royal assent before they became effective. Scotland was still in theory a separate, sovereign Kingdom, but since 1603 it had been a very limited and incomplete independence. It was an unstable situation which was unsatisfactory to both

Scotland and England. To the Scots it was only too apparent that the system meant the predominance of English interests and the neglect of their own. To the English, their control was incomplete if they could no longer rely on the Scottish Parliament supporting the policy of the Ministry.

One of the major contributions of Andrew Fletcher was that he analysed and explained this situation with unflinching lucidity. In one of his speeches in the Parliament of 1703, for example:

> It has been often said in this house that our princes are captives in England; and indeed one would not wonder if, when our interest happens to be different from that of England, our Kings, who must be supported by the riches and power of that nation in all their undertakings, should prefer an English interest before that of this country. It is yet less strange, that English ministers should advise and procure the advancement of such persons to the ministry of Scotland, as will comply with their measures and the king's orders; and to surmount the difficulties they may meet with from a true Scots interest, that places and pensions should be bestowed upon parliament-men and others: I say, these things are so far from wonder, that they are inevitable in the present state of our affairs. But I hope they likewise show us that we ought not to continue any longer in this condition.[3]

Fletcher's remedy was his proposals for 'limitations' on the power of the monarch, and therefore of the English ministers, which would transfer effective control of Scottish affairs from London to the Scottish Parliament.

It was the business of the Scottish officers of State, appointed by London, to try to secure acquiescence of the Scottish Parliament either by argument and persuasion or by the inducements of patronage, pensions and office. This was necessarily a slow and difficult process, especially, as in 1703, when matters of strong national and religious feeling were involved. Because it was a slow process, and because the government wanted to enjoy the support of members once they had been won over or bought, the government preferred long parliaments and infrequent elections. Fletcher, and those who agreed with him in wishing to increase the power of parliament, were in favour of annual elections. George Ridpath, for instance, in the book which I have just mentioned, said that annual parliaments were part of the ancient Scottish constitution, 'for our Ancestors thought that the best method to secure their own Liberties, and those of their Posterity, because they knew well that Parliaments of a long continuance, are liable to be practis'd upon by a designing Ministry'.[4] This is exactly what happened to the Parliament elected in 1703. The longer it continued, the more docile it became in the hands of the Ministry, and there is plenty of evidence to show the way in which it was 'practised upon'.[5]

As the Government in London sought to bring the Scottish Parliament under control, they changed the Officers of State each year in the hope of finding a more successful team. In 1703 the High Commissioner, the personal representative of the Queen and chiefly responsible for securing the safe passage of Government policy, was the Duke of Queensberry. The

Lord High Chancellor, who presided over the debates in the chamber, was the Earl of Seafield. Both were men of considerable political dexterity, who, in the end, became the chief architects of the Union with England. George Lockhart's description of Queensberry was that 'to outward appearance, and in his ordinary conversation, he was of a gentle and good disposition, but inwardly a very devil, standing at nothing to advance his own interest and designs'. Lockhart detested Queensberry because he regarded him as the 'Proto-rebel', the first Scotsman who deserted the Stuarts for the House of Orange. Even so, his judgement of Queensberry's character is close to the general view of his contemporaries. Seafield was the consummate career man, with no strong views of his own but ready to put his talents at the service of the government in office. He was, said Lockhart, 'a blank sheet of paper, which the Court might fill up with what they pleas'd'.[6]

The House divided into three groups or parties, although parties were not then the highly organised and disciplined bodies which they have since become. Those who, for one reason or another, supported the Government were known as the Court party under the leadership of Queensberry. Since the Revolution, the opposition had been in the hands of the Country party, which claimed to represent the national interest and was Presbyterian in religion. It looked for leadership to the Duke of Hamilton, but he often failed them. In spite of many such disappointments, Lockhart did his best to remain loyal to Hamilton, long his leader and patron. 'Never', he says, 'was a man so well qualified to be the head of a party'. He does, however, admit that his opposition to the Union was weakened by his 'too great concern for his estate in England'.[7] Lockhart was not alone in realising this. Sir John Clerk of Penicuik, a member of Parliament and a protégé of Queensberry, recorded in his *Memoirs* that Hamilton 'was so unlucky in his privat circumstances that he wou'd have complied with anything on a suitable encouragement'.[8] As we shall see, it is only too obvious that is precisely what happened. Hamilton's attitude was further complicated by his own claim on the throne, by descent from the royal line, and his ambition to succeed to it. The Election of 1703 brought substantial gains to the Jacobites who now appeared in the House as a third party, calling themselves the Cavaliers, led by the Earl of Home. They were Episcopalians in religion, and were opposed to both the displacement of the Stuart line and to the Presbyterian church settlement in Scotland.

The Cavaliers had been encouraged by the succession of Queen Anne because she was a Stuart and because she was known to be a strong Episcopalian. Queensberry made an attempt to enlist their support in Parliament by holding out hope of the extension of toleration to Episcopalianism; but this soon broke down when they saw that there was no real prospect that he would take the risk of inflaming Presbyterian resentment. After this there was a paradoxical alliance between the Country party and the Cavaliers. They were fundamentally opposed on most issues but were brought together by a common distrust of English influence. To the Cavaliers, English ascendancy meant the Revolution settlement and the continued exclusion of the Stuart line; to the Country party it meant a threat to Presbyterianism and to national independence. Both therefore wanted to resist English interference. This was the factor which brought Fletcher, the opponent of royal power, and Lockhart, the Jacobite, together. They were both Scottish patriots and this is obvious from everything that both of them wrote. Lockhart referred to Fletcher as 'that worthy and never-to-be-enough-praised patriot, . . .' 'a true Scotsman who preferred his country's interest to all considerations whatsoever'.[9]

By instinct Andrew Fletcher was a lone campaigner who did not find it easy to compromise or collaborate. In Lockhart's account of his character, which I quoted in the first chapter, he says that because of this 'he often in Parliament acted a part by himself, tho' in the main he stuck close to the Country party, and was their Cicero'. Among modern historians, William Ferguson describes Fletcher as the leader of the radical wing of the Country party and says that he was ably supported by Montrose, Rothes, Roxburgh and Haddington. This was the group of young noblemen to whom Fletcher addressed his most important pamphlet, *An Account of a Conversation*, in December 1703. They were, Ferguson adds, so completely under his influence that they were popularly called his 'cubs'.[10] John Robertson, on the other hand, denies that Fletcher ever had 'an organised political following in the Scottish Parliament'.[11] There is a sense in which this is true because there was nothing 'organised' in the modern sense about Fletcher's support in Parliament, although it is obvious enough from the record that Fletcher, Hamilton and others were working together in a way which must have been deliberate and planned. It is quite wrong to conclude, as Robertson does, that Fletcher's influence was more intellectual than political. Anyone who reads through any of the contemporary accounts of the sessions of Parliament from 1703 to 1707 cannot fail to be struck by how frequently Fletcher's name appears and how often he takes the initiative and gives a lead. Particularly in 1703 he set the agenda and dominated the atmosphere of the entire session.

Fletcher's influence diminished in the years that followed as the Court 'practised upon' the members and gradually won more support in one way or another. This did not mean that Fletcher was less resourceful or less active. Contrary to some recent assertions,[12] contemporary evidence leaves no doubt that Fletcher resisted the Union and fought to assert the rights of the Scottish Parliament to the end. The reports which Seafield and Mar sent to London about the proceedings mention Fletcher repeatedly and make it quite clear that the Court saw him as their most resourceful and formidable opponent.

The new Parliament, with its first meeting on 6 May 1703, began gently enough. A letter from Queen Anne asked for supplies (or in other words a vote of money through taxation) to pursue the war with France. She suggested that Parliament might consider laws to encourage trade.[13] Queensberry and Seafield, as Commissioner and Chancellor, made speeches to the same effect. Seafield remarked that conditions had deteriorated so much that Scotland had now almost no foreign trade.[14] There was no reference in any of these official pronouncements about the constitutional question or the Succession to the throne. Then, as now, the Government evidently hoped that if they did not mention a question it would go away. They seemed to hope that Parliament would vote supply and in that case they had no further need for it or, failing that, that it could be diverted into questions of trade. At all events, they hoped that it could be brought to accept the constitutional *status quo* and, by default, the English Act of Succession.

After a few days of formal business the issue was joined on 19 May. The Earl of Home as leader of the Cavaliers and in pursuit of their short lived deal with Queensberry, proposed an Act of Supply. This was countered by the Marquis of Tweedale, for the Country party, who presented an Overture that 'before all other business the Parliament might proceed to make such conditions of government and regulations in the Constitution of this Kingdom to take place after the decease of Her Majestie and the heirs of her body as shall be necessary for the preservation of our religion and liberty'.[15]

This was a fundamental challenge to the Government. It proposed in effect that Parliament should not fall into the trap of giving away in advance the bargaining card of supply, nor the more important one of Succession, as means of securing more equitable constitutional conditions than had applied since 1603. There was a long debate on this on 26 May. Many members of the Country party, Ridpath said, 'could not forbear to take Notice, that since our Princes have been under the predominant Influence of another Nation it had been too customary for the Court, as soon as they had obtain'd Money, to Adjourn or Dissolve Parliament, and to forget their Promises of redressing our Grievances'.[16] Fletcher, in particular, pressed this point and the first of his printed speeches is one to this effect.[17] He proposed a vote on the issue on 26 May and it was finally resolved on the twenty-eighth 'by a great majority' that 'Parliament will proceed to make such Acts as are necessary or fit for securing our religion liberty and trade before any act of supply or any other business whatsoever'.[18]

At this early stage in the proceedings, Parliament had asserted itself against the Government which had lost control. The original emphasis, as in Tweedale's Overture, was on religion (which meant the defence of Presbyterianism against Episcopacy) and liberty (which meant freedom from English interference). During the discussion, Hume said, 'Some added Trade',[19] as Fletcher did in his speech, but it was clear that it was not the main point.

On the same day as this assertion of Parliamentary supremacy over the Government, a number of draft acts to be considered before supply were laid on the table. The most important was the Act of Security, which was to become the central issue of the session. An Act proposed by Fletcher was to the effect that after the death of the Queen and heirs of her body (there were, of course, now no such heirs nor likely to be any) all offices civil and military, formerly in the gift of the Sovereign, would in future be appointed by Parliament. Another in the name of Fletcher's colleague, Rothes, proposed to take the power of making peace or war from the Sovereign to Parliament.[20] These were two fundamental points in the effective transfer of power away from the monarch, and therefore from English ministers, to the Scottish Parliament. Fletcher was shortly to propose a comprehensive scheme for this purpose in his famous 'limitations'. (Appendix 'A').

Parliament then turned to the question of toleration for the Episcopalians which had been at the basis of Queensberry's attempt to win the support of the Cavaliers. Ridpath reminds us of the importance of the issue at the time by going into a digression of about 100 pages about the tribulations involved in the attempt by successive Kings in the 17th century to impose Episcopacy on Scotland. Even so, he tells us that many Presbyterians were at first in favour of toleration 'because they thought liberty of conscience to be the Right of Mankind'. They changed their minds when they realised that the object of the Episcopalians was to take over churches and dispossess the present incumbents which would 'put the whole Nation in a Ferment'.[21] The matter was finally decided by Parliament approving 'by 70 votes or thereby'[22] a provision making it treasonable to impugn or alter the Claim of Right, which had declared Prelacy to be 'a great and insupportable Grievance and Trouble to this Nation'. After that, says Ridpath, no more was heard of tolerations.[23] This meant, of course, that the Court was now in a weaker position than ever because they had failed in their desperate attempt to win over the votes of the Cavaliers.

Fletcher distrusted religious enthusiasts of any persuasion and thought that they all tended to encourage arbitrary power in the hope that it would be exercised in favour of their own religion. In a speech which he made about this time (they are not dated or placed in order in the printed collection) he condemned both Episcopalians and Presbyterians with about equal force. The arbitrary power of the King, he argued, had been introduced by the Union of the Crowns. Before that 'no monarchy in Europe was more limited, nor any people more jealous of liberty that the Scots'. The Episcopalians had been chiefly responsible for the extension of the royal prerogative, although 'the peevish, impudent and detestable conduct of the Presbyterians, who opposed these principles only in others, . . . gave them greater force'. He concluded, 'let us not then tread in the steps of mean and fawning priests of any sort, who are always disposed to place an absolute power in the prince'.[24] Fletcher's contemporaries often described him as republican, although he proposed only to limit the power of kings not to abolish them. In view of passages like this, it is strange that no one has ever accused him of atheism or anti-clericalism. At the very least, he was an 18th century moderate, once again ahead of his time. Like many of his countrymen, if he was an atheist, he was a Presbyterian atheist; his distrust of rank and title and his stern morality were evidence of that.

The Court was evidently alarmed by the vote on 28 May and by the tabling of an Act of Security (Appendix 'B') along with the related proposals of Fletcher and Rothes. Their first reaction was to play for time and occupy the House with routine business and private Acts. Meanwhile, they were no doubt active in the background trying to break up the opposition and recruit support, but even the reticent account in the official record shows that the House was increasingly impatient to get down to the real issue. An Act for the Security of the Kingdom was given a formal first reading on 7 June and was debated on the ninth. The Court then filibustered for several sittings, but they could not prevent the House voting on three separate occasions, on the nineteenth, twenty-fourth and twenty-ninth that the Act of Security was to be taken before any other business. On 22 June, the House agreed 'after long altercation' that the four several Overtures (or drafts) of the Act which had been tabled should be printed. One of these was by Montrose, two by the Lord Advocate, Sir James Stuart of Goodtrees, and one by Fletcher containing his proposals for 12 limitations on the power of the Crown. (See Appendix 'A'). It was not until 1 July that the House was at last able to begin the discussion of the Act, paragraph by paragraph.[25]

While this was going on, some recorded episodes showed the temper of the House. Hume tells us that on 9 June, 'Some moved for Perth, because of the Castle here'. Evidently, there was some feeling that now that Parliament was in open defiance of the Court, it might be prudent to move to Perth where they would not have to meet in the shadow of Edinburgh Castle. On 22 June Lord Belhaven and Sir Alexander Ogilvie were arrested for 'scuffling in the House', but were allowed to return a week later after they had apologized. On 30 June, the House ordered a book to be burned by the common hangman because it contained 'many false and injurious reflections upon the Sovereignity and Independency of this Crown and Nation'. The book, *Historia Anglo-Scotica* by James Drake, was dedicated to Sir Edward Seymour, an English Tory, whom we shall meet again in Fletcher's *Account of a Conversation.* English pamphlets abusing Scotland and claiming English supremacy were common enough. That the House chose this moment to denounce one of them was a reflection of the temper of the members. So are the frequent references in Hume and elsewhere to the 'heat' of the debates. Fundamental issues about the future of Scotland were at issue and passions ran high. 'We were often in the form of a Polish diet', wrote Clerk of Penicuik, 'with our swords in our hands, or at least our hands at our swords'.[26]

Of the four drafts for an Act for the Security of the Kingdom, Ridpath says: 'That which was most taken notice of, and came nearest to the Act that the House agreed to, was the Draught given in by Mr Fletcher of Salton'.[27] Even before this, Fletcher had set out one of the essential lines of his argument when he tabled his draft for appointment to be made by Parliament and not the Crown. This idea was now incorporated in the new Overture as one of the twelve limitations. This speech, the second in the published collection, is a good summary of his view on the constitutional weakness imposed on Scotland by the Union of the Crowns of 1603. It exposed the problem with such clarity that it established the basis for subsequent discussion. The constitutional *status quo* was no longer a possibility which could be taken seriously.

The following are some of the key passages in the speech which was presumably delivered on 28 May:

When our Kings succeeded to the Crown of England, the ministers of that nation took a short way to ruin us, by concurring with their inclinations to extend the prerogative in Scotland; and the great places and pensions conferred upon Scotsmen of that court, made them to be willing instruments in the work . . . All our affairs since the Union of the Crowns have been managed by the advice of English ministers, and the principal offices of the kingdom filled with such men, as the Court of England knew would be subservient to their designs: . . . We have from that time appeared to the rest of the world more like a conquered province than a free independent people . . .

Let no man say, that it cannot be proved that the English court has ever bestowed any bribe in this country. For they bestow all offices and pensions; they bribe us, and are masters of us at our own cost . . . And what less can be expected, unless we resolve to expect miracles, and that greedy, ambitious, and for the most part necessitous men, involved in great debts, burdened with great families, and having great titles to support, will lay down their places, rather than comply with an English interest in obedience to the princes' commands? . . .

We all know that this is the cause of our poverty, misery and dependence. But we have been for a long time so poor, so miserable and depending, that we have neither heart nor courage, though we want not the means, to free ourselves.[28]

Fletcher made this speech, which did not hesitate to call a bribe a bribe, in the presence of such men as Queensberry and Seafield who held 'great places and pensions' conferred on them by English ministers on the understanding that they would be 'willing instruments'. Everyone knew that this was true, but it took a Fletcher to spell it out so boldly and unmistakeably.

On 7 July, as Parliament proceeded through the Act of Security paragraph by paragraph, there appears to have been no argument about the opening clauses of the Act. They provided for Parliament to 'act and administrate the government' on the death of the Queen and to 'nominate and declare' a successor if she died without an heir of her body or one already appointed by her and Parliament. These provisions were obviously very much in line with Fletcher's arguments. It was then agreed that Fletcher's proposals for limitations on the royal power should be considered. Fletcher, according to Hume, 'had a long harangue'.[29] (It is IV in the printed collection of speeches.) When Fletcher had first introduced his draft, he had said that before the Union of the Crown 'no monarchy in Europe was more limited, nor any people more jealous of liberty than the Scots'. He now spelled out 'the miserable conditions to which this nation is reduced by a dependence upon the English court'. The limitations would not apply to any prince who was King of Scotland alone but only as long as the two kingdoms shared the same prince. Their purpose was to free Scotland from the influence of English councils and ministers which had been responsible for 'our present miserable and languishing condition'.[30]

The way in which Fletcher proposed to achieve this result was by his programme of twelve 'limitations' which would effectively transfer power from the Court to Parliament. (Appendix A) There would be annual elections. Parliament would choose its own president. Royal assent to laws would be automatic. Peace and war and the negotiations of treaties would require the approval of Parliament. 'All places and offices, both civil and military, and all pensions formerly conferred by our Kings, shall ever after be given by parliament'.[31] This last point was, of course, a vital one because it was because of the control of the Court over these officers and pensions that English ministers had been able to exercise effective control over Scottish affairs.

After Fletcher's speech, Queensberry intervened to say that this proposal was not one which the Queen had under consideration. Then, according to Hume, Fletcher said 'this proves that the Monarch was under English influence'. This indeed is the force of speech V in the printed collection. It was even stronger in its terms than his earlier speeches about the effects of the influence of the English Court. He saw 'the great advantage of that peace which both nations enjoy by living under our prince . . . but it cannot be denied, that we have been but indifferently used by the English nation'. If there was to be no 'other relief from that servitude we lie under by the influence of that court' then Parliament should resolve that after the death of the Queen we will separate our crown from that of England.[32]

Those about the throne, Hume tells us, said that Fletcher deserved to be censured. Hamilton and others spoke up for the liberty of Parliament. There was 'a great hubbub for some time'. Finally, Fletcher's proposal was put to the vote and rejected, presumably because the idea of drastic limitations of the royal prerogative brought the Court and the Jacobite back into temporary alliance. But this was not the end of the matter. The legislation eventually passed by the House as the Act of Security incorporated many of the features of Fletcher's original proposal. Indeed, at the next sitting on 12 July it was agreed that the first meeting of the Parliament after the death of the Queen would have the power of nominating and declaring her successor, which had been the essential point of the preamble to Fletcher's draft.[33]

On 14 July, it was moved that the successor to be nominated by Parliament should be of the royal line. This was agreed, although opposed by Fletcher. It was also agreed that he should be of the Protestant religion.[34] These two provisions taken together so narrowed the field of choice that it must have encouraged Hamilton's own ambitions.

At the next meeting, on 16 July, one of Fletcher's supporters, Roxburgh, proposed a clause which eventually appeared in the Act of Security in substantially the same words and was, in fact, central to its whole purpose. It followed the provision for the nomination and declaration by Parliament of a successor to the throne and read: 'Providing always, that the same be not the Successor to the Crown of England, unless that in this Session of Parliament (or any other Session of this or any ensuing Parliament during her Majestie's reign) there be such conditions of government settled and enacted as may secure the honour and independency of the Crown of this Kingdom, the freedom, frequency and power of the Parliament, and the religion, liberty and trade of the Nation from the English or any foreign influence'.[35] (The words in brackets, and one or two minor drafting changes, were added during the subsequent discussion.)

Parliament had at last come to the nub of the matter. It was a thoroughgoing declaration of independence. The wording was ingenious because it meant that the same successor as chosen by the English would automatically be excluded unless the Scottish Parliament had in the meantime adopted measures, such as those proposed by Fletcher's limitations, which would ensure 'the freedom, frequency and power of Parliament'. Roxburgh's clause accorded so perfectly with Fletcher's original draft and with the whole thrust of his thought that it was obviously part of a coherent strategy.

It was, in fact, argued that Roxburgh's clause was contrary to the vote rejecting the limitations and a long debate followed. When Fletcher proposed that the clause should be put to the vote, the Chancellor, Seafield, intervened as he was speaking to adjourn the sitting. There was, Hume says, 'a great cry and hubbub'. Hamilton at first proposed that they should continue in spite of the Chancellor and draw up an address of protest to the Queen. On second thoughts he withdrew.[36] Vacillation like this was to become typical of Hamilton's behaviour.

It was not surprising that the Court in desperation had brought the proceedings to an abrupt end. Their policy was now in ruins. Queensberry on behalf of the Court had three objectives: first to secure endorsement of Queen Anne's right to the throne, second to obtain supply and third acceptance of the Succession of the Hanoverian line as in the Act of the English Parliament. The first of these he had obtained without difficulty at the beginning of the Session. The vote on Fletcher's resolution of 28 May, deferring supply until fundamental constitutional matters had been resolved, had effectively frustrated him on the second point. Now Roxburgh's clause not only deferred acceptance of the English Succession but raised substantial doubts whether it would ever be accepted. The majority of the House was clearly behind Fletcher's demand for freedom from English control, even if they were not prepared to go the whole way with him on the limitation of the royal prerogative.

When the House next met, four days later on 20 July, there were protests about the precipitate adjournment of the previous meeting. Fletcher said that it had been an illegal encroachment on the liberty of Parliament. In the end, although it took the whole day to achieve it, the House was satisfied with an assurance that the debate on the Act would be resumed at the next sitting.[37] By then, although they clearly had not had time to get instructions from London, they had devised a new tactic. The Lord Advocate, Stuart of Goodtrees, proposed on 21 July a new clause, apparently intended to take the place of Roxburgh's: 'The same person shall in no event be capable to be King or Queen of both Kingdoms of Scotland and England unless a free communication of trade, the freedom of Navigation and the liberty of the Plantations be fully agreed and established by the Parliament and Kingdom of England in favour of the subjects and Kingdom of Scotland'.[38]

It was a measure of Queensberry's desperation that he allowed this proposal to go ahead apparently in the name of the Court. It went well beyond his instructions. Freedom of trade and shipping with England and the Colonies was something which the English Parliament had always been most reluctant to concede to Scotland. Not only that, but the clause contemplated the very unwelcome prospect for England of Scotland escaping from their control by nominating a separate successor. The clause could also be read as an attempt to blackmail the English into making a reluctant concession to avoid something worse. It might also have been an attempt by the Court to introduce indirectly the possibility of a Parliamentary Union, which was never mentioned or advocated during the whole of this Session. The only reference to it was the cancellation of the Commission for the 1702 negotiations towards the end of the session.

On the other hand, Stuart's proposal might have been the outcome of national feeling gaining the upper hand even within the Court party itself, or more of a personal initiative by Stuart than a considered move by the Officers of State as a whole. There is evidence that he was a man of independent mind who did not go along uncritically with his colleagues. When the Union proposal eventually came before Parliament three years later, Stuart is said by Lockhart to have been 'heartily averse' to it. There was at least a rumour that he was the author of a 'protestation' designed as a last ditch attempt to frustrate the Treaty.[39]

A modern historian, P. W. J. Riley, has suggested that the purpose of Stuart's clause was to fend off the time limit involved in Roxburgh's original wording which required suitable conditions of government to be established 'in this session of Parliament'.[40] This is improbable because the easy way to ease the time limit was by the simple amendment to Roxburgh's wording which was in fact inserted, 'or any other session . . . during Her Majesty's reign.'

If the Court hoped to win over the House by offering the hope of concessions on trade, they failed. Ridpath tells us that opinion in the Country party was divided. Some thought that it was an attempt to invalidate the Act of Security by inserting a condition which the Scottish Parliament by itself could not meet because it required the assent of the English. Others thought even if it were agreed it would 'rather be hurtful than advantageous to Scotland'. It might drain away people to the Colonies, Ridpath adds, where too many Scots had gone already and where they were badly treated. Most of the Country party were prepared to add the clause to the Act.[41] It was after all consistent with Fletcher's policy of agreeing to the same successor only on suitable conditions.

Modern commentators, long after the event, very often suggest that the Union was an arrangement in which the Scots deliberately sacrificed their independence for the sake of trade with England and the Colonies. The reaction to the proposal to add this clause on trade is only one of many pieces of evidence to suggest that this is a rationalisation which is contrary to the way that people thought at the time. The majority view, including the trading interest represented by the Convention of Royal Burghs, was that the exposure of Scotland to English trading conditions was more likely to be 'hurtful than advantageous'. Ridpath quotes a pamphlet published at the time which described proposals about the communication of trade as a 'Bate to hook us in under the same Succession with them'.[42]

The two clauses, Roxburgh's and Stuart's, were discussed on 21, 23 and 26 July in a debate where passions ran high. Hume spoke of 'jangling' and Ridpath of 'very great Heats'. There was even a row, in which Fletcher was involved, about the seating arrangements. The final outcome must have been very unwelcome to the Court. So far from Stuart's clause distracting the House from the constitutional reforms envisaged in Roxburgh's, both were added to the Act by votes on 26 July. At least, this is what appears both from the official minutes of that day and from Hume.[43]

The full text of the Act, including Stuart's clause, is printed in Ridpath's account.[44] The official record of Parliament for 1703 contains no text of the Act at all. It does appear at the end of the entry for 5 August 1704 (Appendix B) after the Act had been moved and passed a second time and, this time, received the royal assent.[45] This version omits Stuart's clause. Presumably the implication is that the clause was deleted before the Queen gave her assent. No one at the time seems to have made a fuss about the omission of the clause, which suggests that its removal was surreptitious. John Clerk of Penicuik, who was a follower of Queensberry and thought that the clause was important, has a revealing comment in his *Memoirs*: 'But on passing this Act of Security the clause relating to the liberty of the plantations was by some trick or other left out, for tho it was voted and agreed to, as will be found in the Minutes . . . and tho it was perhaps read with other clauses in the Act in order to have the Royal assent, yet it seems it never had it . . . in none of the printed Acts does it appear, tho by the bye it was chiefly to obtain the benefits of the plantations that the union was agreed to in Scotland, at least it was the chief instrument used for the settlement of the question'.[46] As we have seen, trade with the plantations was by no means generally regarded as an inducement. The obscurity over the precise way in which the clause vanished from the official text no doubt reflects the embarrassment of the Court in handling a clause which was so likely to give offence in England.

After the adoption of the two clauses the House turned to two points which had been covered by the preamble to Fletcher's draft on limitations. The first was how much time should elapse between the first meeting of Parliament after the death of the Queen and the nomination of a successor. Fletcher had proposed twenty days. On 28 July, after considering a number of proposals for a longer interval, twenty days was agreed. The House then turned to the question, who should be responsible for carrying on the government in the interval between the death of the Queen and the meeting of the Estates. Fletcher had proposed that the current members of Parliament assemble and take on the responsibility as soon as a hundred had gathered together. He would have excluded all representatives of the Shires or Burghs who held an office or pension and these appointments would automatically become void. The question now under debate was whether the Privy Council, as the Court proposed, or the Estates should take charge. Ridpath says that the debate was vigorous. The Country party argued that to give power to the Council 'was the same as to lodge it in the hands of the Council of England', a statement clearly in line with Fletcher's arguments. Eventually, on 30 July, a compromise was agreed that the Council and the Estates should act in conjunction. An additional refinement, clearly influenced by Fletcher's proposal, was added on 2 August, that there should always be a majority of members of the Estates who were not members of the previous Council.[47]

On the same meeting on 2 August, which was a Monday, Queensberry ordered an adjournment until Saturday the seventh, on the grounds that some several members would be absent at a meeting of the Convention of Royal Burghs in Glasgow. As Parliament, he said, was now engaged 'upon great and mighty affairs', he wanted the meetings to be as full as possible. Fletcher did not let this pass without a protest about the way in which the Court was delaying the proceedings. This, he suggested, was a deliberate attempt to discourage attendance. It was one more proof of the need for the limitations under which Parliament itself would have the power to decide about adjournments. 'We have been for several days adjourned in this time of harvest, when we have most important affairs under deliberation; that . . . those who have neither place nor pension might grow weary of their attendance . . . But I hope no member of this house will be discouraged either by delay or opposition; because the liberties of a people are not to be maintained without passing through great difficulties, and that no toil and labours ought to be declined to preserve a nation from slavery'.[48]

This was a very real point. Those long sessions were all very well for members who were being paid by the Government in one form or another. Others had to attend Parliament, and pay to live in Edinburgh, at their own expense. Many of them, particularly the lairds with small estates, were not very prosperous. It was a particular hardship for them to attend during the time of the harvest on which their income depended and which they ought to be supervising. There was a natural suspicion that the Government was dragging out the session over August and September in the hope that some of the opposition would decide to go home to their estates. It was for this reason that Fletcher proposed in his limitations that Parliament should meet each year in November and decide adjournments by ballot. The fact that the opposition stuck to its guns over the whole summer of 1703 is another indication of their determination and strength of feeling over the national cause.

Parliament went on to add to the Act two more clauses which had been included in Fletcher's original proposals for Limitations. The first, which had been in his preamble, ruled that all commissions for government appointments (except those of sherrifs and Justices of the Peace) would become null and void on the death of the Sovereign. Fletcher's intention was, of course, to allow the new parliamentary regime to start with a clean slate and decide all appointments by itself. The next clause was an even more outspoken declaration that Parliament meant to assert itself. Following the ninth of Fletcher's Limitations, Parliament now added, as the final clause of the Act of Security, provision for all Protestant men of military age to be provided with fire-arms and to be exercised at least once a month.[49]

In his speech in support of this clause, Fletcher said: 'all acts which can be proposed for the security of this Kingdom, are vain and empty propositions, unless they are supported by arms; and — to reply upon any law without such a security is to lean upon a shadow'. He repeated the classical doctrine on which his Militia pamphlet had been based: 'The possession of arms is the distinction of a freeman from a slave.' His conclusion returned to the reality of the current situation: 'this very act now under deliberation . . . may separate us from England. And if we do not provide for arming the Kingdom in such an exigency, we shall become a jest and a proverb to the world'.[50] It was left unstated whether the arms would be needed for defence against a Jacobite landing or against England.

As a final refinement, Fletcher moved that all military commissions above that of a captain should be cancelled on the death of the Queen. In his speech he said that the arming of the nation would be a sufficient defence when it had been carried out. If the Queen died before this, however, a few bold men at the head of the small number of regular troops might take advantage of the confusion and suspense. 'Since this is probably the last opportunity we shall ever have of freeing ourselves from our dependence on the English court, we ought to manage it with the utmost jealousy and diffidence of such men'.[51] Fletcher's proposal was approved.

Although the Act of Security had now been approved clause by clause, the whole Act was finally 'read, voted and approven' on 13 August. Hume tells us that approval was by a majority of 59 or 60, which was very substantial in a house of about 230. The Act had been before Parliament since its first reading on 7 June and it had been discussed at 19 sittings. In the entire history of the Scottish Parliament no other Act had ever before received such prolonged, careful and detailed drafting and scrutiny. Fletcher described it as 'an act that preserves us from anarchy: an act that arms a defenceless people: an act that has cost the representatives of this Kingdom much time and labour to frame, and the nation a very great expense: an act that has passed by a great majority: and above all an act that contains a caution of the highest importance for the amendment of our constitution'.[52]

Ridpath in his *Account of the Proceedings* said 'the chief design of the Act was to secure the Nation against the pernicious Influence of a Foreign Ministry, which enslaves both our Government and People, and that it was no way design'd to impair but support the Prerogative of the Crown of Scotland'. George Lockhart some years later referred to it in his *Memoirs* as 'that excellent and wisely contriv'd Act of Security . . . which in all probability would have made this nation happy, had all those who were concerned, and assisted to frame and advance it, continued to act by the maxims and motives whereupon this Act was founded, and not basely changed both principles and parties'.[53]

Among modern historians, Hume Brown is not alone in describing the Act of Security as an outstanding example of the 'futility of human counsels', in that it brought about the opposite result from the one intended. It was, he wrote, 'the indubitable expression of the mind of the Scottish nation'; but it brought home to English statesmen the uncomfortable fact that Scotland would no longer tolerate the existing constitutional relationship. Scotland was set on a course that could lead to a return to real, as distinct from sham, independence. It therefore provoked an English reaction which led to the Union and the loss of the independence that the Act was intended to secure. A similar thought seems to be involved in a cryptic remark in Elisabeth Halkett's *Memoir*: 'Though Mr Fletcher disapproved of some of the articles and the whole frame of the Union, as the Act of Security was Mr Fletcher's own work, he had the merit of that great transaction'.[54]

As soon as the Act of Security had been passed, Parliament turned to another of the points in Fletcher's proposals for limitations on the royal prerogative. Like all the others, it was to apply only if Scotland and England continued to share the same Monarch after the death of Queen Anne. It was the sixth of his twelve points and read as follows: 'That the King without consent of Parliament shall not have the power of making peace and war; or that of concluding any treaty with any other state or potentate'. The Act Anent Peace and War, intended to give effect to this proposal, was read on 17 August, discussed on the next two days and approved on the twentieth.[55]

This further Act, like the Act of Security itself, was another declaration of Scottish independence. Since 1603 English governments had many times made wars in Europe without consulting Scotland and in complete disregard of Scottish trading interests. Scotland had contributed in men and money but was again invariably forgotten when the peace treaty was made. Fletcher had complained about it in the first of his *Two Discourses* on Scottish affairs: 'Notwithstanding the great and unproportionable numbers of sea and land soldiers that we were obliged to furnish for the support of the war, yet not one tittle of advantage has procured to us by the peace'.[56] The Act Anent Peace and War was intended to serve notice that Scotland could no longer be taken for granted in this manner, even if the shared monarchy continued.

There was a significant episode in Parliament on 6 September when the Earl of Marchmont, a former member of the Court, introduced an overture for the acceptance of the Hanoverian succession in line with England. The full text is in Ridpath's *Account*. It was not a simple move to accept the same succession as England but a detailed proposal to accompany this with limitations on very similar lines to those in Fletcher's original draft which had not been inserted in the Act of Security. Communication of Trade was included as well but in less peremptory language than Stuart's clause. The Monarch was to be 'holden and obliged to use utmost endeavours to achieve it'.[57]

In spite of this careful attempt to combine the Hanoverian Succession with conditions in line with Fletcher's ideas and the evident mood of the House, the mere mention of Hanover produced a storm of indignation. Ridpath says that it caused 'very great Heats and Debates' and 'General Disgust'. The House even refused to give permission for the proposal to be recorded in the minutes. The episode, says Hume, gave 'a great dash to the interest of Hanover and the Protestant cause'. He thought that the reason for Marchmont's initiative was that Queensberry had been instructed to withhold royal assent to the Act of Security especially because of the clauses on trade and on the arming of the country.[58]

Marchmont had evidently touched a sensitive nerve, for which Ridpath offers an explanation. 'Considering how we have been Treated by the Court of England, since the Union of the Crowns', and the fact that England had settled the Succession without consultation, it was going too far to suggest that Scotland should accept the same Succession 'until we had positive assurance from our Neighbours that our Grievances should be Redress'd'.[59] Scotland had some freedom of manoeuvre as long as the Scottish Parliament kept open the decision over the Succession. If they were to accept the same Succession as England without safeguards, Scotland would be back in the same unsatisfactory state of constitutional weakness. A contemporary pamphlet printed by Ridpath said that England was already ensnared in the Succession while Scotland was still free to decide. 'To be sure they will leave no stone unturned to drag us into it, and into all other Measures as they should think advantageous to their own Nation, though never so distructive to ours'. It added another point which subsequent events were to confirm only too completely: 'Mankind is Frail, Parliaments may be bribed and the English are both able, and never so willing to bribe as at this Juncture.'[60] Fletcher was by no means a solitary voice.

One might suppose that Fletcher had every reason to be pleased with his success. The Court had been utterly defeated in its attempt to use Parliament merely to obtain a vote of money and approval of the same Succession as England. Parliament had demonstrated its independence of mind and determination to escape from subordination to the English Court. Most of his proposed limitations had been embodied in the Act of Security and the Act on Peace and War. Fletcher was, however, not yet satisfied. The Act of Security had stipulated that the same Succession should not be accepted 'unless such conditions of government be first enacted as may secure the freedom of this nation'. But, Fletcher said in one of his speeches, 'this is a general and indefinite Clause'. Now was the time when Parliament should turn to the particulars and enact the details to satisfy the general clause. Otherwise 'this session of Parliament, in which we have had so great an opportunity of making ourselves for ever a free people, is like to terminate without any real security for our liberties, or any essential amendment of our constitution'.[61]

Fletcher had a clear idea what these particulars should be. Parliament should be elected annually, meet over the winter, choose its own president and decide itself when to adjourn, appoint a committee to act when it was not sitting, and, above all, make all the appointments and pensions which had previously been made in the name of the Monarch. He offered two alternative drafts: 'the one containing the limitations by themselves; the other with the same limitations, and a blank for inserting the name of a successor'. He would be satisfied with either, 'being as little fond of naming a successor as any man.'[62] What he wanted, in fact, was a constitutional monarchy with all real power in the hands of Parliament. These were the outstanding points in his twelve limitations which had not yet been included in legislation. Fletcher's persistent attempts to achieve them were probably the main reason why his contemporaries often described him as republican. They no doubt went too far in restricting the royal prerogative to be easily acceptable by the Cavaliers whose voting strength the Country party needed for a majority.

Fletcher made several attempts to introduce discussion of the outstanding points. On 25 August, 'after much debate', the house voted whether to consider overtures for the further security of the Nation or questions of trade. The vote was in favour of trade. On 9 September, Fletcher introduced his two alternative drafts. Both listed the outstanding limitations, but one, although the name was left blank, offered the House the opportunity of naming the successor. Fletcher said in his speech that he had never made court to any prince and hoped that he never would. He thought himself obliged to offer detailed limitations for the security of the Kingdom. 'If we may live free', he continued, 'I little value who is King: it is indifferent to me, provided the limitations be enacted, to name or not name; Hanover, St. Germains, or whom you will'. The House voted to proceed instead with the consideration of an Act on the export of English and Irish wool. Again on 12 September they voted in favour of giving preference to a trade question. The Court had found a successful tactic at least to defer further discussion of Fletcher's proposals. No doubt the representatives of the Burghs, as custodians of the trading interest, felt obliged to give priority to questions of trade.[63]

Meanwhile Parliament was agitated by the failure of Queensberry to indicate the royal assent to the Acts which had been passed, especially the Act of Security. The practice was for the Commissioner to symbolize this by touching the Act with the sceptre. 'This was much urged', said Hume in his entry for 9 September, 'but he was silent'. Next day he records that some members were saying that if any Scotsman had advised the Queen to refuse assent, he was a traitor to his country. Fletcher made three speeches of increasing urgency on the subject (IX, X and XI). He did not dispute that an Act required the royal assent before it had the force of law, but he questioned the right of the Crown to veto an Act by refusing assent. To avoid ministers mistaking 'former bad practices for good precedents' he had an Act of the first parliament of Charles II read. This, at the height of a period of arbitrary rule, asserted the royal prerogative; but it did not declare that the King had the power to refuse assent. Some instances of this had occurred since that Act had been passed, but 'a practice introduced in arbitrary times can deserve no consideration'. Queensberry still remained silent, at least for another few days.[64]

Also on 9 September, Parliament turned briefly to the abortive talks on a Union with England between November 1702 and February 1703. They declared the Commission (that is the Scottish delegation for the negotiation) 'terminat and extinct' and that there should be no new commission without the consent of Parliament. This was the only reference to the idea of Union during the whole of this long session from June to September which had largely been concerned with constitutional issues. Ridpath, who generally supports and reflects the views of Fletcher, makes two comments which are interesting in view of subsequent developments. Firstly, he says that the Country party were very dissatisfied that the nomination of the Commission should have been left to the Court and thought that this was the same as leaving it to England. 'Others', he continues, 'were fully convinc'd that to Unite us in the same Monarchy with England, was the ready way to Entail all our present Grievances . . . and therefore thought no Union practicable but that of an Association, or perpetual Confederacy under the same Monarch, with an entire Reservation of the Sovereignty of each Nation, and a mutual communication of all Privileges, which would make the Union inviolable . . . When the Treaty of Union was set on foot in 1604, the King gave us all possible Assurances that he would do nothing that might in the least impair our Sovereignty'.[65] In other words, in circles close to Fletcher as late as 1703 the word 'union' applied to Scotland and England implied an association which was fully compatible with both countries retaining their sovereignty.

Fletcher made two speeches (XV and XVI) about the Wine Act which authorised the import of all wines and other foreign liquors and therefore repealed an Act of 1700 which had prohibited French wines. It might seem curious that the Court should have introduced such a measure in the middle of a war with France, but they were desperate to raise money through import duty, especially, Fletcher believed, as a means of bribing members of Parliament. He therefore opposed the Act very bitterly. He argues that appointments as collectors of import duties had been taken from their existing holders and given to members of Parliament. It was a way of bribing them to betray the liberties of the country. 'But as there is no crime under heaven more enormous, more treacherous, and more destructive to the very nature of our government, than that of bribing parliaments; so there is nothing more common and barefaced'.[66] Fletcher's eloquence failed and the Act was passed. It could hardly be opposed by the Burghs, and it was tempting also to the Peers and the Barons of the Shires because they had the privilege of exemption from customs duty. Fletcher had in effect been inviting others to follow his example and put principle and the independence of Parliament before privilege and profit.

But Fletcher had another success. His persistence with his proposal for at least one further limitation was at last debated by the house on 15 September. He made what Hume called a 'long and learned discourse', which from what he says about it is clearly XIV. The essential limitation was 'that all places, offices, and pensions, which have been formerly given by our kings, shall, after her Majesty and heirs of her body, be conferred by Parliament so long as we are under the same prince with England. Without this limitation, our poverty and subjection to the court of England will every day increase; and the question we have now before us is, whether we will be freemen or slaves for ever? Whether we will continue to depend, or break the yoke of our dependence? and whether we will choose to live poor and miserable, or rich, free and happy?'[67] It was the longest and most urgent and persuasive of his speeches and it seems to have been effective.

The Court had tabled an Act of Supply for the Government. But, in Lockhart's words, 'the Parliament flew in the face of it', some demanding the royal assent to the Act of Security, others asking, if the Parliament met for nothing else than to drain the nation of money, to support those that were betraying and enslaving it?' Both Lockhart and Hume describe a long and warm debate over the question whether to proceed to overtures for liberty or a subsidy. Roxburgh, according to Lockhart, said that 'if there was no other way of obtaining so natural and undeniable privilege of the House as a vote, they would demand it with swords in their hands'. It was late and the candles were lit. For two hours there were cries of 'liberty and no subsidy'. The troops in the castle had been ordered to stand-by. At length, Queensberry yielded to pressure and it was resolved that the house would proceed next day with Fletcher's overture on liberty.[68]

Next day, 16 September, Queensberry ignored his promise of the night before and resorted to more drastic tactics. He gave the royal assent to the Acts passed during the session except the Act of Security and made a very short speech. It was fit, he said, that the Queen 'should have some time to consider on such things as are laid before her'. A short recess was therefore necessary and he ordered Parliament to be prorogued until 12 October.[69] In fact, it was not recalled until 6 July next year when Queensberry was no longer Commissioner. His last official act in this Parliament had been to resort to this arbitrary way of preventing the debate on the 'particulars' to complete the Act of Security for which Fletcher had been pressing repeatedly for nearly a month.

The 1703 Parliament therefore ended without Fletcher achieving all his objectives, but he had achieved far more than anyone, including the Government, had anticipated. The Scottish Parliament had strongly asserted the national independence of Scotland. They had kept their bargaining power intact by refusing to vote both supply and the same Succession as England. The Act of Security had stipulated that only the Scottish Parliament had the right to 'nominate and declare' the successor to the Scottish throne, and that this successor could only be the same as the English if conditions had been established which would free Scotland from the English interference which had bedevilled her affairs since 1603. In addition, Parliament had asserted its authority over questions of war and peace. All of these were consistent with the ideas which Fletcher advocated in his pamphlets and speeches. As Lockhart said, he was the Cicero of the Country party, in the sense that he was the chief source of their ideas and their most effective spokesman.

Some 20th century English historians have attempted to deny that the Scottish Parliament of 1703 was moved by a strong sense of Scottish nationalism and a will to assert the independence of the country against English encroachment. P. W. J. Riley, for example, accepts that Fletcher's intentions were clear and incorruptible but argues that the rest of the Country party 'merely sought employment'.[70] If that were true, they chose a curious way to ingratiate themselves with Court circles in London. In fact, it is very difficult to be sure about the motives and attitudes of members of that parliament because we do not have the texts of their speeches, except Fletcher's, and no records of how they voted. All contemporary accounts however, even the cautious reticence of the official minutes, make it very clear that feeling in the Parliament was strong, and that a deliberate policy to defend the independence of Scotland was maintained over many weeks of debate and supported by a large majority. They knew that this involved a crisis in Scottish relations with England and they had provided even for military defence in case that should become necessary. As Gilbert Burnet put it: 'A national humour of rendering themselves a free and independent kingdom did so inflame them, that, as they had a majority of seventy in parliament, they seemed capable of the most extravagant things that could be suggested to them'.[71] He was right in this, even if his language has been influenced by a metropolitan cynicism derived from his long involvement with the corridors of power in London. The same might be said of his conclusion: 'great skill and much secret practice seemed necessary to set matters right there'.

Why, asks William Ferguson, 'in the face of the evidence' do these modern historians 'embark on such a futile course' as attempting to play down the significance of the Parliament of 1703.[72] The answer is plain enough. If you can pretend that the strong nationalism of that Parliament was a myth or an illusion, then you have less difficulty in explaining the *volte face* that was imposed on these same members in the three years that followed of 'great skill and much secret practice'. This is of importance to those who wish to argue that the Union of 1707 came about either as a result of an inevitable process or as an act of disinterested statesmanship. The spectacle of a Parliament being induced to change its attitudes by 'secret practice' is not one which accords very happily with either of these contentions.

Fletcher's speeches in the Parliament of 1703 were printed in two editions in that year and again in 1704 in Ridpath's *Account of the Proceedings of the Parliament of Scotland which Met at Edinburgh, May 6, 1703*. In his Preface, Ridpath said of Fletcher's speeches that if there was any force in 'good sense, good language and strong argument', they could not fail to explain to the country where their true interest lay at this critical time. They gave the best account of the Act of Security and the Limitations and of the 'noble efforts of our Parliament to recover our ancient liberty . . . 'The Memory of this Parliament will be precious to the Nation, so long as it has a being'.[73]

10

A Conversation in London, December 1703

'We are an independent nation.'
— Andrew Fletcher

In one of his speeches towards the end of the 1703 Parliament (XIV), Fletcher mentioned 'the perpetual issue of money to England' which was a consequence of the attendance of Scots at the Court in London. As long as government appointments were made there, that was where Scots with political ambitions were obliged to go to seek preferment. This was an abuse which he proposed to end with his limitations which would transfer the disposal of appointments to the Parliament in Edinburgh. Meanwhile, 'by frequenting that Court, we not only spend our money, but learn the expensive modes and ways of living, of a rich and luxurious nation: we lay out yearly great sums in furniture and equipage, to the unspeakable prejudice of the trade and manufactures of our own country'. He was careful to add that he did not think it amiss to travel to England to study their trade and industry. 'But at court what can we learn, except a horrid corruption of manners, and an expensive way of living, that we may for ever after be both poor and profligate'.[1]

When Parliament was adjourned on 16 September, ambitious members had even more reason than usual to rush to London. The Act of Security had challenged the accepted rules of the game. How would the English Court and Parliament react? Some Scots might hope to influence the outcome by argument and persuasion and judicious lobbying. The majority of the visitors to London, however, were no doubt at the old game of trying to secure a profitable place or pension for themselves. Everything was to play for because Queensberry and his team had so obviously lost control of Parliament and failed to carry any of the objectives of their masters in London. Lockhart describes the process: 'all parties strove who should outdoe one another in paying their respect and showing their submission to the good will and pleasure of the Duke of Marlborough and Lord Godolphin: the Queen, indeed, for fashion sake, was addressed to; but such application was made to those two lords, that it was obvious to all the world how much the Scots affairs depended on them.' The great men of Scotland, Lockhart says, were treated like servants, but that was their own fault because they had 'so meanly and sneakingly prostituted their honour and country to the will and pleasure of the English ministry'.[2]

Fletcher himself seems to have gone to London at the end of 1703. He was certainly no suitor for office, but anyone as deeply concerned as he was with the interests of Scotland would naturally wish to see for himself how opinion was moving in London at this crucial time. As far as I can discover, the only surviving evidence that he was then in London is in his next pamphlet, as appears in its full title: *An Account of A Conversation Concerning a Right Regulation of Governments for the common Good of Mankind in a Letter to the Marquis of Montrose, the Earls of Rothes, Roxburg and Haddington, From London the first of December, 1703*. The pamphlet was published in Edinburgh in the next year. The title itself seems conclusive enough, but of course the conversation was almost certainly imaginary, like a dialogue of Plato, with which indeed it was a close affinity of form. Possibly, there was a real conversation which Fletcher elaborated, but it is equally possible that the whole work was a literary convention based only on Fletcher's ideas and imagination. The two English characters in the dialogue sound like portraits from life, but that does not necessarily prove that Fletcher ever actually spoke to them.

Whatever the origin of the *Account*, it is Fletcher's most attractive work as a piece of literature and the boldest expression of his political ideas. In style it anticipates remarkably the best periodical writing of the Augustan age. You might think that he was imitating *The Spectator* of Addison and Steele, if you forget that the first of their papers did not appear until March 1711. I discussed Fletcher's prose style in Chapter 8. In the *Account* it is at its best in idiomatic ease and conversational fluency.

Apart from Fletcher himself, three other characters took part in the conversation, real or imaginary. They were all real people, representative of different political attitudes, one Scottish and two English. The Scot, the Earl of Cromarty, was one of the very few people in Scotland who seems to have been enthusiastically in favour of an incorporating Union and the disappearance of 'the old ignominious names' of both Scotland and England.[3] The two Englishmen, like the Scots, were both Members of their own Parliament. Sir Christopher Musgrave was a high Tory who came to be regarded in England as the head of the party. Burnet describes him as a 'gentleman of a noble family in Cumberland whose life has been regular and his deportment grave . . . of good judgement and of great experience'. Sir Edward Seymour was a prominent member of the House of Commons who had been speaker during the reign of Charles II. He was 'feared more than loved and respected more than esteemed'. As we have seen, an anti-Scottish tract, which the Scottish Parliament ordered to be burnt, was dedicated to him. He was rabidly anti-Scottish. In the dialogue Fletcher attributes to him a remark which he had in fact made in the House of Commons: 'what a pother is here about a union with Scotland, of which all the advantage we shall have, will be no more than what a man gets by marrying a beggar, a louse for her portion'.[4]

Fletcher describes the other three, as 'men of sentiments so different from my own'.[5] He had obviously chosen people with whom he disagreed so that he could set up a good-going argument. Since he was writing the account, he could lead the discussion in the direction that he wanted it to go to cover the subjects that he wanted to cover and make the points that he wanted to make.

He could lead the others in directions that would help his case. Fletcher is clearly in charge throughout. To some extent this sort of dialogue is an unfair technique since one man is writing both sides of the argument. If it is carried out with intellectual honesty, as I think it is in this example, it can help a man to clear his own mind by examining the weak as well as the strong points in his argument. Fletcher allows his opponents to make a vigorous case and speak in their own character. Perhaps we are meant to draw our own conclusion from the fact that the only man who opposes Fletcher on every point and to the end is the anti-Scottish Seymour.

The dialogue falls into four phases, each leading smoothly into the next. In the first, Cromarty, Musgrave and Fletcher set the scene by talking about the beauties and strength of London, 'the greatest city in the world', as Cromarty calls it. Talk of 'the affairs and diversions of the court, together with the recreations and pleasures of the town', leads Musgrave to deplore their 'corruption of manners' which 'has infected the whole nation' . . . 'Where great power, riches and number of men are brought together, they not only introduce a universal depravation of manners, but destroy all good government, and bring ruins and desolation upon a people'. This is a point to which Fletcher intends the argument to return at a later stage. For the present he contents himself with a remark which is certainly the best known passage in all his work: 'I said, I knew a very wise man . . . (who) believed if a man were permitted to make all the ballads, he need not care who should make the laws of a nation'. This was a natural enough observation to make since Musgrave had been riling against 'infamous ballads' that 'tempted to all manner of lewdness', Fletcher himself was not disposed to leave legislation to ballads makers. It is obvious from his speeches and pamphlets that his mind was constantly occupied with ideas about the laws that were needed for 'the general good and interest of mankind'.[6]

The second phase, which is about the limitations, is introduced by the arrival of Sir Edward Seymour. He immediately launches an attack on Fletcher for his opposition to the 'interest of the court' and his proposals for 'Utopias and new models of government, under the name of limitations' in the recent session of the Scottish Parliament. He is heavily sarcastic about the youth of the nobles who had been among Fletcher's supporters (those to whom Fletcher dedicated his *Account*). Their 'long experience and consummate prudence in public affairs could not but produce wonderful schemes of government'. Fletcher replied by arguing that young men were much less likely to be corrupted by bribery. An absolute monarchy could place unlimited power in the hands of a young prince and a limited monarchy could be just as bad if the prince were not accountable.[7]

Fletcher, by asking Seymour why he objected to the proceedings in the Scottish Parliament, then provokes him into displaying his English prejudices. Limitations, Seymour replies, 'tend to take away that dependence which your nation ought always to have upon us, as a much greater and more powerful people'. Fletcher: 'We are an independent nation, though very much declined in power and reputation since the union of the Crowns, by neglecting to make such conditions with our kings, as were necessary to preserve both'. The object of the limitations was to make good that omission. Seymour, 'all in a fret': '. . . Here is a fine cant indeed, independent nation! Honour of our Crown! and what not? Do you consider what proportion you bear to England? not one to forty in rents of land. Besides our greatest riches arise from trade and manufactures, which you want'. Fletcher concedes this last point, but argues that this also was a consequence of the Union of the Crowns. Before that Scotland had a considerable trade which had now decayed. Scotland had been neglected, 'like a farm managaged by servants, and not under the eye of the master'.[8]

When Fletcher then goes on to argue on the familiar grounds that the remedy for this situation is that the Scottish Parliament should 'bestow all pensions and offices both civil and military', Cromarty replies that this would remove all power and authority from the prince. 'I had always thought', Fletcher says, 'that princes were made for the good government of nations, and not the government of nations framed for the private advantage of princes'. There is then more belligerent talk by Seymour who suggests that England would intervene to remove the limitations. Fletcher concedes that England is more powerful, but such a threat would force Scotland to look for allies.[9]

After the second phase had thus discussed the question of the limitations, the conversation in the third phase turns to the possibility of an incorporating union. This had not been raised at all during the 1703 session of the Scottish Parliament, but was evidently now a matter of speculation in political circles in London as a response to the situation created by the Act of Security. Even so, Fletcher is sceptical at this stage that the English would seriously contemplate a 'nearer coalition with Scotland'. He quotes historical examples to show that 'a treaty of union has never been mentioned by the English, but with a design to amuse us when they apprehended any danger from our nation'. The subject is raised by Cromarty who suggests that a union of the two nations might offer an easy remedy. Fletcher disagrees: a union would neither be easy nor a remedy. Scotland would then be poorer than ever. Members of Parliament and men of large estates would live in London and spend their money there. Cromarty objects that Scotland would then be part of Britain and it is the good of the whole body which should then be considered. Fletcher replies, 'If in the union of several countries under one government, the prosperity and happiness of the different nations are not considered, as well as of the whole united body, those that are more remote from the seat of the government will be only made subservient to the interest of others, and their condition very miserable'.[10]

Cromarty suggests that a union would encourage manufactures in Scotland for the whole island as well as for export because of the availability of cheap labour. On the contrary, Fletcher replies, a union 'would certainly destroy even these manufactures we now have'. England can already manufacture more cheaply 'and it is not to be supposed they will destroy their own established manufactures to encourage ours'.[11]

'But sure you will allow', said the Earl, 'that a free commerce with England, and the liberty of trading to their plantations, which cannot be expected without a union, must be of incomparable advantage to the Scots nation, unless you will disown one of your darling clauses in the act of security'. Fletcher's reply to this point is interesting for his views on the trade question and on the clause proposed by the Lord Advocate:

> My lord, said I, the clause you mean is placed there without the condition of a union; and your lordship cannot forget, was brought in by the court as an equivalent for all limitations, and in order to throw out another clause, which declares that we would not nominate the same successor with England, unless sufficient limitations were first enacted. This was done to mislead the commissioners of burghs, who for the most part are for anything that bears the name of trade, though but a sham, as this was. And nothing could be more just than to turn it upon the court by adding both clauses; which sunk your party in the House for a long time after. For my own part, I cannot see what advantage a free trade to the English plantations would bring us, except a farther exhausting of our people, and the utter ruin of all our merchants, who should vainly pretend to carry that trade from the English. The Earl, who knew the truth of these things, was unwilling to insist any longer upon this ungrateful subject.[12]

So Cromarty tried another tack. He suggested that after a union, 'trade and riches will circulate to the utmost part of the island'. Fletcher replied that Wales had been united to England for three or four hundred years, was closer to London than Scotland and had one of the best natural harbours in the whole island. In spite of all that, it was still the only part of the kingdom that had no considerable commerce, 'a sufficient demostration that trade is not a necessary consequence of a union with England'.[13]

Fletcher then spoke in some detail about the English treatment of Ireland. It was not an encouraging example because it suggested that after a union the suppression of any commotion would be used as an excuse to treat the Scots like a conquered people. 'What security can a lesser nation, which unites to a greater, have, that all the conditions of union shall be duly observed, unless a third be admitted for guaranty of the agreement'. At this point in the discussion, Seymour has his outburst about marrying a beggar. Fletcher replies that such language makes him suspect that Seymour is not descended from the noble family whose name he bears. Musgrave explains in more temperate language that England could not permit equal freedom and privileges to Ireland because it might then become a serious rival in trade. Equally they must keep Ireland in a state where it could not separate to set up a distinct government that might be to the disadvantage of England. In that case, replied Fletcher, 'you must own your way of governing that people to be an oppression; since your design is to keep them low and weak, and not to encourage either virtue or industry'.[14]

After Fletcher thus disposed effectively of the arguments in favour of an incorporating union, the discussion then turned to its fourth and final phase, the European dimension. It begins with Musgrave returning to the thought that great cities are 'corrupted by excess of riches and power and tend to disturb the peace'. He asks Fletcher since he is 'an enemy to all great and overgrown power' to suggest into what parts he would divide Europe 'most commodiously to obtain the true ends of governments'. Fletcher suggests that Europe falls naturally into ten geographical regions. The islands of Britain and Ireland might be one such region or government. But Musgrave points out, even if governments of about equal strength were to be established in each of these regions, that would not by itself preserve the peace. Wars have become more widespread, dangerous and destructive. How are they to be prevented?[15]

This brings Fletcher to the most remarkable passage in all of his work, possibly indeed in all of the political philosophy of his time. In an age when it was universally assumed that any advantage to one country must be to the detriment of others, he suggests that the interests of all countries are interdependent and that government should be conducted on that assumption. It is a passage which seems to point, some 200 years before they were realised, at the need for international organisations like the United Nations and the European Community and for a radical change of attitude towards international relations:

> I think mankind might be best preserved from such convulsions and misery, if instead of framing governments with regard only to a single society, as I believe all legislators have hitherto done, we should constitute such as would be no less advantageous to our neighbours than ourselves. You talk strangely, said Sir Chr-
> – as if our advantage were not frequently inconsistent with that of our neighbours. I am of opinion, replied I, that the true interest and good of any nation is the same with that of any other. I do not say that one society ought not to repel the injuries of another; but that no people ever did any injustice to a neighbouring nation, except by mistaking their own interest.[16]

Fletcher then introduced a proposal to abolish war 'as far as may be possible'. This could be achieved if governments with sufficient force to defend themselves were 'rendered either incapable or unfit to make conquests'. If each of the ten portions of Europe had 'ten or twelve sovereign cities well fortified within its territories', it might be very capable to defend itself, and yet altogether unfit for conquest'. This system of 'divers small sovereignties' would be the best means 'to preserve mankind, as well from great and destructive wars, as from corruption of manners, and most proper to give to every part of the world that just share in the government of themselves which is due to them'. Constitutions have so far always been framed with respect to particular nations, 'without any regard to the rest of mankind'. Politicians should consider what it is to be a 'citizen of the world' and think of 'the general good and interest of mankind, on which that of every distinct society does in great measure depend'.[17]

Fletcher in reply to an interjection from Musgrave, says that he does not necessarily mean that the sovereign cities should be republics. They might be the capitals of sovereign and independent kingdoms or countries and united under one monarch. Indeed, a prince might be more capable than a council of delegates of preserving peace among several small sovereignties.[18]

At this point, Fletcher elaborates on the advantages of decentralisation, or, as he puts it, 'the advantage of having twelve cities governing themselves happily and virtuously, instead of one great vicious and ungovernable city'. Musgrave objects that it would be thought unjust to remove the seat of government from London, 'which has been so long possessed of that great advantage'. It is a greater injustice, Fletcher replied 'that one place has so long enjoyed these profits which ought to have been divided among the considerable cities of the nation'. Musgrave remarks that he had not foreseen the use that Fletcher would make of his complaint against the depravation of manners in London, but admits that the conclusion is just. 'If we design to diminish the corruption, we must lessen the city'. This produced a predictable outburst from Seymour, 'What visions have we here? . . . destroy the greatest and most glorious city of the world to prosecute a whimsical project!' 'Do you not think', Fletcher replied, 'the remoter parts of England injured by being obliged to have recourse to London for almost everything? . . . That London should draw the riches and government of the three Kingdoms to the South-East corner of this island is in some degree as unnatural for one city to possess the riches and government of the world'.[19]

Expanding from the example of London to a more general point, Fletcher argues that all governments which control large members of people at a distance are 'violent, unjust and unnatural'. In large countries, the offices of government are overburdened with business, 'most things are abandoned to the rapacity of servants; and the extravagant profits of all great officers plunge them into all manner of luxury, and, debauch them from doing good'. In small countries, 'many men have occasions put into their hands of doing good to their citizens.' As in the cities of ancient Greece, so many different seats of government 'will highly tend to the improvement of all arts and sciences'.[20]

'I perceive now', said Seymour at this point, 'the tendency of all this discourse. On my conscience he has conceived the whole scheme to no other end than to set his own country on an equal foot with England and the rest of the world'.

'To tell you the truth', Fletcher replied, 'the insuperable difficulties I found of making my country happy by any other way, led me insensibly to the discovery of these things, which, if I mistake not, have no other tendency than to render, not only my own country, but all mankind as happy as the imperfections of human nature will admit'.[21]

Then in the conclusion of the dialogue, Fletcher explains how he sees the application of these principles to Scotland and England. In a state of separation, 'my country would be perpetually involved in bloody and destructive wars'. On the other hand if Scotland were united to England 'in any other manner' (by which he clearly means in any manner other than the one he has been describing), 'we must of necessity fall under the miserable and languishing condition of all places that depend upon a remote seat of government'. The union must be based on the equality of the partners with each contributing in due proportion to the joint defence. 'This is the only just and rational kind of union. All other conditions are but the unjust subjection of one people to another'.[22]

This conclusion makes very clear the relationship between Scotland and England which Fletcher thought desirable. The two countries should each be self-governing, and indeed highly decentralised, but they should be 'united' for their joint defence. There is no inconsistency between this and the remark in Fletcher's letter of 1689 (which I mentioned on page 44): 'For my own part I think we can never come to any true settlement but by uniting with England in Parliaments and Trade, for as for our worship and particular laws we certainly can never be united in these'.[23] This is yet another example that 'Union' and 'uniting', in the common usage of the time, meant an association for a common purpose, an association or alliance or an absence of discord. It certainly did not imply any diminuition of autonomy, the 'unjust subjection of one people to another' or dependence on 'a remote seat of government'. An 'incorporating union', necessarily distinguished by the adjective, was something quite different.

Fletcher in this remarkable dialogue covered a good deal of ground. He had explained and justified his proposals for limitations, made a powerful (and I should think unanswerable) case against an incorporating union and developed a coherent argument for highly decentralised government combined with co-operation to preserve the peace. Much of his thought is strikingly modern. This applies especially to his perception that the interests of all countries are interdependent and that each depends in a large measure on the general good of all mankind. So, too, are his concern for the avoidance of war and the support of local particularity and autonomy. His combination of nationalism and internationalism is particularly relevant to Scottish experience and aspiration. His criticism of the concentration of wealth and power in South-East England has, of course, far more force now than it had in his own time.

Most of the dialogue is concerned with the issues which were, or were about to be, on the agenda of the Scottish Parliament, and the primary purpose of the publication was clearly to influence the outcome of the debates on the constitutional issue. Perhaps Fletcher put anti-Scottish animosity into the mouth of Sir Edward Seymour as a device to stir up Scottish resentment or to remind his countrymen of the need for caution in dealing with the English. At the same time, the real-life Seymour did speak like that. Then, as now, English prejudices of that kind existed and had to be taken into account. Also, Fletcher plays fair and offered in the person of Sir Christopher Musgrave a much more reasonable English parliamentarian who was open to persuasion. The personification of these two attitudes adds much to the attractiveness and charm of the dialogue. Cromarty plays a lesser role and has little to say beyond introducing the idea of an incorporating union. Fletcher leaves emotion and abuse largely to the others and relies for his own part on rational argument. Of course, he gives himself the best of it, but on ground of his own choosing, he has much the better case.

It is in the extension of Fletcher's ideas into Europe that he becomes most visionary, to use the word that both he himself and his contemporaries sometimes applied to him.[24] He said himself that the wider ideas grew out of his search for a solution of the problem of Scotland. His European ideas were a projection of his desire to find a means of safeguarding the peace, prosperity and independence of Scotland. The idea of combining decentralised autonomy with cooperation to provide defence and preserve the peace was not beyond realisation for Scotland and England at that time, and indeed Fletcher had offered a practical programme towards it in his proposals for limitations. The same could not be said of the ideas of dividing Europe into ten regions, each subdivided into ten or twelve sovereign city states. Fletcher was describing something which he thought would be an ideal solution, a long-term aim, not an immediate plan for action. And yet, making allowances for our longer experience and more sophisticated ideas about international organisation, there is a suggestion in Fletcher's ideas of the European settlement to which the people of Europe are now feeling their way. There is now widespread support, all over Europe, for Fletcher's ideal of the maximum of decentralised autonomy and particularity, with co-operation to safeguard the 'general good and interest'. Scotland might after all be able to play a role in Europe, not dissimilar in spirit to Fletcher's ideas in 1703.

One of the most interesting, but also paradoxical, modern comments on Fletcher's *Account of a Conversation* is an essay of John Robertson, published in 1987. It is paradoxical because, after summarising the dialogue, it begins with a very perverse judgement: 'Surely it was not a serious contribution to the union debate, but the *jeu d'esprit* of an intelligent man who knows he has lost the real argument, and consoles himself by indulging his eccentric imagination: no wonder Cromarty and his English guests broke off for dinner'.[25] In fact, Fletcher in December 1703 was fresh from his success in the Scottish Parliament where he had won the intellectual arguments. He had not achieved all that he had set out to achieve, but a very large part of it. In the end, Queensberry had adjourned the House rather than face any more of Fletcher's intellectual assaults. In the *Account* itself, Fletcher had certainly won all the arguments, which is not surprising in the circumstances. Is John Robertson perhaps setting up an aunt Sally which he is proposing to knock down? To some extent, because, consciously or otherwise, he eventually reaches the opposite conclusion to the one with which he starts. In the early part of his essay, Robertson chooses to believe that by 1706 the incorporating unionists had won the argument. This is a view which can rest only on a very selective reading of the evidence. In any case, this debate had hardly begun in 1703 and in the *Account* itself, Fletcher produced powerful arguments against such a union which, as far as I can discover, no one at the time was able to refute.

John Robertson suggests that Fletcher's European proposals were a counter argument to Campanella's imperial idea of a universal monarchy to which he had already reacted in his *Discorso delle Cose di Spagna* (See page 67). The Dutch jurist, Grotius, in his *De Jure Belli ac Pacis* of 1623 had replied to the imperial idea with the argument that it should be possible for sovereign states to reach agreements to respect the rights of each other and to refrain from unjust war. French writers of the time had proposed a redrawing of European frontiers to provide stability, with provision for the international arbitration of disputes. Pufendorf, developing the ideas of Grotius, in *De Systematibus Civitatum*, suggested that perpetual alliances or 'systems of states' might consist either of sovereign states under a single king, like Britain under the Stuarts, or of states in agreement amongst themselves, like the United Provinces of the Netherlands or the Cantons of Switzerland. Robertson thinks that Fletcher carried these ideas still further. 'It was thus', he writes, 'Fletcher's remarkable achievement in the *Account of a Conversation* to have articulated such a juristic model of a European state system in the rhetorical guise of a utopia. Out of Pufendorf, by way of More, Fletcher had fashioned a vision of European government to match Campanella's vision of universal monarchy . . . But if Fletcher's plan for the reform of government in Europe was simply a vision, it had served its purpose: it had demonstrated that there was a coherent alternative to incorporating union'.[26]

11

The Parliament of 1704

*'The ill-temper the nation is in . . . through the bad usage
they have met with from their neighbours'.
— Marquis of Tweedale to Queen Anne*

From a Scottish point of view the parliamentary session of 1703 had been an outstanding success with the emphatic assertion of Scottish independence in the Act of Security, even if it had not yet received the royal assent. From the point of view of the Court in London, and of the administration appointed by them to carry out their policy in Scotland, it had been an abject failure. They had failed with both of their main objectives, a vote of supply and approval of the Hanoverian Succession to the throne which would have preserved the constitutional *status quo*, with the English supremacy which that implied. Blame for the failure inevitably attached to Queensberry as Commissioner and the chief agent of the crown in Scotland.

Queensberry, in an attempt to cling to power and discredit his opponents, resorted to a desperate expedient, afterwards known in Scotland as the Queensberry Plot. The key figure in this was a notorious scapegrace, Simon Fraser of Beaufort, afterwards Lord Lovat. Some years before, in pursuit of his claim to the Lovat title and chieftainship of the Frasers, he had raped and forced marriage on the widow of the previous chief, a daughter of the Marquis of Atholl. Fraser, who fled abroad, was condemned *in absentia*. In France he tried to ingratiate himself with the Jacobite court in exile at St Germain and succeeded in obtaining the rare privilege of a private audience with Louis XIV. He assured the King that Scotland was ready to rise to break the royal union with England and restore the Stuarts to the throne. When he came back to Scotland with this objective, he soon found that he was unacceptable as a leader or intermediary. He quickly changed sides and revealed to Queensberry details of what purported to be a Jacobite conspiracy involving Atholl and many of Queensberry's political opponents, but none of his friends.[1]

It is impossible to believe that Queensberry was genuinely deceived. He was well aware of Fraser's outrageous record and of the feud between him and Atholl. As William Ferguson says, 'In sober fact, as the law then stood in Scotland, Simon Fraser of Beaufort's word could not have hanged a dog, let alone have indicted a man for treason'.[2] Lockhart of Carnwath suggests very plausibly that the whole plot was deliberately contrived by Queensberry to discredit his opponents and keep himself in office. Whether he had engineered the plot or not, Queensberry certainly tried to use it for this purpose. Without

106

further investigation, he passed the information secretly to the Queen and told her that Fraser was 'a man of quality and integrity and I dare assure your Majesty there is neither mistake nor trick on his part'. This of a man, in Lockhart's words, 'with whom no honest man in Scotland would converse'.[3]

The trick did not work. In London, Simon Fraser in a moment of drunken vanity told his story to Robert Ferguson, the inveterate plotter. Ferguson warned Atholl and he and the others involved protested vehemently. The Queen, in any case, distrusted Queensberry. Her leading English minister, the Lord Treasurer, Godolphin, had his own good reasons for not welcoming too close an enquiry into clandestine correspondence with the Jacobite court. The whole affair did Queensberry more harm than good and he had become too controversial and unpopular, as well as unsuccessful, to continue as Commissioner.

The English House of Lords took it upon themselves to set up an enquiry into what they described, significantly, as the Scotch Plot. They may have been encouraged in this by a remark of Queen Anne in a speech to the English Parliament on 17 December 1703, when she complained of 'very ill practices and designs carried on in Scotland by emissaries from France'. It was an opportunity for the House both to indulge its animosity and distrust of Scotland and for the Whig majority to attack the Administration and the Tory-dominated House of Commons. The Lords concluded that 'there had been dangerous plots between some in Scotland, and the Court of France and St Germains, and that the encouragement of this plotting came from the not settling the succession to the crown of Scotland in the House of Hanover'. The Lords promised to support, once the Succession was secured, 'an entire and complete union'. That the English Lords should presume to pass judgement on Scottish affairs in this way naturally caused resentment in Scotland where it was regarded, in Hume Brown's words, as 'another proof of insolent assumption'.[4]

The choice of the Queen, or of Godolphin, for a successor to Queensberry, fell on the Marquis of Tweedale, although he had fired the first shot against the Court in the Parliament of 1703. Lockhart's description of him is that he was a 'well-meaning, but simple man', (who) was forced against his will, by his friends and those he trusted (who made a meer tool of him), to enter into many of the bad measures he pursued'.[5] This view of him is consistent with the impression given by surviving correspondence. He does not seem to have any clear objective of his own but to be carried along by events and the manipulations of others.

Fletcher constantly argued that Scotland since the Union of the Crowns had been subordinated to the interest of England because of the monarch's control over all government appointments. These appointments were made on the advice of English ministers and the result was, as Fletcher said in one of his speeches, that the principal offices in Scotland were 'filled with such men, as the Court of England knew would be subservient to their designs'.[6] There is ample evidence that he was right in the correspondence which has survived between English ministers and the holders of the highest offices in the Scottish administration. The tone of the letters from England, although generally polite, is invariably one of command, expecting unquestioning obedience. They exploited to the full the might and majesty of royal power as a very convenient device. Such letters of instruction to Tweedale have been carefully preserved in his family archives in a handsomely bound volume, which is now in the National Library of Scotland.[7] On 11 May 1704 Queen Anne authorised the payment of £3,500 to Tweedale on his appointment as Commission 'for equipage' (or as we might say expenses, although at the time it was a substantial sum of money). Ironically enough, the order is signed by Queensberry, presumably as one of his last official acts. There are orders of 21 June to the 'Commander in Chief of our forces in Scotland, the Governor of Edinburgh Castle' and to John, Duke of Argyll, as 'Colonel and Captain of our Troop of Lifeguard of Horse in our ancient Kingdom of Scotland', instructing them to obey the orders of the new Commissioner. To Tweedale himself there are several letters of instruction, also dated 21 June. The first, although described in the volume as in the holograph of the English minister, Godolphin, is signed in a different hand, that of the Queen herself, 'Your very affectionate friend, Anne R'. It leaves no doubt about Tweedale's principal task: 'the settling of the succession of the Crown of Scotland in the protestant Line will bee a very acceptable service to mee'. It encourages him by a little flattery and a hint of future award: 'Your own modesty and backwardness in the Concerns of your own family will always bee an Argument with mee to have the more regard to them'.[8]

Another document, also of 21 June 1704 and in the hand of Godolphin, is headed 'Instructions'. It gives Tweedale the same two objectives as Queensberry had tried and failed to achieve in 1703, the settlement of the Succession, as adopted in England, and a supply of funds to maintain the armed forces. On the first of these points, he was to use 'all possible Endeavour', and 'for the effecting of this, you are to lett such of the Members of Parliament as you can trust know that we will have no misunderstanding betwixt us and the Parliament concerning Limitations'. An Additional Instruction, in a different hand but of the same date, explain this stratagem in more detail: 'Rather than the succession should not be secured you may consent to appointment of officers of state etc being made by our successor in the same manner as in the Act of 1641, providing always that there be a clause in the Act of Settlement under which both the Act of Peace and War and the above limitations shall cease or be void and null in the event of a Union between the two kingdoms'.[9] The 1641 Act, extracted by the Scottish Parliament from Charles I when he could not resist, had provided for the appointment of officers of state, Privy Councillors and the Lords of Session with the advice and consent of Parliament. The effect of the Additional Instruction to Tweedale was therefore to authorize him to accept the substance of the most crucial of Fletcher's limitations. There is no mention at this stage of royal assent to the Act of Security, presumably because the hope was that Parliament could be persuaded to forget about it on the strength of the concession. The insistence that the concession would end in the event of a Union suggests that the Queen and her English ministers, if they had thought the matter through at all, still envisaged some form of a Scottish Parliament continuing after a Union. It is also a broad hint that the concession was seen as a temporary expedient which would be abandoned as quickly as possible when it had achieved its purpose of keeping control of Scotland through the same Succession to the throne.

According to both Lockhart and Burnet, this tactic was proposed by James Johnstoun, who had been secretary to King William and then Godolphin's principal adviser on Scottish affairs. The idea was to win over Tweedale and a group of members of the Country Party in Scotland by offering them the disposal of offices and appointments on the understanding that they would deliver acceptance of the same Succession as England in exchange for the concession on limitations. The English ministers acquiesced, Lockhart remarks, because they knew that they could easily repeal the limitations in a subsequent Parliament, if they had secured the Succession. 'All this, however, was to be kept a mighty secret'. However contrived, the result was that a number of Fletcher's supporters now went over to the Tweedale administration, under the name of the New Party. They included even those to whom *An Account of a Conversation* had recently been addressed, Montrose, Rothes, Roxburgh and Haddington. It is not surprising that Mar, in a letter to his wife on 16 June 1704, was able to report: 'I saw Saltoun today. He askt for you. Bot he's as ill pleased with our new courtiers as he was with our old'. There is some doubt about the adherence of at least Rothes and Roxburgh to the New Party. They appear several times in Hume's *Diary* speaking on the same side as Fletcher. Lockhart says that they were only pretending to be 'as honest as ever' and their real design was to dispossess Queensberry and his associates.[10]

In fact, the strength of the Court in Parliament was, if anything, weaker than it had been before. Queensberry stayed away but manipulated his following in Parliament through his lieutenant, Mar. All of them were dismissed from office, except Seafield and Cromarty who had the dexterity to worship the rising sun, as Lockhart expressed it. The absent Queensberry made a deal with the Jacobites in which he promised that his followers would vote against the Court on the understanding that the opposition would not press for an enquiry into the Plot. His chief object was to frustrate and humiliate the now holders of office in hope that their failure would eventually bring about his own return to favour. In his letters of instruction to Mar he makes this very plain. On 1 August 1704, for instance, he tells Mar that a failure of Tweedale to carry supply after they had already failed on the Succession, would be the most effective way to disappoint London and expose the weakness of the new administration. 'So you ought to bend your wholl strenth there'.[11] Unionist historians have tried to represent Queensberry as a statesman consistently striving to bring about the Union between Scotland and England. There is nothing in the evidence to support such a view. The only consistency in his devious behaviour is an appetite for the fruits of office. In this respect, he was in the end conspicuously successful.

The 1704 session of Parliament began on 6 July and on that day Seafield wrote to Godolphin. He was not without hope of Succession, he said. He had disposed most of what he called the Old Party to concur in the Government measures. At the same time, he admitted that there was strong support for delaying the question of Succession, possibly by demanding conditions on trade or such matters as the English restrictions on shipping in their Navigation Act and on the import of Scottish cattle, cloth, linen and coal.[12] As events were soon to prove, he was right about the delaying tactic, but quite wrong about the Government's strength in the House.

The House began serious business on 11 July with the reading of the letter from the Queen, which was couched in terms of urgency, if not desperation. 'The main thing that we recommend to you, and which we recommended to you with all the earnestness we are capable of, is the settling of the succession in the Protestant Line as that which is absolutely necessary for your own peace and happiness, as well as the quiet and security in all our Dominions, and for the reputation of our affairs abroad, and consequently for the strengthening the Protestant interest every where'. She was urgent, too, about supply for the forces. 'We are now in a war which makes it necessary to provide for the defence of the kingdom'.[13] Since the Government had failed to secure supply in 1703, there was no doubt that the state of the forces was critical, especially as there was always a possibility of an invasion in the Jacobite interest supported by France. The Commander-in-Chief in Scotland, Lieut-General George Ramsay, wrote to Godolphin on 18 July: 'The small army here is in a manner mouldered to nothing'.[14] The Government's desperation in these two respects, succession and supply, meant that Parliament had two strong bargaining cards in its hands.

The opposition began to play these cards without delay. Already on 11 July, Seton of Pitmedden gave in an Overture of a Resolve (or draft of a resolution) to the effect that there would be no nomination of a Successor in that session of Parliament but a resolution of the conditions of government to take effect after the death of the Queen. This was language which clearly suggested Fletcher's limitations. Seafield as Chancellor immediately moved the adjournment, which Fletcher and two others opposed.[15]

At the next meeting on 13 July, Hamilton adopted the tactic which Seafield had foreseen. He tabled a Resolve: 'That this Parliament will not proceed to the Nomination of a Successor, untill we have a previous treaty with England, in relation to our commerce, and other concerns with that Nation'. Fletcher spoke in support and it was agreed that this draft would be the first for discussion at the next meeting.[16]

Why, one might ask, this sudden change of emphasis when in 1703 questions of trade had a much lower priority than those of the political and constitutional relationship? Possibly the Opposition knew that Tweedale had been authorised to make a concession over the limitations and therefore decided to catch him out on a different point to which he could make no immediate response. Lockhart suggests as much: 'This resolve was compiled and presented, after serious consideration, in order to put a bar upon the succession's being established before the Courtiers had time to work upon and seduce the members. The Court was much surprised and perplexed'.[17] Even, as we see from Seafield's letter, if it was not so much a surprise as Lockhart supposed, it still turned on a point where Tweedale had no instructions and on which the English ministers and both Houses of the English Parliament were especially sensitive and resistant to any concession.

It was a clever tactical move also because it raised matters on which Scotland had substantial grounds for complaint, as few members of the Scottish Parliament would be likely to deny. They are conveniently summarised in a letter which Atholl sent to Godolphin on 18 July: 'the evident decay of our trade since the union of the Crowns, the hardships put on us by the Act of Navigation, the seising of our ship and seamen, the hindering of our planting of colonies, as latly in Darien, the high duties on linnen cloath, xcaet, all wch consideding we are under one heade, was thought most reasonable should be regulat by a treaty before the nomination'.[18]

The debate on Hamilton's draft resumed on 16 July. 'Many members', Lockhart says, 'particularly Mr Fletcher of Saltoun, did elegantly and pathetically set forth the hardship and miseries to which we have been exposed, since the union of the two crowns of Scotland and England in one and the same sovereign, and the impossibility of amending and bettering our condition, if we did not take care to prevent any design that tended to continue the same, without other terms and better security than we have hitherto had'. Hume records that Pitmedden and Roxburgh were among others who spoke for, and Belhaven against, Hamilton's draft.[19]

At this point, Rothes proposed an alternative draft: 'That the Parliament will go in the first place into such conditions and regulations of Government as may be proper to rectifie our constitution and vindicat and secure the Sovereignity and Independency of the Kingdom and then that the Parliament will take into their consideration the Resolve offered for a treaty previous to a nomination'. There was a lively debate which culminated in a proposal to join the two resolutions together. This did not please the Court who had supported the hint of limitations only in the hope of securing the Succession. As Atholl said in his letter of 18 July: 'it was too late, for they had the same fate that the clause in the Act of Security had last year, which was then offered to put off another clause about limitations'. This is clearly a reference to the clause about trade proposed by Stuart, the Lord Advocate, in the session of 1703 (pages 85–87). He is probably right that on both occasions the Court offered a clause as an alternative, to avoid something worse, only to find that it was accepted by the House as an addition. Hume's version of the final text includes the phrase, 'as may free us from the English nation', which does not appear in the official record or even in Lockhart. Either this was a phrase proposed during the debate but not finally accepted or, not for the first time, there has been some discreet censorship of the record.[20]

Seafield tried to avoid taking the vote, but Lockhart says that a 'certain member' (presumably himself) made a very strong speech in which he recalled Roxburgh in the 1703 session saying, 'if the nation was to be so treated, he knew no way to be taken, but to demand the vote with sword in hand'. Seafield yielded and two votes were taken, whether to join the two resolutions and whether to approve the joint resolution. Both votes were carried in the affirmative by a large majority.[21] Already, after only four sittings of the House, the Government had been soundly defeated, and had lost all hope of securing the Succession, even with some concessions on the lines of Fletcher's limitations. The independence of the Scottish Parliament, and a determination to uphold national sovereignty, had been asserted even more emphatically than in 1703.

The spirit of resistance in the House was encouraged by the approval of the people outside. Lockhart says that 'the temper and inclinations of the people were very remarkable' on the day that the joint resolution was passed: 'for, after the Parliament was that day prorogued, the members that had appeared more eminently in behalf of the resolve, were caress'd and huzza'd as they pass'd in the streets, by vast numbers; and the Duke of Hamilton was after that manner convoyed from the Parliament-house to the Abbey, and nothing was to be seen or heard that might but jollity, mirth, and an universal satisfaction and approbation of what was done, and that, by people of all ranks and degrees'.[22]

Gilbert Burnet also describes an atmosphere of strong national feelings among the people at large. 'All was carried with great heat and much vehemence; for a national humour, of being independent on England, fermented so strongly among all sorts of people without doors, that those who went not into every hot motion that was made, were looked on as the betrayers of their country: and they were so exposed to a popular fury, that some of those who studied to stop this tide, were thought to be in danger of their lives . . . . The whole nation was strangely inflamed'.[23]

There was a particular difficulty, Burnet goes on to explain, about the army. Funds were so much in arrears that it could not be carried on much longer. Some had proposed that money should be sent from England, but none of the Scottish ministers would consent to that. 'An army is reckoned to belong to those who pay it: so an army paid from England, would be called an English army: nor was it possible to manage such a thing secretly . . . Men's minds were then so full of the conceit of independency, that if a suspicion arose of any such practice, probably it would have occasioned tumults: even the army was so kindled with this, that it was believed that neither officers nor soldiers would have taken their pay, if they had believed it came from England'.[24]

In this situation, it is not surprising that Tweedale, whose heart was probably not in the business anyway, was quickly reduced to despair. On 18 July, the day after the decisive vote and less than a month after his appointment as

Commissioner, he wrote to Godolphin: 'As I have told your Lordship in former letters, no other could be expected, considering the ferment the nation is in . . . I see not what can be done but to adjourn till such time as I can have her Maj'ies direction how to act now that the main poynt is lost'. In a letter to the Queen on the same day, he was even more outspoken: 'because of the ill temper this nation have been in for some years through the bad usage they have met with from their neighbours in most of these concerns, and has been of late mightily increast by the House of Lords proceedings in the matter of the plot, of which great advantage has been taken, to raise such an aversion in them to the settling of the Succession at this time that they could hardly bear even the mentioning of it'. He went on to offer his resignation and to suggest that the management should be entrusted to some one 'who may be more capable and so more successful than I have been'.[25]

Tweedale's suggestions of an adjournment or a change of Commissioner were evidently both rejected and the session continued under his management. The Court was still to attempt its second objective, supply for the forces. On 19 July the Lord Justice Clerk tabled a proposal for 14 months supply. Hamilton countered with a resolve which linked the prospect of only two months supply with an undertaking that the House would then proceed to draw up 'limitations and conditions of Government for the Rectification of our constitution as may secure the Religion Liberty and Independence of this Nation' and nominate Commissioners to negotiate with England about commerce and other concerns. At the next meeting on 21 July he moved not only that the House should proceed to discuss limitations, but tabled again the Act of Security, which had been passed in the last session but had not yet received the royal assent. On the twenty-fifth there was an involved debate about various ways in which supply and the Act of Security might be linked to make one conditional on the other. Finally, there was a vote between two alternative resolves. The first, moved by the Lord Ross, proposed two months supply at once to be followed by an additional four months when the Act of Security had royal approval and was touched with the sceptre by the Commissioner. The other, moved by Roxburgh, suggested no action on either supply or limitations until the Queen had given instructions about the Act of Security, reserving to Parliament the decision whether to proceed on them, jointly or severally. This was carried.[26]

Tweedale, who was, after all, the Commissioner of the Queen who had so far declined assent to the Act of Security, made an extraordinary admission during the closing stages of this debate. He said that the House knew 'what hand he had in that Act of Security, that he had added more clauses thereto than any other whatsoever, and that he was still in his private opinion of the same mind now as then; but seeing it had pleased the Parliament to fall on other measures than was expected, he behoved to acquaint her Majesty before he could do any thing thereanent'.[27]

Meanwhile he was writing privately to both Godolphin and the Queen herself to urge approval of the Act of Security. On 22 July he told the Queen that the Act 'seems so absolutely necessary to quieten the minds of your people'. He wrote to Godolphin on the same day that the Act was the main thing Parliament insisted on, 'and seemed willing to accept without the clause of communication of trade'. (Presumably, London took the hint and this is the explanation of the mysterious disappearance of the clause from the final printed text. It is also another piece of evidence that most members of the Scottish Parliament did not regard trade as the main issue.) Tweedale wrote again to Godolphin on the twenty-sixth: 'nothing will please but ane Act of Security and the wholl nation is so extremely bent upon it, as that without which they cannot be safe'. He asked Godolphin to use his influence with the Queen and said that, in expectation of a favourable response, he had adjourned Parliament until 3 August.[28]

This advice, or rather pressure, from Tweedale must have been extremely unwelcome in London. So far from agreeing to the Queen's urgent plea for the immediate acceptance of the same Succession to the throne as the English, the Scots were demanding royal approval of an Act which provided for either a separate Scottish Succession or the same Succession but under conditions which would effectively transfer power from the monarch to Parliament, which meant from London to Edinburgh. The Scots wished to restore and maintain their independence which they had largely lost at the Union of the Crowns. But, as Adam Smith remarks, 'no nation ever voluntarily gave up the dominion of any province'.[29] The English wanted to keep their power over Scotland and so secure their back door in the North. Even so, faced with such a strong and united Scottish demand, London decided to yield, at least for the time being. The battle of Blenheim was impending and military uncertainties in Europe were a powerful reason to avoid the provocation of Scotland, at that time.

Accordingly on 5 August, after what Hume calls 'much struggle', Tweedale told the House that he had instructions 'to pass an Act of Security that might sufficiently secure the nation'. This was not enough for Hamilton, who said that 'it was not *An* Act of Security, but *The* Act of Security they were for'. The Act, as passed in the session of 1703, was again read and approved. Tweedale touched it with the sceptre to indicate royal assent. The Government evidently deceived the House by saying nothing about the surreptitious removal of the clause on trade. On page 87 I mentioned Clerk's reference, some years later, to the omission of the clause 'by some trick or other' from the printed texts of the Act. These printed versions probably first appeared long after the event. (The form in which we now have it, in the *Acts of the Parliament of Scotland*, was not printed until 1824, but there were earlier versions.) In 1704 the House was kept in the dark and evidently believed that the Act which now had royal assent was the same, as Clerk said, 'formerly concerted and agreed'. Afterwards, the House, as a mark of their satisfaction with the success of their long and determined campaign, approved an Act for six months supply without dissent. That was also touched at once. The Scottish Parliament and the policy of transfer of power to itself from the monarch, of which Fletcher was the main initiator and advocate, had scored a notable victory.[30]

In these debates, the most important moves were made by Hamilton, in his accepted position as leader of the Opposition and no doubt after consultation and agreement. Fletcher was very active and probably the most effective speaker. It was only for 1703 that we have the full text of any of his speeches, but there are a few quotations and many references in Hume and Lockhart. There are also flashes of Fletcher's temper on more than one occasion. On July 21 he attacked James Johnstone, the Lord Register, as a man with no interest in Scotland (probably in the sense that he owned no land in the country), had been sent by England to manage Scottish affairs. At the next sederunt on the twenty-fifth, when the House was debating the linking (or tacking, in the vocabulary of the time) of the Acts of Security and Supply, the idea was resisted by Johnstone. He argued that it would restrict the liberty of the Queen who might want to consent to one but not to the other. This was too much for Fletcher. Hume quotes him: 'Now it appears that there must be a bargain, and unless the Parliament go into the measures laid down in England, nothing must be done'. He went on to say that 'he knew, and could make it appear, that the Register had undertaken to prosecute the English designs for promotion to himself'. Fletcher, supported by Hamilton, then said that the Queen's letter to Parliament was written when no Scotsman was about her and it must therefore have been written under English influence. Johnstone, denied this, but Fletcher insisted. This led to an exchange of insults. Sir James Hacket said that Fletcher was impertinent and Fletcher replied that anyone who called him that was a rascal. These terms may now sound mild and even childish; but at a time when such words could lead to a duel they alarmed the House. A member moved that both of the offenders should be imprisoned, but it was settled with a rebuke from the Chancellor and an exchange of apologies and undertakings 'not to take notice of it elsewhere'.[31]

Fletcher took a prominent part also in the rest of the business of the session. On 17 July Atholl had proposed that there should be an enquiry into the Queensberry plot and that the Queen should be asked to send the necessary persons and papers to Edinburgh. Tweedale promised to pass on this request. Fletcher, Hume says 'had a long speech reflecting on the House of Peers . . . and commending the House of Commons'. When debate on the subject was resumed on 8 August, Hamilton said that he had a letter from Queensberry to the Queen in which he had alleged that everyone who had voted for the Act of Security in the last Parliament was involved in the Plot. Fletcher said that 'the fountain of our evil was the House of Peers intermeddling in our affairs'. He proposed a Resolve deploring this as 'encroachment upon the honour, sovereignty and independency of this nation'. It was passed by a large majority.[32]

Fletcher took two other initiatives which were not concluded during the course of the session. Both were designed to strengthen the power of Parliament. The first was a draft Act proposing that Parliament should appoint the Commissioners for a negotiation with England, that there should be eight from each of the Estates and that the meetings of the negotiators should be on the

Border. Fletcher had obviously foreseen the risk that the appointment of the Commissioners would be left to the Queen or that all meetings would be in London, where the English ministers would be in the best position to bring influence to bear. In the light of subsequent events, it was unfortunate that the whole question was left open. Lockhart says that the trouble was that Hamilton and Atholl could not be persuaded to agree to the inclusion of Queensberry and Seafield as a compromise between both sides of Parliament.[33]

London had noted the risks that the Scottish Parliament might appoint the negotiators. Wedderburn, a senior official dealing with Scottish affairs in Godolphin's office, wrote to Seafield on 12 Aug: 'It is much desired this session were at an end, for it is thought whatever concessions are made new difficulties will be started'. He was particularly concerned about Fletcher's proposals for the appointment of the negotiators, which, Wedderburn wrote, was 'directly tending, as is thought here, to lodge the Soveraign power in the Parliament of the two kingdomes without the Prince'. He thought that this would encourage the English Parliament also to take over the right of appointing negotiators which had always rested with the Prince.[34] Fletcher's constitutional ideas, and his frank intention of increasing the power of Parliament at the expense of the monarchy, were evidently regarded in England as something which might be dangerously contagious.

Fletcher's other overture, tabled on 19 August, was intended to prevent the Government packing the House by appointing new Peers. He proposed that the numbers of Commissioners of the Shires (or Barons, as they were also called) should be increased by eleven, to match some recent new creations of Peers, and that an additional Baron should be added whenever a Peer was created. At the same meeting, Hamilton tabled an overture, also designed to cut the influence of the Court. This, described as a draft Act on Free Voting, proposed to exclude from voting in Parliament such men in Government employment as army officers, recipients of pensions, collectors and tacksmen of customs.[35]

In addition to the overtures and debates which I have mentioned, the House had dealt with a number of other useful matters and had been conducting a lengthy investigation into Government accounts. This revealed that Queensberry had not accounted for £42,144 outstanding against him in the Treasury accounts for the year 1703 when he had been Commissioner. He was to argue later, in a message to the Queen through Mar, that this had been spent on secret services (and it is not difficult to guess what that meant):

> His Grace wishes his Lordship to remind the Queen of some secret disbursements he made when Commissioner, for which he had secret instructions, but which, because of their nature could not be stated in the accounts with the Treasury. Her Majesty may trust him and order payment or not as she pleases.[36]

Fletcher tabled a Resolve on 16 August that 'all who had misapplied funds should be liable'. This led to a public row between him and Hamilton on 24

August, apparently over the order in which business should be taken. Hume tells us:

> Praiers said be Mr. Meldrum. Rolls called. Minutes read. Moved by the D. of Athol, That the Parliament proceed to the Plot after ending the Accounts. Moved by Salton, To give a 2ᵈ reading to the Act for a fuller Representation of the Barons. Moved by D. Ham., To give a 2ᵈ reading to the Act for Free Voting in Parliament. Salton, That the Member spoke last did contradict himself, for he had been for the Act in favours of the Barons. D. Ham., He craved the Justice of the House,—he had been reflected on by the Member spoke last, and undeservedly, and he offered to go to the bar, if he had said any thing amiss. Salt.,—Such reckoning was for another place. D. Ham.,—He refused not that neither. The Chancellour took notice of both their expressions, and moved, That first Salton should crave M. L. Commissioner and the House pardon, if without any design he had said any thing that gave offence; which after a long struggle he was prevailed with to do, if D. Ham. should do the like, and which both did, and promised on their word of honour, There should be no more of what had passed.[37]

Once again, offence seems to have been taken on what now seems trivial grounds and have escalated rapidly to challenges to a duel. It seems strange that the recognised leader and the intellectual mainstay of the Opposition should fall out publicly with so little cause, especially as both presumably approved of the two overtures in question. The quarrel seems to have led to an estrangement of several months, as appears from a letter which Lockhart sent to Hamilton early in March in the following year:-

> There is one thing that all your Grace's freinds were unanimous in, and requird me to show so much to your Grace and that is they thought it absolutely necessary for promoting the interest of Patrick Steil's club, that your Grace and Salton were again in good understanding. No body will pretend to justifye all his actions and manner of proceedings, but yet he is so useful a member of a party (take him all togather) that your Grace cannot but perceive, how great a disadvantage it woud be, not to have him in concert att this time. The means and and ways how to bring this reconciliation about, must be left, on your Grace's part, to your self, but that it were effected is the hearty wish of all your Grace's freinds, and I have reason to believe Salton is very far from being averss to to it, but on the contrary very desirous of it.[38]

Patrick Steil's was a tavern in Edinburgh where the Country party usually met to plan their tactics in Parliament. This letter is one of the few surviving pieces of evidence, apart from Lockhart's *Memoirs*, of the internal working of the party and of Fletcher's standing in it. Also, it confirms, as appears from the record as a whole, that Fletcher, Hamilton and the rest of the party were accustomed to working 'in concert'.

We have seen plenty of evidence that Fletcher had a quick temper and that he could not stomach a slight or indignity. Hamilton seems to have been much the same. The rigid ideas of the time on the honour of a gentleman tended also to create tension. Hamilton was often indecisive and unpredictable. Fletcher, in Lockhart's phrase, was 'extremely wedded to his own opinion' and reluctant to compromise. Neither man could have found it easy to co-operate with the other. Even making all allowances for these factors, it is difficult to believe that there was not more behind the quarrel than a disgruntlement over the order in which two proposals, both with a similar purpose, should be taken. So far, in this and the previous sessions of Parliament, Hamilton had led the Opposition effectively. His behaviour was quite different in the subsequent session of 1705 and 1706. It is possible that Fletcher already had reason to have doubts about Hamilton's reliability. On 14 September 1704, less than a month after the row in Parliament, Queensberry told Mar in a letter that he was 'strongly of the impression that the present managers have at bottom an understanding with the Dukes of H. and At.', meaning Hamilton and Atholl.[39] Nobody had more experience of this sort of management than Queensberry himself and he had many sources of information. He was certainly right about Atholl who wrote repeatedly to Godolphin during the 1704 session of Parliament and assured him that he was 'a dutiful and faithful servant to her Majesty'.[40]

The meeting at which Hamilton and Fletcher came close to a duel was the penultimate of the session. At the next, on 28 August there was still more business which must have caused much irritation in London. An Act for arming the country was given a first reading. Fletcher and Marischal then proposed a letter to the Queen which was approved. This asked her to send the principal papers about the Plot and expressed great disappointment that the House had not yet seen them. It recalled the resolve (proposed by Fletcher) which declared that the intermeddling of the House of Lords in the matter was an encroachment upon the independence of the nation. For good measure, it added the reproach that nothing could obstruct the measures recommended by Her Majesty more than further encroachments of that nature. After this final shot, Tweedale, no doubt with relief and following the instructions conveyed by Wedderburn, adjourned the session to 7 October. Parliament was not, in fact, recalled until the following year.[41]

The 1704 session of Parliament therefore ended with Scottish independence and the assertion of the power of Parliament over the Queen even more triumphant than in 1703. These causes, of which Fletcher was the most persistent and persuasive advocate, had not been a short lived flicker of resistance, but a campaign sustained over two years against all the pressures which the Court in London, with its monopoly of patronage, had been able to bring to bear. It was a campaign which rested on the enthusiastic support of the people at large. Even Burnet, whose sympathies were with the court after Revolution Settlement, concedes that this was so, and it was to become increasingly obvious in the following years. The Government had been granted financial supply for a very limited period, but it had been completely frustrated in its main objective, the acceptance of the Succession which would preserve the Union of the Crowns and therefore English domination. Instead they had been forced to concede royal approval of the Act of Security which has the

Andrew Fletcher of Saltoun
1653–1716
(*After William Aikman*)

James Douglas, 4th Duke of Hamilton
1658–1712
(*Artist unknown: After Sir Godfrey Kneller*)

James Douglas, 2nd Duke of Queensberry and 1st Duke of
Dover, 1662–1711
Commissioner, 1703 and 1706–7
(*Attributed to Sir John Baptiste de Medina*)

John Hay, 2nd Marquis of Tweeddale
1645–1713
Commissioner, 1704
(*Attributed to J. J. Voet*)

John Campbell, 2nd Duke of Argyll and 1st Duke of Greenwich
1678–1743
Commissioner, 1705
(*By William Aikman*)

James Ogilvie, 1st Earl of Seafield
1664–1730
Chancellor, 1703 to 1707
(*By Sir John Baptiste de Medina*)

John Erskine, 6th or 11th Earl of Mar
1675–1732
Secretary of State, 1705 to 1707
(*By Sir Godfrey Kneller*)

John Ker, 5th Earl and
1st Duke of Roxburgh
?–1741
(*Artist unknown*)

George Lockhart of Carnwath
1681–1732
(*By Sir John Baptiste de Medina*)

Gilbert Burnet,
Bishop of Salisbury
1643–1715
(*Artist unknown*)

opposite intention, to secure 'the honour and sovereignty of this Crown and Kingdom . . . from English, or any foreign, influence.'

Of course, it was to be expected that England would struggle to maintain its dominance. Their main weapon was money and the control of patronage, including the disposal of funds raised within Scotland itself. In the circumstances of the time, when the classes who sat in Parliament had few alternative sources of income, it was a very powerful instrument. As Fletcher said in 1703, 'And what less can be expected, unless we resolve to expect miracles, and that greedy, ambitious, and for the most part necessitous men, involved in great debts, burdened with great families, and having great titles to support, will lay down their places, rather than comply with an English interest in obedience to the prince's commands'.[42] Perhaps it is more surprising, and an indication of the strength of Scottish national feeling, that so many held out against the pressures for so long, than that a majority eventually succumbed.

Given the sensitivity of bribery, and the fact that it was necessarily conducted in secret with the minimum of written evidence, it is remarkable how much hard evidence has survived.[43] Much of it dates from the period between the end of the session of 1704 and the approval of the Treaty of Union in 1707, when pressure of this kind was at its most intense. In November 1704, for example, Alexander Ogilvie wrote to Seafield:

Pitmedden younger pretends a great keyndness to your Lo. and says most seriouslie to me that if your Lo. will obtain him a pension of one hundred pounds per annum, he will be your servant and give you a suitable returne.[44]

This refers to the Seton the younger of Pitmedden who had played an active part in the 1704 session in support of the Hamilton and Fletcher line. His offer to sell his services was presumably successful because he now changed sides and became one of the most effective speakers on the Government side and the author of a pamphlet in favour of the Union. Some modern historians take him seriously as if he were speaking and writing from conviction and not for payment. N. T. Phillipson, for instance, describes him as 'the Union's chief spokesman'.[45] Two of the other pamphleteers on the same side were also in Government pay. William Paterson, the chief architect of both the Darien Scheme and the Bank of England, was recommended to the Queen by Queensberry in July 1700 for a gratuity of £100 on the understanding that he would support the Government with his pen.[46] The most prolific pamphleteer of all on the Union question was Daniel Defoe, the English novelist, who was sent to Edinburgh in 1706 as a spy and propagandist.[47]

By far the most important and extraordinary of the Court's successes in recruiting supporters by bribery was the Duke of Hamilton himself. As we shall see, his behaviour in Parliament became increasingly erratic and damaging to the Scottish cause after the 1704 session. It is difficult to find any explanation for it, other than deliberate sabotage of the cause he was supposed to be leading and for which he was receiving the acclamations of the people in the Edinburgh streets. There are many unmistakeable indications that his motive was mercenary. Shortly after the 1704 session on 12 December 1704, Roxburgh wrote from London to Baillie of Jerviswood:

> I have been told by a friend of Duke Hamilton's, and one that knows him well, within this eight-and-forty hours, that if the Queen has a mind for this business, Duke Hamilton was vain and necessitous.[48]

On the same day, James Johnstone also wrote from London to Jerviswood:

> In short, you may setle the Sucession upon limitations, if you please, if the Court will still venture to grant them, or you may accept of a Union. If you will do neither, you may expect all the mischief that can be done you; for, as it was said, you and your independence are not so great but that you must depend either on France or England, and sure they will not suffer you to depend on France, if they can help it . . . . The spirit here runs upon conquest or union.[49]

Clearly very murky waters lay ahead. To the carrot of bribery was added the stick of military intimidation.

James Johnstone, who at the time as Lord Register was a key figure in the conduct of Scottish affairs in London, wrote again to Jerviswood on 15 February 1705:

> Duke Hamilton's friends are so gross as to intimate to great men here that he is *Chambre à Louer*. But for all that's to be done now, I find its thought scarcely worth the while to make the Purchase.[50]

All the evidence suggests that Hamilton soon found a way to prove that his support was worth the purchase and that he sold a great deal more than his vote.

12

The Parliament of 1705

'Contrair to our expectations the Treatie has cairied.'
— Earl of Mar

The success of the Scottish Parliament in extracting royal assent to the Act of Security served notice that Scotland could no longer be taken for granted as a dependency. As Daniel Defoe expressed it in his *History of the Union*: '. . . the measures taken in Scotland seemed to be well grounded, and their Aim well taken . . . . This effectually Settled and Declar'd the independency of Scotland, and put her in a Posture fit to be treated with, either by England, or by any other Nation'.[1] The Act of Security offered an escape from the situation in which Scotland had been placed since the Union of the Crowns and which Andrew Fletcher had repeatedly and eloquently exposed. Defoe, who was after all, a paid agent and propagandist for the English cause never mentions Fletcher but he tacitly concedes that Fletcher was right about this. After 1603 he says, Scotland was 'in a political though not in a legal sense, always under the management of the English court . . . it had the subjection without the advantages'.[2] In fact, another passage of his *History* amounts to a good summary of Fletcher's essential argument:

> The Scots had been very sensible of the visible decay of trade, wealth and inhabitants in this country, even from the first giving away their Kings to the English sucession; and, as the sinking condition of their Nation was plainly owing to the loss of their court, concourse of people, the disadvantages of trade, and the influence the English had over their Kings; so it was as plain, there was no way to restore themselves, but either better terms of Union and Alliance, or a returning back to their separate self-existing state.[3]

The question now was the English reaction. After centuries of effort, they had succeeded in neutralising Scotland and reducing her to control; they would be unlikely to allow Scotland to reassert her independence if they could help it. According to Burnet, the state of affairs in Scotland was 'aggravated very odiously all England over' by false rumours that France was already supplying great quantities of arms to Scotland.[4] In both Houses of Parliament, members seized the opportunity to attack the Lord Treasurer, Godolphin, as the man responsible for Scottish affairs and for the royal assent to the Act of Security in particular. 'The tories resolved to attack him', Burnet says, 'and that disposed the whigs to preserve him; and this was so managed by them, that it gave a great turn to all our councils at home'.[5] The Act eventually adopted by both

Houses was as much as anything a diversion by the Whigs to save Godolphin, but it also amounted to an ultimatum to Scotland.

This was 'an Act for the effectual securing the Kingdom of England from the apparent dangers that may arise from several Acts lately passed by the Parliament of Scotland', commonly called the Aliens Act. It provided, first of all, for the authorisation of 'such persons who shall be nominated by Her Majesty' to 'treat and consult' with Scottish commissioners 'concerning the Union of the two Kingdoms', provided that the Scottish Parliament took similar action. The second part of the Act was much more aggressive in tone and amounted to what we should now call the imposition of sanctions. It related not to Union (still of course a vague term, capable of a great range of interpretations) but to Succession. Unless the Crown of Scotland had been settled in the same manner as in England by 25 December 1705, from that date all Scots (except those in the Forces or already settled in England) would be treated in England as aliens and incapable of inheriting property. From the same date no cattle, sheep, coal or linen (the main articles of trade) would be imported into England.

The penalties or sanctions in the Act (following the Commons' Bill as finally accepted also by the Lords) therefore applied pressure on the Scots to accept the English Succession. This was evidently the solution which the English preferred but which had been successfully resisted in the last two sessions of the Scottish Parliament. It is true that the Scottish Act of Security, with its strong element of Fletcher's limitations, offered a possibility of the Scottish Parliament so asserting itself that the worse effects of 'subjection without the advantages' might be avoided, even with the same Succession. Even so, the same monarch would always place severe limitations on Scottish independence, from the extent of the royal prerogative, especially in foreign relations. The terms of the Aliens Act suggest that both Houses of the English Parliament believed that Scotland could be kept under control as long as the Scottish Parliament could be brought to accept the English Succession.

As Bruce Lenman has recently pointed out, the threats in the Act were directed particularly against the Scots nobles, 'the key group in the Scottish legislature because of their immense influence on the lairds and burgesses who made up the other two orders'. Since 1603 some Scottish nobles, including the Duke of Hamilton, had acquired estates in England as a result of intermarriage. Such property was now directly threatened. Many nobles had a financial interest, through their land holdings, in trade in the products now liable to embargo. The Aliens Act served notice on the Scottish nobility that they must expect to suffer financially if the Scottish Parliament failed to comply with English wishes. It is therefore not surprising that Burnet observed that 'it was the nobility, that in every vote turned the scale for the union: they were severely reflected on by those who opposed it; it was said, many of them were bought off, to sell their country and their birthright'.[6]

The Act was of doubtful legality since Queen Anne was still Queen of both Scotland and England and the English courts had long established that the *post nati* (Scots born after 1603) could not be regarded as aliens in England since they owed allegiance to the same monarch. Defoe said that the Act 'in a manner declar'd open war with Scotland' and that it was 'the most impolitic, I had almost said Unjust, that ever past that great Assembly'. He added that 24 warships were fitted out to prevent the Scots trading with France and that all concerned with the general good of both Kingdoms now foresaw that war between them was unavoidable.[7]

Feelings between the two countries were exacerbated still more by the *Worcester* episode. This was an English ship seized in the Forth in retaliation for the seizure of a Darien Company ship at London. Some remarks by members of the English crew gave rise to the suspicion that they had committed piracy against another Darien ship. In a trial, which began on 5 March 1705 in Edinburgh, Captain Thomson Green and 14 members of his crew were found guilty of piracy and murder and condemned to death. The Queen intervened in their favour, but the Scottish Privy Council, afraid of provoking the people at large, allowed the Captain and two of his officers to be hanged. It seems to have been a miscarriage of justice in which 'a wild desire for retaliation against England . . . blinded even the coolest of the Scots to the simplest laws of evidence. In England indignation was proportionally great'.[8] 'Never', wrote Defoe, 'two nations, that had so much affinity in circumstances, have had such inveteracy and aversion to one another in their blood'.[9]

It was in these difficult conditions that John, second Duke of Argyll, was appointed by the Court to replace Tweedale as Commissioner for the 1705 session of the Scottish Parliament. Since the New Party of Tweedale and his friends had failed, the Court had little choice but to try again the old guard of Queensberry and his associates. On the other hand, there were difficulties in simply reappointing Queensberry as Commissioner. Resentment against him over the Plot was still unresolved in Scotland and the Queen greatly disliked him. She wrote to Godolphin: 'I own it goes mightily against me, it grates my soul, to take a man into my service that had not only betrayed me, but tricked me several times, one that has been obnoxious to his own countrymen these many years and one that I can never be convinced can be of any use.'[10] Argyll was therefore to some extent at least, a substitute or front man for Queensberry. Lockhart indeed says that Queensberry used Argyll 'as the monkey did the cat in pulling out the hot roasted chestnuts'.[11] At the same time, Argyll, although young and inexperienced, had attributes which made him valuable to the Court. From his ancestry alone he had enormous prestige and influence among Scottish Presbyterians. The English Earl Hardwicke, in a note to Burnet's *History*, says: 'He managed well for the Court, and was from the beginning zealous for the Union'.[12]

Although Queensberry's followers were now once again in office, he himself stayed on for some time in London. According to Lockhart, he pretended sickness and gave one excuse after another, to avoid returning to Edinburgh at the beginning of the Parliamentary session. Lockhart suggests two motives. He wanted to see 'how affairs were like to go, and whether or not he might venture himself in Scotland', but also he wanted to show that Argyll could not manage Parliament without Queensberry's help. Lockhart acknowledges, with regret and dismay, that Queensberry's influence was very real, even 'over men of sense, quality, and estates; men that had, at least many of them, no dependence upon him'.[13] Seafield, in one of his private letters to Godolphin, on 8 June 1705, admitted as much: 'There is litel hops of success nou if the D of Q come not doun.'[14]

Godolphin's intention had been that Argyll should work along with Tweedale's associates to try to combine the votes of both the New and Queensberry's old Court Party. As soon as he arrived back in Scotland from London, Argyll rejected this idea and called for the dismissal of the men of the New Party. On the grounds that a 'faithless friend is worse than a professed enemy', he insisted on their places being given to 'such as have always been firm to the Revolution'. He threatened to resign over this. Then, when he got his way, he agreed to carry on but demanded an English peerage. (He became Earl and then Duke of Greenwich). With his strange blend of arrogance and sycophancy, self-confidence and professed diffidence, he must have exasperated his masters in London. When he was given two alternative messages from the Queen to Parliament, one calling for Succession and the other for a Treaty, he insisted on instructions on which he should adopt. When the Queen opted for a version which gave priority to Succession, he reported that this had made it more difficult to secure either of the objectives. He was a shameless believer in the use of patronage to buy votes. On 20 June 1705 he told Godolphin that his failure to supply ten or twelve thousand pounds to pay arrears of pensions had 'cost the Queen above twenty votes'. He noted that certain members holding pensions or posts had voted against the Government and therefore asked the Queen's approval to sack them.[15] At a later stage when he was asked to come back to Scotland in 1706 to help to secure the approval of Treaty of Union in Parliament he wrote to Mar:

> My Lord, it is surprising to me that my Lord Treasurer, who is a man of sense, should think of sending me up and down like a footman from one country to another without ever offering me any reward. Thier is indeed a sairtain service due from every subject to his Prince, and that I shall pay to the Queen as fathfully as anybody can doe; but if her ministers thinks it for her services to imploy me any forder I doe think the proposal should be attended with an offer of a reward.[16]

Argyll wrote this when he was with Marlborough's army in Flanders. As Lockhart said of him; 'His head was more upon the Camp than the Court.'[17] Probably his robust, direct military style and sense of discipline, and his complete lack of shame towards the use of bribes, helped him to muster support for the Government in Parliament. Certainly, it was during the 1705 succession, when Argyll was Commissioner, that the Government (meaning the Scottish ministers and officers of state appointed by London) began to achieve a majority. Also the Parliament was now in its third session. The longer a Parliament continued, the more opportunity the Government had to bring pressure to bear on the members. It was for this reason that the first of Fletcher's limitations called for the election of a new Parliament every year.

In accordance with Argyll's insistence, Tweedale's friends in the New Party were dismissed so that the old Government stalwarts of the Queensberry era could return to office. The 'half a dozen' as Argyll contemptuously called them,[18] Tweedale, Roxburgh, Rothesay, Belhaven, Selkirk and Baillie of Jerviswood, now called themselves the *Squadrone Volante*. It was a name which proclaimed both their fashionable enthusiasm for the literature and language of Italy and their intention to exercise their freedom to vote as they pleased. The group was, in fact, larger than the half dozen office holders dismissed by Argyll. Marchmont, one of its members, claimed that they numbered 34.[19] Leven, the Governor of Edinburgh Castle and very much a place-man and supporter of the Court, wrote about them at a later stage in a letter to Godolphin of 26 October 1706. He said that the Squadrone had 15 or 16 members but that Montrose actually joined the Government and influenced two or three others to do likewise. 'Besides these', he added, 'we have found ways since we have came from England to persuade several of that party to join with us in the matter of the Union.'[20]

The one exception to the clearance of office holders was the indispensable Seafield who remained Chancellor, as he had been under both Queensberry and Tweedale. 'He was finely accomplished; a learned lawyer, a just judge; courteous and good natured;' wrote Lockhart, 'but withall so intirely abandon'd to serve the Court measures, be what they will, that he seldom or never consulted his own inclinations, but was a blank sheet of paper, which the Court might fill up with what they pleas'd.'[21] The large number of Seafield's letters which have survived confirm this view of his character. Hume Brown, who edited a volume of these letters, came to the same conclusion: 'It seems to have been Seafield's maxim from the beginning of his public life to accept the powers that were and, in his own interest, to serve them to the best of his ability: in his letters it is his constant refrain that he considered it his sole duty to give effect to the wishes of the authorities by whose grace he held such offices as he did.'[22]

Seafield was not alone, even if he was the most consistently successful, in thus acting as the docile sycophant to such men as Godolphin, the Lord Treasurer of England, who held power in London. The Scottish nobility of the period are generally intelligent and articulate in their letters, but many of them grovel abjectly when they write to ministers in London. They do this because they are desperate for Government appointments or pensions, all of which lay in the gift of the Monarch in London who was surrounded and advised by English ministers. As Fletcher had repeatedly argued, it was a system which was inevitably corrupt and demoralising. 'As long as Scotsmen must go to the English court to obtain offices of trust or profit in this Kingdom . . . what less can be expected, unless we resolve to expect miracles?'[23]

With the restoration of Queensberry and his followers to office and the emergence of the Squadrone Volante the parties in the Scottish Parliament had assumed the dispositions which were to persist for the remaining two sessions. The Government or Court Party included all the officers of state and other holders of posts conferred by London in the name of the Crown. They were likely to be supported by such men of 'Revolution Principles' who were afraid that flirtation with opposition might lead to the risk of a Jacobite restoration. The Squadrone had intellectual pretensions as well as hopes of a return to office. As the Jerviswood correspondence shows, they agonised over the best way to serve their own interests, and sometimes those of Scotland as well, in a private debate of considerable intelligence and sophistication. Several of them had been early supporters of Andrew Fletcher. Eventually, and for a variety of motives, but mostly because of the carrots which Seafield dangled before them, they persuaded themselves to the opposite conclusion.

Neither of these parties had, of course, anything like the formal structure, discipline or organisation of modern political parties, even if the court had the powerful weapon of patronage. The opposition had even less organisation. As a whole it looked to Hamilton as its leader but it had two distinct elements. Andrew Fletcher, although he acted very much as an individual, was in effect the main spokesman and intellectual inspiration of the first of these, known as the Country Party. Their object was to restore Scottish independence and curb English influence in Scottish affairs. As part of this policy, they aimed at the transfer of effective power from the Monarch to Parliament. The second element were the Jacobites, known as the Cavaliers, whose object was the restoration of the Stuart line. Their leaders were Atholl and Hume, and Lockhart of Carnwath was an important member. Although the Cavaliers agreed with Fletcher about the need to assert Scottish independence against English interference, they certainly did not share his 'republican' instincts. They were prepared to entertain ideas of a negotiation with England, because they hoped that this would mean the indefinite postponement of the Succession question. To add to this confusion, the terms 'Country' and 'Cavalier' were sometimes used interchangeably.

Hamilton as a leader, apart from his prestige, had the advantage of being acceptable to both the Fletcher and the Jacobite wings of the opposition. As we have seen, there were already misgivings about his reliability. Lockhart notes that before the 1705 Parliamentary Session, Hamilton had frequent private meetings with Mar, a leading associate of Queensberry, and that 'great familiarity and confidence' appeared between them. Lockhart thought that this was the reason for Hamilton showing 'less zeal and forwardness in this ensuing than in former Parliaments'.[24]

For the 1705 Session Hume of Crossrigs' *Diary* is less informative than in the previous two. He missed a number of meetings because he was ill and even for the others his entries are briefer and less detailed. On the other hand, we have very full reports which Seafield sent to Godolphin. They fully confirm Fletcher's allegation that the system of appointment by the Court subjected the Scottish administration to English supervision and control. Not content with these official reports, Godolphin's ministerial colleague, Robert Harley, was also receiving reports from a secret agent, William Greg, which have survived in the papers of the Duke of Portland. Greg's reports are evidently coloured by a desire to show that his sympathies were with his English employers. This leads him frequently to snide observations about Fletcher who plays a prominent part in his reports. He refers to Fletcher in one of his letters to Harley as 'the madman, as I remember your Honour once rightly called him'.[25] Even so, his letters have the advantage of sometimes giving verbatim quotations from some of Fletcher's speeches.

The session began formally on 28 June with Argyll as Commissioner and Seafield as Chancellor. Fletcher, beginning the session as he meant to continue, was at once on his feet with a constitutional point. He objected to Baillie of Jerviswood's election as a member for Clydesdale (or Lanark as it is called in APS) on the grounds that he was Treasurer-Depute. Since Baillie had lost the post in the Argyll reshuffle, the point lapsed, but Fletcher had called attention to a means by which the Government could attempt to buy parliamentary votes.

Business began on 3 July with the reading of the Queen's letter. In the previous two years she had asked for the settlement of Succession and supply. This year, she again gave first place to Succession, but added a new point, a Treaty for Union. On Succession she offered an inducement, and tacit acceptance of the general idea of limitations, by saying that she was 'ready to give Royal Assent to such Provisions and Restrictions as shall be found necessary and reasonable in such a case.' On the other point she said, 'We are fully satisfied . . . that great benefits would arise to all our Subjects, by an Union of Scotland and England, and that nothing will contribute more to the composeing of differences and extinguishing the heats, that are unhappily raised and fomented by the enemies of both Nations . . . . We earnestly Recommend to you to pass an Act for a Commission to set a treaty on foot between the kingdoms.'[26]

Parliament showed no disposition to follow the Queen's recommendations. In fact at the next meeting on 6 July, Annandale made proposals of quite a different kind. He suggested that Parliament should consider 'such limitations and conditions of government as shall be judged proper for the next succession in the Protestant line' and at the same time a committee should be appointed to consider the coin of the Nation and the state of commerce and trade. The first of these might have been seen as a step towards the settlement of the Succession, even if it used Fletcher's term, limitations, which the Queen's speech had carefully avoided. The point about coinage and trade, however seemed likely to set the Parliament off for weeks in debates which had nothing to do with the Court's objectives. There would have been nothing surprising about this if it had been moved by the opposition, but Annandale had just been appointed as one of the two Principal Secretaries of State.

Burnet offers an explanation. He says that there had been a disagreement between the ministers. Annandale was for an immediate attempt to secure the Succession. The others thought that this was likely to fail and that they should try for the Union. That was popular because it 'seemed to be a remote thing; there would be no great opposition to a general act about it.' Some, says Burnet were sincerely in favour of Union. Others thought that the negotiation would take years, during which they would be continued in their appointments, as it was impossible to frame a treaty that would pass both Parliaments. This course was therefore agreed and Annandale was so offended that he took no further part in the councils of his colleagues.[27] It is not surprising to find Argyll writing to Godolphin to recommend that Mar, 'who had done her Majesty very good service in this Parliament', should be appointed in Annandale's place. Annandale, who does not seem to have grasped that the rules of the game required obedience, gave every appearance of being surprised and disgruntled by his dismissal.[28]

Burnet's account fully accords with the impression given by the letters of Argyll and Seafield. The preference of the Court was for the Scottish acceptance of the English Succession. The Union was very much a second best, intended to secure the same result by another means, the continued control of Scotland by the English Court. They decided to go for Union only because they were afraid that they would fail, as in the previous two years, to carry the English Succession in the Scottish Parliament. Seafield, in his letter of 8 June to Godolphin, wrote: 'I know the succession is most desirable, but I am verie afraid it will not succeed at this time, . . . whereas that of a treatie seems more probable to succeed.'[29]

The idea of a treaty, or in modern language negotiation, was likely to succeed in Parliament because it was sufficiently vague to combine the votes of many different interests. At this stage, there was no clear idea of what the outcome might be. For some, it was an opportunity to press for the end of English interference and discrimination against Scottish trade. For others it was an opportunity to postpone the decision about Succession. 'The Jacobites concerned all heartily agreed in this', Burnet says, 'it kept the settling the sucession at a distance, and very few looked at the motion for the Union, as anything but a pretence, to keep matters yet longer in suspense.'[30]

Annandale's proposals, on 6 July did in fact divert the House from the Government's objectives. Marischal proposed that they should deal first with the question of currency and trade. Mar countered with the proposal that before any other business the House should deal 'with circumstances as to England and how to enter into a treatie with them.'[31] When these two proposals were put to the vote, trade and currency was carried by what Hume of Crossrig called 'a vast plurality.'[32] For several meetings the House duly engaged itself exclusively with these matters.

The debate on currency provoked a quarrel between Fletcher and Roxburgh which very nearly involved them in a duel. There are laconic accounts in the letters of Mar and Seafield but Greg gives us the most detailed and vivid version. The trouble began when Baillie of Jerviswood was speaking in favour of Law's proposal on currency. At an earlier stage, Greg had remarked that Fletcher had showed 'ill nature and spleen' against Baillie because of his apostasy from the Country Party. Fletcher rose to the attack again, with what Greg called 'his usual ill-nature', and described the proposal as 'a contrivance to enslave the nation.' Roxburgh came to Baillie's defence and said that 'a gentleman ought at least to be treated with good manners'. At this, Fletcher 'fell into a passion'. The Commissioner ordered both to be confined to their chambers, but, adds Greg, 'the Laird who boasts that he never made his Court to any King or Commissioner, made no bones of breaking it.' He was however persuaded by his friends 'to return to his cage'.[33]

Fletcher had even stronger grounds for resenting the defection of Roxburgh from the Country party to the New party and then to the Squadrone. He had been one of Fletcher's closest political associates in 1703 and one of those to whom *An Account of a Conversation* was addressed. With the short fuse of Fletcher's temper, it is therefore not surprising that the quarrel broke out again at the next sederunt of the House. The Commissioner ordered that both should be put under arrest, but they slipped out next morning and met on the sands of Leith in response to Fletcher's challenge. Roxburgh said that he could not fight a duel because of a weakness in his right leg. Fletcher produced pistols, but by this time Horse Guards had arrived. The two seconds composed the quarrel and fired the pistols in the air.

By the standards of today, this whole affair is absurd as well as deplorable, but the early 18th century had different ideas of appropriate behaviour in such matters. It shows once again, Fletcher's pride, irascibility, prickly temper and courage. His readiness to take slights, real or accidental, to such extremity at least had the advantage of showing that he was not a man to be trifled with. Probably it was one of the reasons why his contemporaries regarded him with such respect. Of course, duelling was by no means uncommon in the early 18th century. Of the men discussed in this book, two died as a result of duels, Hamilton in 1712 and Lockhart of Carnwath in 1732.

In his letter of 16 July about this affair, Mar says that he expects that next day will be decisive in Parliament. 'We'll be bussie upon what cairies, either Treatie or Succession, We have trifled all this time, . . . This is like to be a hote day in Parliament.'[34] What in fact happened on 17 July was that Hamilton proposed that the House should again adopt the same Resolve as they had passed, against the wishes of the Government, on the same day in the previous session:

> That this Parliament will not proceed to the nomination of a successor till we have a previous treaty with England in relation to our commerce and other concerns with that Nation. And further, It is Resolved That this Parliament will proceed to make such Limitations and Conditions of Government for the rectification of our Constitution and may secure the liberty Religion and Independence of this Nation before they proceed to the said nomination.[35]

Hume tells us that this was much debated with some members very properly objecting that the discussion on trade had not been completed. Even so, it was approved by about 45 votes. Belhaven, who had spoken against the Resolve on the previous year when he was part of the administration, voted for. Montrose, Tweedale and the 'rest of that party', that is the Squadrone, voted against.[36]

This vote was a serious reverse for the Government as Seafield admitted in a letter next day to Godolphin, in which he reported the outcome of a meeting between Argyll and his colleagues: 'We all aggreed that there remains nothing now to be done concerning the succession in this session of Parliament, and that wee ought to endeavour to have ane act for a treatty in such terms as that wee might hope to have some success. So wee are to try what influence wee can have upon the members of Parliament for obtaining ane act for a treatty, leaving the nomination to the Queen, and, if we cannot prevail in that, to joyn that there be a good nomination. If this cannot carry, wee will be necessitat to bring the session the a close as soon as wee can'.[37]

At this early state in the session therefore, the Government were already contemplating as complete a defeat as in the previous two. They did not need to anticipate much difficulty in finding a majority for an Act to authorise a 'treaty' or negotiation with England since even Fletcher and the opposition generally were in favour of a negotiation to try to resolve difficulties in the relations between the two countries, including the long standing English discrimination against Scottish trade. A significant point in Seafield's letter is that the Government would not have been content with an Act authorising a treaty unless the 'treaters' or Commissioners (that is the negotiators), were men on whom they could rely. They could achieve this either by leaving the appointments to the Queen, which meant effectively to her English advisers and their Scottish friends. Alternatively, if the choice were left to Parliament, that would be acceptable, provided they managed a majority for 'a good nomination', or, in other words for men who could be relied upon to follow the Government line. This was obviously much less dependable than leaving the choice to the Queen.

At this point, perhaps I should say a word about the usage of the term, 'treaty', in the early 18th century. Among the meanings identified by the *Oxford English Dictionary* are:

2.   The treating of matters with a view to settlement; discussion of terms, conference, negotiation.

3.   a)   A settlement or arrangement arrived at by treating or negotiation.

   b)   A contract between two or more states, relating to peace, truce, alliance, commerce and other international relation.

The Dictionary says that 3(b) is now the prevailing sense and that 2 is now rare and obsolete. It quotes the *Encyclopaedia Britannica* to the effect that the word has been commonly employed in sense 3(b), a contract between two or more states, since the end of the 17th century. In the early 18th century the word can be found in both senses, meaning negotiations as well as their result. It is clear from the context in contemporary Scottish documents that the most common usage then was still in the sense of negotiations. The Acts of the Parliament of Scotland, for instance, on 5 September 1705 refer to 'An Act for sending ambassadors from this Kingdom to foreign treaties'.[38]

For about the next six weeks, after their reverse on 17 July, the Government continued to suffer a series of defeats. On 20 July Mar and Lothian both presented drafts to authorise a treaty, but this was countered by a series of other proposals. Tweedale offered a draft letter of reply to the Queen. Roxburgh, still apparently to some extent under the influence of Fletcher's ideas, in spite of their recent quarrel, presented a proposal anent the way of changing officers of state in the event of the Queen's death. There were a number of defeats on matters of trade, which proposed restrictions on imports from England, presumably (although it was not stated) as a retaliation against the English Aliens Act.[39]

Queensberry at last returned to take personal command of his followers, taking the oath as Lord Privy Seal on 24 July. On that date there was a vote on whether to proceed with Tweedale's draft letter or with the question of trade. The latter carried. So far the Parliament had been making little progress in any direction. The opposition were trying to avoid the discussion of measures which they found distasteful; but the Government was also deliberately playing for time. In a letter of 1 August Seafield acknowledged Godolphin's approval of the attempt to go for a treaty since Succession has once again failed. He reported that all the 'servants' (a significant word for the officers of state) were agreed that they 'should yet try if wee can gain a majority to be for a treatty, and that, in order to have time, wee may proceed to some acts of trade and limitations.'[40]

Lockhart was well aware of the dangers of allowing the Government to procrastinate. He thought that if the opposition had forced the matter of the treaty to a vote early in the session, 'they might easily have either rejected it altogether, or at least framed and clogged it as they pleased, and chosen such members as they had a mind to be commissioners for meeting and treating with the commissioners from England.' He adds that he had always been of the view that 'if anything for the Country's interest was to be attempted in a Scots Parliament, it must be at the beginning of the session.' Otherwise, members become weary of attendance and slip off home to their country houses. Meanwhile the Court 'who had the purse and the power' were steadily winning support.[41]

In the same letter of 1 August, Seafield reported an important debate on the previous day, the first substantial discussion of the Act for the treaty. Lothian proposed the first reading and Fletcher replied with what Hume called a 'long harrangue' and Seafield, 'high and studied speeches'. According to Greg, Fletcher argued that 'there was no way left to make the Scots a happy people, but by separating from England and setting up a King of their own.' He proposed that he should be neither Stuart nor Hanoverian but the 'Prince of Prussia, who was of our religion, and able besides, by his powerful interest abroad, to secure us from any uneasiness from a jealous neighbour.'[42]

Presumably this was more a debating point than a serious proposal, allowing Fletcher once again to expose the dangers of sharing a monarch with England.

Turning to the question more immediately at issue, Fletcher argued that it was inconsistent with Scottish independence and sovereignty to treat with England unless the English Parliament first rescinded the threatening provisions of the Aliens Act. He proposed a Resolve that it was inconsistent with 'the honour and interest of this independent Kingdom' to appoint commissioners until England proposed the same 'in a more neighbourly and friendly manner.' Hamilton proposed an additional clause to the effect that the House should now proceed to questions of trade, rectifications of the constitutions and limitations in the terms of the Resolve proposed on 17 July. 'The Throne', Hume wrote, 'was all for a Treaty'; but when it was put to the vote, proceed with the Treaty or with the limitations, it was limitations which carried but now only by 4 votes (as compared to the majority of 45 on 17 July). On 2 August it was resolved to devote the next few meetings to trade and then subsequently to proceed to limitations.[43]

The trade proposals included the Overture for an Act prohibiting all imports from England, but attention focused on a proposal for the creation of a Council of Trade. The way in which this was appointed would be a precedent for any appointment of the Commissioners for a Treaty, and the Court therefore fought hard for appointment by the Queen. They lost by a margin of 9 votes on 10 August. The next question was whether the nomination of the members of the Trade Council should be by the whole House together (as the Government preferred) or separately by each of the three Estates. It was decided that each Estate should choose seven members on a proposal by Marchmont, seconded by Hamilton and 'pressed' (as Hume writes) by Fletcher and Belhaven. 'Wee are in hopes', Seafield reported to Godolphin 'to carry both the nobility and burrows'. This is an interesting indication that the Government were least confident of the Commissioners of the Shires (of which Fletcher was one), the only part of the Parliament that was representative, if only of a very restricted class. Although Seafield does not mention it, the House also passed a clause excluding from the Council members of Parliament who were also tacksmen or collectors of customs and excise. We do not know who moved this but it is very much in line with Fletcher's constant pressure to reduce the political influence of men who were paid servants of the Crown.[44]

On 10 August also, Parliament displayed its national feelings in three decisions about books. They awarded 4,800 pounds (presumably pounds Scots, but even so, a substantial sum) to James Anderson W.S. for his *Historical Essay showing that the Crown and Kingdom of Scotland is imperial and independant*, and the same amount to James Hodges whose writings also 'served the interest of the nation.' At the same time, books by the Englishman, William Atwood, were ordered to be burnt by the hangman on the grounds that they were 'Scurrilous and full of falsehoods' . . . 'reflecting on the honour and independancy of this nation.'[45]

The meetings devoted to limitations, which followed, brought several proposals which were highly distasteful to the Court. By now, the term, 'limitations', which Fletcher had originally introduced in 1703, was generally employed, even in the official record, to include any measure intended to strengthen Parliament at the expense of the Crown. The House proceeded with three such measures on 15 August. Rothes moved his Act, first presented on 20 July, for the appointment by Parliament, after the death of the present Queen, of the Officers of State, the Lords of the Privy Council, Exchequer and Treasury, and the Lords of Session and Justiciary. Fletcher again presented his twelve limitations in the same wording as his original proposal in 1703. (Appendix A) He proposed that they should be treated as a Claim of Right which would not require the royal assent. Seafield remarked in his letter of 18 August to Godolphin that Fletcher's proposals would have plainly constituted a republic (although Fletcher had not, in fact, proposed the abolition of the monarchy but only the transfer of its powers to Parliament). Seafield added that Fletcher made a 'long formall speech, holding out the necessity and advantage of such a government' and that several spoke in his support. Greg reported that Fletcher 'harrangued the House above half an hour and spoke particularly to each of his twelve limitations.' Lockhart tells us that when Stair spoke against the tenth limitation (no general indemnity nor pardon without the consent of Parliament), Fletcher replied that this was no wonder. If it had been in force, 'His Lordship had long e're been hanged, for the advices he gave King James, the murder of Glenco, and his conduct since the Revolution.'[46]

The Cavalier Party presented an Act for changes in the constitution of Parliament to take effect immediately in the lifetime of the Queen. This provided for the election of a new Parliament every three years and the exclusion from membership of tacksmen, farmers of taxes and recipients of royal pensions. Seafield says in his letter of 18 August that he and his colleagues decided to join with the New Party (or Squadrone) in support of the Rothes proposal in the hope of frustrating any curtailment of the royal powers in the current reign. All three proposals were given a first reading and it was decided by vote that the Rothes proposal should be taken first at the next meeting.[47]

In his letter of 18 August, Seafield also says that he was informed on the morning of the sixteenth that Fletcher proposed in addition to present the Act which he had introduced in 1704 for an increase in the number of Commissioners for the Shires and also to move that any limitations proposed for the successor should take effect in the current reign. When the meeting began, it was plain that the feeling was against considering any increase in membership before limitations had been first considered. Fletcher therefore suggested that the Rothes Act should apply at once. This was resisted by Stairs and Belhaven who argued that it would be hard on the Queen, who was already restricted by the Claim of Right, to impose additional restrictions on her. Fletcher was seconded only by the Earl of Hume, at which, according to Seafield, he 'was so angry that he went out of the House, but I know he will return to our next meeting.'[48]

In the debate which followed, the Court argued strenuously that Parliament should not go beyond the Act of 1641 which gave the House the right to approve or reject a list of nominations to offices presented by the King or his Commissioner. 'To loadge the nomination in the Estates', Seafield argued, 'was to divest the soveraign of all power and to extirpate the monarchy and constitute a republict.' Fletcher's absence did not prevent the presentation by others of his by now well established argument. 'There was a great deal said', Seafield records, 'for loadging it in the Estates as the only remedy to prevent English influence on the sucessor and to prevent the nobility and gentry goeing up to London to seek places, qch did ruine our private estates and fortunes, and exhaust the wealth of the Kingdome.' Seafield's reply that nomination by Parliament would 'run ourselves in all confusion and disorder' did not prevent the vote going against him and the Government. It was decided by a majority of 16 that nomination should lie with Parliament. Another clause was approved providing for the nomination of the Lords of Session and Justiciary in the same manner and the whole Act was passed on 21 August.[49]

'The next limitation proposed', Seafield reported to Godolphin, 'was that of a triennial Parliament and the excluding of the managers, collectors and farmers of the revenue from being members of Parliament.'[50] This proposal was very much in line with Fletcher's ideas, although it was a compromise which retreated a little from the proposal in the first point of his original twelve limitations for annual elections. It was supported by both the Cavaliers and the New Party who commanded a majority as long as they voted together. Against the members of the Government, who argued that this was a new restriction of the royal prerogative and an alteration of the constitution, it was decided by a majority of 16 votes that the measure would take effect in the current reign. There was then a vote whether the existing Parliament would continue for one more year (as proposed by Hamilton) or for three. The latter was carried by a majority of 32. Hamilton then proposed that the General Receivers of the revenue should also be excluded from the membership of the Parliament. Seafield saw this as a personal attack on himself because the Receiver, Sir Alexander Ogilvie, was a near relation and always followed his lead in Parliament. He had been warned in advance and was able to defeat the amendment by 87 votes. The whole Act, however, passed on 22 August by what Seafield himself called 'a considerable majority'.[51]

The session of 1705 had now been meeting for nearly two months without the Government achieving any progress towards the three objectives set out in the letter from the Queen, the settlement of Succession, a treaty for Union and supply. On the contrary, Parliament had continued to assert the Fletcher spirit by approving a series of measures in line with the limitations which he had originally proposed in 1703. As we have seen, they had again passed, on 17 July by a majority of 45 votes, a resolution calling for limitations to secure 'the liberty, Religion and Independancy of this Nation'. On 10 August they had decided by a majority of 9 that the members of the Council of Trade should be appointed by Parliament and not by the Queen. On 16 August they voted (by a majority of 16 according to Seafield or 23 according to Greg) in favour of the appointment of Officers of State by Parliament and on 22 August for triennial Parliaments. These last two measures alone, if they received the royal assent and were carried out, would have been sufficient by themselves to achieve Fletcher's fundamental objective of achieving a real transfer of power from the Court to the Scottish Parliament.

In discussing these developments in a letter of 26 August to Godolphin, Seafield said that he could not approve of what the New Party (or Squadrone) had done. Clearly they had so far voted with the Cavaliers and Country Party in favour of these limitations. 'Yet', he adds, 'I doe not discurage them to expect a share of her Majesties favour if they will not insist to have the royal assent to the acts for limitations, and if they will give a suplie and a plan act of treatie'.[52] In other words, he was prepared to overlook their assertion of independence and hold out some prospect of reward, provided they did not in the end frustrate the essential objectives. If the Government could secure Supply and, above all, an Act to set the Union negotiations in train, they would be able to ignore the limitations. The Government could refuse royal assent and, in any case, the negotiations could produce a new situation where the limitations would be quite irrelevant. In spite of two months of Parliamentary reverses, the whole tone of Seafield's letter suggests something close to confidence that he would be able to carry the New Party with him and therefore achieve a Government majority in the end. The Government had been playing for time and using all the means available to it to mobilise support for the vote on the proposal for Union negotiations.

On 2 August, the House had decided to devote a few meetings to limitations and a few to questions of trade. By 24 August, this had been done and they therefore now turned to Supply and the Treaty. There was a temporary digression when the Queen's reply to the Address on the Plot was raised, but the heat had now gone out of this question, and Queensberry was able to dispose of it without much trouble. The Government argued for an immediate Act of Supply on the grounds that otherwise the army would have to be disbanded. Seafield says that there were many speeches against this for the usual reason that it was imprudent to grant supply until the bills which the House wanted, those on trade and limitations, had been passed and received the royal assent. There was also a need to consider counter measures to the economic boycott which the English Aliens Act would impose on 25 December. After much hard bargaining, in which Seafield clearly saw the attitude of the New Party as crucial, it was agreed that the next sederunt would proceed to consideration of an Act for a Treaty with England previous to all other business.[53]

The debate on the Treaty began on 25 August on the basis of the draft which Mar had tabled on 20 July. He afterwards claimed in a letter to his wife that it was finally passed almost without the alteration of a word.[54] The draft attributed the initiative to the Queen: 'Considering with what earnestness the Queen's Majesty has recommended settling of the Succession and also a Treaty as the most effectual way for extinguishing the heat and differences that are unhappily raised betwixt the two Nations.' It emphasised that what was proposed was a negotiation between 'her two independant Kingdoms of Scotland and England.' It excluded 'any alteration of the Worship Discipline and Government of the Church of this Kingdom as now by law established', and it provided that nothing proposed or agreed by the Commissioners appointed by the Act would have any effect until it was confirmed by an Act of the Parliament of Scotland.[55] One important point was left open in the original draft, whether the Commissioners were to be appointed by the Queen or by Parliament. The point was crucial because appointment by the Queen would mean a spurious negotiation in which both sets of negotiators would be men acceptable to the English ministers and who could therefore be relied upon to follow their policy.

On 25 and 28 August there were, in the words of APS, the official record, 'long debates' on the draft. The opposition, in which Fletcher took a conspicuous part, had several lines of defence. In the first place there was the threatening language in which the English Parliament had presented the proposal as an ultimatum. Greg says that the whole day was 'spent in making angry speeches against the Parliament of England.' He continues: 'Mr Fletcher was the first who vented his spleen in his usual fierce and violent manner against the usage done this nation, as injurious, insolent and unneighbourly; and advanced that the English Act of Parliament, in the terms it was conceived, struck at the sovereignty and independency of the Kingdom of Scotland.' Greg adds that Stair 'for once, agreed with Fletcher.'[56] Lockhart says that Fletcher made a 'pathetick' (which in the usage of the time meant moving and emotional) speech denouncing 'the scurrilous and haughty procedure of the English' and urging the Parliament, 'as became Scotsmen' to throw out the proposal with indignation until it was proposed 'in more civil and equal terms.'[57]

APS records that Fletcher tabled a draft address to the Queen on those lines as an alternative to proceeding with the Act. Atholl proposed as another solution of this difficulty that a clause should be added to the Act prohibiting the departure of the Commissioners from Scotland until the English Parliament had rescinded the clause in their Aliens Act which declared that the Scots were aliens. Eventually (but not until 4 Sept) the Government extricated itself by a compromise. It was agreed that the negotiations would not begin before the English Parliament rescinded the offensive clause. A vote was taken on whether this should be stated by an amendment to the Scottish Act or in a separate letter to the Queen. The latter was agreed by a majority, according to Seafield, of 3 or 4.[58]

On 29 and 30 August the House was occupied with other matters, private business, personal petitions and the like, and the Queen's reply to the Address from the 1704 session about the Plot. Evidently the Government was again playing for time, perhaps awaiting instructions on the awkward matter of the offensive tone of the English Act.[59]

The debate on Mar's draft resumed on 31 August. Hamilton proposed an additional clause: 'That the Union to be treated on shall not derogat any wayes from any fundamental laws ancient privileges offices rights dignities and liberties of this Kingdom.' This, of course, raised the crucial issue. As Lockhart remarks, the clause was one which had been used in previous Acts for Union negotiations from the time of James VI. Both he and Seafield are quite specific that the purpose on this occasion was to rule out an incorporating Union and to restrict any negotiations to a federal arrangement. According to Lockhart, the clause was 'vigorously opposed' by the Government precisely because it would exclude them from 'treating on an entire or incorporating Union; of which the abolishing of our Parliaments, and subversion of our constitution, was a necessary consequence. And it was this kind of union England designed and desired; because it riveted the Scots in perpetual slavery, depriving them of any legal method to redress themselves of the injuries they might receive from them, by keeping them poor and under their chains.'[60]

Seafield says that the Cavalier Party 'spoke much against ane incorporating union', and that the New Party agreed with them, after some hesitation. He had, however, several friends whom he could not entirely influence in everything, but in this he prevailed and managed to secure a majority against the clause. According to Lockhart, the majority was only 2 votes and this could have been avoided since 6 or 7 of the Cavalier and Country Parties were absent. He thinks that if the Court had lost this vote, they would have abandoned the idea of the Treaty; 'by which means the nation had been free of that fatal thraldom to which 'tis since subjected'.[61]

It is very doubtful that the English Government would have abandoned their objectives so easily. They and their Scottish appointees had after all patiently soldiered on, despite constant reverses, in the successive parliamentary sessions of 1703, 1704 and, so far, 1705. They might certainly have changed their tactics since they had only resorted to the idea of union after their repeated failure to secure the same Succession to the throne, their preferred alternative method of maintaining the neutralisation and control of Scotland. At all events this majority of 2 votes was the first real success of the Court in these three sessions of the Scottish Parliament. It was an important psychological victory which gave confidence to the Court and demoralised the opposition. It prepared the way for the extraordinary events of the following day.

It is unfortunate that we do not have the texts of any of the speeches or even the names of the speakers from this debate or for the session generally. Because of ill health, Hume of Crossrig had missed several of the sederunts and his diary becomes less informative for this session. As always, the APS gives only a bare outline of the decisions. We have to rely mainly on Lockhart or on the letters of Seafield. Although they are writing from opposite sides, their accounts coincide remarkably in all essentials but they are not always as detailed as we would wish. Fletcher published his speeches only for the session of 1703 and no pamphlet is attributed to him for 1705. It is clear from the references to him in Hume, Lockhart, Greg and even, exceptionally, APS that he took a prominent part in the whole session. His views on the crucial issue debated on 31 August can be deduced from his published writings, but we have no confirmation, although it a safe assumption, that he was one of those that, in Seafield's words, 'spoke much against ane incorporating union'.[62]

The debate on the Act for a Treaty continued on 1 September in a long, involved and finally dramatic meeting. According to Hume, Fletcher proposed that the clause about the church should be omitted, presumably because it was a transparent attempt to reassure the Presbyterians. Fletcher, apparently because of lack of support, let this proposal fall.[63] Atholl then moved the addition of his clause prohibiting the departure of the Scottish Commissioners until the English had rescinded the offensive clause in the Aliens Act. The House agreed that the English Act should be rescinded before negotiations began, but an alternative proposal to Atholl's was also tabled, that the Act be 'plain and simple' and that the clause in the English Act be considered separately. This alternative eventually passed by a majority of 12, but before the vote was taken Atholl read a Protestation that the Commissioners should not leave the Kingdom before the clause in the English Act had been rescinded and invited other members who agreed to add their declaration. This was an established procedure to allow members to have their views on a particular matter recorded in the minutes which otherwise generally gave no names. It was obviously tedious and time-consuming. Of the nobles, 24 (including Hamilton) adhered, 37 of the members for the shires and 18 for the burghs. Lockhart was among the adherents, but not Fletcher. In the vote between the two amendments to the Act, Atholl's version was defeated by 12 votes.[64]

The sudden and unexpected *volte face* which followed is recorded laconically in APS. It was moved that the House should now consider whether nominations of the commissioners be left to the Queen or by Parliament. A proposal to delay this decision, because it was already late in the day after a long sederunt, was defeated. It was then carried that nominations be left to the Queen. Hume, who is a little more informative about this meeting than for a large part of the session, adds the information that it was Hamilton who took this startling initiative and that Fletcher opposed it 'most bitterly'. Hume adds also the majority for nomination by the Queen was 'about 40'. After this the whole Act was put to the vote and approved. Again before the vote Atholl insisted on again making his Protestation. Hamilton no longer adhered, but the numbers of those who did were about the same as before, Nobles 22, Shires 33 and Burghs 18.[65]

Lockhart has a fuller account of these events. He says that while the rolls were being called on the first of Atholl's Protestations, many members left after recording their vote. It was already late and they expected that there would be no further business that day. Hamilton seized this moment to propose that nomination be left to the Queen. Lockhart continues:-

This, you may be sure, was very surprizing to the Cavaliers and Country party; 'twas what they did not expect would have been moved that night, and never at any time from His Grace, who had, from the beginning of the Parliament to this day, roared and exclaimed against it on all occasions; and about twelve or fifteen of them ran out of the house in rage and despair, saying aloud 'twas to no purpose to stay any longer, since the Duke of Hamilton had deserted and so basely betray'd them. However, those that remained opposed it with all their might, and a hot debate arose upon it, wherein the Cavaliers used the very arguments that the Duke of Hamilton had often insisted on upon this and the like occasions.[66]

Greg adds his usual jeer at Fletcher: 'It will be easily believed, that Fletcher fell into one of his fits, when he saw the nomination was like to go as it went, and so impudent was he, as to say, that the giving the nomination to the Queen was in effect complimenting the English ministers (and particularly, my Lord Godolphin) with it. This went not without a reprimand from the Chancellor, who snubbed the madman roundly.' Fletcher was, of course right about this and everyone knew it. As it happens, an English visitor, Joseph Taylor, was in the House on that day and wrote an account of the debate. He gives particular attention to Fletcher as one of 'the principall leading men of the High party, or those which oppos'd the Court', and says that he spoke well 'but with a great deal of passion'. He describes the final stages of the debate:

The next great point was, whether the Queen or parliament should have nomination of Commissioners: Fletcher oppos'd the Queen, for says he, you had as good leave it to my Lord G—d—in, and we know that our Queen is in England, under the Influences of an English Ministry, and 'tis not to be expected that the Interest of Scotland should be so much considered by her, as the inclinations of an English Parliament, Another Gentleman said, he would vote the parliament should nominate, it not being to be expected she would disoblige her English Parliament, being engaged in a long and expensive warr, for that the English were able to supply her, but they being poor, and not able to assist her, the English would certainly have the greater influence. H—— contrary to the expectation of his party, voted the Queen to nominate, giving this reason, with his usuall haughty and bant'ring Ayr, that the Parliament was too much in heats and feuds, and could never agree upon proper persons, but the Queen, who was free from partiality, might doubtless make a good choice, but added he, if she should make a bad one, wee will be safe, for all must return to them again, and they might send the Act back to the place from whence it came; which show'd a sting in the taile of his Complement. 'Twas carry'd the Queen should nominate by 4 Voices,

After the sederunt several supporters of the Court came to Taylor's lodging. They 'seemed mightily pleas'd at what was done; and told us we should now be no more English and Scotch, but Brittons. And thus we merrily spent the night, in drinking to the Success of the treaty and happy union'.[67]

According to Lockhart's account, Hamilton's motion, in the absence of the twelve to fifteen members, passed by a majority of eight. In comparison to the usual voting pattern this is more probable than Hume's figure of about 40, especially as even Seafield claims no more than a 'considerable majority' for the final vote on the Act and says that both the Cavalier and New parties 'shew a great inclination to have the Act throwen out'.[68] Lockhart comments (although it is a phrase that he used also of other events) 'from this day may we date the commencement of Scotland's ruine'. He adds that it was the more enraging that both of the crucial votes (those on the first restricting clause and on the nominations) were lost by small majorities and in the absence of several members of the opposition. He says that he is certain from his own knowledge (and he was one of the Commissioners himself) that the English, knowing the reluctance of the Scots to enter into an incorporating Union, would not have pressed it if even two or three of the Scottish Commissioners had opposed it. He continues:-

> But to consider the Duke of Hamilton's part in this affair a little more particularly: 'Tis true, some reports had been whisper'd about, from the beginning of the Parliament, that His Grace's behaviour in this point would prove as it did, and many were uneasy at the great familiarity that appeared betwixt him and the Earl of Mar; but yet all were unwilling to believe any thing that was amiss of one who had stood so firm, and done such service to his country, especially in this point, whereupon he had so frequently, nay, not many days before it fell out, expressed and declared his opinion and resolution. But the following particular will make his conduct the more unaccountable. That very morning on which this affair was concluded, about forty or fifty of the Cavaliers being met together, had under consideration, whether it would be most proper to chuse the commissioners in a full House, or that every Estate should separate and chuse such as should represent themselves; and inclined to prefer the last, because they were sure to carry what Barons they pleased, but might run the hazard of losing all the other way. Yet such was their confidence in, and deference to, the Duke, that before they would determine themselves positively in it, they dispatched the Earl of Strathmore, George Lockhart of Carnwath, and George Home of Whitfield, to acquaint His Grace of what had passed amongst them, and desire his opinion: but His Grace being abroad when they came to wait upon him, the message was not communicated to him, till just as the Parliament sat down. Mr. Lockhart meeting him accidentally in the outer house, delivered his commission; to which he gave this answer: "Tell "these gentlemen, 'twill be time enough for us to consider on "that affair; for it shall not be in this day." I never yet could hear of any reasonable excuse he made for this his behaviour.[69]

Hamilton's sudden reversal astonished the Government managers, in Edinburgh at least, as much as it did the opposition. Mar wrote to his wife on 7 Sept:

> Bussiness here has taken a mighty turn since I wrote last. Contrair to our expectations the Treatie was cairied as we had a mind, the Act I presented not haveing almost a word altred. The Queen has got the nomination of the treaters, and the Duke of Hamilton proposed it first, which has made his pairtie mad at him.[70]

Seafield's report to Godolphin contains no suggestion that he had any prior knowledge of Hamilton's intentions but only that he, as Chancellor, took the opportunity when it was offered to him.[71] It must have been difficult for him to believe his luck in this sudden turn of events. He wrote to Godolphin on 21 Sept: 'Perhaps everything is not so well done as wee wished, yet the Parliament has had ane issue very farr beyond what in reason we could have expected as matters stood at the beginning of the Parliament and a considerable time thereafter'.[72]

What was Hamilton's motive? Lockhart suggests that it was because he 'had a great mind to be one of the treaters himself' and thought that this was the best way to recommend himself to the Queen's favour.[73] Clerk of Penicuik, who was a Protégé and close associate of Queensberry, says much the same. Nomination by the Queen was, he writes in his *Memoirs*, 'a proposal of the Duke of Hamilton, who from that piece of independence expected the Honour of being appointed by the Queen.'[74] This interpretation is consistent with a conversation with Hamilton which Seafield reported to Godolphin on 15 August. Hamilton had shown a great concern to be chosen as one of the Counsellors for Trade and had spoken about it almost to the whole nobility, even those in the Government service, including Seafield himself. Seafield reminded him that he had taken a leading part in taking the nomination of the Council of Trade away from the Queen. She would think her servants unfaithful, Seafield continued, if they now appointed him. 'On the other hand, had he assisted us in procuring the nomination to be left to her Majesty, I should very readily have concurred in recommending him to be named.'[75] Perhaps Hamilton was now taking Seafield at his word. In spite of this, it is difficult to believe that Hamilton would sacrifice his Party, and any reputation he might have for consistency in his political principles, for the comparatively empty honour of nomination as one of the Commissioners for the negotiation, which he might have secured, in any case, if it had been left to Parliament. On more than one occasion at a late stage, when the treaty itself was under debate, he similarly abandoned his Party interest at a crucial point. He continued to be accepted as the recognised leader of the Cavaliers and bask in the applause of the Edinburgh crowd who saw him as the hero of the national cause. He seems to have played a treacherous and ingenious double game which finally destroyed the cause which he professed to lead. Indeed a modern English historian, who has written on this period, G. M. Trevelyan, has said of the Union that Hamilton was 'the instrument, under Heaven, of its almost miraculous passage'. During this entire time Hamilton was speaking and acting as the leader of a Party committed to the opposite. As Trevelyan says, 'so noble was his almost royal person, so high was his prestige, that his followers, though they murmured at each fresh betrayal of their cause, had never the heart to renounce him in earnest.'[76]

So what was the motive? Clerk of Penicuik, in his passage about Hamilton goes on to say, 'I knew that this Duke was so unlucky in his present circumstances that he wou'd have complied with anything on a suitable encouragement.'[77] On pages 119–120 I quoted some of the indications in the *Jerviswood Correspondence* that it was well known in the circle around Roxburgh that Hamilton was offering to sell his services to the Government.

Johnstone (who was then Lord Clerk-Register and well placed in Government circles in London) wrote on 13 January 1705:

> I have had suspicions, but now I am certain, that Duke Hamilton is tampering by the means of Harley with the Lord Treasurer . . . . He must have his debts payed.[78]

There is confirmation of this from another source. Robert Harley, along with the Duke of Marlborough and the Earl of Godolphin, was a key minister in the English Government in the early years of Queen Anne. He became Northern Secretary of State in 1704 and built up a secret service. Among his agents were the William Greg, quoted frequently in this chapter, and Daniel Defoe, the novelist and pamphleteer, who was sent to Edinburgh to influence the debate on the Union in 1706. Another seems to have been Col. James Graham (He lived in Westmoreland and was the brother of Lord Preston and the intimate friend of Lord Sunderland. Both of these men were prominent Jacobites, a connection which probably brought him into contact with Hamilton.) Graham reported to Harley about a conversation with Hamilton in Preston on 30 March 1705. Hamilton had said that he desired the Treaty 'as much as any man in either Kingdom and will to his power promote it.' He wanted 'to demonstrate his service and inclinations for the Queen's services and to give undeniable proof of it . . . . He doth desire that from my Lord (Godolphin) or you he may be fully instructed to what point his skill or service may be required, and may be plainly informed without reserve how he may be most useful.' Graham goes on to say that Hamilton is in England, to see about an estate in Staffordshire which has fallen to him, and to suggest that Harley should take advantage of this opportunity to meet him.[79] We do not know if this meeting took place. We can judge only by Hamilton's conduct in Parliament. A letter has, however, survived which suggests that he was fully conscious of the effects of his behaviour. He wrote from Holyrood to Graham on 11 September, a few days after his *volte-face*: 'Our Parliament is now drawing to a close. I have done her Majesty signal service in it'.[80]

On 6 October, Hamilton wrote again to Graham, this time from Kiniell Castle:

> As deeds surpass words, so do my actions. You know best what you said to me, and what authority you had for it. If the consequences should be the re-establishing of my adversaries, you should think yourself and me not justly dealt with. I have done my part, and I hope that I have hurt neither my country nor my friends, though I have angered some of them. I have ever wished for a good understanding between the two Kingdoms, and, if my advice had been listened to, these difficulties would not be what they are.[81]

There is clearly a suggestion here that Graham had acted as an intermediary in arranging some sort of deal between Hamilton and the English ministers.

We do not know what instructions Hamilton may have received from Godolphin or Harley. Even without any, he knew what their policy objectives were and the way to earn favour and reward was to help to achieve them. The more unexpected, spectacular or decisive the method, the stronger claim an appropriate reward and, as we know from many sources, Hamilton was desperate for money. Either Hamilton himself or his manipulators in London had evidently decided that he could be most effective not by an open change of front, but by continuing to pretend to lead the opposition and working for opportunities to sabotage and undermine it. The emptying and exhausted House on the evening of 1 September was such an opportunity which he exploited with skill and determination. This tactic was so secret, as it obviously had to be, that not even the Scottish Officers of State seem to have known about it in advance. Any deal that Hamilton may have made, he made directly with London.

The real mystery is why the Cavalier Party and the opposition generally did not see through Hamilton after 1 September and then repudiate his leadership. If his anxiety to sell himself for money was so widely known to the Squadrone men around Roxburgh, as is evident from their letters, and to such a back bench member as Clerk of Penicuik, is it possible that hints of it never reached the ears of his own supporters? Lockhart in his *Memoirs* makes his disapproval and dismay over Hamilton's conduct very plain, but he never suggests that his motive was money. No doubt he was reluctant to believe that of his leader whom he respected and admired. There is no record either that Fletcher ever made any such comment, although his quarrel with Hamilton (mentioned in the last chapter) suggests that he had reasons for distrusting and disliking him.

The fact was that Hamilton's standing, prestige and abilities were such that the opposition could not afford to reject him, even when they were dismayed by his behaviour. For most of the time, he gave every impression of being a very effective Party leader. Even his opponents recognised that. Clerk, for instance, said in his *Memoirs*: 'The Duke of Hamilton was the head of the Jacobites, and indeed, a man every way fitted to be the Head of a popular discontented Party. He was a man of courage, and had a great deal of natural Eloquence, with much affability in his temper.'[82] Lockhart worked closely with Hamilton as one of his chief supporters in Parliament. He uses almost the same phrase as Clerk, 'Never was a man so well qualified to be the head of a party', and speaks too of his courage, of his 'clear, ready and penetrating conception'. He could not be surprised because he always had his wits about him. Although he was cautious about entering into a new design, once he had taken it up, 'nothing could either daunt or divert his zeal and forwardness.'[83] Modern historians have suggested that Hamilton's conduct is to be explained by lack of resolution, because he was torn between his political convictions and his desire to protect both his claim to the Scottish throne and to the estates in England which he had acquired by marriage. The evidence of his contemporaries seems to suggest that Hamilton was not vacillating or indecisive, but was precisely the sort of man who had the nerve and skill to follow the course of action that would serve his interests, even if it meant an elaborate deception and the abandonment of his party, his principles and the national interest.

After the dramatic events of 1 September, the Parliamentary session continued for another three weeks. On 4 September the House resumed the question of the English Aliens Act. Fletcher presented the draft of an Address to the Queen and an Overture of an Act was also tabled to the effect that the Commissioners would not enter into a Treaty until the offending clause of the English Act had been repealed. It was decided by vote to proceed by way of an Order and an Address and not by an Act and Address. The two former were then approved unanimously. The order simply stated that the Commissioners would not begin the treaty until this condition had been met and the Address explained the point to the Queen. It is not clear whether the Address as approved was the same as Fletcher's draft. It is a dignified, but firm, statement of the impossibility of undertaking negotiations with England while the offending clause of the Aliens Act remained in force.[84]

There were further indications at the next meeting on 5 September that Parliament had not been completely demoralised by Hamilton's *volte-face*. Two overtures for Acts were presented. One, moved by Fletcher, proposed that all imports from England should be prohibited. The other, an Act for sending Ambassadors to foreign treaties, was proposed by Marischal and given its first reading. This was concerned with a long standing abuse which Fletcher had addressed in his published writings. Since 1603 Scotland had been involved in English foreign policy by virtue of sharing the same monarch. It had contributed men and money to the prosecution of the wars in which England engaged. On the other hand, Scotland was not consulted in making of foreign policy and was not included in the negotiation of peace treaties, which took no account of Scottish interests. The new Overture proposed to remedy this by insisting on Scottish participation in future foreign negotiations. It was a move which was in line with the sixth of Fletcher's limitations (that Parliamentary approval should be required for the making of peace or war and in the conclusion of treaties). The discussion on the proposal spread over three days on each of which Fletcher spoke. He had the satisfaction, says Greg, 'of railing at the courtiers, in a long winded harangue made for that purpose'. The act, now described with more precision as one for 'Ministers for Scotland to be present at foreign treaties wherin the Kingdom may be concerned', was approved on 11 September.[85]

Most of the rest of the session was taken up with private business. The proposal for a ban on imports from England was referred to the new Council of Trade and six months supply was at last approved on 8 September. On the twenty-first Argyll touched with the sceptre, to indicate royal assent, the Acts on a Treaty with England, on the Council of Trade, Supply and four of the economic measures. The Acts of limitations, that is on the appointment of Officers of State, triennial Parliaments and Scottish representation in foreign negotiations, were all ignored and Parliament was then promptly adjourned.[86] The Court, having given assent to the measures which suited its purposes and ignoring those which asserted Scottish independence, had now stifled further discussion by the adjournment. Again, there is no record of Fletcher's reaction, but it is not difficult to imagine.

In writing to Godolphin on 21 September, Seafield said: 'Seing her Majesty hath the nomination of the treatters for both Kingdomes, much depends upon this, and I am very hopefull that the English will make a right use of this opportunity, and that your Lordship, under her Majesty, will have the honour to establish what hath been so much desyred and difficult to obtain'.[87] He did not exaggerate the difficulties. It had taken the Court three years of parliamentary time to secure a vote which gave them an opportunity to remove the risk, from their point of view, of Scotland escaping from the control which had been imposed on it by the settlement of 1603.

13

The Negotiation of the Treaty of Union. 1706

'You see that what we are to treat of is not in our choice, and that we see the inconvenience of treating an incorporating union only.'
— Earl of Mar to William Carstares, 9 March 1706

As Seafield remarked at the end of the 1705 session of the Scottish Parliament, the English now had an opportunity to achieve 'what hath been so much desyred and difficult to obtain', that is some secure means of keeping Scotland under the control of the Court in London. Both Parliaments had now agreed to the appointment by the Queen of the commissioners for a negotiation. She and her advisors were now in a strong position because they could appoint to both sides men who could be relied upon to support their objectives. In the end, they would have to come up with proposals that both Parliaments could be induced to accept and no one supposed that would be easy. Even the Scots who were most committed to the policy of the Court were in favour of a cautious and gradual approach. Stair told Mar that 'great mischiefs' might follow if the Queen died before the Succession was settled. He therefore thought an attempt should be made to secure free trade in exchange for acceptance of the English Succession before moving to an incorporating Union at a later stage.[1] William Carstares was afraid that the 'urgeing of an incorporating Union now will furnish pretexts to delay the setling of of the sucession upon which the quiet of our countrey seems very much to depend'.[2]

The first obstacle was the prior condition advocated by Fletcher and firmly asserted by the Scottish Parliament, the withdrawal of the objectionable clauses in the English Aliens Act. This depended on party political manoeuvering within both Houses of the English parliament and on delicate calculation of party advantage. As a modern English historian P. W. J. Riley has put it, the politicians 'were not negotiating union for the sake of posterity, they were concerned with the political balance at Westminster in the immediate future'.[3]

A newly-elected English Parliament met for the first time on 28 October 1705. It had a Whig majority which might have seemed favourable to the proposals for Union. The Whigs had been in favour of a Union during the reign of William when they had been closely involved with the Court. When they lost this position on the accession of Anne, they had turned against the idea and suspected that it was only likely to strengthen the Court to their own disadvantage. On the other hand, the Tories had an instinctive aversion to the whole idea of Union. 'They saw no advantage to be gained by it and found the prospect of closer connection with a presbyterian kingdom repugnant.'[4] It was common ground between the parties that they had no intention at all of allowing Scotland to recover effective independence. 'The English would not tolerate an independent Scotland', as Riley says.[5]

In view of the complexities of the calculation, both Houses delayed consideration of the issue until the end of the session. Since the Aliens Act had been a Whig measure, the Tories thought that they could safely aim at earning some credit with the Court by proposing the repeal. They were surprised, Bishop Burnet tell us, when the Whigs agreed and the repeal of the offensive clauses passed both the Commons and the Lords by 20 December.[6] It seems that the Whigs had decided that their interests would best be served by going along with the negotiation and using their majority to play a dominant part in the English negotiating team. Since the English Whig *Junta* had close association with Queensberry and he was likely to dominate the Scottish side, they presumably calculated that in the long run Union could be made to strengthen the Whig position. Lord Somers, who had played a leading part in obtaining the Aliens Act, was now active in its repeal and was afterwards a key figure in the negotiations.

Burnet adds that the repeal of the aggressive clauses of the Aliens Act removed the fear of a war against Scotland. 'All the northern parts of England, which had been disturbed for some years, with apprehensions of a war with Scotland, that would certainly be mischievious to them, whatsoever the end of it might prove, were much delighted with the prospect of peace and Union with their neighbours.'[7] Similar apprehensions had been expressed by Roxburgh in a letter of 26 December 1704: 'I am thoroughly convinc'd that if we do not go into the Sucession, or an Union, very soon, Conquest will certainly be, upon the first Peace.'[8] By the last phrase he meant, of course, that as soon as the English armies were free from Continental engagements, they would turn their attention to Scotland.

The way was therefore now clear for the Queen to appoint the two Commissions, each of 31 members. The Scottish one was appointed on 27 February 1706 and the English on 10 April. Argyll, whose handling of the 1705 Scottish Parliament had done great service to the Court, did not join the Commission. Either he had decided that he preferred to pursue his military career in Flanders with Marlborough or he was offended by the omission of Hamilton to whom he had promised a place. His family interest was represented by his brother, Lord Archibald Campbell, and some other adherents. The Squadrone was excluded. With one notable exception, George Lockhart of Carnwath, the Commission was mainly composed of Queensberry and his adherents. They included some younger men on whom he could rely, like John Clerk of Penicuik, or had bought, like William Seton of Pitmedden. Others, like the Earl of Sutherland, lost no time in asking for a reward for their services. He wrote at once to Mar to ask for a post in the Treasury.[9] As a 19th century historian, James MacKinnon, expressed it, 'The chief end of the nomination was not to elicit the mind of Scotland on a most momentous question, but to secure a parliamentary majority to the inevitable surrender to the English demand for incorporation, alias "an entire Union" '.[10]

The English Commission, which unlike the Scottish did not require to be chosen from an unrepresentative minority, was an impressive gathering of the Establishment. It included, apart from other members of both Houses, The Archbishops of Canterbury and York, the Keeper of the Great Seal, the Lord Treasurer, five Dukes, two Secretaries of State, the Chancellor of the Exchequer, the Speaker of the House of Commons, the Attorney-General, the Solicitor-General, the Advocate-General and two Lord Chief Justices.

Lockhart tells us that he was surprised to find himself included in the Scottish Commission. He assumed that it was because he was the nephew of Lord Wharton, an influential English Whig and a member of the English Commission, and they hoped by this appointment 'to carry him off.' That this was indeed the intention has some confirmation in a letter which Sir David Nairne, Deputy-Secretary in London for Scottish affairs, wrote to Mar on 7 Oct 1706: 'I told my Lord Wharton that we were not very sure of his nephue. He told me that he promised to be for the Union'. Mar knew better. He wrote to Nairne on 7 October: 'Mr. Lockhart still keeps companie with the opposeing partie, and I am assured by most people that he's to be against us.'[11] Lockhart intended at first to refuse a service so contrary to his own inclinations but consulted Fletcher, Hamilton and others of his political associates. They advised him to join the Commission, keep quiet and listen so that 'he might make discoveries of their designs, and thereby do a singular service to his country'.[12] This was no doubt helpful to the opposition, since the intention of the Commission was to keep their proceedings and the draft Treaty secret until the Parliamentary debate began.

Another member of the Scottish Commission who has left an account of his involvement is John Clerk of Penicuik, a member of the Scottish Parliament and then a young protégé of the Duke of Queensberry. This is in his *Memoirs* which did not appear in print until they were published by the Scottish History Society in 1892. He was a reluctant recruit because he knew that the idea of Union was highly unpopular in Scotland and he thought it unlikely to succeed:

> This choise, however honourable to me, was very far from giving me the least pleasure or satisfaction, for I had observed a great backwardness in the Parliament of Scotland for an union with England of any kind whatsoever, and therefor doubted not but, after a great deal of expense in attending a Treaty in England, I should be obliდged to return with the uneasy reflexion of having either done nothing, or nothing to the purpose, as had been the case of former Commissioners appointed for this end. I was, in short, upon the point of refusing the Honour conferred upon me, and the rather that my Father, whom I always considered as an Oracle seldom mistaken, seemed not to approve of it. However, as at last he grew passive, and that the Duke of Queensberry threatned to withdraw all friendship for me, I suffered my self to be prevailed upon, and to take journey for London with other Commissioners, and arrived there on the 13 of Aprile 1706.[13]

Clark's reference to an Union 'of any kind whatsoever' is another indication of the fact that the Scots at least saw the term 'Union' as embracing a wide range of possible agreements between the two countries. At one end of the scale was what the English called an 'entire and complete' and the Scots an 'incorporating' union. That is a term which had a reasonably precise meaning. It meant the sort of arrangement which was in fact negotiated in 1706 and approved by the two parliaments in 1707. It was incorporating in the sense that formally the two Parliaments would cease to exist separately and would be incorporated into one Parliament of Great Britain. Since the Scottish members would form only a very small minority in the new Parliament, the Scots were well aware that in practice the English Parliament would continue as before, apart from the addition of a few Scottish members, but that the Scottish Parliament would cease altogether.

The term which the Scots of the time used to describe the other possibilities, a 'federal' union, had no such precision. Once again, we have to take account of the gradual change in the meaning of the words. Just as 'treaty' in the early 18th Century usually meant negotiation and 'union' was a vague term meaning any form of agreement or concord, so 'federal', according to the O.E.D., meant 'of or pertaining to a covenant, compact or treaty'. It was simply the adjective derived from the Latin 'foedus', meaning treaty, agreement, alliance or promise. The Dictionary describes this meaning as now obsolete, but it cites examples of its use in this sense from 1660 to 1825.

The modern meaning of the word is defined by the O.E.D. as 'of or pertaining to, or of the nature of, that form of government in which two or more states constitute a political unity while remaining more or less independent with regard to their internal affairs'. The Dictionary adds, 'This sense arises from the contextual meaning of phrases like *federal union*, in which the adjective was originally used in sense a.' (That is the original meaning as I described it in the previous paragraph). The first example of the new usage cited by the Dictionary was in fact in the Scottish Parliament in 1707 when Seton used it when he spoke of Sweden and Denmark as 'united by federal compact' under the same King.

Apart from the Scandinavian example, the negotiators of 1706 might also have in mind the examples of Switzerland and the United Provinces of Holland. In fact, it has been suggested that Marlborough's difficulties with a conflict of authorities there was one reason why the English were opposed to what we should now call federalism.[14] Burnet refers to such examples: 'The Scotch had got among them the notion of a federal union, like that of the United Provinces, or of the cantons in Switzerland: but the English resolved to lose no time in the examining or discussing of that project, for this reason, besides many others, that as long as the two nations had two different parliaments, they could break that Union whenever they pleased; for each nation would follow their own parliament.'[15]

That the Scots, or some of them had given some thought to the implications of federalism of this kind appears from another passage in Clark's *Memoirs*:

The first grand point debated by the Commissioners for Scotland amongst themselves was whether they should propose to the English a Federal union between the two nations, or an Incorporating union. The first was most favoured by the people of Scotland, but all the Scots Commissioners, to a Man, considered it rediculous and impracticable, for that in all the Federal unions there behoved to be a supreme power lodged some where, and wherever this was lodged it hencefurth became the States General, or, in our way of speaking, the Parliament of Great Britain, under the same royal power and authority as the two nations are at present. And in things of the greatest consequence to the two nations, as in Councils relating to peace and war and subsidies, it was impossible that the Representatives or their suffrages in both nations cou'd be equal, but must be regulated in proportion to the power and richess of the several publick burdens or Taxations that cou'd affect them; in a word, the Scots Commissioners saw that no Union cou'd subsist between the two nations but an incorporating perpetual one. But after all the truble we gave ourselves to please the people of Scotland, we knew at the time that it was but losing our labour, for the English Commissioners were positively resolved to treat on no kind of union with us but what was to be incorporating and perpetual.[16]

Although this passage can be read in more than one way, it might mean that the Scottish commissioners had considered something on the lines of a modern Federation. In fact, it is unlikely that many people in 1706 had any such precise constitutional arrangement in mind when they used the word 'federal'. It was then as vague as the word 'Union' also was, which is why 'union' had to be qualified by some such adjective as 'incorporating' to make the intention clear. By 'federal union' the Scots of the time (as will appear from the conduct of the first stage of the negotiations) meant no more than a treaty arrangement for co-operation between the two countries, each of which would remain separate with its own Parliament.

In fact, this idea of federation, amounting to no more than a treaty relationship or alliance, was defined by James Hodges in his book, *The Rights and Interests of the Two British Monarchies* (1703): 'A Confederate or federal union is that, whereby Distinct, Free and Independent Kingdoms, Dominions or States, do unite their separate interests into one common interest, for the mutual benefit of both, so far as relates to certain Conditions and Articles agreed upon betwixt them, retaining in the mean time their several Independencies, National Distinctions and the different Laws, Customs and Governments of each . . . Concerning which, we are to consider, that the word Union in this Federal Sense, is a general Term of very large comprehension.'[17] It was to this James Hodges that the Scottish Parliament awarded a grant of 4800 pounds Scots on 10 August 1705 in recognition of his writings.[18] We know also that Fletcher approved of the book and thought its arguments against an incorporating Union were unanswerable.[19]

As we have seen in the last chapter, the issue between the two possibilities, incorporation or treaty between two continuing states, arose over the amendment proposed by Hamilton on 31 August 1705: 'That the Union to be treated on should no ways derogate from any fundamental laws, ancient privileges, offices, rights, liberties and dignities of this Nation.' This was incompatible, and was deliberately intended to be, with any notion of incorporation. It was for this reason that the Government exerted itself to defeat it. They were able to do so, but only by 2 votes, after Seafield and his friends displayed a large number of ingenious, but rather desperate, arguments.[20]

As Clark says, the English were determined to insist on incorporation. They made this plain even before the two Commissions were appointed. Mar, who had busied himself lobbying in London after the end of the Scottish Parliamentary session of 1705, reported to Cromartie on 28 November: 'I find here that no Union but an incorporating relishes. I know your Lordship has long thought that the best. I wish you could perswade others of it too.'[21] Cromartie is in fact one of the very few Scots that we know had advocated an 'entire' Union. We know of two others, Roseberry and Stair.[22] All three were appointed to the Scottish Commission. On 9 March 1706 Mar replied to Carstares, who was worried that insistence on an incorporating Union might delay the settling of Succession: 'They (the English) think all the notions about foederal unions and forms a mere jest and chimera. I write this freely to you, though it is not fit this should be known in Scotland, for fear of discouraging people, and making them despair of the treaty. You see what we are to treat of is not in our choice, and that we see the inconveniences of treating an incorporating union only.'[23]

The first meeting of the two Commissions was held, in the Council Chamber of the Cockpit in Whitehall, on 16 April 1706. It was purely formal, but at the next meeting, on 22 April, the English wasted no time in making clear their demands. (The official minutes which are admirably brief and lucid are printed as an appendix to Vol XI of the Acts of the Parliament of Scotland). They made some procedural proposals, in line with the practice in the abortive negotiations of 1702–3. All proposals were to be in writing; no agreed point would be binding until all matters had been adjusted; the proceedings were to be kept secret during the negotiations. There followed a proposal of substance, which in fact embraced the whole matter:–

> That the two Kingdoms of England and Scotland be for ever United into one Kingdom by the name of Great Britain. That the United Kingdom of Great Britain be represented by one and the same Parliament.

They also proposed that the English Act of Succession would apply to the United Kingdom.[24]

On 24 April the Scots countered with a radically different proposal of four points:–
1. Succession according to the English Act.
2. Reciprocal exchange of rights and privileges between the two Kingdoms.
3. "Free exchange and Intercourse of Trade and Navigation between the two Kingdoms and Plantations."

4. All Laws and Statutes in either Kingdom contrary to these terms of Union to be repealed.[25]

There was no reference to uniting into one Kingdom or to the incorporation of the two Parliaments into one. In other words, even if this proposal was described as one of federal union, what it in fact meant was the confirmation of the 1603 *status quo*, two separate countries with separate Parliaments but with the same monarchy. The Scots were offering to accept the same Hanoverian Succession as England in exchange for free trade and the repeal of English discriminatory legislation such as the Navigation Act.

Even this Scottish offer was a substantial concession. For three years the Scottish Parliament had resisted the strenuous efforts of the Court to induce them to accept the same Succession as England. They had resisted because, as Fletcher had so often argued, the same Monarch meant in effect that English ministers had control over the Scottish executive. For the same reason, the Court regarded Scottish acceptance of the Succession as their main objective in Scotland. Queen Anne, like her predecessors on the throne, had a fondness for the idea of closer union, but it had generally been opposed by English ministers and English Parliaments.

This had changed by 1706. In the letter which Mar sent to Carstares from London on 9 March, he reported that the arguments in favour of pressing for Succession in preference to an entire Union now carried very little weight with the English. 'They tell us plainly, they will give us no terms that are considerable for going into succession, if any, without going into an entire union.'[26] What was the reason for this change of attitude? Probably it was the very success of the Scottish Parliaments in 1703, 1704 and 1705 in demonstrating that it was an instrument which could assert an independent Scottish policy and reject English control. This was the purpose of Fletcher's Limitations and successive Acts of the Scottish Parliament had moved steadily towards their realisation. In 1705 Hamilton's *volte face* had given the Court a victory over the nominations of the Scottish Commissioners; but in the same session Parliament had passed Acts for the appointment of Officers of State by Parliament, triennial Parliaments and Scottish representation in foreign negotiations, all measures very much in line with the spirit of the Limitations. The actions of the Scottish Parliament had persuaded both English Houses that Scotland could escape from its harmless impotence if they did not take drastic measures to assert control. They were in a stronger position to do so because the success of Marlborough's armies in Europe had increased English self-confidence and power. Also, since the sitting Scottish Parliament was now more than three years old, the Court had had plenty of time to win over members by the arts of 'management'.

To return to the negotiations in the Council Chamber of the Cockpit on 24 April. When the Scottish Commissioners had presented their four points, the English withdrew and then returned to reply:

(They) are so fully convinced that nothing but an entire Union of the two Kingdoms will settle perfect and lasting friendship between them, and they therefore think fit to decline entering into any further consideration of the Proposal now made by the Lords Commissioners of Scotland, as not tending to that end.

Having thus refused even to discuss the Scottish proposal, they asked for a reply to their own.[27]

The Scottish response, at the next meeting on 25 April, was to abandon any attempt to defend their own proposal and to accept the English one. They did enter the proviso that there should be 'full freedom and intercourse of trade and navigation and communication of priviledges and advantages.' The English assured them that this would be a 'necessary consequence of an entire union.'[28]

This immediate collapse of the Scottish position was to be expected from a group of negotiators hand-picked as supporters of the Court, with the single exception of Lockhart. As the passage from Clerk's *Memoirs*, which I quoted above, shows, the Scottish Commissioners had decided in advance that the so-called 'federal' approach was 'ridiculous and impracticable' and that the only Union which could survive was one that was 'incorporating and perpetual'. Incorporation would be perpetual because the Scots would have surrendered any means of establishing and asserting an independent point of view. The Scottish Commissioners had made a gesture by opening with a proposal which would have preserved the Scottish Parliament because they knew that it 'was most favoured by the people of Scotland'; but it was no more than a gesture and an excuse with which they could later use to justify their surrender. They wanted to be able to argue that they had at least tried.

Lockhart was, of course, present, but he 'had orders from his friends to sit silent and make his observations'. His account agrees substantially with that of Clerk and of the official minutes. (In fact it is striking how often Lockhart's version of events is confirmed by the other evidence). He does, however, add another point. Seafield, as the Scottish spokesman, was asked by his colleagues to introduce the Scottish proposal with an apologetic little speech which gave the argument away before it started. 'By making this proposal, they did not reject the other proposal (of an entire Union) made by your Lordships, but are of opinion this scheme would be most effectuall to facilitate the English Succession's being establish'd in Scotland'. Making the proposal in such a manner was, Lockhart says, 'a bare-faced indignity and affront to the Scots nation and Parliament.' He adds that the Scottish commissioners were 'so sensible of the meaness' of their statement, and of the effect it would make if it became known, that they took care to exclude it from the minutes.[29]

Lockhart has his own explanation of the reason why Queensberry and his followers supported an incorporating Union. 'It was this kind of Union', he says, 'England designed and desired; because it rivetted the Scots in perpetual slavery, depriving them of any legal method to redress themselves of the injuries they might receive from them, by keeping them poor and under their chains. On the other hand, the Duke of Queensberry, Earl of Stair, and all that were throughly on a Revolution foot, were inclined the same way, because they were conscious of their own guilt, and afraid, some time or other, a Scots Parliament (if reserved even under a federal Union) might take them to task, and punish them as they deserv'd; whereas if it were out of their power, and the Scots representation stifled and suppressed by the much greater majority of the English representation in one and the same Parliament, they expected to be protected against the just resentment of a injured and exasperated nation'.[30]

After the Scottish acceptance of 'one and the same Parliament', the rest of the negotiation was concerned mainly with details of taxation and the size of the Scottish representation in the new joint Parliament. There was no discussion of the English representation, because it was assumed, curiously enough, that the new Parliament would simply consist of the English Parliament continuing with no change except the addition of some Scottish members. As William Ferguson has remarked, the further proceedings of the negotiators resolve themselves into matters, which, as the English Commissioners had said of free trade, were necessary corollaries of an incorporating Union, or were inducements to ease the acceptance of the proposals by both Parliaments.[31]

On 29 April, the next meeting after the Scottish abrupt acceptance of incorporation, the English made another sweeping proposal, although it fell into the category of necessary corollary. They proposed the application throughout the new United Kingdom of the 'same Customs, Excises, and all other taxes, and the same Prohibitions, Restrictions and Regulations of Trade'. It was agreed to set up a committee of eleven members from each side to consider these matters and draw up accounts of revenues and debts for both countries. The point here was that England had much greater revenues, but also much greater debt.[32]

The Scots produced a counter proposal on 9 May. In effect they agreed to the English proposal of 29 April about the same taxes and trade regulations but with two modifications. They made no reference to Excise and suggested that an Equivalent should be allowed to compensate Scotland for assuming a proportion of the English debt. Next day, the English noted that the Scottish statement did not refer to Excise and insisted upon their proposal of 29 April, 'without which there cannot be an entire Union'. They did however agree to the idea of an Equivalent. On 13 May the Scots agreed to equality of excise on beer, wine, spirits and some other drinks (which the English chose afterwards to regard as 'all excisable liquors'), but proposed an exception on some other commodities for a limited period. The English replied that they were inclined to assent to this, 'in such cases where it may be done without prejudice to the Trade or Manufactures of England'.[33]

The Scots returned to their proposal for a 'General Exception for Excise and other Burthens' on 17 May, no doubt arguing that the Scottish economy was not strong enough to bear the same levels as the English. On 18 May the English gave them an 'assurance that it cannot be supposed that the Parliament of Great Britain will ever lay any sort of Burthens upon the United Kingdom, but what they shall find of necessity at that time for the preservation and good of the whole, and with due regard to the circumstances and ability of every part of the United Kingdom and to allow of any supposition to the contrary would be to form and set up an unanswerable argument against the Union itself.' With this grandiloquent, if unenforceable, statement, the Scots felt obliged to be content. 'On a basis of that understanding,' they agreed 'not to insist further at present', but to leave the matter to the Parliament of Great Britain.[34]

The Queen came in person to the meeting of 18 May to hear what progress had been made and to 'recommend very earnestly' the bringing of the whole affair to a happy conclusion. The meetings of 23, 24 and 25 May were taken up with the details of the minor exemptions which the English had agreed to accept, including the Salt duty.[35]

It was the turn of the Scots on 29 May to make some sweeping proposals which were afterwards embodied in the Treaty using much of the language of the original proposal. These very far-reaching points were as follows:–

1. All Scots laws would remain in force but would be alterable by the Parliament of Great Britain. Those which concerned public policy and Government might be made the same throughout the United Kingdom; 'but that no alteration be made in the Laws which concern Privat Rights, except for evident utility of subjects within that part of the United Kingdom now called Scotland'. (Once again it is eloquent of the nature of the Union, more a take-over than a merger, that it was not thought necessary to state that the Laws of England would continue in force).

2. The Courts of Session and Justiciary would remain 'in all time coming', but would be subject to such regulations for the better administration of Justice which might be made by the Parliament of Great Britain. The other Scottish Courts would also remain, but would be subject to alteration by Parliament.

3. No legal causes in Scotland would be cognoscible by the English Courts of Chancery, Queen's Bench, Common Pleas 'or any court in Westminster Hall.' No English Court would have power to review or alter the acts or sentences of the Scottish Courts, 'or stop the execution of the same'.

4. A Court of Exchequer would be set up in Scotland (This was a court to deal with fiscal matters).

5. The Scottish Privy Council would continue until the Parliament of Great Britain thought fit to alter it.

6. All heritable offices and jurisdictions would be reserved to their owners.

7. The rights and privileges of the Royal Burghs would remain entire.[36]

In spite of the wide-reaching implications, the English agreed to all of this at the next meeting on 30 May. The minutes record no comment or discussion, but there must have been intense negotiations behind the scenes. These provisions were skilfully contrived sweeteners to appeal to the classes represented in the Scottish parliament, and in the team of negotiators, by safeguarding their vested interests. The guarantees for the continuation of Scottish law and the Scottish courts, in spite of the loss of control over legislation, protected the interests of the lawyers. There was no provision for appeals to the House of Lords (which subsequently became the practice) and the implication of the Scottish proposal was that the Scottish legal system would continue to be self-contained. The last two proposals were blatant appeals to other sections of the membership. The heritable jurisdictions (inherited rights to administer justice) cried out for reform, but they were the property of the lairds and nobility who made up most of the Parliament. The same groups could aspire to membership of the Privy Council. The rights of the Burghs were less objectionable than the jurisdictions, although many of them were restrictive enough; but once again their representatives sat in Parliament. There was also some protection elsewhere in the draft for industries, such as salt, which were under aristocratic ownership. The Scottish negotiators may have disregarded the interests of their country, but they certainly looked after themselves.

On 5 and 7 June the Commissioners again dealt with detailed points about the temporary exemption of Scotland from the duty on salt. The English were prepared to 'consent' that there should be exemption for seven years, but proposed elaborate arrangements to make sure that duty was paid on any salt or salted fish exported to England. The Scots agreed with provisions about avoidance of double duty on imported salt and on an 'Equivalent' after the seven years. The English agreed to these points on 15 June except that the Equivalent on the salt duty would apply only to the proportion of the duty which was applied to the payment of the English debt.[37]

Meanwhile the negotiations were also concerned with another very basic point, the number of Scottish members who would sit in the new Parliament. On 7 June the English being, as they said, 'extremely desirous to come to a speedy conclusion', proposed that Scotland should have 38 members in the House of Commons. The Scots proposed a separate conference (in effect a sub-committee) to consider the question and this was agreed. On 14 June the Scots insisted on a larger number. At the next meeting on 15 June, the English, 'to show their inclinations to remove everything that would of necessity be an obstruction', proposed that Scotland should have 45 members in the Commons and 16 Peers in the Lords.[38]

This proposal meant that Scotland would have 45 seats in a House of Commons of 558 and that all but 16 of the 154 of Scottish Peers would lose their automatic right to sit in Parliament. The ratio of taxable capacity between the two countries was 38 to 1 in England's favour and of population probably about 5 to 1. The English proposal for the Commons amounted to about 12 to 1 as a sort of compromise between these two criteria. If we accept the undemocratic view of the time that property was more important than people, this might not seem ungenerous. Burnet in fact argues that the Scots were very favourably treated because, as he puts it, the Scots with only a fortieth part of the tax burden were granted nearly an eleventh part of the legislature. It meant, of course, that Scotland would not merely be absorbed but overwhelmed in the new Parliament. The bargain was even worse in view of the quite irrational basis of the English representation, including rotten boroughs and the like. If some attempt was made to relate Scottish representation to property and population, English membership remained unchanged. Cornwall alone, with 44 members, would now have nearly as many as the whole of Scotland. Burnet puts the 16 Scottish Peers in perspective by remarking that the Church of England had 26 Bishops in the House of Lords.[39]

On 18 June the Scots accepted the English proposals for both Commons and Lords. They made no further comments about the former but were concerned about the status of Scottish Peers after the Union. (Of the 31 Scottish Commissioners 14 were Lords, an Estate which had on average attendance 67 seats out of the total of 226 in the Scottish Parliament). They accepted the proposal that only 16 of their number would sit in the House of Lords, 'provided all Peers of Scotland after Union be reckon'd and declar'd Peers of Great Britain' and that they enjoy all the immunities and privileges which were enjoyed by Peers of England, and that Scottish Peers would take the same rank and precedence as those of the same order and degree created in the United Kingdom after the Union. There was further discussion of the finer points of this on 19, 21, 2 and 25 June. It was finally confirmed that the English accepted the Scottish understanding that Scottish Peers, apart from the 16, would have all the privileges of peerage except that of sitting in Parliament.[40]

It might seem that this was a fuss about a trivial matter of social vanity. In fact there was a real privilege at issue which was likely to act as a powerful inducement on the Scottish Lords to vote for the Union. Unlike the English Peers, the Scottish Lords did not enjoy immunity from arrest and civil process, including debt, except during the sittings of Parliament. The poverty which made them vulnerable to bribery also made them susceptible to the offer of freedom from the debtors' prison as more than adequate compensation for their loss of the automatic right to sit in Parliament. It is said that before the Union, at the end of each session, the Canongate Jail of Edinburgh was crowded with Scots Lords.[41] From the number of times that the privileges of Peers were discussed and the care which the Scottish negotiators took over the precise definition, it is clear that this was a point which they took very seriously.

Some other matters, of more general effect, if less immediate bearing on the fate of the Treaty in the Scottish Parliament, were quickly dealt with. On 17 June, the English proposed that coin, weights and measures should be standard throughout the United Kingdom and should be those already established in England. They also proposed that laws and statutes in either Kingdom which were contrary or inconsistent with the Union should be null and void. The Scots accepted both of these points on 21 June, with two provisions on the first of them. They proposed that consideration should be given to the losses of private persons through the change of coinage and that the Mint in Edinburgh should continue. At the same time they proposed that the Company of Scotland, Trading to Africa and the Indies (that is the Darien

Company) be continued or, if judged inconvenient for the trade of the rest of the United Kingdom, the private right in it should be purchased from the proprietors. (It was an unfortunate precedent that the Scots should propose the abolition of a Scottish institution, simply on the grounds that the English found it inconvenient).[42]

The English responded to the clear hint about the Company of Scotland and offered some hope of compensation to the private persons over the coinage on 25 June in the context of the Equivalent. They agreed on 1 July that the Mint in Edinburgh should continue.[43] The Equivalent was in fact the main matter which still had to be settled, and it was to be one of the strongest inducements to persuade the members of the Scottish Parliament to accept the Treaty. As we have seen, a committee of eleven members from each side had been appointed on 24 April to look into the implications of common taxation, and on 13 May the English had agreed to an Equivalent to compensate the Scots for, in effect, accepting responsibility for repaying part of the English national debt. The committee, after frequent meetings, had recommended that the Equivalent should be £398,085.10 sh., 'according to the proportion which the present Customs and Excise in Scotland do bear to those upon excisable liquor in England'.[44]

At the meeting on 25 June, the English said that they agreed with this sum. Also on account of the increase in trade and people, which they thought would be the 'happy consequence' of the Union, they proposed that an account should be kept of the duties paid in Scotland so that an Equivalent could be calculated and the portion used towards the payment of the English debt. Commissioners for the administration of the Equivalent were to be appointed by the Queen and it was to be spent in the following way:–
1. On the public debt of Scotland.
2. The English were of the opinion that the Company of Scotland was 'inconsistent with the good of Trade in the United Kingdom' and they 'insist that it ought to be determined.' They proposed therefore that the Equivalent should be used to pay for the capital stock of the company plus interest at 5% per annum. The Company then 'shall be dissolved and shall cease'.
3. The remainder was to be used for compensating private losses on the conversion of the currency and then to encourage fisheries and other manufacturers in Scotland 'as may most conduce to the general good of the United Kingdom.'[45]

The Scottish public debt seems to have consisted mainly of outstanding payments of salaries and allowances to Officers of State and other officials, most of whom were members of Parliament. The shareholders in the Darien Scheme were numerous, but those with substantial holdings were of the classes represented in Parliament. Some members, including the leaders of the Squadrone Volante or New Party, were among the most prominent in the affairs of the Company and had most to gain from the windfall compensation for what had seemed likely to be an absolute loss. The Equivalent in other words, was a direct appeal to the self-interest of the members of the Scottish

Parliament as a means of persuading them to vote in favour of the ratification of the Treaty. It was a curious proposal in that the sophistication of the basis of the calculation was well beyond the capacity of the statistical information then available. Even if we accept the validity of the calculation at its face value, the fundamental assumptions behind it are difficult to justify. The Equivalent itself is said to be compensation to Scotland for accepting part of the responsibility for the English debt. But then it was to be repaid by charging the people of Scotland higher duties on their wines, beer and spirits, the proceeds of which would go to the British Treasury. The Equivalent itself is to be spent not on the generality of consumers of the 'excisable liquors', but mainly on the minority of the population who were represented in Parliament. They would receive payment either of money already due to them from the Treasury or compensation for their shareholding in the Company which had been seriously hampered in its operation by the English government and was now to be abolished at the behest of that same Government.

The Equivalent was simultaneously several things at the same time, creative accounting of a high order of ingenuity. It was compensation for accepting part of the English debt and for the abolition of the Company of Scotland (to say nothing of the loss of the Scottish Parliament), but it was to be repaid by the Scots themselves whenever they bought a drink. Sir Walter Scott wrote of this cynical provision:–

> This large sum of money in fact belonged to the Scottish nation, being the compensation to be paid to them for undertaking to pledge their revenue for a part of the English national debt. So that, in fact, the Parliament of Scotland was bribed with the public money belonging to their own country. In this way, Scotland herself was made to pay the price given to her legislators for the sacrifice of her independence'.[46]

On the day after the English had made their proposals for the Equivalent, 26 June, the Queen once again appeared at a meeting of the Commissioners. She urged a speedy conclusion because the Scots 'cannot without great inconveniency be much longer absent from that Kingdom'.[47]

On 28 June, the Scots agreed to the arrangements proposed for the Equivalent with two 'Additions and Explanations', that the calculations should be entered in the minute book and that the Commissioners for the Equivalent should have power to inspect the books of the Collectors of Revenue. They also made a proposal on quite a different matter, that the crosses of St Andrew and St George should be joined in the flag of the United Kingdom. (This is a curious proposal because James VI had introduced such a flag by proclamation in 1606.[48] Perhaps the Scots were afraid that the English, on the model of weights, measures and currency, might want to adopt the Cross of St George for the whole of United Kingdom). The English proposed that five Commissioners from each side should now be appointed to draft the Treaty and the Scots agreed. On 3 July, the English agreed to the Scottish points about the Equivalent, which was to be payable on ratification of the Treaty by both Parliaments. They also agreed about the flag.[49]

While the drafting of the Treaty was going on, the English raised a number of evidently last minute thoughts on 11 July. They proposed that the Union should take place on 15 May 1707 (apparently assuming that ratification by both Parliaments would be complete by then), that members of the English Houses of Parliament should be members of the British Houses (a point which had so far been taken for granted) and that the Scottish members should take the oath in the form in force in England. The Scots agreed on 13 July apart from some minor points about the oath which the English accepted.[50]

On 16 July the draft of the Treaty was read and on 22 July it was signed and sealed. Next day the Commissioners went to St James Palace to present the Queen with the Treaty which was to take effect 'if your Majesty and the Parliament of both Kingdoms shall think fit to approve and confirm the same'. In his speech on behalf of the English Commissioners the Lord Keeper, William Cooper, referred to the risk of war if the Union did not go through. The 'great and main consequence of the Treaty' was 'the continuation of peace and tranquility in this Island upon a Descent of the Crown, instead of the bloodshed and distraction which would probably follow upon the fatal division of it'. The Lord Chancellor, Seafield, on behalf of the Scottish Commissioners made a similar reference. He spoke of the Treaty as 'necessary for establishing the lasting peace happiness and prosperity of both nations'.[51]

Mar drew some satisfaction from the fact that, although the Scots were on the left in the procession to the Council Chamber, they stood at the Queen's right during the ceremony. Clerk of Penicuik, perhaps equally clinging to a small straw of satisfaction, records that Seafield's speech 'excelled the other' because it was spoken without hesitation, but that the Lord Keeper, 'was miserably mangled in the delivery, and at last he was forced to draw it out of his pocket and read it.'[52]

This whole negotiation was concluded with quite remarkable speed, between 16 April and 22 July, with the actual drafting completed in 18 days. Such despatch over a matter so far-reaching in its consequences was unexpected. Burnet makes the point: 'The Union of the two Kingdoms was a work, of which many had quite despaired, in which number I was one; and those who entertained better hopes, thought it must have run out into a long negotiation for several years: but beyond all men's expectations, it was begun and finished within the compass of one.'[53]

It is true, of course, that it was not a real negotiation since both sides had been selected and appointed by the Court to produce the expected result, and, for the most part, depended on royal patronage for their appointments and much of their income. As we have seen, the Scots conceded at once the essential point of substance, federation or incorporation, or in other words, separate or united Parliaments. After that, they made some show of defending Scottish interests but there were very few concessions. As the English said, free trade was a necessary consequence of an 'entire' union. Apart from a few temporary exceptions, Scottish trade was to carry the same customs and duties as the English although it was much less able to support them. On representation in the House of Commons, the Scots succeeded in raising the original offer only from 38 to 45. The continuation of the Scottish legal system, heritable jurisdictions and the privileges of the Royal Burghs cost the English nothing. Even the major financial inducement of the Equivalent was to be more than repaid by the Scottish acceptance of the English rate of Excise.

These facts, and the speed with which proposals were made and accepted, tend to bear our Lockhart's account of the way in which business was conducted within the Scottish group. The English, he says, 'cannot be blam'd for making the best bargain they could for their own country, when they found the Scots so very complaisant, as to agree to everything that was demanded of them, managing all matters in a private club, so that when the Scots commissioners met amongst themselves, a paper containing an answer to the last demand of the English commissioners was presented by the Chancellor or one of the two Secretaries, which being read, was immediately approved of, was then given in to the general meeting, without being discoursed upon (as matters of such weight and importance did require) and the commissioners allow'd copies or the least time to consider what was contain'd in it; and thus they drove on headlong to a conclusion.' Lockhart adds that the Equivalent was the 'mighty bait, . . . a swingeing bribe to buy off the Scots Members of Parliament from their duty to their country'.[54]

Lockhart's phrase, 'managing all matters in a private club', suggests a small inner group of Commissioners from both sides who negotiated everything in advance of the formal meetings. The speed and ease with which the business was despatched certainly suggest management of this kind. There is some evidence that there was no social contact between the two Commissions apart from their formal meetings. This comes from a letter from James Erskine in Edinburgh to his brother, the Earl of Mar, on 3 August 1706, about 11 days after the signature of the Treaty.

> My Lord Justice Clerk [that is Cockburn of Ormiston who was one of the Scottish Commissioners] arriv'd yesternight. He makes no secret of the Treaty, and says he knows of no engadgment he is under to do it. People talk several odd things of it which they lay in Carnwarth's name. I don't know if he be the author of them; but Kelly tells me he was informed by him that none of the English during the Treaty had one of the Scots so much as to drink a glass of wine with them. People are generally much disatisfy'd still that the terms agreed to are keept secret.[55]

This does not sound very much like the usual social climate of international negotiations. It is possible that a small inner group managed the business in secret, but that the English avoided social exchange with the other Scottish Commissioners. The nature of the affair as something imposed, stage managed and contrived might have made it awkward to have any general conversation about what was going on. In any case, since the Scots at the time spoke quite differently from the way they wrote, members of the two delegations would have difficulty in understanding one another.

It is evident that the stage managers, the Officers of State of both Kingdoms, their Secretaries and officials, conducted it with great skill. Certainly they had behind them the ground work of the earlier abortive negotiations; but, even so, their efficiency is impressive and so is the concision and lucidity of the official minutes. The way in which the package was assembled with the minimum concession or cost on the part of England with the maximum appeal to the self-interest of the members of the Scottish Parliament showed great political skill.

It is easy to see the advantages which England obtained from the Treaty. In the first place, it greatly reduced the possibility of a Jacobite restoration. Scotland could no longer take a separate monarch and ally itself with France or with any other country that might be hostile to England. As Daniel Defoe expressed it picturesquely in his *Review*: "the Union is a mountain thrown on the grave on the late King James and his Roman Posterity, which covers them so deep, as that all their Party will never be able to dig them up again.'[56] The Union secured the northern frontier of England and allowed her to pursue her interests in Europe and beyond without having to look apprehensively over her shoulder. It opened up new sources of men for the forces, of revenue from the customs, and a new market for English trade. To quote Defoe again, from the first of his pamphlets, *At Removing National Prejudices Against A Union with Scotland*: 'It must be allow'd to say, without the least Partiality, that the Advantage is *wholly on England's* side, whose Power is by the Addition of *Scotland* so fortif'd, that it must be her own Fault, if she does not make a different Figure in all the affairs of Europe, to what she ever did before.'[57] (This was, of course, in a pamphlet directed at an English audience and published in London before he came to Edinburgh). The Union was a bloodless annexation of Scotland achieved by England with remarkably little cost, and with her institutions, coinage, weights and measures and all the rest of it continuing as before.

The first article of the Treaty provided for the two Kingdoms of Scotland and England to be united into one Kingdom by the name of Great Britain. Other articles refer to 'that part of the United Kingdom now called England' and similarly to Scotland. It would seem therefore that its intention was to abolish the separate identity of both countries and their Parliaments and to create a new entity, Great Britain, represented by a newly created British Parliament. It has been interpreted in this way by distinguished constitutional lawyers. A. V. Dicey for instance, in *The Law of the Constitution* writes: 'Though the fact is often overlooked, our Parliaments both of England and Scotland did, at the time of the Union, each transfer sovereign power to a new sovereign body, namely, the Parliament of Great Britain'.[58] The practice gave a different impression. The fact that English institutions and the English Parliament continued unchanged, with the addition of some Scottish members and the extension of its authority to include Scotland, suggested simple annexation. The name, England, continued in use, but was now understood to include Scotland as well. The power of England had not been diminished but increased. For Scotland, the matter was very different. Scotland had surrendered the potential to manage her own affairs to a Parliament in which she would have an ineffective minority. It is true that the Treaty preserved the Scottish legal system and the rights of the Burghs. (The Kirk and the Universities were to be the subject of a separate Act). The Union was therefore a great deal less 'entire' than the word suggests. Indeed two constitutional historians, the English A. V. Dicey, and the Scottish R. S. Rait, concluded in their joint study of the effect of the Union, which was written from a strongly unionist point of view, that: 'the supreme glory of the Act, (they mean the Acts ratifying the Treaty) is that while creating the political Unity it kept alive the nationalism both of England and Scotland.'[59] 'Supreme glory' is rather excessive in language, but it is true that the Union did not destroy the two national identities, although it has put that of Scotland under very strong pressure.[60] Under the treaty, Scotland retained many of her institutions, which for the next 150 years or so were more important than Parliament in their effects on the life of the people. Even so, it was a Parliament which increasingly claimed absolute sovereignty to do as it pleased without a written constitution, constitutional court, or machinery to review the Treaty or prevent violations of it. In practice, there was nothing to stop this Parliament setting aside even the guarantees embodied in the Treaty itself.

When he was trying to persuade the Scots to accept the Treaty, Defoe argued that it would be the 'foundation' of the new Parliament of Great Britain and that therefore Parliament could not break it without dissolving itself.[61] Whether Defoe believed this or not, it was not an idea which seems to have given pause to anyone else. Burnet's comment is more to the point, 'where a supreme legislature is once acknowledged, nothing can be unalterable.'[62] The incorporating Union meant that the extended English Parliament could intervene in Scotland, even, if it wished, in the matters which the Treaty had preserved. On the other hand, Scotland was left without any constitutional defence or means of expressing her views. That this implication was very quickly realised in Scotland, and that news of the negotiations reached Edinburgh very quickly (in spite of the intended secrecy) appears from a letter which Robert Wodrow sent on 30 May 1706 to George Serle in London for George Ridpath:

> I have a great many melancholy thoughts of living to see this antient Kingdome made a province, and not only our religiouse and civil liberty lost, but lost irrevocably, and this is the most dismall aspect ane incorporating union has to me, that it putts matters past help. Though many a time we have been over run and our civil and religious rights invaded, yet at the next turn we had them restored some way, as 1572, 1638, 1688. But now, once lost, ever lost.'[63]

In a letter which Robert Burns wrote to Mrs Dunlop on 10 April 1790 he wrote: 'Alas have I often said to myself, what are all the boasted advantages which any country reaps from a certain Union, that can counterbalance the annihilation of her independence, and even her very name'.[64] It is a legitimate question. What persuaded the Scottish Commissioners to accept, and the Scottish Parliament afterwards to ratify, so unequal a bargain?

As we have seen, Lockhart thought that the key figures, like Queensberry and Seafield, were anxious to see the Scottish Parliament suppressed so that it could not call them to account for their actions. Whether or not they were afraid of such a possibility, the fact is that they had built their whole careers on identifying themselves with the court, which meant English, interest. As the editor of Seafield's letters says of him: 'It seems to have been Seafield's maxim from the beginning of his public life to accept the powers that were and, in his own interest, to serve them to the best of his ability: In his letters it is his constant refrain that he considered it his sole duty to give effect to the wishes of the authorities by whose grace he held such offices as he did.'[65] Men like this were unlikely to change course when the English made it plain that they would discuss only an incorporating Union. When it came to ratification by Parliament, the financial inducements aimed at the members themselves had a powerful effect, especially as most of them were chronically poor. Many had invested all that they possessed in the Darien scheme. They thought it had gone for ever, but now here was an opportunity to recover the loss plus interest at 5%.

Were there other motives beyond cynical self interest? Writing from an admittedly Unionist point of view, Hume Brown concludes: 'With the correspondence of the time before us it is difficult to escape the conclusion that the men who were chiefly responsible for carrying the Treaty — Queensberry, Seafield, Argyle, Mar, Roxburgh, Baillie and the rest — were sincerely convinced that Union was the only possible solution of the relations between the two Kingdoms, though its immediate results led certain of them subsequently to believe that they had been mistaken.'[66] This begs the question by the use of the word, 'Union'. There was no real dispute that Union in the sense of a Treaty relationship was desirable; incorporation was another matter. Before the negotiations in 1706 very few Scots expressed themselves even in their private letters (as far as the surviving examples go) in favour of incorporation. There were some exceptions such as Cromartie and Roseberry. Stair and Carstares were in favour, but thought it unwise to press it too soon.[67] Clerk of Penicuik, as we have seen, said that all the Scots Commissioners thought a Federal Union was 'ridiculous and impracticable', but their discussion seems to have been about a more formal arrangement than a treaty of co-operation between two sovereign countries. That is what most Scots of the time understood by union, when the word was not qualified by 'incorporating'. It is also what the Scottish Commissioners formally proposed, if without insistence.

I think, however, that it is fair to say that the correspondence of the time, which is voluminous, articulate and intelligent, does suggest that the men involved were not entirely moved by self-interest, but had thought deeply and were concerned about the fate of Scotland. The evidence does not give any clear or straight forward answer to the question of why such an arrangement was negotiated or ratified. The common modern belief in that it was a bargain in which Scotland bartered her independence for the sake of free access for trade to England and the Plantations. A letter which Roxburgh sent to Baillie of Jerviswood on 28 Nov 1705 is often quoted in support of this view. He said that he thought that a Union would pass in the Scottish Parliament and said why: 'The motives will be, Trade with most, Hanover with some, ease and security with others, together with a general aversion at civill discords, intollerable poverty, and the constant oppression of a bad Ministry, from generation to generation, without the least regard to the good of the country'.[68]

'Trade, with most', but all the evidence is to the contrary. As we shall see, the trading interest, represented mainly by the Burghs, were overwhelmingly against the Treaty precisely because they were convinced that it would ruin Scottish trade. They, in fact, agreed with the case developed by Fletcher in *An Account of a Conversation* or elsewhere. Wealth would be attracted from Scotland to London; trade regulations would suit English interests and not Scottish; 'the Union would certainly destroy even these manufactures we now have' because of the flood of imports from England. Scotland would become like Wales, which after three or four hundred years United with England 'is still the only place in that Kingdom, which had no considerable commerce'.[69] Fletcher and the Burghs were in fact right. The effect of the Treaty for years afterwards was exactly as they had predicted. Defoe as a propagandist for the Union had argued that its effect on trade would be beneficial. When some twenty years later he described the condition of Scotland in *A Tour Thro' the Whole Island of Great Britain* (1727), he admitted that 'this is not the case, but rather the contrary'.[70]

Sir Walter Scott, whose description of the transaction of the Union accords more closely with the evidence than the majority of historians who have written about it, puts the point about the trade very justly:

> The persons who were interested in commerce complained that Scotland was only tantalised by a treaty which held out to the kingdom the prospect of a free trade, when at the same time, it subjected them to all the English burdens and duties, raising the expenses of commerce to a height which Scotland afforded no capital to defray; so that the apprehension became general that the Scottish merchants would lose the separate trade which they now possessed, without obtaining any beneficial share in that of England.[71]

Burnet, who was an enthusiastic supporter of the Union (and as Bishop of Salisbury a member of the House of Lords at the time) has a passage in his *History* which is curiously similar to Roxburgh's letter of 28 November. They may, of course, have discussed these matters. He puts the trade point in rather more cautious language. The failure of the Darien scheme had 'made the trading part of that kingdom see the impossibility of undertaking any great design in trade; and that made them the more readily concur in carrying on the union'. He then goes on, in effect, to explain the point which Roxburgh had made about 'the constant apprehension of a bad Ministry'. As he puts it, 'The wiser men of that nation had observed long, that Scotland lay at the mercy of the ministry, and that every new set of ministers made use of their power to enrich themselves and their creatures at the cost of the public; . . . The poor noblemen and the poor boroughs made a great majority in their Parliament, and were easily to be purchased by the court: so they saw no hopes of a remedy to such a mischief but by an incorporating Union with England.'[72] The mischiefs which Burnet describes are the same as those which Fletcher had constantly denounced from the Parliamentary session of 1703 onwards, and against which he had proposed the Limitations. It is difficult to see how anyone could suppose that the arrangements negotiated in the Treaty were any remedy against them. The Scots would have even less control over their own affairs and as the pamphlet, *United and Separate Parliaments*, (discussed in the next chapter) remarked, 'It is much easier to corrupt 45 Scots at *London*, than it is to corrupt 300 at *Edinburgh*.'[73]

At this point, Burnet also mentions the powerful influence of the financial inducements. Thoughts of accepting the Union 'were much quickened by the prospect of recovering what they had lost in the ill-concerted undertaking of Darien.' He adds that Godolphin, the Lord Treasurer, was particularly anxious to promote the Union because there had been talk of impeaching him for allowing the royal assent to the Scottish Act of Security. The Scottish members of Parliament, 'had learned from England to set a price on their votes, and they expected to be well paid for them: the Lord Treasurer did also bestow himself in this matter with an activity and zeal that seemed not to be in his nature'.[74]

But this carries us no further forward in the search for a compelling motive, apart from personal financial gain, which might have moved the Scottish Commissioners to acquiesce in the Treaty. One possibility might be the security of the Protestant religion which the Hanoverian Succession was intended to safeguard. Many Presbyterians were tempted by this, but they were torn in two directions. The Treaty would mean government by an overwhelmingly English, and therefore Episcopalian, Parliament, with more bishops than Scottish peers in the House of Lords. Precisely the Presbyterians who were most concerned about the security of Protestantism were the most worried that a united Parliament would make a new attempt to impose Episcopalianism on Scotland. On the other hand, Scottish Episcopalians tended to be Jacobites and therefore irreconcilable to the Hanoverian Succession. It was because of the complexities of the religious aspect that the question of church government had been expressly excluded from the Treaty negotiations. A separate Act was introduced at a later stage to guarantee the Church of Scotland; but, in the meantime, the position of the church was not an inducement but an obstacle to the Treaty. As Defoe said in his *History of the Union*, 'the most dangerous rock of difference, on which this Union could split, and which could now render it ineffectual, was that of religion.'[75]

If neither religion nor trade were clear motives for the Scottish acquiescence, there was another, the fear that the alternative was military conquest and the imposition of worse terms by the English. I have already quoted Roxburgh's remark in Dec 1704, 'if we do not go into the Sucession or a Union, very soon, conquest will certainly be, upon the first peace'.[76] In fact, on 17 July 1703, Godolphin in a letter to Seafield had sent a polite but unmistakable threat of the use of military force. He objects to the Scottish Act transferring decisions on peace and war from the crown to Parliament and continues:

> Pray, my Lord, allow mee for argument's sake to suppose the case were now hapned.
> England is now in warr with France. If Scotland were in peace and consequently at liberty to trade with France, would not that immediatly necessitate a warr betwixt England and Scotland also, as has often been the case before the two nations were under the same sovereign. And though perhaps some turbulent spiritts in Scotland may bee desiring to have it soe again, if they please to consult history, they will not find the advantage of those breaches has often been on the side of Scotland. And if they will give themselves leave to consider how much England is increased in wealth and power since those times, perhaps the present conjuncture will not appear more favorable for them, but, on the contrary, rather furnish arguments for enforcing the necessity of a speedy union between the two nations, which is a notion that I am sorry to find has soe little prevalency in the present Parliament of Scotland. And I hope your lordship will not bee offended with mee if I take the freedom to bee of opinion they may possibly be sorry for it too when the opportunity is out of their reach.
> I had not time to write so fully upon this subject by the last pacquett to my Lord Commissioner, and therefore would desire the favour, if you please, that you would communicate this letter to him, and excuse the great freedom of it from, my Lord, your lordship's most humble and obedient servant, Godolphin.[77]

Fletcher, although his temper was explosive and easily ignited, was deeply concerned with the preservation of international peace. We have seen that he proposed in *An Account of a Conversation* a scheme to keep the peace in Europe by a system of small countries 'united together for the common safety', but each 'incapable of conquest'. In one of his speeches in the 1703 Parliament he said, 'No man in this house is more convinced of the great advantage of that peace which both nations enjoy by living under one Prince', a view which was consistent with his wish to see Scotland as one of the independent small countries of which Europe should consist. At the same time, just as he believed that the possession of arms is the distinction between a free man and a slave', so nations required arms to defend their freedom. For this reason, he proposed as the ninth of his Limitations that all men of the nation between 60 and 15 should be armed and a similar provision was included in the Act of Security.[78] It was this threat that Scotland would take measures to reassert her independence and defend it, that provoked the English Parliament to reply by threatening the economic sanctions of the Aliens Act.

The rearming proposal in the Act of Security was necessary because Scotland had become virtually disarmed as a consequence of the Union of the Crowns. Scots were recruited into the English army and navy for service in European wars, but hardly any forces were maintained in Scotland itself. In one of his speeches advocating rearmament, Fletcher said that Scotland must not continue to be unarmed, alone among the nations of the world: 'to continue without arms, is to be directly in the condition of slaves.' . . . 'All acts which can be proposed for the security of this Kingdom are vain and empty propositions, unless they are supported by arms.'[79] As Godolphin said in his letter, England had 'increased in wealth and power' since 1603. The opposite had happened to Scotland and it was therefore more vulnerable than ever to English threats of force.

The pamphleteers of the time discussed the risk that England would resort to force. James Hodges analysed the probable consequences in his book, *War Betwixt the Two British Kingdoms Considered* (1705). He admitted that Scotland was in no position to resist attack because of impoverishment and neglect of military preparations since the Union of the Crowns, but conquest would expose England to the dangers of maintaining a standing army in a hostile country.[80] From the other side, Daniel Defoe reached very similar conclusions. In the first of his essays *At Removing National Prejudices Against a Union* (1706), which was addressed to an English audience, he recognised the change in relative strength brought about by the Union of the Crowns:–

But some say, we are too strong for the *Scots* now, and there is no fear that ever they shall invade our Country any more; for that our Wealth and Strength is so much increased, that we are able to crush them presently, and can always keep the War *out of our own country*; that as we are become more powerful, the *Scots* are become weaker, as we are richer, they are poorer than ever, and therefore the case alters.

But he saw danger for England as well:

If ever this Matter should break out into a War, it will be the most bloody, implacable and cruel, that ever happened between the Nations. The *Scots* are poor, and that may be allow'd beyond what we pretend to; but there are such circumstances attending Scotland, and which render her a Nation which the other powers of *Europe* will so gladly embrace, that we have unforeseen Events to encounter with in such a Breach[81]

Another of his pamphlets, *The Advantages of Scotland, by An Incorporate Union with England* (no date, but evidently 1706) was, as always, anonymous but it professed to be written by a Scot. (Defoe was in the habit of changing his identity and nationality to suit his argument). Here he gave as one of the advantages of the Union that it would secure a lasting peace 'with the Nation in the world most capable of destroying us.'[82]

It was, therefore, I think, not mere rhetoric that the Lord Keeper in presenting the Treaty to the Queen said that its 'great and main consequence' was 'the continuation of peace and tranquility, instead of 'bloodshed and distraction'. The Scottish Commissioners in 1706 were under no illusion. They knew, as is evident from the tone of their letters at the time, that they had either to accept what England was prepared to offer or risk invasion and the imposition of still worse terms. One of them, Sir John Clerk of Penicuik, summed up the matter some years after the event in his *Observations on the Present Circumstances of Scotland* (1730, but not published until 1965):

But here a melancholy scene presented itself, for so long as the Succession to the Croun of Great Britain remain'd unsettled and that Her Majesty Queen Anne was not likely to live long, many in Scotland expected such a scene of misfortunes as had been felt dureing the Civil Wars in the reign of King Charles the First and in the end that the whole country would fall under the Dominion of England by right of conquest. The Union of the tuo Kingdoms was then thought of as the best expedient to preserve the honour and liberties of Scotland and likeways the peace of the whole island, for as the councils of Britain wou'd then be united, the Succession wou'd naturally devolve on one and the same person. This was the principal motive both in Scotland and England for bringing about the Union. There were indeed other reasons which had greater influence with many of this country, such as the prohibition of our black cattle in England, a general mismanagement and decay of trade, want of money to engadge in other projects and an inability for enlarging our trade or improving our manufactories, and (which was worse) a moral certainty that England wou'd never allow us to grou rich and pouerfull in a separat state. It was likeways a very strong motive for some to favour the scheme of Union when they considered what had been more than once complained of in our Parliaments — to wit, that we were in a state of absolute bondage to England, tho' under the appearance of national liberty supported by our oun Parliaments and Privy Councils.[83]

This is an aspect of the matter which has been played down by both sides ever since. It is not flattering to be seen either as a bully or as the weaker party who capitulates. Perhaps for the same reason, or because they were anxious to place the Union in as favourable a light as possible, historians have also tended to disregard it. T. B. Smith in a book published in 1962, however, stated the harsh facts with precision:

The Scottish Commissioners in 1706 were certainly negotiating . . . under the implied threat, if negotiations failed, of invasion by one of the great captains of history at the head of a veteran army, backed by the military resources of one of the most powerful states in Europe.[84]

This view is now becoming more generally accepted than the old rationalisation, or evasion, that the Union was an exchange of independence for trading concessions. Gordon Donaldson, for instance, in 1974:

England was not going to permit a disruption of the existing union, and the scanty and ill-trained Scottish regiments could not have resisted Marlborough's veterans.[85]

P. W. J. Riley, who made a thorough study of the evidence from the English point of view, published in 1978, comes to the same conclusion: 'Contrary to an apparently reasonable hypothesis, trade considerations seem to have exerted no influence worth speaking of . . . The English would not tolerate an independent Scotland.' He sees 'anarchy, civil war and English conquest' as the only alternative to the Union that was then available.[86]

14

United and Separate Parliaments (1706)

*'Their 45 Scots Members may dance around to all Eternity,
in this Trap of their own making'.
— Andrew Fletcher*

We have almost no information about Fletcher's activities during the whole period when the Treaty was under negotiation. None of his letters for the period have survived and there are very few references to him in the letters of others. There is, however a very interesting and relevant pamphlet published at that time which has been attributed to him on very impressive authority. This is *State of the Controversy betwixt United and Separate Parliaments*. It appeared as an anonymous pamphlet in 1706 and was reprinted in the same year. It was not included in the collected *Political Works* of Andrew Fletcher, which were published in several editions in the 18th Century, but the first of them only in 1732, sixteen years after his death. The pamphlet was not reprinted again until Sir John Dalrymple included it as an Appendix to his *Memoirs of Great Britain and Ireland*, published in 1788 with a new edition in 1790. It did not appear in print again until I brought out an edition for the Saltire Society in 1982.

Dalrymple explained that the pamphlet had been brought to his attention by another Andrew Fletcher. (He was the grandson of the Patriot's brother who became a member of the British Parliament and died in 1779):

> The late Mr. Fletcher of the house of commons once put into my hands, as related in common with him to Mr. Fletcher of Salton, whose family he represented, a treatise on the Union of States, which he found among the papers of his ancestor, but not written with his hand, desiring my opinion whether it was his composition. I thought that it was. Afterwards I found a copy of this paper in the advocates library, and on it, in the hand writing of Mr. Thomas Ruddiman, librarian, who was the cotemporary of Mr. Fletcher, and eminent for historical erudition, industry, and accuracy, the following note, "supposed to be written by the Laird of "Salton."[1]

R. A. Scott MacFie in his *Bibliography* also accepts that the pamphlet is Fletcher's. 'The style', he says, 'is more jerky than was usual with Fletcher, but it may have been composed hurriedly. The ideas are in harmony with what he expressed elsewhere.'[2]

The opening paragraph of the pamphlet made it clear that it was written or published between the end of the negotiations (if that is the appropriate word) on 11 July 1706 and the opening of the debate on the Treaty in the Scottish

Parliament on 3 October. It is quite specific about this: the 'Commissioners have concluded a Treaty' and it 'is to be laid before the Parliament of Both Nations'. Although the text had not yet been published and was in theory secret, the writer shows an accurate knowledge of its contents, the Equivalent, the treatment of national debts, the 45 members in the Commons and the 16 Representative peers, and so on. He also knows, and strongly disapproves, that the issue of united or separate Parliaments was taken at the very beginning of the negotiations and that the Scots yielded without an argument. They had done this, 'though its known to every Body, that many of the greatest and wisest Men of this Nation are absolutely against a United Parliament, as a measure most likely to frustrate the Treaty . . . This was not the way of treating with Men at Freedom, and with Commissioners called together by one and the same Authority. This was the only grand point of the whole Treaty; and the anticipating it thus, was yielding the whole Cause.'[3]

The pamphlet is in favour of quite a different concept of Union, a form of good understanding, an alliance, or co-operation between the two countries. Both would keep their own separate parliaments to safeguard their own interests, but would share a Prince to prevent wars between them and provide for common defence. If it is objected that this would mean continuing 'in the same unhappy State' as Scotland has been since the Union of the Crowns, the fact is that there are already laws awaiting the royal assent which would do much towards curbing these evils. All this is very similar to the argument of *An account of a Conversation*, even to the extent of referring to Wales as an example of the ill usage of a dependent territory, remote (but less remote than Scotland) from the seat of government.[4]

The core of the argument was that the loss of the Scottish Parliament would mean the loss of any means of protecting Scottish interests whenever they were different from the English. If it were accepted that the Treaty of the Union could destroy the Scottish Constitution, 'there is an end forever, of all the Security which the Scots can have for any of their reserved Interests . . . It is plainly beyond the power of Men, to make such a provision of Security as may not be undone in an united Parliament.' For this reason, there could be no confidence that the Scottish Presbyterian Church would survive, that the Equivalent would be paid, that the final appeal in law suits would not be carried to the House of Lords in London, or that Scottish trading interests would not be sacrificed to the English.[5] The author of the pamphlet had understood the implications of subordination to a Parliament that was about to evolve the doctrine of parliamentary sovereignty which recognises no limitations to its absolute power.

Not only the general line of argument, but also much of the language, strongly suggests the hand of Fletcher, especially some of the more pungent phrases about the consequences which would follow the loss of the Scottish Parliament. 'The Scots deserve no pity, if they voluntarily surrender their united and separate interests to the Mercy of an united Parliament, where the English have so vast a Majority . . . It is much easier to corrupt 45 Scots at

London, than it is to corrupt 300 at *Edinburgh*; and besides, there will be no occasion of corrupting them, when the Case shall occur of a difference betwixt the South-Britons and the North-Britons; for the Northern will be out-voted, without being corrupted . . . This will be the Issue of that darling Plea, of being one and not two; it will be turned upon the Scots with a Vengeance; and their 45 Scots Members may dance round to all Eternity, in this Trap of their own making.'[6]

All of this sounds like Fletcher, but there are other passages which are contrary to his known views and attitudes. 'I am not for over-loading the Power of the Prince with unusual Limitations, especially during the Administration of so gentle a Government as we live now under at present . . . It's true, in so far as an Act of Parliament is requisite, the Assent of the Crown must be had; but if a Scots Parliament does exert themselves according to their Duty, they have a gracious Queen who will do them Justice.'[7] Unless this is meant as heavy irony, and it does not sound like it, it could not have been written by Fletcher who distrusted hereditary monarchy, who saw the royal power as a cover for English interference in Scottish affairs, had worked tirelessly for Limitations and proposed as the fourth of them 'that the King shall give the sanction to all laws offered by the estates.' It is true, of course, that the pamphlet of 1706 was explicitly written to rally opposition to the Treaty. In the face of a real threat to the very survival of the Scottish Parliament, the refinement of limitations was no longer the immediate issue and there was no point in offending the Queen unnecessarily.

There are some contemporary references which show that Fletcher was believed to be writing about the Union at about this time. The first is a letter in the Jerviswood correspondence written to Roxburgh on 19 April 1706, just as the negotiations in London were beginning: 'I'm told that Salton is writing against the Union, till at least a new Parliament be called, instructed for that effect; and I have grounds to think he has the Advocate's assistance.'[8] (That is the Lord Advocate, Sir James Stuart, who, although a member of the Administration, opposed the Union to the end.)

While the negotiation was still going on, Mar's brother, James Erskine, wrote to him from Edinburgh on 22 June about Fletcher's reaction:

> This town is still very thin. Salton came to it two or three days ago, and is in a great rage against the Union. I supped with him yesternight all alone. After a great deal of talk about it he desire me to read the 3rd section of Mr Hodge's 1st book on that subject, and if it did not convince me how pernicious ane incorporating Union is he would know what to think of me. He does not believe any of you to be cordially for it except the Dallrymples, and for their paines he swears they ought all to be dragged at horse's taills. I fancy he is out in the reckoning he makes of people's inclinations for it. He believes that the nation is generally so averse to it that it will not stand out one sederunt in the Parliament, and that the promoters of it will think themselves happy if they can get it quickly smothered; but that he and those against it will endeavour to bring it in and have it debated that they may oppose it forever . . . He is as angry at the squadrone and at the D(uke) of H(amilton) as

ever . . . Salton told me twice thrice that he was sorry you had to do with such a business as this Union.'⁹

Mar replied to his brother on 18 August: 'I hope Salton and I shall still be on speaking terms tho' not of the same oppinion in this measure of the Union. I have not forgot his case of instruments.'¹⁰ This is a pleasing instance of friendship surviving political difference. Mar had evidently promised to do some shopping for Fletcher in London. I do not know what the instruments were, but I imagine that they were mathematical. Erskine wrote again to Mar on 20 April:

> I had one accidental conversation with Salton lately on the Union. He urged his old argument which he believed invincible that the Parliament could not ratify ane Union unless called expressly for that effect. I pulled out of my pocket the proclamation calling this present Parliament when the ratifying of ane Union is the principall thing it is conveened for. Salton, for as much as one would believe he has thought on that mater, had never as much as dreamed that such a thing was in the proclamation. His answers to it were not very satisfying. He turned angry, and so I said no more, but he concluded in his ordinary strain that it was a damn'd villanous Union and so much the more because those who pretended to carry it on were certainly against it in their minds. I told him that I had seem him once or twice last spring very positive in some such things and afterwards was forc't to own that his intelligence had not been so good. Ay but I'm sure of this, said he. Thus we ended as to the Union and fell a talking of books and buildings of houses.¹¹

Erskine ended his letter by referring to a 'little book' against the Union: 'written (as they say) by Wylie of Hamilton. Salton's argument I just now mentioned and the Covenant is what he principally insists on.' This does not sound like *United and Separate Parliaments*.

These two letters of James Erskine are useful not only for Fletcher's first reaction to the proceedings in Whitehall but as one of the few records that we have of Fletcher's conversational, as opposed to parliamentary, style. He was evidently forceful and passionate but capable of transition to calm and civilised conversation about such things as books and houses. Erskine misunderstood Fletcher's point about the calling of the Parliament. Fletcher's argument, which was put forward by him and others in course of the debate, was that Parliament had no power to make a fundamental change in the constitution if it has not been specifically summoned and elected for that purpose. The document which Erskine produced was presumably the Queen's commission for the 1706 session, which was of a Parliament elected under quite different conditions in 1703.

What then are we to conclude about the authorship of *United and Separate Parliaments* from all this conflicting evidence? John Dalrymple's reasons for accepting it as Fletcher's cannot be lightly set aside, although none of it is conclusive. Nor is the omission of the pamphlet from the *Political Works*; but, as I mentioned in Chapter eight, John Robertson has drawn attention to remarks in Fletcher's catalogue of his library which make it very probable that the *Works* contained everything which he had published up to September 1708. When I wrote an Introduction to *United and Separate Parliaments* in 1982, I said that on the whole we might agree with the later Fletcher, Dalrymple, Rudiman and Scott MacFie that it was indeed by Andrew Fletcher. My doubts are now stronger than they were, not so much because of the evidence from the library catalogue (which was not available in 1982) but from the content of the pamphlet itself. Certainly there are passages which in thought and verbal force sound like the authentic Fletcher, but it is difficult to believe that he could have brought himself to utter the sychophantic references to the Queen. Apart from that, the pamphlet generally does not have the fluency or lucidity of Fletcher's acknowledged works. Taking all these points together, I think that the probability is that *United and Separate Parliaments* was a work of collaboration to which Fletcher contributed some passages. We have seen that there was talk in April 1706 of collaboration between Fletcher and Stuart. Lockhart presumably supplied information about the negotiations. Others such as Ridpath and James Hodges, may have contributed as well. As we have seen from Erskine's letters, and would in any case expect, Fletcher was indignant about the Treaty and full of arguments against it. Even if *United and Separate Parliaments* was partly, or even largely, written by others, there is no doubt that most of it reflected his ideas and his sense of outrage.

15

The Reaction to the Treaty

'No incorporating Union was the word."
— Daniel Defoe

The negotiation (if that is the right word) between two groups of men each hand-picked by the Court for the purpose was comparatively easy. The more difficult stage of the Treaty was still to come, approval by both Parliaments, or more precisely by the Parliament of Scotland where the outcome was highly uncertain. The English Parliament had been opposed to ideas of Union with Scotland in the past, but the draft Treaty offered them the permanent security of their northern border and the subjection of Scotland to England at a very low price. The English Parliament and constitution were to continue virtually unchanged, except for the addition of an insignificant minority of Scottish members. It was quite different in Scotland. The Scottish Parliament was to be asked to vote for its own abolition and, in some ways at least, the absorption of Scotland by England. The Scottish Peers, but not their English equivalents, were to lose their automatic right to a seat in Parliament. Scottish trade was to be exposed to the full pressure of English competition and made to carry the unfamiliar burden of English duties designed to suit English conditions.

Since it was the attitude of the Scottish Parliament which was uncertain, the Court decided to put the draft before them first. This left the last word with the English Parliament and saved them from the possible embarrassment of seeing the Scots reject a document which they had approved. The Scottish Parliament faced with this momentous task still had the same membership as in the three successive sessions of 1703, 1704 and 1705. These were the men who had endorsed so many of the arguments of Andrew Fletcher and had asserted a spirit of Scottish independence by passing the Act of Security in two successive Parliaments. They had resisted all attempts by the Court to induce them to accept the English Succession to the throne. Fletcher knew what he was doing when he made a proposal for the election of a 'new Parliament every year' the first of his Limitations. The longer the same Parliament sat, the more time the Court had to win over support by bribes, promises, appointments and other forms of pressure. This Parliament was now in its fourth year of such a process. Burnet remarks in his *History*: 'The poor noblemen and the poor boroughs made a great majority in their parliament, and were easily to be purchased by the court".[1] In the circumstances, it is remarkable that so many held out for so long.

The surviving correspondence has some eloquent examples of the way in which the process worked. Argyll as Commissioner had shown considerable dexterity in managing the Session of 1705. 'On his return from Scotland he was received with much honour in London and made an English Earl'.[2] He had then returned to Marlborough's army in Flanders. In 1706 the Court swallowed their dislike of Queensberry by recognising that as Commissioner he was the man most likely to succeed in carrying the Union; but they wanted the help of Argyle as well. His reply to a summons from Mar was direct and to the point:

'My Lord, it is surprising to me that my Lord Treasurer, (Godolphin) who is a man of sense, should think of sending me up and down like a footman from one country to another without ever offering me any reward. Thier is indeed a sairtin service due from every subject to his Prince, and that I shall pay the Queen as fathfully as any body can doe; but if her ministers thinks it for her service to imploy me any forder I doe think the proposal should be attended with an offer of a reward.'[3]

Argyll wrote this from the camp at St Louis la Tere on 18 July. By 17 September, Sir David Nairne was able to report to Mar:

'My Lord Treasurer told me this morning that my Lord Malborrow has got now the Duke of Argyle in a very good humor on making him or promising to make him Major-Generall, upon which his Grace has promised to goe to the Parliament and serve the Queen in the affaire of the Union.'

In the same letter, Nairne added that Marlborough 'to please the Earle of Stairs', (another of the Court's leading supporters in the matter of the Union) had made his son a Brigadier.[4] Argyll was not content with his military promotion alone. Mar wrote to Nairne on 13 October:

'He is very desireous to have his brother made a peer of Scotland, and made us all promise to write to the Treasurer of it, which I have done.'[5]

During the whole of the 1706 Session of Parliament, Mar as Secretary of State was very conscientious and thorough in keeping London informed about the debates in Parliament and the situation in Scotland generally. His letters have survived and are an important source, especially for the period of the crucial debate. Before it began, he wrote to Godolphin on 16 September about the prospects, although he thought it was hard to make a reliable conjecture before the Parliament met. He was much concerned about the attitude of the Lord Advocate, Sir James Stuart, the one member of the Administration who remained adamantly opposed to the Union and had become a close associate of Andrew Fletcher. Mar suggested that Godolphin might write a letter to be shown to Stuart to the effect 'that the Queen expects all in her service wou'd act vigorously for the Union, else they can not expect her favour, nor to continue in her service.' This sort of threat was usually effective, since the Queen was the sole source of patronage, but Stuart stuck to his guns and offered to resign his place 'without any grudge'.[6]

In his letter of 16 Sept Mar also said that he had rather better hope of success since he returned to Scotland from London. He thought that opinion against the Union had everywhere abated and that the more the terms were known, the more people would be won over. Either he was speaking only about the narrow circle of Parliamentarians who might be tempted by the Equivalent or he was misled by wishful thinking. All the evidence shows that the movement of opinion was in the opposite direction. The pamphlet, *United or Separate Parliaments*, proves that some knowledge of the terms of the Treaty had leaked; but the Government seems to have been fairly successful in keeping them secret from the public at large until the parliamentary session began on 3 October. An outburst of rage and indignation began as the nature of the Treaty spread from that day onwards, and before long Mar himself was reporting it. Daniel Defoe arrived in Edinburgh early in October as a spy, propagandist and agent for the English Government. His instructions from Robert Harley, Speaker of the House of Commons and Secretary of State, required him to report constantly on the true state of things and do all he could to secure the passage of the Union. He was to take the 'utmost caution that it may not be supposed you are employed by any person in England: but that you came there upon your own business, and out of love to the Country'. In the first of his letters from Edinburgh which has survived, dated 24 October, he spoke of a 'Most Confused scene of affaires' and 'General Aversion to the Union.' There were mobs in the streets that made him fear for his life. A 'Terrible Multitude' with a drum at their head marched down the High Street shouting: 'all Scotland would stand together, No Union, No Union, English Dogs, and the Like.'[7]

When he came to write his *History of the Union*, first published in Edinburgh in 1709, Defoe gave a more detailed account of the state of the public opinion in Scotland. Looking back to the past, he thought that 'never two nations, that had so much affinity in circumstances, have had such inveteracy and aversion to one another in their blood.' Things had reached the point where there must either be Union or there was 'no other way left, to prevent the most bloody war that ever had been between the two nations.' Against this general background, he makes it very plain that the great outburst of indignation followed the publication of the Articles of the Treaty when Parliament assembled. 'Nothing was to be heard now, but of slavery to the English, running away with the Crown, taking away their Nation, and the like.' This feeling drew together 'Parties and peoples whose interests and principles differed as much as light and darkness', Jacobite and Presbyterian, Cameronian and Catholic. 'And such was the clamour against the Treaters, that I verily believe . . . had the articles of the treaty been published before the treaters came home . . . there was not many of them would dared to have gone home, without a guard to protect them.'[8]

The Government had evidently been prudent in delaying the publication of the Articles to the last possible minute. Defoe expresses surprise at what seemed to him a sudden change of mood when the conditions of the Treaty became known. 'Such convulsions as these agitated the whole Kingdom; and it was the unaccountable thing that ever was known, to find a nation, that but a few months before, were earnestly crying out for a Union, and the nearer the better . . . now fly in the face of their masters, and upbraid the gentlemen, who managed it, with selling and betraying their country, and surrendering their constitution, sovereignty and independency to the English.'9

There is no evidence at all that the Nation at large had ever cried out for a Union; but in any case there is the familiar question of what the word meant. As I have already argued, when Fletcher and others spoke about union with approval they meant something very different from the terms of the Treaty of Union, something ranging from a federal arrangement to an agreement to co-operate on certain matters. Defoe should have understood the point, because he goes on to describe the Scottish attitude in words which Fletcher would have readily accepted;-

'And thus now stood the debate, — no incorporating Union was the word: Let us have an Union with England with all our Hearts; but no incorporation; let us keep our Parliament, keep our Sovereignty, keep our independency, keep our constitution; as for all the rest, we are ready to Unite with you, as firmly as you can devise.'

But Defoe also understood that this Scottish position was unacceptable to England: 'It could not be expected, England whose considerations for uniting were peace, strength and shutting a back door of continual War, and confusion from the North' . . . should communicate trade 'and leave the main things yet precarious and uncertain.'10 This implies that the English thought that they were buying the permanent security of their northern border for the price of concessions on trade. Perhaps this view helps to account for the widely accepted belief that the Scots made a deliberate choice in 1707 to barter their independence for trading advantages. The weight of contemporary evidence is opposed to this interpretation. Indeed, one of the most frequent arguments against the Treaty from the trading community itself was precisely the contrary one that the Treaty would be harmful to Scottish trade. As Defoe says, 'the merchants, the burghs, the county people, all cryed out of oppression, and of ruin and destruction in trade.'11

Among the flood of addresses against the Union which poured into Parliament from all over Scotland, the one which made the point about trade with most authority was that from the Convention of Royal Burghs, since they represented the trading interest. They began by making the familiar point that they were not against 'an honourable and sole Union with England, consisting with the being of this Kingdom and Parliament thereof without which we conceive neither our religious nor civil interests and trade, as we now by law enjoy them, can be secur'd to us and our posterity.' They continued, 'far less can we expect to have the condition of the people of Scotland, with relation to these great concerns, made better and improv'd without a Scots Parliament.' On the other hand, the extinction of the Scottish Parliament meant that 'our religion, character, government, claim of right, laws, liberty, trade and all that's dear to us' was in danger of being encroached upon by the English in a British Parliament where the 'mean representation' allowed to Scotland could not secure Scottish interests.

They objected to the imposition of English taxes 'which is a certain insupportable burden' and to the regulation of trade by English laws, 'considering that the most considerable branches of our trade are differing from those of England, and are and may be yet more discourag'd by their laws.'[12]

A recent writer, Brian Levack, has made a very thorough study of the various proposals from 1603 onwards for economic, religious, legal and political union between the two countries. In the earlier part of the period, the Scots, but not the English, showed some interest in an agreement to remove barriers to trade. Apart from the abortive personal initiative of James VI, and the imposed Cromwellian settlement, there was no suggestion of parliamentary Union until after 1668. After that date, Levack points out, 'all English proposals for union, and indeed all formal union projects, made provision for a union of parliaments. It is not coincidental that very few English objections to the union on economic grounds arose after this time. Englishmen would continue to oppose Scottish proposals for a federal union in which there would be a limited communication of trade, for this would have allowed Scotland to secure numerous commercial benefits without assuming any new burdens.'[13]

The English, in other words, were not prepared to relax their discrimination against Scottish trade, such as the Navigation Acts, unless they secured control over Scottish economic policy. As Levack realises, this meant that the Scots now found themselves in a radically different situation from their earlier discussions in which they had envisaged an economic 'union' in the sense of a mutual dismantling of barriers to trade. 'Instead of the reduction of trading barriers by the joint action of two separate parliaments which would retain control of the commercial and economic life of their respective countries, they were now dealing with the proposed assumption of the economic control of their country by a parliament dominated by Englishmen. In the same way that a united British parliament threatened their law and their church, it also threatened their economic independence.'[14] This is, in fact, an understatement. A separate Act was passed to safeguard the Scottish church. The Treaty itself contained some guarantees for the continuation of the Scottish legal system. Apart from some minor and temporary exceptions from duties, there was nothing at all in the Treaty to protect Scottish trade from regulations designed to suit English conditions and to promote English trade. There was therefore nothing unreasonable or surprising in the opposition of the Scottish trading community to the Treaty.

Both Mar and Defoe thought that the Treaty had most to fear from the opposition of the ministers of the Kirk. On 7 November 1706 Mar wrote to Nairne, 'One thing I must say for the Kirk, that if the Union fail it is oueing to them'.[15] Even when the Treaty had been ratified by both Parliaments and was in force, Defoe wrote in a letter of 10 June 1707 about the 'Rigid and Refractory Clergy who are the worst Enemies of the Union.'[16] The Church of Scotland had good reason for their opposition. The Treaty proposed to subject Scotland to the control of a Parliament which was not only overwhelmingly Anglican and Episcopalian, but even had the Bishops sitting in its Upper

House. In England the tradition was for one state church throughout the Kingdom which, since the Reformation, was 'strictly subordinated to the state and served its purposes.'[17] The Kirk had resisted the imposition of such an arrangement during the whole of the 17th Century; the Treaty now seemed to impose a new and more dangerous threat. It was because the Government recognised the force of this feeling that they introduced a special measure of reassurance in a separate Act.

In fact, the Treaty was unwelcome not only to the Kirk, but to virtually all shades of religious and political opinion in Scotland. To the Covenanters, it represented a final betrayal of the covenants. At the other end of the scale, the Episcopalians and Catholics tended to be Jacobites and one of the main aspects of the Treaty would be Scottish acceptance of the Hanoverian Succession. In Parliament from 1703 onwards Jacobites, like Lockhart, had made common cause with the Country Party and the republican, or near-republican, Fletcher. Both the Royalists and the anti-Royalists wanted to preserve the independence of Scotland and therefore agreed in resisting the encroachment of the English Court. As Defoe noticed, a common antipathy to the Union now brought together all shades of belief from Covenanter to Jacobite. All other differences of opinion seem to have been subsumed by the same sort of patriotism or nationalism that first appeared in the Declaration of Arbroath of 1320. The language of the Addresses, which now descended in a flood upon Parliament, expressed the general view:- 'An incorporating Union . . . is contrary to the honour, fundamental laws and constitutions of this Kingdom . . . and destructive to the true interest of the nation.'[18] Like Wodrow,[19] people understood that there would be no easy escape from such a union once accepted. Defoe quotes a letter from the Presbytery of Hamilton to Carstares as Moderator: 'As to the disposition of the people, the plain truth is, that they are generally most averse from the Union; and many have expressed themselves broadly enough against it, as what they fear may prove an irremediable evil, if it should be concluded, wishing that some stop might be put to it.'[20]

The ministers of the Kirk did not necessarily feel this antipathy more strongly than other people; but they were, in Hume Brown's words, 'the most influential body of men in the country.'[21] In the General Assembly they and their lay leaders had a national forum which was far more representative of the people than Parliament itself. Their pulpits in every parish in the country gave them a then unrivalled instrument to express and influence public opinion. In the words of Brian Levack: 'The Kirk had achieved a considerable amount of independence from the State and in the views of some was superior to it . . . The fact that the Scottish Church had served as a major source of national cohesion since the Reformation, filling a role that the weak and subservient Scottish Parliament could not play, made the preservation of the Church an issue of extreme national importance.'[22]

If the outcome had depended on public opinion, the Treaty would have been soundly rejected as soon as its terms were known. As it was, the Government had to win over, after four years of manipulation, a majority from the 220 or so members of Parliament in whose election only a minute proportion of the population had participated. Even so, the Government managers were not entirely confident of success at the beginning of the parliamentary session. Mar wrote to Nairne on 4 October 1706: '. . . by all appearance wee may have good hopes, and very quicklie the faite of the Union will be seen, tho' I cannot yett say that wee are possetivlie shure of succeeding.'[23] Seafield was rather more confident, but clearly thought the 20 or so votes of the *Squadrone Volante* (or New Party) crucial. He wrote to Godolphin on 14 October: 'I have taken al the methods I was capable to use to keep the Neu Pairtie from conjoining with our Torie Pairtie, and the Marques of Montrose has concurred most activlie in this, and I doubt not bot that they will al concur with us, which, I think, will make the cariing the Union certain.'[24]

As the Jerviswood *Correspondence* shows, the *Squadrone* had agonised over their position for months. They had gradually moved towards acceptance of the Union, partly because they entertained the hope that this would help them to return to office. There is a letter from Roxburgh of 28 Nov 1705, which is very frequently quoted, in which he more or less reaches the conclusion that the Treaty would pass in the Scottish Parliament: 'The motives will be, Trade with most, Hanover with some, ease and security with others, together with a general aversion at civill discords, intolerable poverty, and the constant oppression of a bad Ministry, from generation to generation, without the least regard to the good of the country.'[25] In fact, the *Squadrone* were finally persuaded to support the Union by various 'methods'. They were given the impression that they would be given the management of the Equivalent payments to the Darien company. In this they were deceived after the treaty had been safely approved, as Mar told Nairne is one of his letters.[26] Mar also tells us that Fletcher and the Justice Clerk supported them in their anger over their disappointment. There was also a rumour, which Mar mentions more than once, that they were to be re-established as royal favourites if the Union was completed.[27] Straight-forward bribery was also involved.

It was to be expected that the Court, which had been struggling to gain control of the Scottish Parliament since 1703, would make a special effort now that the Union negotiators had put final victory within their grasp. There is undeniable evidence that this involved a sum of £20,000 sent to Scotland between the conclusion of the negotiations and the opening of the final session of the Scottish Parliament. The first account of this is in an Appendix to Lockhart's *Memoirs*. As a member of the British Parliament in 1711 he became aware of a matter uncovered by a Parliamentary Commission enquiry into the public accounts, and he reprints a number of documents presented under oath to the Commission. These show that the Queen authorised the Treasury on 12 August 1706 to lend £20,000 to pay debts due to Government servants. Two letters to Godolphin as Lord Treasurer of England were signed by Queensberry, Seafield and Mar. Loudoun and Glasgow acknowledge that the money was sent to Scotland in two separate instalments of £10,000. It was not to be announced because it 'might probably make some noise if the letter were read in the Treasury before the meeting of the Parliament and before the treaty is well-received'. Lockhart prints an account of the disbursement to individuals 'exhibited on oath by the Earl of Glasgow'. They range from £12,325 to Queensberry 'for equipage and daily allowance' to a paltry £11.2.0 to Lord Banff.[28]

Two letters have survived in private archives which fully corroborate Lockhart's account, although he could not have been aware of them. The first is dated 20 July 1707, addressed to Queensberry and signed by Seafield and Glasgow. It was evidently intended to be read to Godolphin as an explanation of the use of the £20,000. The matter was so delicate that it ends 'Your grace may be pleased to burn this letter when you have read it to my Lord Treasurer'. Godolphin obviously insisted on keeping the letter unburnt because it remained with his family papers until it was sold to the British Museum in 1892. He could produce it as a receipt if he was challenged and it gave him a powerful hold over the Scottish noblemen involved. The letter itself suggests that between £12,000 and £13,000 could be attributed to Queensberry's equipage and daily allowance but it was 'impossible for us to do more, for what was given to the Duke of Atholl, Marquiss of Tweedale, Earls of Roxburghe, Marchmont, Ballcarray, Dunmore, Cromarty and singly or evenly others in small soumes, its impossible to state these soumes without discovering this haill affair . . . which hath been hitherto keeped secret.' This 'would be of no use, unless it were to bring discredit upon the management off that parliament".[29].

The other letter of 22 March 1711 is from Glasgow to Robert Harley, by that time Earl of Oxford. This refers to the enquiry mentioned by Lockhart. Glasgow says that the Commissioners for the public accounts have asked him for a true account. He explains that the money had not appeared officially in the Treasury of Scotland 'for if it had been known that there had been a farthing sent from England to Scotland it would have totally disappointed the carrying on of the Union'. He had been instructed by Queensberry to disburse the money on his orders; 'I being enjoined to carry on this matter with the greatest secrecy and privacy, for if ever it had been in the least discovered during the haill session of the Union Parliament, the Union had certainly broken, and I had been infallably 'De Witted', our mob and generality of Scotland being so incensed against the Union'. (Jan De Witt was a Dutch statesman of the 17th Century who was torn on pieces by an angry mob). Glasgow asks for Oxford's comments, which he will 'punctually obey', and ends with one of these passages of grovelling sycophancy which are so disagreeable to read in the letters from Scottish politicians to their English counterparts[30].

The recipients of these payments include the people that Mar and Seafield describe as particularly helpful in securing the passage of the Union, Marchmont, for instance, who received £1,104.15.7 and Montrose who got only £200. Other leaders of the *Squadrone* are included, Tweedale (£1,000) and Roxburgh (£500). Leven, (who had been one of the negotiators) reported in a letter of 26 October 1706 that Montrose had joined the Government side and influenced two or three of the *Squadrone* to do likewise. 'Besides this,' he added, 'we have found ways since we came from England to persuade several of that Party to join with us in the matter of the Union.'[31] Everyone on the list produced by Glasgow voted for the Union, except Atholl, who was so influential that he was worth an attempt to win over.

It is true that the original purpose of this advance of £20,000 was to pay the debts of the civil list. Queensberry's expenses may have been legitimate, although, according to Lockhart, he received payment twice.[32] The secrecy with which the whole transaction was handled, until four years after the Union came into effect, and the general tone of the letters, leaves no doubt about the nature and purpose of the payments. Even when there was a legitimate debt, the Court could make or withold payment depending on the way the applicant voted in Parliament. In a letter of 8 October to Godolphin, Mar reports a request from Tweedale for a payment owing to him for his time in the Queen's services. Mar replied that he would do his best, but added that 'much would depend on himself to make it in my power or not'. In the same letter, Mar begs for the appointment of his brother as a Lord of Session, and he assures Godolphin that he has always put himself under the Lord Treasurer's 'protection and direction'.[33] The manipulator assures his master that he is also one of the manipulated.

Even allowing for the change in the value of money and the scarcity of it among the Scottish nobility, £20,000 is a shamefully low price for the sale of one's integrity and country. Lockhart makes an indignant comment: 'It is abundantly disgraceful to be any manner of way a contributor to the misery and ruine of one's native country; but for persons of quality and distinction, to sell, and even at so mean a price, themselves and their posterity, is so scandalous and infamous, that such persons must be contemptible in the sight of those who bought them, and their memories odious to all future generations'.[34] In his *Tales of a Grandfather*, Sir Walter Scott added: 'It may be doubted whether the descendants of the noble lords and honourable gentlemen who accepted this gratification would be more shocked at the general fact of their ancestors being corrupted, or scandalised at the paltry amount of the bribe'[35] All of this is fair comment, but the £20,000 was, of course, by no means the only bribe or inducement. I have already mentioned some examples of these and will refer to others as they occur.

The consequence of this process of management or corruption was that the Court purchased a secure majority in Parliament and had no need to worry about persuasion or argument. Seafield and Mar reflected increasing confidence, as the session proceeded, that they could be sure of success. Fletcher and others argued vigorously against the Treaty article by article, but gradually the Government hardly bothered to respond. As Lockhart expresses it: 'the Courtiers had ears and would not hear, hearts and would not understand, nay, mouths but would not speak. Few or not answers were to be made, but a vote requir'd.'[36] Curiously enough, some modern historians, perhaps misled by Defoe's *History of the Union*, have given the opposite impression. They would have us believe that the unionists won the intellectual argument and that Fletcher and his friends gave up in despair.[37] There is abundant evidence in contemporary accounts, such as Hume's *Diary* and the letters of Mar, that this is simply untrue.

We have noticed that Godolphin in 1703 made an unmistakable threat of military intervention if the Scots did not accept the Union and that many contemporary commentators saw a real risk of war. With a Parliament now reduced to submission, it might be supposed that force was no longer to be contemplated; but troops were in fact moved to the Border and the North of Ireland, and Godolphin was still a key mover in the business. On 26 November 1706 Sir David Nairne in London wrote to Mar:-

> You bid me not to write to any body of what was desired of my Lord Treasurer by the joint letter, yet I cannot help telling your Lordship that the affaire was finished this day and I write of it this post to the Earl of Glasgow. But it's good you know it both for your own sake and mine. The troops on the Boarders are three regiments of foot, and in the North of Ireland, three of horse, one of foot, and one of dragoons, and they have the necessary orders; but all relating to this affaire must be kept very private.[38]

(I remark as an aside that the mysterious reference in the first sentence must be to the secret transfer of the two instalments of the £20,000. Lockhart prints two 'joint letters' to the Lord Treasurer on the subject signed by Queensberry, Seafield, Mar, Loudoun and Glasgow. They nominate Glasgow as the man to whom the money is to be sent.)[39]

Nairne wrote to Mar again on 10 December:

> There is 800 horse marched from this to the Borders by advice of the Duke of Marlborrow, for he thinks they will be more useful then thrice there number of foot.[40]

These miliary preparations were probably intended not so much to intimidate Parliament as to protect if from the indignation of the population. In fact, the Court's representatives in Scotland had requested military protection. On 26 October, Leven, as Governor of Edinburgh Castle wrote to Godolphin about the 'mob in the streets' and their 'repeated huzzas and acclamations of praise' to Hamilton. He was sure that there was a majority for the Union in Parliament, but concluded: 'I humbly conceive it would be of great advantage to have some forces in the North of England near the border, for the troops here are few in number.'[41] As the news of the Treaty and of the management of Parliament spread, there were widespread protests and riots. In a well-known passage of Walter Scott's *The Heart of Midlothian*, one of the characters says that 'when we had a king and a chancellor and parliament men o' our ain, we could aye peeble them wi' stanes when they werena gude bairns.'[42] This was exactly what the Edinburgh crowd now did or threatened to do. The rest of the country could demonstrate and draw up written protests; but the Edinburgh people could make their feelings known very directly to those now called upon to debate the Treaty. Hamilton, who was assumed to be the leader of the opposition to the Treaty was cheered whenever he appeared. The crowd followed him to and from the House, as Defoe says, 'shouting and crying out, God bless his grace for standing up against the Union, and appearing for his country and the like.' On the other hand, 'the Queen's representative, the High Commissioner, had all the insults, reproaches and indignities offered him that they durst.'[43] All the negotiators of the Treaty, or 'treaters', were liable to a similar reception. Mar wrote to Nairne of 17 November: 'I'm not verie timerous and yet I tell you that every day here wee are in hazard of our lives. Wee cannot goe on the streets but wee are insulted.'[44]

Lockhart says that as soon as the terms of the Union were known, the nation became 'universally averse' to it.[45] All contemporary accounts, even, as we have seen, private letters from servants of the Court, agree that this was so. Defoe, as a propagandist for the English Government tried every trick in the book, but when he wrote his *History of the Union* he described the mood of the Country in these terms:-

That the figure of Scotland would make in the British Parliament would not like a Kingdom, but like a province; that one country in England, viz Cornwall, sent up as many members, one excepted, as the whole Kingdom; and this was an external badge of their subjection, and the like.

This was a general cry, and began to be very popular: The people cried out, they were Scotsmen and they would be Scotsmen still; they contemned the name of Britons, fit for the Welshmen, who were made the scoff of the English, after they had reduced them. Scotland had always had a name and fame in foreign Courts: they were naturalised in France, enjoyed for many years great priveleges there, and honours bought with the blood of their ancestors; and they would never give away their birthright, though some of the nation had been driving a bargain for themselves, at the price of selling their country. Thus they filled the mouths of the common people, who would go about the street crying, 'no Union', and call the treaters traitors, and soon began to threaten them to their faces.[46]

16

The debate on the Treaty.
3 October 1706 to 16 January 1707.

'A Sovereign Independent Monarchie shall disolve its constitution
and be at the disposall of England'.
— Duke of Atholl

The Court, after spending August and September in building up support in the manner described in the previous chapter, were ready to face Parliament by the beginning of October. Queensberry as Commissioner had very precise instructions.[1] His prime business was to carry the 25 articles of the Treaty with as little alteration as possible, and any alteration was to be submitted to the Queen. If a majority opposed the Treaty, Parliament was to be adjourned. Any proposal for a federal Union or for Succession with Limitations was to be rejected. The settlement of the Church question was to be left to the House.

The Parliamentary session began on 3 October with the reading of a letter from the Queen which advocated the Union in glowing terms. 'We shall esteem it as the greatest glory of our Reign . . . An entire and perfect Union will be the solid formulation of lasting Peace. It will secure your Religion Liberty and property, remove the animosities amongst yourselves and the jealousies and differences betwixt Our two Kingdoms; It must increase your strength Riches and Trade, and by this Union the whole Island being joyned in affection, and free from all apprehension of different Interests, will be enabled to resist all its Enemies, Support the Protestant Interest everywhere and maintain the Liberties of Europe.' The speech went on to say that the question of Church government had been referred to both Parliaments in the Acts providing for the negotiation. 'You now have an opportunity for doing what may be necessary for security of your present Church government after the Union within the Limits of Scotland'. The articles of the Treaty were then read and ordered to be printed. Hamilton proposed, and it was agreed, that the official minutes of the negotiation should also be printed.[2]

Serious discussion of the Treaty began on 12 October, when Mar proposed that the articles should be considered one by one. The opposition, evidently aware that the Court had now contrived a majority, tried to find a diversion. Stewart of Pardivan proposed that the Kirk should be asked to call a fast over the whole country. Mar says that Stewart was a 'foolish fellow', but that he was supported by Hamilton, Atholl, Marishall, Balmerino, Saltoun, Kilmarnock, 'and all that set'. Hume of Crossrigs adds 'this occasioned a long jangle'. The intention as Mar realised, was to delay and frustrate the Union by provoking

187

the resistance of the Kirk. Sir Thomas Burnett, following a line long advocated by Fletcher, moved that members should first consult their constituents before deciding on a matter of such importance as the Union. The meeting seems to have ended in some confusion. The minutes record that it was agreed that the records of all former 'Treaties' should be laid on the table and that Parliament would proceed to the consideration of the articles at the next sederunt. When the House met again on 15 October, however, Fletcher, Hamilton, Atholl and Belhaven challenged whether this latter point had in fact been decided. When 'proceed or delay' were eventually put to the vote, 'proceed' carried by 66 votes.[3]

The vote on 15 October was the first real trial of strength after the Government's efforts of the summer and it gave great satisfaction to their leaders. Seafield wrote to Godolphin next day: 'What occurred yesterday in Parliament gives so good hopes of success that wee thought it necessarie to accquant you with it by this flying packet.' He was particularly pleased by the recruitment of the members of the New Party or *Squadrone Volante*, such as Tweedale, Rothes, Roxburgh, Haddington, Marchmont and Jerviswood, who had formerly supported Hamilton and Fletcher. Mar was even more confident, writing to Nairne that they could have carried the vote even without the *Squadrone* who brought only 18 votes. He thought that Hamilton had been on the point of giving up without a vote. Now that the Opposition saw that they had lost all hope of a majority, he thought they would try 'some foolish extravagant thing if they can bring it about.'[4]

Mar was right in the sense that the Opposition was now bound to respond to the Government's tame majority by looking for some other device to bring public opinion to bear. Lockhart says that Fletcher and other members of the Country Party 'took a great deal of pains to expose the unreasonableness of the several articles as they went thro' them; but the Courtiers very seldom made any reply, having resolv'd to trust to the number of led-horses, and not to trouble themselves with reasoning'. In this manner, although there were on some days long debates which went on after night-fall, Parliament for the rest of October proceeded to go through the articles without taking votes on them. Mar reported to Nairne on 17 October that Fletcher said that the 'wholle nation are grown rogues'. He had not yet spoken much, but Mar thought that he was reserving himself until they started to take votes.[5]

Meanwhile, as the news of the Treaty and of the situation in Parliament spread, the temperature of public resentment was rising strongly. In his letter of 17 October Mar had said that 'the mob of this town are mad and against us.' From the beginning of the session the crowd in the streets had been cheering Hamilton and abusing the supporters of the Union. On 23 October the unrest broke into open riot. Daniel Defoe who was an eye-witness, described it in the first of his letters from Edinburgh which I quoted in the previous chapter. He says that he found 'the wholl City in a Most Dreadful Uproar and the high street Full of the Rabble', all crying out against the Union. They attacked the house of Sir Patrick Johnston, a former Lord Provost, who according to Defoe, had been one of the most popular men in the town before he became one of the 'treaters'.[6] Eventually order was restored by calling in the troops from the Castle, an unprecedented step.

When the riot was discussed in Parliament on 25 October, Fletcher moved that the presence of troops in the town was an encroachment on the privileges of Parliament. He said that the people in the streets were 'the true spirit of this country, for the Reformation and Revolution were both brought about by them'. After a long debate, in which Fletcher was supported by his usual friends, the Government prevailed with a resolve thanking the Council for their action and recommending that the Guards should stay in the town.[7]

Mar had concluded too soon that Fletcher was saving his fire. On the 28, when the Fast-day was again discussed, he said that if he told what he knew about members of the Commission of the Kirk who were also members of Parliament, they 'would be ashamed to hold up their faces'. Next day he said ('in passion', according to Mar) that the 'treaters' 'had betray'd their trust'. When challenged, he said that he could find no 'softer words'. Under pressure he in the end apologized to the extent of saying that he was sorry if he had offended any one. It was 'no small mortification to him', wrote Mar, 'to be oblidg'd to beg pardon'.[8]

More signs of public discontent with the Treaty were now appearing. On 26 October Mar reported to Godolphin that 'the humor in the country against the Treaty or Union is much increased of late'. He blamed this principally on the Ministers who were preaching about the dangers to the Kirk, and on the opposition who were persuading the people that they would be burdened with taxes. He was still confident that 'the Union will certainly do in the Parliament' but he was afraid 'some people may commit some foolish irregular thing either before it pass or after it'. Three days later he told Nairne that in every shire Addresses to Parliament were being drawn up and 'all against the Union'. There were stories, which he hoped were only 'braggs' that the country would rise and not allow Parliament to finish the Union. 'I'm creedibly inform'd that the Duke of Atholl's men are to muster this week'. Nairne replied on 1 November that people in England would find it difficult to understand how any arguments could be brought against a communication of trade (as though that were the whole story). He observed, rather wistfully, that the mob might change sides, if that particular was understood. Rather more to the point, he enclosed the approval of a request from Queensberry for the payment of 1,000 marks a year to the Earl of Hopetoun. He had 'behaved mighty well, and therefor the Queen granted it very freely'.[9]

On 30 October the House completed the process of going through the Treaty article by article as a first reading and without taking votes. On the same day, Hamilton made the point that the English Sacramental Test meant an inequality since Scots would be debarred from employment in England but not the English in Scotland. According to Hume, this was 'as momentous, referred to further consideration'.[10]

At the Sederunt on 1 November, therefore, the Government was now ready to begin to go through the Treaty again with the object of bringing each article to the vote. Before this could be debated, they had the irritation of the arrival of the first of the Addresses that Mar had mentioned. They were from Midlothian, West Lothian and Perthshire, protesting against the Union as 'contrary to the honour and independency of the Kingdom'. From now on, each sederunt began with the receipt and reading of Addresses like this against the Union from all over the country, from shires, burghs and parishes and from all social classes. From the shires they were signed by 'Barons, Freeholders, Heretors and other Gentlemen,', in other words by the landowners and gentry; from the burghs by the Magistrates, Town Council, Deacons of Crafts and burgesses at large; from the parishes by Heretors and other Inhabitants.

Defoe prints the text of the Address from the Burgh of Dumfermline as 'a specimen of the manner how these addresses were usually signed'. It is signed by 13 members of the Town Council, 28 merchants, 16 wrights, 6 masons, 4 shoe-makers, 11 fleshers, 31 weavers, 17 tailors, 7 smiths and 9 baxters. In addition, Andrew Symson, Notary Public, added a note in Latin, presumably because of the solemnity of the occasion, certifying that another 36 people wished to add their names but could not write.[11] Long before any form of quick or easy communication, this rejection of the Union, with such unanimity and on such a scale, was a demonstration of popular will, virtually without parallel.

After the reading of the first of these Addresses, Marchmont proposed the approval of the first article. The Opposition put up a stiff resistance. Mar admits that he was too 'weary and hungry' to be able to write his usual letter to Nairne that night. It had been a hard two days. On the second of them the House met between 10 and 11 in the morning and continued after dark until 8 in the evening. 'It grew at last so late and every body faint with hunger, for most of us had eat none that day'. The Court therefore had to abandon hope of bringing the article to the vote on the same day. Since it was the article that provided for the uniting of the two kingdoms into one, the vote on it was, of course, the moment of crucial decision.[12]

Hume tells us that one of the lines of the opposition argument was in favour of a recess to allow members to consult with their constituents before such a momentous matter was put to the vote. Lockhart says that many speeches argued that an 'incorporating Union was altogether inconsistent with the honour of this nation, and absolutely destructive to its interests and concerns both civil and religious'. Some argued that the Union would be a precedent dangerous to liberty. If the Scottish Parliament could alter or subvert its constitution, might not a British Parliament do the same? Hamilton asked, 'shall we in half an hour yield what our forefathers maintain'd with their lives and fortunes for many ages?'. Belhaven made his famous, emotional speech about his vision of the murdered Caledonia, which Mar says 'was made pretty ridiculous'. He adds that 'Fletcher gave us two of his study'd speeches, which certainly we'll have 'eer long in print as allso Bellhaven's'.[13]

Mar was right about Belhaven's speech, which was printed both as a pamphlet and by Defoe in his *History*. Defoe also printed the most celebrated of the few speeches made in favour of the Union, that of Seton of Pitmedden. Early in this century, the historian Hume Brown, wrote that he was 'one of the ablest supporters of the Union. Measured, compact and logical, his contributions to the debate were at once full of matter and inspired by a grave sense of the national issues at stake'.[14] He omits to mention that Seton had sold his services to the Court. (See page 119).

Seton's speech turned mainly on the argument about trade. Since it is the only speech in favour of the Union of which, thanks to Defoe, we have the full text, it may have contributed to the belief that this was the decisive issue. 'This nation being poor, and without force to protect its commerce, cannot reap great advantage by it, till it partake of the trade and protection of some powerful neighbour nation, that can communicate both these . . . By this Union, we will have access to all the advantages in commerce the English enjoy . . . and we will have our liberty, property and religion, secured under the protection of one Sovereign, and one Parliament of Great Britain'. He asserted these points without any supporting argument and without any attempt to reply to the very strong case which had been made by Fletcher and others, including the trading community itself, against the subjection of Scotland to a trading policy designed for English conditions and to the control of a Parliament in which the English would have an overwhelming majority. Seton does not seem to have had much confidence in his own arguments because he prefaced them by saying that, having been one of the Commissioners who negotiated the Treaty, he thought that he had to explain himself. 'Though his reasons', he said, 'could not convince any member, yet they might serve to vindicate his conduct to posterity'.[15] This sounds to me more like a guilty conscience than a 'grave sense of the national issues'.

Of Fletcher's speeches in this session we have no record. If they were printed as pamphlets, no copy is known to survive. Defoe, as a propagandist for other side, dealt with the most formidable of his opponents by pretending that he did not exist. There is no reference at all to Fletcher in the whole of the 600 odd pages of Defoe's *History of the Union*, except in two of the voting records which he includes as an appendix. It is very clear, however, from the references to him in Mar's letters and Hume's *Diary* that Fletcher took a very active part in the debates and made many of what Mar called his 'studied speeches'.

Defoe says of the Opposition's conduct of the whole debate, 'From article to article, they disputed every word, every clause, casting difficulties and doubts in the way of every argument, twisting and turning every question, and continually starting objections to gain time; and, if possible, to throw some unsurmountable obstacle in the way'.[16] Defoe did not intend this to be praise, but it is an unconscious tribute to the determination and resourcefulness with which the Opposition resisted the Union, in spite of the frustration of the Government's newly purchased majority whenever a vote was taken. Many of the key moves in this resistance were made by Fletcher and many of the arguments, as we can see from the many Protestations made in the debate, derived from his ideas.

On the second day of the debate, 2 November, the Court introduced a proposal to deal with one of the objections which had been raised by the opposition. If the House voted for article 1, which provided for the union of the two Kingdoms, what would happen if the royal assent was then given to this and the nation would be united to England on no terms or 'at best upon such as England of themselves should condescend to give us afterwards'? To dispose of this the Court conceded that the vote on each article would have no binding effect until all the articles had been approved. They proposed that article 1 should be approved and that the house should then turn to the question of the Church.[17] This concession was one of the very few that the Court made.

Generally, Lockhart said, 'the Courtiers were not at the pains to solve the doubts, and answer the objections raised by the Country party, so they continued the same method throughout the whole remaining part of the session, allowing the Country party to argue some little time upon the matter under the House's consideration, and then moving a vote upon it'.[18] Even so, on this crucial article they had great difficulty in bringing the matter to the vote. They had to accept postponement on November 1 and 2, which was a Friday. On Monday 4, they finally got their way, at the cost, wrote Mar, 'of a great deal of wrangling and loud speaking'. The article was approved by 32 votes, according to Mar, or 33 according to the Minutes. 'A good plurality but fewer than we expected. What with the addresses and the humor that's now in the country against the Union, several members left us, tho' I'm hopeful many of them will come about again'. From this decision onwards, the names of those voting on both sides are recorded in the minutes. It is clear from this that the Court had recruited most support from the nobility on whom they had concentrated their efforts, 46 of them were for and 21 against. In comparison, the other two estates were fairly evenly split; Shires, 37 for, 33 against; Burghs, 33 for, 29 against. As has often been remarked, it was the nobility who were mainly responsible for the acceptance of the Treaty. As Burnet expressed it, 'it was the nobility, that in every vote turned the scale for the union: they were severly reflected on by those who opposed it; it was said, many of them were bought off, to sell their country and their birthright'.[19]

Before the vote was taken, there were two gestures of defiance. Annandale, whom Mar had been trying hard to recruit, moved a Resolve, which was clearly based on the ideas for which Fletcher had been arguing for the last four years. It began by rejecting the proposal for an incorporating Union, to which the nation was 'generally averse' and which was contrary to the fundamental constitution and Claim of Right. Such a Union would not promote friendly relations between the two countries, but on the contrary 'distractions and animosities' which would lead to 'fatal breaches and confusions'. It therefore offered two alternative solutions. Either there might be a Union (in the customary sense of cooperation) over 'Succession, Wars, Alliances and

Trade', which would preserve 'the Sovereignity and independency of our Crown and Monarchie . . . as now established'. Alternatively, incorporating Fletcher's ideas of Limitations and using the language of the 1703 Act of Security, the same succession as England could be accepted, 'upon such conditions and regulations of government as shall effectively secure the Sovereignity and Independency of this Crown and Kingdom'. According to Lockhart, Annandale realised that in the new circumstances there was no longer any chance of a majority for such a proposal, but thought it worth while to let it lie on the table as a sign to England that different solutions were possible.[20]

The second gesture was a Protestation by Atholl 'for himself and others who shall adhere' that an incorporating Union was contrary to the honour, interest, fundamental laws and constitution of the kingdom. 67 members adhered, including, of course, Andrew Fletcher. The publication of the names of the adherents in the minutes along with those voting for and against the first article was described by Hume as 'an extraordinary method'.[21] It was the first time that it had been done. Either it was a recognition of the vital importance of the votes which were now being taken or a means of intimidating members by reminding them that the Government was taking a careful note of their conduct.

On 6 November the Court introduced the measure which they hoped would reconcile the Kirk to the Union, the 'Act for Security of the true Protestant Religion and Government of the Church as by law established'. The Earl of Glasgow also tabled an Act of Supply to raise money for the armed forces. Much time was taken up recording the adherents to Atholl's protestation and with more Addresses against the Union, including one from the Convention of Royal Burghs. Even so the Act of Supply was passed on 8 November and 'touched' by the Commissioners to indicate royal assent on the 9th. In the previous three years, Parliament had always declined to vote supply early in the Session because that meant losing their own means of forcing the Government to keep the House sitting and to allow the discussion of measures which Parliament, but not the Government, wanted. The easy passage of the Act showed how different the situation now was. The Government could now count on an assured majority. For once, the main business before the House, the approval of the Treaty, was something which the Government wanted to force through. Mar mentions an additional reason. A rumour had gone around that the Government had decided to abandon the Treaty and were resorting to their familiar tactic of seeking supply so that they could close the session. The rumour, he concedes, made it easier to have the Supply Act approved. He saw it as a very good day's work. It took pressure off the Government 'and it pleases the troops, so makes them sure to us'.[22]

The Act on the Kirk did not go through quite so easily. As Mar said, the Opposition tried to load it with amendments that would make it unacceptable to the English Parliament. Belhaven proposed one such amendment, to exempt Scots after the Union from the Sacramental Test in England. This would have removed the inequality to which Hamilton had drawn attention on 30 October.

As long as the Test was in force, A Scot in England after the Union could not hold office, or even go to a university, without taking an oath of allegiance to the Church of England. There was no similar restriction on the employment of Englishmen in Scotland. Belhaven's amendment was clearly in the Scottish interest. Even so, the grip of the Government on their majority was now so strong that they were able, after a long and strenuous debate, to defeat the amendment by 39 votes. Another amendment, which was less likely to be opposed in England, was passed. This provided that the Universities of St Andrews, Glasgow, Aberdeen and Edinburgh 'shall continue within this kingdom for ever' and that their Professors would be members of the Church of Scotland.[23]

The rest of the Act aimed at similar permanence. The Church of Scotland, as it was then constituted, was 'to continue without any alteration to the people of this land in all succeeding generations'. The Act was to be regarded as an indissoluble part of the Union and succeeding sovereigns were to subscribe and swear to it on their accession.[24] These solemn undertakings did not reckon with the doctrine of parliamentary sovereignty, which was to evolve in England. According to this, Parliament could always do as it pleased without being restricted by previous undertakings or by anything else, except royal assent which became an automatic formality. Even so, the Act 'as far as words could go, safeguarded for all time the National Church of Scotland, as it had been established at the Revolution'.[25] It was calculated to calm the anxiety of those who felt that the Union would put the Kirk at the mercy of the overwhelming Anglican majority in the British Parliament. It strengthened the hands of the minority within the Kirk who, like the acting Moderator, William Carstares, supported the Union. On the other hand, it did nothing to lessen the resistance to the Union on wider grounds of national interest which were as strong within the Kirk as in the country as a whole.

The Church Act passed on 12 November by 112 votes to 38, a majority which clearly included many of the opponents of the Union. Before the vote was taken Belhaven entered a Protestation that there could be 'no real and solid security' to the Church of Scotland 'by any manner of Union by which the Claim of Right is unhinged, our Parliament incorporated and our distinct Sovereignty and Independency intirely abolished'. Fletcher voted against the Act and adhered, along with 23 others, to Belhaven's Protestation. Mar was well pleased with the outcome because 'the great rock wee were most afraid to spleet on was the Church'.[26]

I should at this point mention two side issues in which Fletcher was involved. It appears from letters exchanged between Nairne in London and Mar in Edinburgh that Ridpath had written a report, which appeared in the newspaper, the *Flying Post*, about Fletcher's speech on 29 October in which he had said that the 'treaters' were traitors. Nairne and Mar were incensed by what they saw as Ridpath's exaggeration and both wanted complaints to be raised against him with a view to his punishment. Ridpath was the author of several pamphlets against the Union and of the book about the parliamentary session of 1703 in which he had praised Fletcher with enthusiasm (See pages 76 and 95).[27]

On 9 November Fletcher, in the incongruous company of the Earl of Glasgow, was appointed a member of a group of six charged with the responsibility of looking into the progress made by James Anderson in the work recommended to him by Parliament. This evidently refers to a Resolution of 21 September 1705 which authorised a payment of 3,600 pounds Scots to Anderson to enable him 'to print and carry on an account of the ancient charters and seals of the Kingdom before James I'. Anderson did, in fact, in due course produce a handsome volume of this kind, and so it seems that the efforts of the group of six were fruitful. Here then is the Parliament of Scotland, in the middle of a debate which was to lead to its own abolition, concerned with the preservation of the historical records of Scotland and setting up what we might call an all-party committee for the purpose. It was by no means the last time when authorities in Scotland have had more regard for the relics of past independence than the harsh realities of the present.[28]

The House returned to the Treaty on 14 November, when the Lord Register moved that the second article should be approved, but that this would have no effect until all the other articles had been approved by both Parliaments. This was another crucial turning point because article 2 approved the same Succession to the throne as in England. Article 3, providing for 'one and the same Parliament' of Great Britain, was yet another. At this point, Fletcher introduced another long and heated debate by proposing that consideration of these two articles should be deferred until article 4 and all the other articles on trade and taxation had been considered. He evidently hoped to defer for as long as possible, or if he could frustrate, the decisions on Succession and the abolition of the two separate Parliaments. The debate lasted until it was almost dark, but a vote to proceed to article 2 was carried by 26 votes.[29]

The debate resumed next day with more struggle than Mar expected after winning the procedural vote. Annandale reminded the House of the terms of his Resolve of 4 November, which had proposed the acceptance of the English Succession but on conditions similar to Fletcher's Limitations. He was supported, Mar says, by Hamilton 'and most of that side', which presumably included Fletcher. Hamilton then made another proposal, in which he was supported by Atholl, Annandale, Fletcher and others. He drew attention to the flood of Addresses against the Union which were now pouring into Parliament. These, he said, called for a letter to the Queen to inform her of 'the general aversion of the nation, appearing by the multitude of Addresses presented', and to ask for a recess and a new Parliament to settle the Succession. Otherwise he was afraid that there was a danger of civil war. Mar replied by trying to discredit the Addresses. They were signed mostly by the 'commonallitie' who had been misled by falsehoods from people disaffected to the Government. In any case, they could not be said to be representative of the nation because a quarter of it had not signed them. 'Parliament', he added, 'was the fitt judge to consider of the terms of the Union'. Argyll said that the Addresses were of no other use than to make kites.[30]

In fact, the remarkable number and unanimity of the Addresses against the Union, expressing, Lockhart says, 'the inclinations and earnest supplications of the people', were causing disquiet in London. Nairne wrote to Mar on 14 November:

'Whey has there not been some pains taken to gett counter counter address from some places? I hope there wold be as many and as good hands at them as at the other. It wold have been of mighty use here, for I finde people here, I mean coffee house company, begin to droop or despond to hear of soe much doeing against the Union without doors and soe litle for it.'

Mar replied on 19 November that it was thought better not to attempt to obtain Addresses in favour of the Union. 'It was past time to gett verie many, and few wou'd look worse than non.'[31]

No doubt the Government would have countered if they could have done so without stirring up more trouble for themselves; but they were faced with a great revulsion of feeling among the people at large, and they knew it. Contrary to Mar's allegation, the Addresses were signed by people of all classes, by lairds in the shires and merchants in the burghs, as well as by ministers and humble members of their congregations in parishes all over the country. All of these Addresses firmly rejected the Treaty, with the single exception of that from the burgh of Ayr which was more equivocal in tone. Defoe says that it 'had some seeming softness in it', and Hume that it was 'very discreet, and craving some amendments may be made of the Articles of Union, and seems to incline for the Union.'[32] Nothing like this could be said of all the others which left no doubt of their complete rejection of the Treaty.

The flood of Addresses was an extraordinary and unprecedented event which should be celebrated as a milestone in political history. I do not think that there had ever before been such a unanimous, peaceful and rational demonstration of the views of a people on an important political issue. It showed the great strength of national feeling in Scotland, and the wide-spread literacy and political sophistication. Democracy did not then exist anywhere. It was a time when it was still possible to argue unashamedly that ordinary people who were not landowners or members of Parliament had no right to express views on matters of state. Mar implied this in his speech on the Addresses and Defoe was explicit in one of his pamphlets in support of the Union. He argued that those who had no right to vote for members of Parliament, and that meant the great majority of the population, had no right to seek to influence them: 'they can have no Right to direct those who they have no part in constituting . . . (they) are meddling with what they have no Right to be meddling with, nor are any way concerned in'.[33] At a time when such views were accepted, conventional wisdom, long before the general franchise, referenda or public opinion polls, it is impressive that the Scottish people sought to bring their opinions to bear in documents that were lucid, forceful and succinct.

I return to the debate on 15 November about article 2, which led to an unseemly procedural wrangle about the form of the vote. When this seemed to be settled and the government attempted to call the vote, 'Fletcher was full of a studied speech', which he insisted on finishing. He was supported by Hamilton and the rest of his party. Mar's account continues: 'Wee wou'd hear non of them speak; and so with their bauleing to be heard and ours to stope them the Houss cam in a great confusione'. The article was finally put to the vote and passed by a majority of 58, which suggests that there was more support for the Protestant Succession than for the Union. Marischall entered a Protestation which again repeated the words of the Act of Security, based on Fletcher's Limitations, that no Successor could be designated unless Parliament settled and enacted such conditions of government as 'may secure the Honour and Sovereignty of this Crown and Kingdom, the freedom frequency and power of Parliament, the religion liberty and trade of the Nation from English or any foreign influence'. Fletcher, naturally, was among the 46 who adhered.[34]

The House turned on 18 November to the remaining crucial article, the third, which provided for 'one and the same Parliament of Great Britain'. Fletcher's Resolution to proceed first to the fourth and following articles was again put to the vote and rejected. There was a long debate which lasted until after dark. The question of how much confidence Scotland could have in a British Parliament was raised. Fountainhall asked what security was there for the observance and performance of the Treaty? Hamilton proposed that the Scottish members should have a right of veto in 'matters essential and fundamental in the Union' and that any encroachment of the Treaty would automatically render it void. This was a difficult one for the Court. It showed that the Scots had understood that they would have no means of redress once the Treaty had been passed, and that the British Parliament might easily disregard any of the few safeguards of Scottish interests which it contained. In effect, they were calling the bluff of one of the points which Defoe had made in his propaganda. In his *Fourth Essay at Removing National Prejudices* of 1706 he argued that the Scots could have complete confidence in the Treaty because the British Parliament, which was established by the Treaty, could not violate it without destroying the whole basis of its existence and therefore dissolving itself. Stair, generally regarded as the best mind on the side of the Court, could think of no better reply than to move that the matter should be deferred until all the articles had been approved.[35]

Before the vote was taken, Annandale lodged another Protest. This was in similar terms to the one which he had made on 4 November, but it omitted the references to Succession and ended: 'And therefore I do Protest That this shall not prejudge the being of future Scots Parliaments and Conventions within the Kingdom of Scotland at no time coming'. The Court, who had evidently expected to recruit Annandale, were puzzled by his increasingly strong support of Scottish independence. Nairne told Mar on 21 November that the Queen was taking particular notice of it. There were 54 adherents to his Protest and article 3 passed by 30 votes. With the passage of this article, Mar remarked, 'the hardest of our work is over'.[36]

That night the coach of the Commissioner was stoned as he returned to Holyrood and one of his servants was injured. Mar, in reporting this, showed alarm at the increasing and widely spread unrest. He was certain that there had been a mustering of men in arms in various parts of the country, especially in the south, and he believed that nothing had prevented an armed rising but the season of the year and the bad weather. Defoe agreed: 'At last it came to downright insurrection and rebellion; which, had not circumstances and the season particularly prevented, had risen up to blood, civil war, and all the terrible consequences of an enraged and divided nation'.[37]

When the House met next day, 19 November, the Chancellor reported the attack on the Commissioner. It was agreed that the Committee on the Equivalent would consider appropriate measures and that the Magistrates, who seemed to have been avoiding action, would be asked to proceed with the trial of those arrested after the riot on 23 October. Unrest had now spread beyond Edinburgh. A mob in Glasgow on 7 November virtually seized the city and the Provost fled to Edinburgh in fear for his life. Order was restored after some weeks by the intervention of the dragoons. A small band of protesters left Glasgow to raise the country. While this was going on, there was a movement of insurrection throughout Ayrshire and the South West. On 20 November, an armed crowd of near to 2 or 3 thousand, according to Lockhart, or a rabble of about 200, according to Defoe, entered Dumfries, burnt a copy of the Treaty and affixed a proclamation to the town cross. This denounced the negotiators of the Treaty as 'either simple, ignorant or treacherous, if not all three'. Ratification of the Treaty by Parliament would be 'contrary to our fundamental, liberties and priviledges' and would not be binding on the nation. They intended to acquit themselves 'as becomes men and christians'.[38]

On 26 November Mar reported to Nairne that 'musters and rendezvouses' were being held in several places, particularly in the south and west, and that there was talk of several thousand armed men descending on Edinburgh to force Parliament to abandon the Union. He urged that the Queen should order as many troops as could be spared to be held ready in the north of England and Ireland. The Chancellor made a report to Parliament on 29 November and moved the approval of a Proclamation against 'tumultuary and irregular meetings'. Even Lockhart voted for this and there were only 4 votes against. Fletcher abstained. An Act was also approved to suspend the clause in the Act of Security which provided for the arming of fencible men and the exercising of them once a month at least. All were now ordered to return, on pain of high treason, to 'their habitations and lawful employments'. According to Lockhart, however, it was not so much these measures which frustrated the armed descent on Edinburgh as the intervention of the Duke of Hamilton. Lockhart says that Covenanters from the south-west and Jacobites from the north were ready to make common cause against the Union. Seven or eight thousand armed men were ready to rendezvous at the town of Hamilton for an advance on the Capital, but a few days before the appointed time, the Duke sent messages throughout the country calling off the venture for the time being. This was the second time, and not the last, when he had come to the rescue of the Court at a critical point.[39]

To return to the proceedings in Parliament on 19 November, the Government moved the approval of Article 4 as providing for 'full freedom and Intercours of Trade and Navigation'. Atholl countered this by proposing that the British Parliament should meet in Scotland at least once every three years, but it was agreed to defer this until Article 27 was under consideration. Fletcher then made a long speech, according to Hume, showing the disadvantages of the communication of trade. He said that there were many branches of trade and moved that each should be considered separately. The debate ran over into the next sederunt when the Article was approved by 156 to 19, a great increase in the Government's majority, presumably because even many opponents of incorporating Union saw no objection to freedom of trade by itself. Mar says that Fletcher was so angry when the Article passed that he ran out of the House.[40]

For the next two months, against a background of increasing unrest in the country, Parliament continued to work systematically through the rest of the 25 Articles. The first four had conceded the major points of principle but they were short and clear. Those which followed, dealing with matters of trade, customs and excise and finance, including the Equivalent, were more detailed and complicated. It appears from Mar's correspondence that the Court's servants in Edinburgh did not expect to be able to carry them, even with their tame majority, without some clarifications and amendments. Mar wrote to Nairne on 23 November: 'We shall endeavour in all the articles to keep as near the Treaty as possible. But our people here, even those who have hitherto gone along with us, are so skittish and have advanced so far on amendment to be made that we have little hope of carrying the Treaty without alterations'. There is much talk of a 'memorial' which is evidently a paper he and his colleagues had sent to London seeking permission to make some limited concessions. 'Wee long for an ansuer to the memoriall, and pray God it may be a satisfieing one, else I confess I would be affraid of our success', he had written on 19 November. The reply came two days later, but was not completely satisfying. It evidently recommended that the Scots should trust the Parliament of Great Britain to put right some of the anomalies which the Scots had identified. 'That is not the language of this place just now, and one wou'd be staired att if they said so in the Houss. For the British Parliament is what frights most of our Scotish members that wee are forced to manage'.[41]

There is another example of the methods of this 'management' in Mar's letters at about this time. He wrote to Nairne on 28 November:

'My Lord Northesk has all this Parliament behaved very well. He is Sherief of Angus, and wou'd gladly have it for his own life and his son's. The Commissioner desir'd me to write of it to you that you may lay it before the Queen . . . this will show in that country that the Queen favours those who go into the measure of the Union, which few of the peers of that country do'.[42]

In this situation, the obvious tactic for the Opposition was to work for amendments that the English Parliament might reject so that the whole question could be re-opened. The Court had to steer a delicate course between trying to please the Scots by concessions in the Scottish interest, while avoiding anything that would be unacceptable to the English. Fletcher took a leading part in moving amendments that might wreck the Treaty. On 5 December he moved that Scotland should be permanently free from the tax on malt and on the 7th that Scotland should not be subject to English debts. This last point arose over article 15, a particularly long and complicated article which proposed the Equivalent in compensation for Scotland's acceptance of a share of the liability for debts contracted by England before the Union. The first clause of this was put to the vote separately. Since it provided for the payment of the Equivalent, the financial sugar on the treaty, it is not surprising that it passed by what Hume called a 'vast number'. Only 27 voted against, including Fletcher, Atholl and Marischall, but not Hamilton or Belhaven.[43]

The remorseless advance of the Court's majority through the Treaty often moved Fletcher to fury. Articles 6 and 8, on customs duty, regulations on trade and the duty on salt, had been referred to a committee because of the many objections which they provoked, and which eventually led to detailed but comparatively trivial, amendments. Even so, the Court pressed on and passed Article 14, which also referred to duties, without waiting for the report of the committee. This roused Fletcher to what Mar called a 'vast heat'. There was another row on 10 December when the Court proposed to take the first report of the committee on Article 6. Fletcher argued that all the reports should be read and printed before any part of them was put to the vote. This, Hume says, was 'stuck to tenanciously' by Fletcher, Hamilton and Annandale. They spoke so often that Argyll, supported by Mar, said that anyone who transgressed the rules of the House should be censured. It was resolved that the Chancellor should in future stop those who transgressed. On 17 December a quarrel between Fletcher and Stair delayed proceedings for an hour while each accused the other of lying. Both were at length persuaded to apologise and to give their words of honour that they would not 'resent it without doors'.[44]

On 24 December Mar was able to tell Nairne that he believed that they were now in sight of land. The Court had been narrowly defeated once or twice on unimportant points of detail or procedure; but, by and large, they had carried the day. They had gone through troublesome passages on such matters as the malt tax, the salt duty and export premiums on the export of meal. On all these points, amendments or additions to the Treaty had been passed, but not of a kind likely to cause difficulty in the English Parliament. They had succeeded in defeating all amendments of that kind, even if they were favourable to Scotland. The Professors of Mathematics of the Universities of Edinburgh and

Aberdeen had reported on 7 December that the calculation of the Equivalent was just.[45]

Addresses continued to descend on Parliament. Two of these aroused special comment. One from Ayr, which I have already mentioned, was notable because it was the only one that did not utterly reject the Union. Another from the Presbytery of Hamilton was described by Defoe as 'of an extraordinary nature'. It pleaded that no incorporating Union should be concluded until a General Assembly of the Church had been called; 'the National Church established by law hath an undoubted right to be consulted'.[46] This may have seemed a strange notion to Defoe as a newcomer to Scotland, but it was perfectly in accordance with what George Davie has recently described as the 'Reformation ideal of a constitution finely balanced as between church and state: a constitution by which they would govern themselves through the cooperation of a pair of mutually critical but mutually complementary assemblies, the one concerned with politics and law, the other with the distinguishable, but nevertheless inseparable sphere of ethics and faith'.[47] It was certainly arguable that the General Assembly had a right to be consulted on a matter of such consequence as the Union which radically affected all aspects of Scottish life. The General Assembly could also legitimately claim to be far more representative than Parliament of the people at large.

The Chancellor referred to the Addresses in a statement which he made to the House on 27 December. He claimed that they had been given due consideration. (A number of them had, in fact, been read at the beginning of nearly every sederunt, but the Government had paid no further attention to them). Nevertheless, he continued, certain people had now sent letters to the subscribers of the Addresses asking them to assemble in Edinburgh and await replies. He therefore proposed a Proclamation prohibiting 'all such unwarrantable and seditious convocating'. It was passed by 112 votes to 62. Lockhart made a Protest that the Proclamation did not prejudge the rights and privileges of the Barons, Freeholders and Heretors.[48]

The language of Lockhart's Protest was an allusion to what the Opposition in fact intended and which was something more formal and dramatic than the Government may have realised. It was a proposal, put forward by Atholl and Fletcher, which Hamilton, at first, professed to support. The idea was based on a precedent from the time of the minority of James V. As many of the barons, freeholders and heretors (in other words, the landowners) as could come to Edinburgh wait as a body on the High Commissioner and ask him to send a National Address to the Queen. A draft was drawn up for the purpose. It informed the Queen of 'the almost universal aversion to the Treaty' and, 'to prevent such a chain of miseries as is likely to be the consequence of a forced Union', asked her to discountenance the Treaty and call a new Parliament and General Assembly of the Church.[49]

By the time appointed 500 landowners had assembled in Edunburgh and more were arriving. Once again, Hamilton found a way to frustrate the plan. At the last minute he told his colleagues that he could not support the Address unless a clause was added indicating willingness to accept the Hanoverian Succession. This was, of course, repugnant to many of those who had assembled and it inevitably produced dissension among them. All attempts to reach a compromise failed. Hamilton and Atholl were now at loggerheads and the landowners eventually returned home, 'highly enraged at being thus baulked'.[50]

Apparently undistracted by this latest turmoil, Parliament returned on 30 December to the detailed consideration of article 15 which dealt with the Equivalent. They had debated the article clause by clause, the first on 7 December and another six on 26 December. The main outstanding issue was the position of the African and Indian Company of Scotland, in other words, the Company of the Darien Scheme. Article 15 of the Treaty provided that part of the Equivalent of £398,085. 10. 0 should be used to pay for the capital stock of the Company plus interest. After the passing of an Act in the English Parliament to raise this money, the Company would neither trade nor license to trade, and it would 'be dissolved and cease' when the payment was made. In an Address to Parliament the Company had protested against the proposal to abolish it, maintaining that their continuation 'upon the same foot with the East India and other trading Companies in England, is in no way inconsistent with the trade of the United Kingdom'. This very reasonable point was ignored. As something of a sweetener, an amendment passed on 30 December provided for payment to the Company being given priority even over the payment of the Scottish public debt, and giving them the right to continue trading if payment was not made to them within 12 months.[51]

Defoe comments that even at this stage people in Scotland were so far from being convinced that the Union would take effect that the value of the Company's Stock was very low and it was being sold 'for trifles'. 'Several people offered to sell their whole interest for ten per cent on the original stock, though at the same time they saw, that if the Union took place, the whole principal money, with interest, was to be repaid them'.[52] Although it was obvious by this time that the Scottish Parliament was about to approve the whole Treaty, it seems that people at large still found it impossible to believe that something so widely detested could possibly be imposed on them.

By 31 December 1706, Parliament had reached article 18 about the continuity of laws. This was approved and another attempt to exempt Scots from the English Sacramental Test was rejected. This exemption would have been entirely reasonable. The Test obliged all applicants for public office in England to take an oath of adherence to the tenets of the Church of England. It meant that no Scotsman could take public office in England without changing his religion, but there was no such restriction on Englishmen taking employment in Scotland. The Court's success in defeating an amendment to prevent this discrimination is another proof of the strength of their control over their vote. Defoe comments that it was a vital point because the English Parliament attached such importance to the Test that to ask for an exemption 'would be to ask something which they knew would not be granted, and consequently put the treaty to a stop'.[53]

For the meetings in January, which dealt with the remaining seven articles, two of our sources dry up. Mar had conscientiously sent a long report for each day's proceedings up to 31 December, but there is a complete break between then and 1 February. Presumably he continued to write the letters but they have been lost. Hume of Crossrigg's *Diary* also peters out at about the same time because illness kept him from the House. For the next nine meetings, which completed the approval of the Treaty, we are therefore deprived of the two sources which so far had given some information about Fletcher's part in the debates. For this period Lockhart is mostly concerned with extra-parliamentary activity. The *Acts of the Parliament of Scotland*, as usual, give an outline of the proceedings, but no speeches and no names, except in the voting lists. Defoe in his commentaries on the minutes sometimes summarises points made in the debates. He seldom says who made them and he continued his policy of never mentioning Fletcher, an unconscious tribute perhaps to the force of his arguments.

The House approved a few amendments to these remaining articles. On article 20, which preserved all heritable offices, the word 'superiorities' was inserted. This, says Defoe, 'bound down Scotland to the private tyranny and oppression of the heretors and lairds'.[54] This is fair comment. The article preserved one of the most unsatisfactory of Scottish institutions and the amendment made it worse. Like Article 15 on the Equivalent, 19 on the legal system, 21 on the priveleges of the Burghs and 23 on those of the Peers, Article 20 was a blatant appeal to the self interest of precisely the classes who were represented in Parliament. They were all part of the inducement to them to vote for the Treaty. Defoe mentions another. Before the Union the salary of the law lords of the Court of Session was £200 per annum; it was to be £500 afterwards.[55]

One of the amendments was a concession to Scottish sentiment. A proposal to add a clause to article 20 was accepted as an addition to the 24th. This provided for the keeping in Scotland 'in all tyme coming' of the Scottish Crown, Sceptre and Sword of State and the public records of the Kingdom. Defoe is probably right that the reason for this amendment was to still a rumour, which was disturbing the people, that these symbols of Scottish nationhood were to be removed on the completion of the Union. Most of the other proposals for amendments were rejected. They included, once again, the proposal that the Parliament of Great Britain should meet in Scotland at least once every three years. Two amendments about the rights of Scottish Peers were also rejected. One (which sounds like a Fletcher idea) would have denied them immunity from proceedings for debts incurred in Scotland before the Union. The other would have given all Scottish Peers the right to sit in the House of Lords, although only the elected 16 could vote.[56]

Another Act intended to curb demonstrations against the Union was hurriedly passed, and touched with the sceptre, on 2 January 1707. This adjourned the sittings of the law courts until 4 February. The purpose, as Defoe explained, was to remove a pretext for people gathering in Edinburgh during the final stages of the debate on the Union.[57]

With the approval of the whole Treaty now within sight, the Opposition made a vigorous last stand over Article 22. As Hume Brown has said, 'Of all the Articles of the Treaty none was more galling to the national pride.'[58] It was this article which would reduce the Scottish representation in the new Parliament of Great Britain to 45 members in the Commons and to 16 Peers, elected from their number, in the Lords, while leaving the English representation unchanged. The article, Defoe says, was 'vigorously opposed'. There were many 'long speeches' over three days, 7, 8 and 9 January. Defoe summarises some of the points made, but does not tell us who made them. Even at this late stage, it was argued that the whole of the Scottish Parliament, like the English, should remain intact, meeting if need be alongside the English one. A more sophisticated proposal, and one which was difficult to refute, sounds like Fletcher with his concern for constitutional equity and precision. Before England required Scotland to reduce her representation to one which bore a proportion to population or to revenue from taxes, she ought to reduce her own representation by the same criteria.[59] Such criteria were notoriously disregarded in England with rotten boroughs and the like until the Reform Acts of the next century.

Before the vote, with its inevitable outcome, was taken on article 22, a series of protests were made. Atholl made a powerful general statement of the case against the article and indeed against the Treaty as a whole. We do not know who drafted the Protest, but it was such an important statement that it was probably approved by the leading men of the Opposition. Its force, clarity, logic and national feeling all suggest the hand of Fletcher. The text began by noting that the 160 Scottish Peers in Parliament were to be reduced to 16 and joined to the English House of Lords in which England had 180. This was a 'very unequal' representation for country 'as independent and as free a Nation as the other'. It amounted to forfeiture and was dishonourable and disgraceful. Similarly, the representation of the Shires and Burghs was to be reduced from 155 to 45 and joined to the 513 English members of the House of Commons. Scotland could have no influence in the joint Parliament because of the vast disproportion of these numbers. 'From all of which it is plain and evident that this from a sovereign Independent Monarchie shall disolve its Constitution and be at the disposal of England whose Constitution is not in the least to be altered by this Treaty'.[60]

The Protest then referred to the Addresses which showed the 'generall dislike and aversion to the incorporating Union'. There had been not one Address in favour. Accordingly this and the following Articles should not be approved until the queen had been informed of the will of the people. She might then call a new Parliament to seek 'an Union upon honourable just and equall terms which may Unite them in affection and interest the surest foundation of peace and tranquillity for both Kingdoms.'[61] The opposition, in other words, were in favour, as they had been from the beginning, of a union in the sense of a treaty of friendship and cooperation which preserved the independence and separate parliaments of the two kingdoms. Other Protests were made by Buchan, Lockhart and Walter Stewart on behalf of the interests of the Nobility, the Shires and the Burghs and by Erroll and Marischall on behalf of their great hereditary offices as High Constable and Great Marshall of the Kingdom.[62]

Atholl's Protest evidently struck home because the 8 and 9 of January were largely taken up with a debate about it, Marchmont protested against the Protest as 'presumptions illegal and unwarrantable'. Balmerino, in turn, protested against Marchmont's counter-protest as 'highly reflecting on many noble and worthy members.' This battle of Protest against Protest in the end reached a stalemate. It was decided that none of the Protests would be printed or inserted in the Minutes but that they would be recorded in the records of Parliament.[63]

As impressive as was this demonstration against the Treaty, it fell short of what had in fact been planned. Hamilton had proposed that when Article 22 was reached, Annandale should again propose the settlement of the Crown on the House of Hanover. When this was rejected, all opposed to the Union should adhere to a Protestation against it and then leave the House in a body. They would then have a National Address, signed by as many people as possible, despatched to the Queen. Hamilton was convinced that this demonstration that the Union did not rest on a 'secure and legal basis' would persuade the English to drop the measure. Lockhart, who gives us an inside account of this episode, prints the text of this Protestation. He says that it was probably drafted by Sir James Stuart, the Queen's Advocate, who, although a member of the Court, had remained bitterly opposed to the Union.[64]

The document begins by challenging the right of Parliament to overthrow its own constitution without a convention of the Estates, 'cloathed with a more than ordinary power'. It refers to the 'unprecedented number' of Addresses against the Union and to the offer of accepting the Hanoverian Succession as a better method of establishing a good understanding between the two nations. Many reasons for rejecting the Union are then rehearsed. Among them are the overthrow of the fundamental constitution and the surrendering of the power of the Scottish Parliament 'to the entire Parliament of another nation'. It would tend 'to ruin the trade and subjects of this kingdom, by engaging them into insupportable customs and burdens upon foreign trade and home consumption, and by involving the trade of Scotland under the regulations of the trade of England', which would be ruinous to Scotland because conditions there are so different from the English.

The conclusion went much further than an appeal to the Queen; it was nothing less than a declaration of independence and a refusal to accept the proposed British Parliament. The signatories declared that they refused to 'lessen, dismember, or part with our Parliament, or any part of the power thereof', and would refuse to accept 'pretended laws, acts or resolves of 'any pretended Parliament of Great Britain'. They declared that it would be lawful for them, 'as our ancestors in the like cases have usually done, to vindicate and assert our ancient rights and liberties'.[65]

According to Lockhart, Hamilton went to great pains to enlist support for this proposal. The revival of the idea of accepting the Hanoverian Succession caused difficulty with the Jacobites, but Hamilton was able to persuade most of them that this was a necessary tactic and that the text of the Protestation did not commit them to the Succession. Atholl was not convinced on this point, but agreed to take part in the measure of leaving the House. 'It caused', says Lockhart, 'an universal joy, and great numbers of gentlemen and eminent citizens flock'd together that morning about the Parliament House to attend the separating members, and assist them in case they should be maltreated as they came from the House. But all their hopes soon vanished and came to nothing'. Once again this was because of the behaviour of Hamilton. He first refused to go to the House on the pretext of toothache. When he was eventually persuaded to go there, he asked who was to present the Protestation. It had naturally been assumed that this would be Hamilton himself since he had made the proposal and was in any case the acknowledged leader of the Opposition. He refused to take the lead, although he said that he would be the first to adhere. So much time was spent in arguing the point that the business of the House had proceeded so far that the opportunity was lost.[66]

Not surprisingly, Lockhart tells us that this third act of sabotage by Hamilton (or rather fourth, counting the acceptance of the nomination of the Commissioners by the Queen in the previous year) caused great rage among his supporters. It was the last straw. 'No other measures were concerted, and every one did that which was good in his own eyes; and in a few days great numbers of those had appeared zealously against the Union, deserted the House in despair.'[66] The wonder is, of course, that they had tolerated and followed him so long, even if, in Lockhart's phrase, he was 'the person of the first quality and most interest in the nation'. He must have had such qualities of charisma and plausibility that they blinded his followers to his actions. It was true that these four episodes, disastrous as they were, always appeared as unexpected exceptions and that for the rest of time Hamilton acted the part of a determined leader of the opposition to the Union, and as such basked in the cheers of the crowds in the streets.

I have already discussed in Chapter 12 the other mystery, why did Hamilton behave with such extraordinary vacillation or duplicity?. Of this last episode, Lockhart says that Queensberry, or someone sent by him, called on Hamilton on the night before the crucial day and threatened him that 'England would lay the blame of it upon him, and he would suffer for it', if he went ahead with the plan.[67] This tends to confirm that England had some hold on him, either by means of his English estates or otherwise. There are two possibilities. He may throughout have been acting a part with the deliberate intention of misleading and betraying his followers. This would have required an extraordinary degree of cold-blooded and ruthless skill. On the other hand, he may have been pulled in opposite directions by his political instincts and by his self-interest. If so, at the decisive moments, when the Court jerked the reins, it was always his self-interest which prevailed. In either case, the result was that the nominal leader of the Opposition effectively undermined and destroyed it.

I mentioned on page 117 a public quarrel in Parliament between Hamilton and Fletcher in 1704. Perhaps Fletcher realised at an early stage that Hamilton was not to be trusted. Although they were nominally on the same side politically they evidently remained estranged for at least some time. In 1705, before the 26 March, Lockhart in the course of a long letter (which I have already quoted) to Hamilton about the political situation strongly recommended a reconciliation:

> There is one thing that all your Grace's freinds were unanimous in, and requird me to show so much to your Grace and that in thy thought it absolutely necessary . . . that your Grace and Salton were again in good understanding. No body will pretend to justifye all his actions and manner of proceedings, but yet he is so useful a member of a party (take him all together) that your Grace cannot but perceive, how great a disadvantage it would be, not to have him in concert att this time. The means and ways how to bring this reconciliation about, must be left, on your Grace's part, to your self, but that it were effected is the hearty wish of all your Grace's freinds, and I have reason to believe Salton is very far from being averse to it, but on the contrary very desirous of it'.[68]

We do not know what came of this suggestion or what were the personal relations between Hamilton and Fletcher in the 1706–7 Session of Parliament. Fletcher's name does not appear in the list which Lockhart gives of those with whom Hamilton first discussed his plan for the Protestation and walk-out over Article 22.[69]

After this episode, the remaining three Articles of the Treaty were approved on the 10 and 14 January. The Act Ratifying and Approving the Treaty of Union was read on the 15th. Next day the Act for Securing the Protestant Religion, 'which is inserted in and ratified by the above Act' was passed and touched with the sceptre. The Act ratifying the Treaty was then put to the vote. It passed by a majority of 41 with the breakdown of the vote very similar to that on the first Article more than two months before. Of the nobility 42 were for and 19 against; Shires 38 for and 30 against; Burghs 30 for and 20 against. Lockhart is the source of the well known episode that when Seafield as Chancellor signed the Act, 'he returned it to the clerk, in the face of Parliament, with this despising and contemning remark, "Now there's ane end of ane old song"'.[70] Stair, who had provided the intellectual leadership for the Court, died suddenly on the following night; 'his spirits', says Burnet, 'being quite exhausted by the length and vehemence of the debate.'[71]

Defoe described this outcome (for which he as an English propagandist and agent had worked hard) as 'contrary . . . to the expectation of all the world'. The Parliament of Scotland had 'a long, a troublesome, a dangerous, and I must own a very uncomfortable debate, step by step, and article by article, from the third of October to the fourteenth of January, with very little intermission; for never was business closer applied, more strenuously pushed, or more vigorously opposed'. He contrasted this with the smooth passage of the Treaty in the English Parliament. The debate there began in the House of Commons on 22 January and the articles were passed one by one 'without any opposition, amendment or alteration, no not in the least'. It had passed through both Houses by 4 March and was approved by the Queen on the 6.[72]

There was the same contrast between the two countries in their reactions when the Treaty came into force. Queensberry had been stoned by the crowd in Edinburgh; but, when his work as Commissioner was complete, he made a triumphal progress through England to London in April 1707. Clerk, who accompanied him, says that in all the English cities he passed through, he was received 'with great pomp and solemnity' and the 'joyful acclamations of all the people,' When he arrived at Barnet, on the outskirts of London, 'he was met by the Ministry of England and most of the nobility then attending the two Houses of Parliament. Their Retinue consisted of 46 coaches and above 1,000 Horsemen.' On may 1, when the Treaty came into force, the Queen and both Houses of Parliament went to a service in St Paul's 'with the greatest splendour.' Clerk says that he 'observed a real joy and satisfaction in the Citizens of London, for they were terribly apprehensive of confusions from Scotland in case the Union had not taken place. The whole day was spent in feastings, ringing of Bells, and illuminations, and . . . at no time Scotsmen were more acceptable to the English than on that day.'[73]

It was quite different in Scotland. Harie Maule wrote to Mar from Edinburgh on May 1:

> There is nothing so much taken notice of here today as the solemnity in the south part of Britain and the want of it here. The first tune of our musick bells this day was 'Why should I be sad on my wedding day'.[74]

The different reactions in England and Scotland were significant and inevitable. For England, the Union meant the achievement of an ambition, pursued since the days of Edward I, to reduce Scotland to English domination. For Scotland, it meant the loss, in a particularly humiliating and shameful manner, of the independence which they had maintained against heavy odds for hundreds of years.

17

Last Years (January 1707 to 15 September 1716)

'Lord have mercy on my poor country that is so barbarously oppressed.'
— Andrew Fletcher

After the ratification of the Treaty on 16 January 1707, the Scottish Parliament remained in session for another two months. For one thing, the House had to be ready to respond to any amendment that might have been proposed to the Treaty by the English Parliament. Consequential arrangements had to be made, on the assumption that the Treaty would come into force, such as the method of election to the new Parliament of Great Britain and the payment of the Equivalent. There was a now a last chance to dispose of routine Scottish business. Although Parliament was in its last agonies it still found time on to turn its attention again to the work of John Anderson on the Scottish historical records. As I mentioned on page 195, Fletcher had been appointed to a committee to look into this in November of the previous year. Their report was evidently satisfactory because Parliament passed an order on 12 February to 'encourage and enable' Anderson to continue with his work on ancient charters and seals. Payments of £590 sterling for work already done and of £1,050 to enable him to complete the task were recommended.[1]

In the memoirs and diaries of the time there seems to be reference to only one intervention by Fletcher during these two months. On 20 January it was proposed for the Government that the 16 Peers and 45 members of the commons should be elected from the present Parliament, a slightly dubious interpretation of Article XXII of the Treaty, and an admission that the government was unwilling to risk a new election against a background of general indignation. Hume tells us that Fletcher moved that no Peer or eldest son of a Peer should be eligible to represent a Shire or a Burgh. Fletcher was plainly trying to curb the influence of the nobility but his motion was defeated by 13 votes.[2]

Fletcher presumably took part in other debates of which no detailed record survives, apart from the skeleton narrative of the *Acts of the Parliament of Scotland*. One matter on which his feelings can well be imagined was a proposal by Argyll that expenses should be paid to the Commissioners who negotiated the Treaty on a scale of £1,000 for each Peer, £500 to each other member, £400 to the Secretary and £400 to each of two accountants. After two days of debate a scale of about half of these figures was approved. Defoe has a comment:

> This proposal was ill received indeed, and a horrid clamour raised at it without doors: the people who had been hot against the Union took hold of it with

unbridled raillery, reproaching the treaters in a most indecent manner, exclaiming at the very thing itself. Now the nation might see they said what they had been doing at London, and what they had been pursuing ever since that they had sold their country for a sum of money, and they were beginning to share it among them.[3]

Defoe gives us no names; but Fletcher, who had always denounced the mercenary motives of the negotiators, must surely have been one of the most outspoken. This melancholy session of the Scottish Parliament, Seafield's end of an auld sang, finally reached a conclusion on 25 March 1707. Queensberry, as Commissioner, said: 'the Publik Business of this Session being now at an end, it is full time to put an end to it.' Parliament was accordingly 'adjourned to 22 April next.' It has not yet met again.[4]

There is a story, quoted by G. W. T. Ormond in his biography and ultimately deriving from an anecdote recorded by Lord Elibank, that Fletcher left Edinburgh, and perhaps Scotland, immediately after the House rose:

On the day of his departure, his friends crowded around him, entreating him to stay. Even after his foot was in the stirrup, they continued their solicitations, anxiously crying, 'will you forsake this country?' He reverted his head, and darting on them a look of indignation, keenly replied 'It is only fit for the slaves that sold it' then leaped upon the saddle and put spurs to his horse, leaving the whole company struck with a momentary humiliation, and (blind to the extravagance of his conduct) at a loss which most to admire, the pride of his virtue, or the elevation of his spirit[5]

This has a ring of truth about it. At that moment Fletcher's bitter feeling of indignation and sorrow at the loss of the independence of Scotland, and particularly at the sordid manner of the loss, must have been overwhelming.

Fletcher does not seem however to have left Scotland at once. Among the pitifully few letters to him or from him which have survived at Saltoun is one of about this time, 21 April 1707, to Fletcher from D. Gregory in London. It throws some light indirectly on Fletcher's feelings at the time and gives a hint of other matters about which we have very little evidence. The letter begins by referring to an interest which Fletcher had expressed in the design of Covent Garden Church and gives a reply from no less than Sir Christopher Wren to a technical question which had arisen over the construction of some outbuildings at Saltoun. The letter continues:

Dr. Arbuthnot and I are very much obliged to you for your kind remembrance of us. We miss no opportunity of all grateful remembring you and hope to see you here for all that has happened and if you are resolved not to come to London, I hope to see you at Salton.[6]

At first glance, this looks like no more than a trivial note of social courtesy, but there are several points of interest about it. The writer is almost certainly David Gregory (1661–1708), a member of a very accomplished family from

Banffshire, a mathematician and astronomer. He became Savilian Professor of Astronomy at Oxford and was living in London at about this time where he was friendly with the Dr Arbuthnot (1667–1735) who is mentioned is the letter. Arbuthnot was another Scottish émigré in London, a fashionable physician who became the personal doctor of Queen Anne. He was well known as a writer, wit and satirist, and was a friend of Pope, Gay and of Jonathan Swift (who mentions him frequently in the *Journal to Stella*). The letter then is clear evidence that Fletcher was on terms of intimate friendship with two Scotsmen in London who were moving in the highest literary and intellectual circles, and he could casually ask Wren for his advice on some trivial question of building.

We know from other evidence that Fletcher himself some years earlier enjoyed London society and was well received there, whether at the Grecian Tavern or elsewhere (See page 58). If his *Account of a Conversation* is largely fictional, it presumably reflects the sort of conversation to which he was accustomed in London as well as Edinburgh. At the end of his *Discourse* on Militias, he praises the English and describes London as 'that great city, the pride and glory, not only of our island, but of the world.'. At the same time, of course, he objected to London drawing the 'riches and government of thee three Kingdoms to the South-east corner of the island.'[7]

It was natural enough that Gregory should have supposed that Fletcher would now be reluctant to go back to London after 'all that has happened'. His letter is evidence that Fletcher inspired not only respect but affection among his friends and acquaintances. Most of what we know about him concerns his public and political activity. In this, his integrity, determination and firmness are undoubted, but he also appears as harsh, quick-tempered and reluctant to suffer easily fools, knaves and those who disagreed with him. We might suppose that such a man was more likely to make enemies than friends. Further evidence of the more attractive side of his personality appears from a letter on an unlikely subject in this connection, his imprisonment by his political opponents.

In March 1708 a considerable French fleet set sail from Dunkirk with the object of making a landing in Scotland in the Jacobite interest.[8] It came to nothing, largely because it was frustrated by the weather, but it naturally alarmed Whitehall. A large number of people in Scotland were arrested and among them, Andrew Fletcher. He was certainly no Jacobite, but opposition to the Union made strange bedfellows and the authorities were taking no chances. Mar wrote from Whitehall on 29 March to his brother, Lord Grange:-

> There are more people ordred to be taken up and amongst the rest your friend, Mr Fletcher, who I'm sure will be very angrie; but if he is innocent, as I hope he is, his friend the Highland Duke, is the occation of it and there was no saying against it.[9]

From his prison in Stirling Castle, Fletcher sent to Mar on 14 April 1708 one of the very few of his letters which have survived. It shows him in an unexpected light. He is ironic, but relaxed, playful and generous to his opponents, in spite of the fact that he has been imprisoned without proper cause:-

> My Lord: Your friendship shows itself by effects not words. My Lady Mar has put herself to so much trouble about me as gives me more than my confinemennt. But my greatest mortification was from the civilitys I received from Collonel Ariskin to whom of late I never showed common ones. All that I could say for myself was that my prejudices were never personal. You see what uneasyness one falls under by imprisonment, when even kind things done him turne to be of a different nature, especialy to a man who sees himself in no capacity to returne them. You may tell my Lord Colvin we are not locked up here at night, and that we drank all yesternight of the Collonel's good wine and continued till this morning, that he can find no such company in Scotland, and that for his excuse we shall perswade the Collonel to say that he is confined. I am with great sense of your obligations, my Lord, your most humble servant, Fletcher.[10]

There is a clear hint in this correspondence that Mar was well disposed towards Fletcher personally, even if they were poles apart, at that time, over the Union. I have already quoted the letter which Mar wrote to his brother from Stamford on 18 August 1706 when he was on his way back to Scotland after the Union negotiations: 'I hope Saltoun and I shall still be in speaking terms tho' not of the same opinion in this measure of the Union. I have not forgot his case of instruments.'[11] I emphasise 'at that time' because Mar, in common with many of the others who had made the Union, very quickly began to regret it.

A whole succession of events soon brought home to the Scots of all parties that, in the words of *United or Separate Parliaments*, they were now in a trap of their own making in which they could dance around to all eternity.[12] For example by December 1707, the Scottish Privy Council was abolished. Grange wrote to Mar about the 'consternation and surprize' which this caused in Scotland. 'All sorts of people, Unioners and Anti-Unioners, Episcopal and Presbyterian are thunder struck.' Fletcher and others were pointing to it as an effect of the 'happy union'.[13] Scottish prisoners were transferred to London. The English treason law was applied to Scotland. English excise officers flooded into Scotland. The historian, Hume Brown, though a Unionist, says of the period: 'Throughout these years every interest of Scotland was regarded and treated purely and simply with reference to the exigencies of political parties in England. There was not a class in Scotland which had not reason to complain of a breach of the Articles of Union, and to regret that it had ever been accomplished.'[14] On 14 June 1708, Mar wrote to the Queen: 'I think myself obleidged in duety to lett your Majestie know that so farr as I understand the inclinations and temper of the generallity of this country is still as dissatisfied with the Union as ever, and seem mightily sowr'd.'[15] Within a few months of the completion of the Union, Mar was as opposed to it as Fletcher himself. By 1713 Scots of all parties had reached the same conclusions. A motion for the dissolution of the Union was moved in the House of Lords by one of those most responsible for managing its acceptance in Scotland, Seafield, by then the Earl of Findlater. It failed by only four votes.

To return to 1708, Fletcher was not transferred with the other prisoners to London and seems to have been released fairly soon, although we do not know exactly when. This comparitively lenient treatment was due to the intervention of Mar. He wrote from Whitehall to his brother, Lord Grange, on 16 April:

> I leave the incloased to Salton open that you may read it and then deliver it. I cou'd not wryt it to him, but you may let him know that he cou'd not be sett at libertie just now because those who were taken up upon the same account, I mean the Duke of Athole's letters, are ordred up here with the rest, but as soon as they are gone he'll be sett at libertie, tho' he wou'd not speak of this. I know not what he'll think of it, but here 'tis thought a mighty favour, and I assure you I bestir'd myself for him, tho' I fancy I'll hardly get thanks.[16]

Fletcher was evidently at liberty and preparing to leave Scotland by August. As I mentioned on page 70, he wrote a list in his library catalogue of 'Books put in a box to be sent to London. August 1708' and another of items 'Left in the great drawer of my cabinet. Sept 1708.'[17] This looks very much as if he was making careful arrangements not for a short journey but for a long, if not permanent, absence. Unfortunately, we have no other evidence to throw any more light on this. Was his disgust over what had happened to Scotland so strong that he could no longer bear to live there? If so, London seems a strange choice, unless he was only passing through on his way to France or somewhere else. Since most of the books in the box had a bearing on the constitutional issue did he have some idea of pursuing the argument in London? Was he perhaps only proposing to send the books for sale because they had become painful reminders of a lost cause? We simply do not know, not even if he in fact left Scotland in September 1708 or changed his mind.

There is, however, firm evidence that Fletcher was in Holland by June 1710. In April of that year his brother, Henry, signed an agreement on his behalf with James Meikle. Under this agreement, Meikle, described as a wright of Wester Keith (which is close to Saltoun), was to travel to Holland. He was to learn there the 'perfect art of sheeling barley' and 'how to accomodate, order, and erect mills for that purpose'. He was then to return to Scotland and pass on these new skills to Saltoun and to no one else. Andrew Fletcher was in Holland at the time and involved in the enterprise, as appears from a letter which he sent from the Hague to Meikle on 18 June 1710:

> I received yours of the 14th, and doubt not but you have got the barley before this comes to your hand; as for those big pieces of iron work you speak of, which will be necessary for setting up a mill for sheeling barley, pray have them made, and every thing else which you think necessary to buy in this country, and take care that they be ready, as soon as may be. As for the time of your sailing it is uncertain, but you must be at Rotterdam by the time the ships fall down, which I shall have

timely advertisement of, and come to bring you away; I believe you may expect me about Friday or Saturday the 27th or 28th of this month, so let all be ready against then, and advize with Mr Morison if you find difficulty in any thing.[18]

This piece of industrial espionage led to the setting up in Saltoun of the first barley mill in Scotland, long operated there with great success. During his exile in Holland Fletcher had noticed mills of this kind which husked barley to make it edible as meal and as an ingredient for broth and other dishes. You could say that one of Andrew Fletcher's contributions to Scotland was that he made possible the traditional recipe for Scotch broth.

Because of this episode, it is often said in the reference books and elsewhere that after the Union Fletcher devoted himself to agricultural improvements, particularly in the production of linen and the milling of barley. In fact, there is no evidence that Andrew Fletcher himself was actively engaged in these activities. Most of the credit is due to his sister-in-law, Margaret Carnegie of Pittarow, who married his younger brother, Henry. He wrote to his son, also called Andrew, then a student at Leyden, on 22 Nov 1714 in a postscript to a letter from Margaret: 'she says you need not trouble yourself to inquire anything about the making of Barley, for she has taken pains on it since you went away and is perfectly master of it and the mill goes extraordinarly well.'[19] A remark by Andrew Fletcher about Margaret is recorded in the anonymous *Recollections respecting the family of the Fletchers of Saltoun*, published in 1803. It records that Andrew: 'observing the many domestic virtues of this Lady, when thy spoke of marriage, said, 'my brother has got the woman that should have been my wife.'[20] This is the only scrap of evidence which has survived about Fletcher's attitude to, or relationships with, women. Too much should not be read into this, since very little of the surviving record is concerned with his private life. Certainly he never married, and it is possible, I suppose, that his attitude was influenced by an early disappointment. The rivalry, if such it was, does not seem to have led to antagonism between the two brothers. The surviving letters between them, which I shall summarise later in this Chapter, do not suggest any bitterness or tension, although the tone of Henry's letters is generally more respectful than warm.

Fletcher was back in Scotland at the end of 1711, to judge from a letter which George Lockhart of Carnwath sent to him from London on Christmas day. By this time, Lockhart was a member of the British Parliament and had been appointed a member of a Commission to enquire into the 'affairs of the Scots Forage'. This concerned contracts to supply forage for mounted troops in Scotland in 1708. The future Prime Minister, Robert Walpole, was involved and was expelled from the Commons and sent to the Tower. Fletcher had evidently written 'with some warmth' to Lockhart to complain that his name had appeared in one of the documents submitted to the Commission. Lockhart in reply assured Fletcher that no malice was intended and that the Commission was obliged to investigate all complaints submitted to it, even if they were groundless. He added: 'the rules and orders of the house are you know very misterious (if I may use that expression) or uncertain, and generally unknown, especially to us Scotsmen.' Although we do not have Fletcher's letter, it seems that he was in Scotland at the time because Lockhart refers to a report sent to his agent in Edinburgh, with the implication that it would be easy for Fletcher to have a look at it.[21]

Fletcher was however in London by February 1713. On the 3rd of that month Henry wrote to him 'at Mr Duras's in Charles Street, near St James Square' to report the death of their mother on the previous day. He said that she had always kept her reason entire. She left 500 marks to the poor in Saltoun and 1,500 for the widows of Episcopal ministers.[22] There is an incidental reference in a letter which Lockhart wrote in London on 29 April: 'Mr Fletcher has been very ill of a fever and is not out of danger yet', the first indication that his health was declining.[23]

He was still in London on 13 December of the same year when he wrote to his brother to say that Bishop Burnet had left in his will 20,000 marks to Aberdeen and the same to Saltoun. We do not know if he stayed on in London for the next year or so, but we do know that he left London for Holland in May 1715. His nephew told his mother in a letter, 'my uncle come from London the 6 May NS and was in the Hague 8 May. He did not look very well then but has since recovered and is now very well'.[24]

This letter is part of the only sustained correspondence involving Fletcher which has survived, preserved until recently in Saltoun House and now in the National Library of Scotland. It is between Henry and Margaret Fletcher at Saltoun, their son (the student at Leyden, later to play a prominent part in the affairs of Scotland as Lord Milton) and Andrew Fletcher, the Patriot, now in the last two years of his life. It is a correspondence in which constant, but undemonstrative, family affection is taken for granted. Henry and Margaret's letters are marked by parental anxiety for the good behaviour of their son, especially as his brother, Robert, has been a disappointment. 'Let us have some contact with you', Henry wrote on 21 June 1715, 'for we expect none from your brother, whose confirmed miscarriages have put his mother almost in her grave.'[25]

Irene J. Murray, who edited some of these letters for the Scottish History Society, says of Andrew Fletcher's that 'they most clearly reveal the witty, rather caustic, man who must have been so familiar to his contemporaries. And even in these private letters, his true patriotism, his love for his country which was above and beyond party interest, comes clearly through, and stands far above sickly sentiment.' She adds that Fletcher is 'a fascinating combination of high ideals, lofty motives, quick-temper and shrewd common sense.'[26] It is typical of his wit, as of his attitude to monarchy, that he writes of the 1715 Rising: 'The pretender has bin in Scot. now a month and a half; and is, they say, taking all the pains he can to ruine his owen affairs; which convinces everybody who formerly did not believe it that he is of the Family.'[27]

Fletcher left Holland for Paris where he arrived on 25 October 1715. He found that 'all things are excessively dear and bad' but there were more 'curious books' than he had imagined and more learned men than anywhere else in the world. There is a good deal in the correspondence about the current situation in Scotland with Henry passing on the news and Andrew saying rather surprisingly, that he is kept well informed by the British Ambassador, Lord Stair, the son of his old opponent in Parliament. There is also much discussion of books with Andrew sending detailed requests to his nephew to buy a good number at a sale in Holland. The books, mainly in Latin or Greek, are for the most part poetry, history and works on law. Some are intended for the younger Andrew's law studies and others, presumably, to fill gaps in the already substantial library in Saltoun. Henry, at his brother's request, sends a detailed description of a Highland targe. Andrew says that he is 'reading with extraordinary application and delight Daniel's history of France which, bar his Machines, the Sants and the Pope, in one of the best writ historys extant.'[28]

The correspondence turns to arrangements for the nephew to meet his uncle in Paris. Henry in his letters to his son takes a very respectful and deferential attitude towards Andrew; but he was after all a man of distinction as well as head of the family and laird of Saltoun. He writes, for instance: 'take heed that all that you say to your uncle be perfectly true and that you use not the least dissimulation, for he will very quickly find you out and will have no kindness for your afterwards'. On the other hand: 'You may see and learn more in 2 months when he is in Paris, than you would do in six if he were not there.'[29] Both father and uncle were anxious that the visit to Paris should not interfere with the younger Andrew's studies, but by mid-July 1716 the college vacation would have started and all would be ready. Andrew sent advice about clothes and in particular on the need for a black suit because of the mourning for Louis XIV. He would meet the coach when it arrived in Paris.[30]

It did not work out like that. By the time the younger man reached Paris, his uncle had to send him a note: 'I have ben very ill of a loosnes, and tho' I hope I am now upon the mending hand, yet I desir you may quit your company and come to me alone. I have therefore sent my footman with this line that he may call you a coach and bring you hither straight.'[31]

The planned stay in Paris had to be abandoned and it was now a question whether Fletcher had enough strength left to get back to Saltoun. On 21 August 1716 he wrote to his brother from his old lodgings at Mrs Duras's in Charles Street in London: 'Your son and I arrived here on Saturday at night, but so late we could not writ that night. I may very well say that without his help and extreem kind assiduity I had never bin able to come here, but would have bin obliged to stop by the way with a thousand inconveniencys and to the great hazard of my health: which is still very bad, and the looseness no ways stopt. But I stil hope I may recover some strength to be able to get to Salton.'[32]

Henry wrote back on 28 August: 'I am persuaded your own air will do you good, and that you can be no where so well as in your own House, where you will be better cared for than among strangers. All here will make you as well-come as your heart can wish.' A few days later, Andrew dictated, and then signed, his last letter: 'My recovery being not only uncertain but almost desperate I thought fit whatever might happen to send you this. I design to make no formal will seeing what I have will naturally go to you. I only desire that Two Hundred Pounds sterling value may be employed in relieving the most necessitous poor Scots prisoners and others who are rendered miserable by the late Rebellion.' He gave instructions also for other charitable payments, and one to 'Mr Alexander Cunningham to whom I have been much obliged and from whom I have received many kind services these many years, and to whom your Son has been much obliged and may still be more.'[33]

There are several references to this Alexander Cunningham in Fletcher's letter to his nephew during the previous few months. He was evidently also living in Leyden and was to come on the visit to Paris. Fletcher invariably asked his nephew to pass on his good wishes to Cunningham and he obviously had a high opinion of his scholarly knowledge of books. Since Fletcher mentions in one of the letters that Cunningham is 'going for Venice',[34] he was probably the Alexander Cunningham who was appointed British envoy to Venice in 1715. He was born in Selkirk in 1654 and completed his education in Holland where he met the political émigrés, including presumably Fletcher. His chief claim to fame is a history of Britain from 1688 to the accession of George I, written originally in Latin.[35] Since he enjoyed the patronage of the Duke of Argyll, he might seem an unlikely candidate for the friendship of Andrew Fletcher; but the warmth of the references in these letters and the terms of the bequest leave little doubt that he must have been very close to him. It is symptomatic of how little is known of Fletcher's private life that this connection only becomes apparent at this final stage.

Fletcher was attended by his friend, Dr Arbuthnot, and Alexander Cunningham, who had presumably travelled with him from Paris, was also with him at the end. His nephew had the melancholy task of writing an account of his last hours. He said that Fletcher had suffered much pain with great fortitude and talked about his approaching death with 'as much easiness and indifference as ever he talked about the publick news'. Almost the last words which he spoke distinctly were: 'Lord have mercy on my poor Countrey that is so barbarously oppressed.'[36] He died in London on 15 September 1716 and his body was taken back to Scotland by sea for burial in the family vault below the Kirk of Saltoun.

18

Andrew Fletcher Today

'The debate in which he was involved has never been closed, but continues.'
— *Gordon Donaldson*

It is very clear from contemporary accounts, and from nearly everything that was written about him for the next 200 years or so, that Andrew Fletcher's reputation as the Patriot derived from his activities in Parliament, and his unflinching and determined defence of Scottish independence. This reputation continues to this day. Fletcher's name is certainly no longer a house-hold word. With the neglect of Scottish history in our schools, it is probable that most people in Scotland have never heard of him. There are, however, many who respect his memory. This is evident from the existence of the Andrew Fletcher Society and the commemoration every September by the Saltire Society in the Kirk of East Saltoun, where a succession of distinguished speakers have considered various aspects of his life and influence. In these circles at least, even larger claims are made for Fletcher today than were made in the past. Lord Murray, a former Lord Advocate, in his speech in East Saltoun in 1982, said that without Fletcher's 'courage and integrity, Scotland could hardly be alive today.' Even more recently in an article in *Chapman*, the poet, Tom Scott, said of Fletcher that he was the greatest man of his time in Scotland, 'one of the most important in our history,. . . who led the struggle to prevent Scotland becoming Scotshire.'[1]

On the other hand, the traditional view has been challenged. In the first of several essays which John Robertson has published in recent years about Fletcher, he argued that his real significance had been 'obscured by a nationalistic posterity's preoccupation with his supposed role as leader of patriotic opposition to the Treaty of the Union.' Fletcher, he says, 'was ill-fitted for any conventional political role. He positively alarmed his contemporaries. Not only had he a violent past; he was secular, cosmopolitan and formidably learned, the possessor of a magnificent library; perhaps most disturbing of all, he was utterly ingenuous. Isolation was the natural price of such qualities — isolation from those whose views were close to his own as much as from opponents. Reputed a militant republican, his connections with republican circles are shadowy; and despite his fearless criticisms of the crown's ministers, he never had an organised political following in the Scottish Parliament.'[2] Robertson goes on to argue that 'Fletcher's contemporary significance was intellectual rather than political'. I shall return to that point; but, in the first place, is it true that Fletcher was ineffective as a practising politician?

Of course, there is a good deal of truth in Robertson's description of Fletcher, 'cosmopolitan and formidably learned' and the rest; but I know of no evidence that he 'alarmed' his contemporaries. The recorded comments of the time, as we have seen, suggest respect, admiration and a, sometimes grudging affection. Perhaps Robertson is judging Fletcher by his own, or 20th Century, standards; the contemporary reaction was quite different. It is the contemporary admiration which is the root of Fletcher's long-enduring reputation.

As for Fletcher's 'shadowy' connections with republican circles, the fact is that Fletcher never described himself as a republican. It was his opponents, such as Burnet and Clerk of Penicuik, who used the term as a pejorative label. Fletcher certainly distrusted the hereditary power of monarchs and wanted to transfer it to Parliament. 'He was', wrote Lockhart, 'an enemy to all monarchial governments, at least thought they wanted to be much reformed.'[3] In *An Account of a Conversation*, Seymour suggests that Fletcher's proposal for a European settlement implies the establishment of republics. Fletcher denies this; he was talking about either 'Kingdoms or Countries'. He goes on to discuss the matter in a way which shows that he saw advantage in the Union (by which he means alliance) of several small sovereignties under one Prince.[4] Fletcher did not object to the institution of monarchy and he was fairly indifferent who the monarch might be, as long as he or she was only a constitutional figure-head with the real power vested in Parliament. Fletcher, therefore, was not an out and out republican and there is no reason to suppose that he aspired to lead any such movement.

The extent to which he had 'an organised political following in the Scottish Parliament' is also a fairly complex matter. In his Saltoun address Geoffrey Barrow said that Fletcher 'was quintessentially independent, wholly incabable of being a party politician.' He goes on to quote in support one of the letters which Fletcher sent to his brother in June 1716: 'For the via di mezzo was always ruinous. The Torys and the Jacobites are idiots and mad-men. And the whig Party are some of them traitors to their country and others half witted. God have mercy on this country.'[5] A plague on all their houses, but he was then writing nine years after the Scottish Parliament was abolished and not of the situation in which he himself had been involved.

Certainly, Fletcher was an individualist who was reluctant to compromise. He must have been a difficult colleague but that does not necessarily mean that he was ineffective. As he was one of these colleagues, Lockhart of Carnwath was in a good position to know. On page 207 I quoted a letter which he sent to Hamilton in March 1705. It reflects both the difficulty of working with Fletcher and his value to the cause: 'no body will pretend to justifye all his actions and manner of proceedings, but yet he is so useful a member of a party (take him all to gather) that your Grace cannot but perceive, how great a disadvantage it would be, not to have him in concert att this time.'[6] When, some years later, Lockhart came to write his *Memoirs* he summed up Fletcher's position in the Country Party in a passage which I have already quoted on page 6.

He had a penetrating, clear and lively apprehension, but so extreamly wedded to his own opinions, that there were few (and those too must be his beloved friends, and of whom he had a good opinion) he could endure to reason against him, and did for the most part so closely and unalterably adhere to what he advanc'd (which was frequently very singular) that he'd break with his party before he'd alter the least jot of his schemes and maxims; and therefore it was impossible for any set of men, that did not give up themselves to be absolutely directed by him, to please him, so as to carry him along in all points. And thence it came to pass, that he often in Parliament acted a part by himself, tho' in the main he stuck close to the Country party, and was their Cicero.[7]

This has the ring of truth of a statement by a man who knew what he was talking about. It is also entirely consistent with all the other evidence. By 'their Cicero', Lockhart presumably means that Fletcher provided the party with intellectual inspiration and made most of the best speeches. As we have seen, he was certainly not alone in the five year struggle in the Scottish Parliament to preserve the independence of Scotland; but it is clear from the references to him in the correspondence and memoirs of both friend and opponent that he was universally regarded as the most formidable spokesman. He lost the support of the young peers to whom he addressed *An Account of a Conversation*. Political parties in the modern sense, with a formal structure, whips and all the rest of it, did not then exist. Even of the much looser organisation which was called the Country Party, Fletcher was never the recognised leader, but he was the source of most of its ideas and a constant force behind its endeavours. He clearly had a political following in a real, if not in a formal, sense.

The debates in the Scottish Parliament during these fine years largely derive from Fletcher's analysis of the gross imperfections of the 1603 settlement and from his proposal for Limitations to assert the authority of the Scottish Parliament. Even if the Limitations were never adopted in their entirety, they were largely included in the Act of Security, and the Act anent Peace and War. They set the tone and established the agenda of the whole prolonged debate. John Robertson in fact acknowledges this when, having denied that Fletcher had a political role, he goes on to say: 'To a remarkable extent Fletcher's writing can be seen to have established the framework for the debate on 'the condition of Scotland' in the years preceding the Union: those who were to support the Union no less than its opponents adopted Fletcher's analysis of the crisis as their starting point.'[8]

Nor did Fletcher confine himself to intellectual influence from the side lines. As we have seen, he was one of the most frequent and persistent participants in the debates in Parliament and one of the most resourceful in proposing new initiatives and new tactics. He continued this role to the end, even after the Treaty of Union had been passed. Not for the first time, popular tradition, which regards Fletcher as the chief opponent of the Union, is closer to the truth than much scholarly speculation.

Robertson seems to have been misled by two essays by Nicholas Phillipson, to which he refers in a footnote, to conclude that 'Fletcher's contemporary significance was intellectual rather than political'.[9] In one of these essays, Phillipson had written: 'The irascible, anglophobic Fletcher took no part in this final debate about the Anglo-Scottish Union; its paradoxes were clearly too much for him'.[10] As I remarked on page 104, Robertson describes Fletcher's *An Account of a Conversation* as 'the *jeu d'esprit* of an intelligent man who knows that he lost the real argument', and this of a work written in December 1703, when Fletcher was fresh from the triumph of the 1703 Session of Parliament. Robertson, in the same essay goes so far as to say: 'The incorporating unionists did not of course win the argument on intellectual merit alone.'[11] This, in the light of the actual course of events and the universal rejection of the Union by the population at large, is a statement wholly remote from any reality. I can only suppose that Phillipson and Robertson have been deceived by Defoe's *History of the Union*. His propagandist device of omitting all reference to Fletcher has worked nearly 300 years later and persuaded them that he took no part in the final stages of the debate. More recently, Robertson seems to have changed his view. In his most recent essay on the subject, he recognises that Fletcher 'continued vehemently to oppose incorporating union, doing his best to disrupt the last Scottish Parliament as it voted through the clauses of the Union Treaty'.[12]

If John Robertson has been sceptical about Fletcher's role in the Scottish Parliament, no one has been more emphatic about the importance of his intellectual influence on the evolution of political thought. In this, he was following the work of Caroline Robbins, published in 1959, and of J. G. A. Pocock, published in 1965 and 1975. As I mentioned in Chapter 8, they saw Fletcher as contributing to, and going beyond, the thought of English and Irish writers in the Aristotelian and Florentine humanist tradition, the Commonwealth Men and Real Whigs. In the words of Pocock, 'Fletcher was a Scot, one of the first of a long line of percipient North Britons who understood the language of English controversy better, in some respects, than the English themselves'. Or, as he wrote elsewhere, Fletcher's writing 'represents an advance, in terms of historical explanation, over anything of which Harrington was capable. Fletcher really is talking about the rise of the modern state and the effect of money upon society'.[13] Similarly, Robertson says of Fletcher's *Discourses* that 'the classic civic social prescriptions are combined with a commitment to economic development virtually unprecedented in the civic tradition'.[14]

This view of the importance of Fletcher's intellectual influence has recently been challenged by Roger L Emerson: 'Dr Robertson unduly magnifies the significance of Fletcher, who had few followers in his own time and who actually complained about the attention which Scots were paying to science and metaphysics around 1700'.[15] (This cryptic remark about Fletcher's complaint is presumably a reference to the pamphlet on education of 1704 which has been attributed to him and which I discussed on pages 72–73). It is easy to see why Emerson might think that Fletcher's intellectual influence has been exaggerated. After all, Fletcher wrote only a few short pamphlets in which many of his ideas are little more than hinted at. His economic ideas in particular, to which Robertson attaches so much importance, are very briefly stated. The only ideas which he developed at length are those in his speeches in Parliament about the political and constitutional relationship between Scotland and England.

On the other hand, there is a good deal of evidence that Fletcher's influence was long-lasting. The fact that his *Political Works*, first published in 1732, had new editions in 1737, 1749 and 1798 is one sign of this. So are the frequent references to him, almost always in a tone of respect and admiration. Some times this comes in unexpected places. For example, the pamphlet of 1752, which led to the building of the new town of Edinburgh, quotes Fletcher's *Second Discourse* in a way which suggests that he is an authority who carries weight. It calls him, 'a very spirited and manly author'.[16]

On page 2, I referred to David Hume's description of Fletcher in his *History* as 'a man of signal probity and fine genius'.[17] As far as I know, this is the only reference which Hume made to Fletcher by name in any of his writings. George Davie had shown, however, that it is possible to read Hume's Essays as an extended reply to 'Fletcher's philosophical defence of the small nation idea' and that Adam Smith and John Millar carried on the same discussion. If this is so, it is not inconceivable that it was Fletcher's interest in economic questions that influenced Hume and Smith to turn their minds in that direction.[18] Nicholas Phillipson says of Hume's essay 'Of a Perfect Commonwealth' that it is 'a startingly Fletcherism model'. Elsewhere he even suggests that Fletcher had a hand in a document on reform in the 1780s; but since he had been long dead by that time, Phillipson must be confusing him with another member of the family unless, as Bruce Lenman, suggests, Fletcher's name was being used to add posthumous authority. I discussed in Chapter 1 the interest which Rousseau and Boswell took in Fletcher. As is usual, they were more concerned about his role in Parliament in defence of Scottish independence than in his writing and his ideas.[19] Caroline Robbins, having traced similarities between the thought of Fletcher and men like Molesworth, Trenchard and Pownall, finds practical expression of their ideas in the constitutions of several of the American States. She also traces similarities between the ideas of Fletcher and those of Hutcheson, Wallace, Smith and Adam Ferguson.[20] Hutcheson is recognised as one of the founding fathers of the Scottish Enlightenment. As Bruce Lenman has pointed out, he was an Ulsterman and a Real Whig of the Molesworth circle and therefore shared this connection with Fletcher.[21]

Bruce Lenman has also remarked that 'the posthumous career of Andrew Fletcher of Saltoun is a neglected subject'.[22] This is true, but it is very often impossible to be sure if resemblances are the result of direct influence. It was not the habit of writers in the 18th Century to state their sources or give references. We cannot be certain that Hume in any particular essay had a passage of Fletcher in mind, even if it looks like it. The resemblances between the general approach of Fletcher and that typical of the Scottish Enlightenment, as I said in Chapter 8, is so strong that there is a strong presumption of a chain of influence and response. There is the same willingness to apply analytical intelligence to all the problems of society and the same habit of searching for explanations by speculating on the probable course of historical development.

To give another example, there is much about Thomas Paine's celebrated work, *Rights of Man* (1791), which is reminiscent of Fletcher in his attitude to sovereignty, for example, as in his opposition to monarchy and aristocracy. Twice, Paine makes the point that a hereditary ruler is as absurd as a hereditary author or mathematician.[23] Is this coincidence, or had he heard of Fletcher's joke about the hereditary professor?[24] Did Robert Burns know from his reading that 'we're bought and sold for English gold', or from oral tradition, which is often a more reliable guide than the historians?

It is quite likely that Paine was familiar with the work, or at least the reputation, of Fletcher because his name was evoked more than once by the Scottish supporters of the French Revolution. In 1796, a 'Scot named Watson', one of a group of Scottish and Irish Jacobins in France published an Address 'To the People of Great Britain'. In it, he asked: 'Had Wallace died, had Buchanan and Fletcher written, had Ossian sung in vain?'[25] Ossian is in strange company in this group of national heroes, but, of course, at the time he was regarded as an exemplar of primitive virtue. The mention of Fletcher is the same breath as Wallace elevates him to the Pantheon of heroic fighters for Scottish freedom, but the allusion is to his writing. Two years later, Thomas Muir of Huntershill was in France, after he had escaped from Australia to which he had been deported because of his agitation for reform. He wrote a memorandum to Talleyrand, then Foreign Minister of France. In this he describes the political situation in Scotland and says: 'The Union between England and Scotland had been accomplished, in spite of Fletcher, by English bribes'.[21]

On page 2, I quoted Sir Walter Scott's description of Fletcher as 'one of the most accomplished men, and best patriots, whom Scotland has produced in any age'. Other people at the time wrote about Fletcher in very similar terms. In 1823 an edition was published in Aberdeen of *An Historical Account of the Ancient Rights and Power of the Parliament of Scotland*. It was incorrectly attributed to Fletcher, although it is almost certainly by George Ridpath. The Introduction refers to Fletcher as 'our Scottish Patriot' and defends him against the very legitimate accusation that he was undemocratic in his attitude to the people at large. 'In Fletcher's time the tenants, tradesmen and mechanics, were, for the most part, ignorant of the principles of free government'; but now, 'their information, both political and religious, fully entitled them to a participation in all the advantages of a Free Constitution'.[27] The anonymous editor is right to remind us of the need for historical perspective in judging such matters. The fact that this was published when the first Reform Act was still nine years ahead, shows, I think, that Fletcher's authority was once again being called in aid by supporters of parliamentary reform.

To give one more example, James Aikman in the 1820s wrote a translation from the Latin of George Buchanan's *History of Scotland* and continued it himself to 1707. He quotes extensively from Fletcher's published speeches, calls him 'the Patriot' and gives a reference to his *Political Works*. He says of his parliamentary performance, echoing Ridpath: 'Fletcher of Saltoun exerted, with triumphant efficiency, his eloquence, characterised, says a late writer, by a nervous and concise simplicity, always dignified and often sublime; whose speeches may be classed among the best and finest specimens of oratory which the age had produced'.[28]

On page 65 I discussed the breach in the almost universal admiration of Fletcher by Hugh Millar and Lord Macaulay in the middle of the 19th century. This hardly seems to have dented Fletcher's reputation. John Hill Burton's *History of Scotland* was published in parts between 1853 and 1870. He follows Macaulay in contrasting Fletcher's detestation of tyranny and arbitrary power with his advocacy of slavery for the 'humble children of the soil'. Unlike Macaulay, he emphasises that Fletcher's proposal was not made for the benefit of the higher classes, but of the poor people themselves, whose drastic condition required a drastic remedy. He notes that conditions at the time were so bad that Fletcher's proposal caused no surprise and no reaction. Burton's summary of Fletcher's character was that he was the 'leader and high priest' of the Country Party, 'a man of high genius and stern courage, governed by a haughty, independent, and unmanageable temper . . Altogether, few men have so united in their persons whatever was dignified in old classic patriotism, and in medieval chivalry'.[29] If anything, the traditional view of Fletcher had become, in the 150 years since his death, even more lyrical and enthusiastic. One might distrust such a reputation, as John Robertson evidently does, but the fact is that it had a firm foundation in Fletcher's determined, eloquent and resourceful resistance to incorporating Union.

One might expect interest in Fletcher to increase as opposition to that Union increases. This has, in fact, happened. Scottish Home Rule only became practical politics with the extension of the franchise. It was not until the 1880s that the Scottish Home Rule Association was formed, the Liberal Party in Scotland adopted Home Rule as a policy and the Government, in response to agitation, restored the office of Secretary of State for Scotland. G. W. T. Omond's biography, *Fletcher of Saltoun*, was published in 1897 and Ramsay MacDonald's essay on him in 1893.[30] At about the same time, (it is undated, but according to the NLS catalogue it was published in 1888) Fletcher's *An Account of a Conversation* reappeared in print. This was under the title of *Home Rule for Scotland as advocated by Andrew Fletcher of Saltoun (Our First Home Rule Statesman)*. This had been reprinted as a pamphlet from *The Leader*, a periodical devoted to the causes of Home Rule for Scotland and Ireland. According to the Introduction: 'Scotsmen have never forgotten, and will cease to be Scotsmen when they forget, the noble figure of Fletcher of Saltoun, who led the unhappily futile opposition to the incorporating union with England'. It looked forward to the realisation of Home Rule in the three Kingdoms, 'for the sake of England as much of the sister countries'.[31]

In the same way, the publication in 1935 of W. C. MacKenzie's *Andrew Fletcher of Saltoun; His Life and Times*, the first full-length biography, was at the time of the MacDiarmid Renaissance and the formation of the SNP.

In fact, a note on the jacket of the book said that its publication was 'particularly opportune, in view of the ever-increasing ferment in Scotland over the questions of her national status and political future'. On the other hand, the work of Caroline Robbins and J. G. A. Pocock from 1959 onwards, which drew attention to Fletcher's importance as an original thinker, was a consequence of their interest in the political thought of the 17th and 18th centuries. The association between an interest in Fletcher and the movement for constitutional reform became apparent again in the 1970s with the rise of SNP and the developments which led to the Scotland Act. The Andrew Fletcher Society was founded at that time. David Daiches's *Fletcher of Saltoun, Selected Writings* was published in 1979 and the Saltire Pamphlet edition of *United and Separate Parliaments* in 1982. The Saltire Society erected a plaque to Fletcher at East Saltoun Kirk in 1955, and from the late 70s the annual commemoration by the Society has attracted a steadily increasing audience and a succession of notable addresses.[32]

In his address at Saltoun in 1979 Gordon Donaldson, the Historiographer Royal, said that Fletcher was 'a failure, an honourable failure', in the sense that the main cause which he supported, Scottish independence, did not in the end carry the day in the Scottish Parliament of the time. Despite that, and unlike most failures, he has not had a bad press. Donaldson suggested two reasons. The first was 'the qualities of the man himself, his lack of selfishness and his single mindedness'. the second was that 'the debate in which he was involved has never been closed, but continues'.[32] This is a point which Allan Massie has also made:

> Fletcher opposed the Act of Union to the end . . . He remains a figure of enduring importance, however, because his arguments, though directed to the immediate political crisis, remain the best exposition of the case against the Union. Anyone arguing that case finds himself returning to Fletcher for refreshment.[34]

In other senses, Fletcher did not fail. Despite all that he could do, the Scottish Parliament has stood adjourned since 25 March 1707; but this is still a live issue to the point where the demand for its restoration is probably now irresistible. Fletcher's reputation and the continuing force of his arguments have contributed to that result. Some of the things he advocated have been achieved. He saw the need, if only in a very rudimentary form, for society to tackle the problem of poverty and provide for unemployment, sickness and old age. This principle has long been accepted by most people in most countries, even if there are now moves to turn back the clock. He struggled hard to transfer power from the Monarch to Parliament. Again this principle has been widely accepted, although in the British case the result has been to transfer power, not to Parliament, but to a Cabinet and even, more recently, to an individual Prime Minister. Bruce Lenman, in his Saltoun address in 1987, pointed out that patronage and government by secrecy still flourished in Britain and that the elective dictatorship of a Prime Minister, usually based because of the voting system on a minority vote, had far more absolute and centralised power than any Monarch in the past. His conclusion was that 'the issues which concerned Fletcher in his time are just as relevant today, and in some ways a great deal more urgent'.[35]

Developments in Europe have also given a new relevance and topicality to the ideas, which Fletcher expressed in *An Account of a Conversation*, about the combination of European co-operation with the decentralised autonomy of small states. As Neal Ascherson has remarked, 'when Fletcher wrote his "Account", this prospect was utopian. Today is is not.'[36] This thought has recently been carried further by John Robertson in an important essay published in the magazine, *Chapman*, in September 1990, which may be summarised by the following quotations from it: 'What has emerged from recent scholarship on Fletcher is, quite simply, a new recognition of his intelligence. Eccentric he could be, but he knew an enormous amount about European history and affairs; and he wrote about them with notable sophistication . . . Fletcher's agenda remains very much to the point . . . Over the 1980s the recognition that Scotland belongs in Europe has provided increasingly good reason to renew the argument for self-government . . . Fletcher's point in 1704 was that unless small nations such as Scotland deliberately combined to establish a new political order throughout Europe, greater powers would continue to dominate the continent, and England would be free to go on dominating Scotland. Given the structure of the EEC, this danger is very real: the integration of Europe proceeds on French and German terms, under a strongly federal, centralised EEC. A separate Scottish presence within the EEC, aligning itself with the smaller nations of the community, is thus desirable in its own right, representing a more constructive response to France-German predominance than Mrs Thatcher's little Englander obstructiveness . . . The point of Andrew Fletcher's vision of Europe suddenly seems quite clear: there is now an opportunity to form a Europe of regions and smaller nations, confederally united on terms calculated to present the emergence of any new imperial power. The challenge to constitute a Scottish political community that will help to form such a Europe, the most ambitious of the challenges which Fletcher set his contemporaries, has finally become ours'.[37]

Many of Fletcher's ideas and aspirations, therefore, are still of value to us. English pressure was too much for the Scotland of his day and Europe as a whole has had to go through centuries of turmoil before it was ready to meet the Fletcher vision. Scotland and Europe may now, at last, be on the brink of achieving a settlement with a recognisable affinity to Fletcher's proposals for a 'right regulation of Governments for the common good of mankind'.

Appendix A: Fletcher's Limitations

Text from a speech by Fletcher in Parliament in 1703, printed in *The Political Works of Andrew Fletcher, Esq. of Saltoun*, edition of 1737, pages 283 to 286.

1. THAT elections shall be made at every Michaelmas head-court for a new parliament every year; to sit the first of November next following, and adjourn themselves from time to time, till next Michaelmas: That they chuse their own president, and that every thing shall be determined by ballotting, in place of voting.

2. THAT so many lesser barons shall be added to the parliament, as there have been noblemen created since the last augmentation of the number of the barons; and that in all time coming, for every nobleman that shall be created, there shall be a baron added to the parliament.

3. THAT no man have vote in parliament, but a nobleman or elected member.

4. THAT the king shall give the sanction to all laws offered by the estates; and that the president of the parliament be impowered by his majesty to give the sanction in his absence, and have ten pounds sterling a day salary.

5. THAT a committee of one and thirty members, of which nine to be a quorum, chosen out of their own number, by every parliament, shall, during the intervals of parliament, under the king, have the administration of the government, be his council, and accountable to the next parliament; with power in extraordinary occasions, to call the parliament together: and that in the said council, all things be determined by ballotting in place of voting.

6. THAT the king without consent of parliament shall not have the power of making peace and war; or that of concluding any treaty with any other state or potentate.

7. THAT all places and offices, both civil and military, and all pensions formerly conferred by our kings shall ever after be given by parliament.

8. THAT no regiment or company of horse, foot, or dragoons be kept on foot in peace or war, but by consent of parliament.

9. THAT all the fencible men of the nation, betwixt sixty and sixteen, be with all diligence possible armed with bayonets, and firelocks all of a calibre, and continue always provided in such arms with ammunition suitable.

10. THAT no general indemnity, nor pardon for any transgression against the publick, shall be valid without consent of parliament.

11. THAT the fifteen senators of the college of justice shall be incapable of being members of parliament, or of any other office, or any pension: but the salary that belongs to their place to be increased as the parliament shall think fit: that the office of president shall be in three of their number to be named by parliament, and that there be no extraordinary lords. And also, that the lords of the justice court shall be distinct from those of the session, and under the same restrictions.

12. THAT if any king break in upon any of these conditions of government, he shall by the estates be declared to have forfeited the crown.

Appendix B: The Act of Security

Acts of the Parliament of Scotland, Vol. XI, pages 136–7

ACT for the Security of the Kingdom

OUR SOVEREIGN LADY The Queens Majestie with advice and consent of the Estates of Parliament Doth hereby Statute and Ordain That in the event of her Majesties death or of the death of any of her Majesties heirs or successors Kings or Queens of this Realm This present Parliament or any other Parliament that shall be then in being shall not be dissolved by the said death But shall and is hereby Required and Ordained if assembled to Sit and Act in manner aftermentioned notwithstanding of the said death And if the said Parliament be under adjournment the time of the said death It shall notwithstanding meet precisely at Edinburgh the twentieth day after the said death excludeing the day thereof whither the day of the said adjournment be sooner or later And It is further Statute and Ordained That in case there shall be no Parliament in being at the time of the death foresaid then the Estates or members of the last preceeding Parliament without regaird to any Parliament that may be indicted but never met nor constituted shall meet at Edinburgh on the twentieth day after the said death the day thereof excluded And further provideing that in all or any of the said cases if there shall happen to be any vacancie of members by reason of death or promotion the Barons or Burghs concerned shall have power to choose and supply the said vacancie in the accustomed manner As Likewayes that in all or any of the said cases no person who hath been, is or shall be then papist and hath not purged himself of popery by takeing of the Formula set down in the third act of the Parliament One thousand and seven hundreth before the said death shall be capable to be a member of or to elect or be elected to the said Meeting of the Estates of Parliament And sicklike that no English man nor forreigner haveing a Scots title and not haveing an Estate of Twelve thousand pounds yearly rent within this Kingdom shall in the event foresaid have place or vote in the said Meeting of Estates And the said Estates of Parliament appointed in case of the death foresaid to continue or meet as above are hereby Authorized and Impowered to act and administrat the Government in manner aftermentioned That is That upon the death of her Majestie leaveing heirs of her own body or failieing thereof lawful successors designed or appointed by her Majestie and the Estates of Parliament or upon the death of any succeeding King or Queen leaving lawfull heirs and successors as said is the said Estates of Parliament are Authorized and Impowered after haveing read to the said heir or successor the Claim of Right and desired them to accept the Government in the terms thereof to require of and administrat to the said heir or lawful successors by themselves or such as they shall commissionat the Coronation oath and that with all convenient speed not exceeding thirty dayes after the meeting of the said Estates if the said heir or successor be within the Isle of Brittain Or if without the same not exceeding three moneths after the said Meeting in order to their Exerciseing the regal power conform to the Declaration of the Estates containing the Claim of Right And also in case of the said heir or successor their being under age which as to the exercise of the Government is hereby declared to be untill their attaining to seventeen years compleat to Provide for order and settle within the space of Sixty dayes after the said meeting a Regencie for the Kingdom untill the said heir or successor take the Coronation oath and do actually enter to the Exercise of the Government The Regent or Regents to be so appointed allwayes haveing the Claim of Right read to him or them as above and he or they takeing at his or their entry the Coronation oath and to continue for such space as the said Estates shall appoint After the entry of which heir or successor to the Exercise of the Government in manner foresaid or the settling the Regency in case of under age the said Estates of Parliament shall only continue to sit and act for the space of three moneths unless they be sooner lawfully adjourned or dissolved by the said heir or successor being entered or by the Regent or Regents lawfully settled as said is And further upon the said death of her Majestie without heirs of her body or a successor lawfully designed and appointed as above Or in the case of any other King or Queen thereafter succeeding and deceasing without lawfull heir or successor the foresaid Estates of Parliament Conveened or Meeting are hereby Authorized and Impowered to Nominat and Declare the Successor to the Imperial Crown of this Realm and to settle the succession thereof upon the heirs of the said successors body; The said successor and heirs of the successors body being allwayes of the Royal line of Scotland and of the true protestant Religion Provideing allwayes that the same be not successor to the Crown of England unless that in this present Session of Parliament or any other Session of this or any ensueing Parliament dureing her Majesties reign there be such conditions of Government settled and enacted as may secure the honour and sovereignty of this Crown and Kingdom, the freedom frequency and power of Parliaments, the religion liberty and trade of the Nation from English or any foreigne influence With power to the said Meeting of Estates to add such further conditions of Government as they shall think necessary the same being consistent with and no wayes derogatory from those which shall be enacted in this & any other Session of Parliament dureing her Majesties reigne* And It is hereby Declared That the said Meeting of Estates shall not have power to nominate the said Successor to the Crown of this Kingdom in the event above-expressed dureing the first Twenty dayes after their meeting Which twenty dayes being elapsed they shall proceed to make the said nomination with all convenient diligence And It is hereby expressly Provided and Declared That it shall be high treason for any person or persons to administrat the Coronation oath or be witnesses to the administration thereof but by the appointment of the Estates of Parliament in manner abovementioned or to own or acknowledge any person as King or Queen of this Realme in the event of her Majesties decease leaveing heirs of her own body untill they have Sworn the Coronation oath and accepted the Crown in the terms of the Claim of Right, And in the event of her Majesties decease without heirs of her body untill they swear the Coronation oath and accept on the terms of the Claim of Right and of such other conditions of government as shall be settled in this or any ensueing Parliament or added in the said Meeting of Estates and be thereupon Declared and Admitted as above Which Crime shall be irremissible without consent of Parliament And because in the foresaid interval of twenty dayes betwixt the said death and meeting of the Estates of Parliament in case there be no Parliament assembled for the time It is necessary that the administration of the Government be provided for in that interim Therefore It is hereby Declared That in case of the death of her Majestie or of any succeeding King or Queen of this Realm then and in all or either of the events abovementioned the foresaid Administration shall be in the hands of such of the members of the Estates of Parliament and such members of the Privy Councill last in being as shall be at Edinburgh the time of the said death or shall come to Edinburgh before the said twentieth day and shall meet in the Parliament house there Which members of the Estates and the said members of the said Privy Councill are hereby Impowered to Sit and Act in the said interim for preserveing the peace and quiet of the Kingdom allennarly and till the said meeting of the Estates and no longer Thirty of the said members of the said Estates and members of the former Councill being a quorum the plurality being allwayes of the Estates who were not of the former Councill And It is hereby further Statute and Ordained That all Commissions granted to the officers of State Lords of Thesaury and Exchequer President of the Privy Councill and all other civill Commissions that are now granted dureing pleasure shall by the decease of the King or Queen reigning become null and void Excepting Sheriff's Steuarts and Justices of Peace in their respective bounds And for a further Security of the Kingdom Her Majestie with advice and consent foresaid Statutes & Enacts That the whole Protestant Heretors and all the Burghs within the same shall furthwith provide themselves with fire arms for all the fensible men who are Protestants within their respective bounds and those of the bore proportioned to a bullet of fourteen drop weight running And the said Heretors and Burghs are hereby Impowered and Ordained to Discipline and Exercise their said fensible men once in the moneth at least The said heretors allwayes takeing the oath of alleadgeance and assureance As also such heretors or fensible men who are suspect of popery are hereby appointed when required to take the Formula mentioned in the Act of Parliament one thousand seven hundreth and that before the Sheriff of the shire or any other Judge within whose Jurisdiction they reside And It is hereby likewayes Statute and Ordained That upon the decease of Her Majestie or any of her heirs or successors the Commissions of all officers of the standing forces above a Captain shall immediatly become void and null And that the Captains of the several troops and Companies and Lieutenants of those who shall have belonged to the Collonells Lieutennant Collonells and Majors do continue to command their respective troops and companies without extending their command any further under the pain of treason till further orders from the said Estates or Committee in the intervall And further Her Majestie with advice and consent foresaid Requires and Ordains all officers and souldiers who shall happen to be on dayly pay at the time of the decease foresaid to Continue in or immediatly repair to their respective garrisons & quarters and not to remove from thence but by order of the said Estates or Committee abovementioned upon pain of treason And Lastly Her Majestie with advice and consent foresaid Rescinds Casses and Annulls the Seventeenth Act of the Session of Parliament one thousand six hundreth and ninety six years and all other Laws and Acts of Parliament in so far as they are inconsistent with this Act.

The clause included in the Act as passed by Parliament in 1703 and 1704, but omitted when the Act received the royal assent (see Chapter 9, page 87 and Chapter 11, page 114) is given as follows in George Ridpath's *Proceedings of the Parliament of Scotland*, page 246, at the position marked ★ in the text above:

And farther, but prejudice of the Generality aforesaid, It is hereby specially statuted, enacted and declared, That it shall not be in the Power of the said meeting of the Estates, to name the Successor of the Crown of England, to be Successor to the Imperial Crown of this Realm; nor shall the same Person be capable in any event to be King or Queen of both Realms, unless a free Communication of Trade, the Freedom of Navigation, and the Liberty of the Plantations be fully agreed to, and established by the Parliament and Kingdom of England, to the Kingdom and Subjects of Scotland, at the sight, and to the satisfaction of this, or any ensuing Parliament of Scotland, or the said meeting of the Estates.

Appendix C: The Treaty of Union

1 The Articles of Union agreed in London on 22nd July 1706 by the Commissioners of Scotland and England. (*Acts of the Parliament of Scotland,* Vol. XI, pages 201 to 205)

I. THAT the two Kingdoms of Scotland and England shall upon the first day of May next ensuing the date hereof, and for ever after be United into one Kingdom by the name of GREAT BRITTAIN and that the Ensigns Armorial of the said United Kingdom be such as Her Majesty shall appoint And the Crosses of St Andrew and St George be conjoyn'd in such manner as Her Majesty shall think fit, and us'd in all Flags, Banners Standards and Ensigns both at Sea and Land.

II. THAT the Succession to the Monarchy of the United Kingdom of Great Brittain, and of the Dominions thereunto belonging after Her most Sacred Majesty and in default of Issue of her Majesty, be remain and continue to the most Excellent Princess SOPHIA Electoress and Dutchess Dowager of HANNOVER, and the Heires of Her body being Protestants, upon whom the Crown of England is Setled by an Act of Parliament made in England in the Twelfth year of the Reign of his late Majesty King William the Third Entituled an Act for the further Limitation of the Crown and better securing the Rights and Libertys of the Subject, and that all Papists, and persons marrying Papists shall be Excluded from, and for ever incapable to Inherit, Possess or Enjoy the Imperial Crown of Great Brittain and the Dominions thereunto belonging, or any part thereof, and in every such Case the Crown and Government shall from time to time Descend to, and be Enjoyed by such person being a Protestant, as should have Inherited and Enjoyed the same, in case such Papist, or Person marrying a Papist was naturally Dead, according to the Provision for the descent of the Crown of England made by one other Act of Parliament in England in the first year of the Reign of their late Majestys King William and Queen Mary Entituled an Act Declaring the Rights and Libertys of the Subject, and Settling the Succession of the Crown.

III. THAT the United Kingdom of Great Brittain be Represented by one and the same Parliament to be Stil'd the Parliament of Great Brittain.

IV. THAT all the Subjects of the United Kingdom of Great Brittain shall from and after the Union have full freedom and Intercours of Trade and Navigation to, and from any Port, or Place within the said United Kingdom, and the Dominions and Plantations thereunto belonging. And that there be a Communication of all other Rights Privileges and Advantages which do, or may belong to the Subjects of either Kingdom, Except, where it is otherwise Expressly agreed in these Articles.

V. THAT all Ships belonging to Her Majestys Subjects of Scotland at the time of Signing this Treaty for the Union of the two Kingdoms (tho' Forreign Built) shall be deem'd and pass as Ships of the Built of Great Brittain, The Owner, or where there are more Owners, one or more of the Owners, within Twelve Months after the Union, making Oath that at the time of Signing the said Treaty the same did[1] belong to him, or them, or to some other Subject, or Subjects of Scotland to be particularly nam'd, with the places of their respective abodes, and that the same doth then belong to him, or them, and that no Forreigner directly or indirectly hath any share, part, or interest therein Which Oath shall be made before the Chief Officer, or Officers of the Customs in the Port next to the abode of the said Owner, or Owners, And the said Officer, or Officers shall be Impowered to Administer the said Oath, And the Oath being so Administred shall be attested by the Officer, or Officers who Administred the same, And being Registred by the said Officer, or Officers shall be delivered to the Master of the Ship for security of her Navigation, and a Duplicat thereof shall be transmitted by the said Officer, or Officers, to the Chief Officer, or Officers of the Customs in the Port of Edinburgh to be there Entred in a Register, and from thence to be sent to the Port of London, to be there Entered in the General Register of all Trading Ships belonging to Great Brittain.

VI. THAT all parts of the United Kingdom, for ever, from and after the Union shall have the same Allowances and Encouragements, and be under the same Prohibitions Restrictions and Regulations of Trade, and lyable to the same Customs and Dutys on Import and Export, and that the Allowances, Encouragements, Prohibitions, Restrictions, and Regulations, and Regulations of Trade, and the Customs and Dutys on Import and Export, Settled in England when the Union Commences shall from, and after the Union, take place throughout the whole United Kingdom.[2]

VII. THAT all parts of the United Kingdom be for ever, from and after the Union lyable to the same Excises upon all Excisable Liquors,[3] and that the Excise settled in England on such Liquors when the Union Commences take place, throughout the whole United Kingdom.

VIII. THAT From and after the Union all Forreign Salt which shall be Imported into Scotland shall be Charg'd at the Importation there with the same Dutys as the like Salt is now Charged with being Imported into England and to be Levied and Secur'd in the same manner,[4] But Scotland shall for the space of Seven Years from the said Union, be Exempted from the paying in Scotland for Salt made there, the Duty, or Excise, now payable for Salt made in England, but from the Expiration of the said Seven Years shall be Subject and Lyable to the same Dutys for Salt made in Scotland, as shall be then payable for Salt made in England to be Levied and Secur'd in the same manner, and with the like Drawbacks and Allowances as in England,[5] And during the said Seven years, there shall be paid in England for all Salt made in Scotland, and Imported from thence into England, the same Dutys upon the Importation as shall be payable, for Salt made in England to be Levied, and Secur'd in the same manner as the Dutys on Forreign Salt are to be Levied and Secur'd in England, And that during the said Seven years, no Salt whatsoever be brought from Scotland to England by Land in any manner, under the penalty of forfeiting the Salt and the Cattle and Carriages made use of in bringing the same and paying Twenty Shillings for every Bushel of such Salt, and proportionably for a greater or lesser quantity for which the Carrier, as well as the Owner shall be lyable joyntly and severally and the person bringing or carrying the same, to be Imprison'd by any one Justice of the Peace by the space of Six Months without Bail; and untill the penalty be paid, And that during the said Seven years, all Salted Flesh, or Fish, Exported from Scotland to England, or made use of for Victwalling of Ships in Scotland, and all Flesh put on board in

Scotland to be Exported to parts beyond the Seas which shall be Salted with Scotch Salt or any mixture therewith, shall be forfeited and may be Seiz'd, And that from and after the Union the Laws and Acts of Parliament in Scotland for Pineing, Curing and Packing of Herrings White Fish and Salmon for Exportation, with Forreign Salt only, and for preventing of Frauds in Cureing and Packing of Fish be Continued in Force in Scotland subject to such alterations, as shall be made by the Parliament of Great Brittain, and that all Fish Exported from Scotland to parts beyond the Seas which shall be Cur'd with Foreign Salt only, shall have the same Eases Præmiums and Drawbacks as are, or shall be allowed to such persons as Export the like Fish from England, and if any matters or fraud relating to the said Duty's on Salt shall hereafter appear which are not sufficiently provided against by this Article, the same shall be subject to such further Provisions as shall be thought fit by the Parliament of Great Brittain.

IX. THAT whenever the Summe of One Million Nine Hundred Ninty Seven Thousand Seven Hundred and Sixty three pounds Eight Shillings and Four pence half penny, shall be Enacted by the Parliament of Great Brittain, to be raised in that part of the United Kingdom now call'd England on Land and other things usually Charg'd in Acts of Parliament there for granting an Aid to the Crown by a Land Tax, That part of the United Kingdom now called Scotland, shall be Charged by the same Act, with a further Summe of Forty Eight Thousand pounds, free of all Charges, as the Quota of Scotland to such Tax, and so proportionably for any greater, or lesser Summe raised in England by any Tax, on Land, and other things usually Charg'd together with the Land And that such Quota for Scotland, in the Cases aforesaid be rais'd and collected in the same manner as the Cess now is in Scotland, But subject to such Regulations in the manner of Collecting as shall be made by the Parliament of Great Brittain.

X. THAT during the Continuance of the respective Dutys on Stampt Paper, Vellome and Parchment by the several Acts now in force in England, Scotland shall not be Charg'd with the same respective Dutys.

XI. THAT during the Continuance of the Dutys payable in England on Windows and Lights which Determins on the first day of August One Thousand Seven Hundred and Ten, Scotland shall not be Charged with the same Dutys.

XII. THAT during the Continuance of the Dutys payable in England on Coales Culm, and Cynders which determins the Thirtieth day of September One Thousand Seven Hundred and Ten, Scotland shall not be Charg'd therewith for Coales Culm and Cynders consum'd there, But shall be charg'd with the same Dutys as in England, for all Coal, Culm, and Cynders not consum'd in Scotland.

XIII. THAT during the Continuance of the Duty payable in England on Mault which determins the Twenty fourth day of June one Thousand Seven Hundred and Seven, Scotland shall not be Charg'd with that Duty.

XIV. THAT the Kingdom of Scotland be not Charg'd, with any other Dutys laid on by the Parliament of England before the Union Except those Consented to in this Treaty, in regard it is agreed that all necessary Provision shall be made by the Parliament of Scotland for the Publick Charge and Service of that Kingdom for the year One Thousand Seven Hundred and Seven Provided nevertheless that if the Parliament of England shall think fit to lay any further Impositions by way of Customs, or such Excises with which by virtue of this Treaty Scotland is to be Charg'd Equally with England In such Case Scotland shall be Lyable to the same Customs and Excises and have an Equivalent to be Settled by the Parliament of Great Britain[6] and seing it cannot be supposed that the Parliament of Great Brittain will ever lay any sorts of Burthens upon the United Kingdom, but what they shall find of necessity at that time for the preservation and good of the whole and with due regard to the Circumstances and Abilitys of every part of the United Kingdom, Therefore it is agreed that there be no further Exemption insisted on for any part of the United Kingdom, But that the Consideration of any Exemptions beyond what are already agreed on in this Treaty shall be left to the Determination of the Parliament of Great Brittain.

XV. WHEREAS by the Terms of this Treaty the Subjects of Scotland for preserving an equality of Trade throughout the United Kingdom, will be lyable to several Customs and Excises now payable in England which will be applicable towards payment of the Debts of England Contracted before the Union, It is agreed that Scotland shall have an Equivalent for what the Subjects thereof shall be so Charg'd towards Payment of the said Debts of England in all particulars whatsoever in manner following vizt That before the Union of the said Kingdoms the summe of Three Hundred Ninty Eight Thousand and Eightie Five pound Ten shillings be Granted to her Majesty by the Parliament of England for the uses aftermentioned being the Equivalent to be answer'd to Scotland for such parts of the said Customs and Excises, upon all Excisable Liquors, with which that Kingdom is to be Charg'd upon the Union, as will be applicable to the payment of the said debts of England according to the proportions which the present Customs in Scotland being Thirty Thousand pounds p^r Anñ do bear to the Customs in England Computed at One Million Three Hundred Forty one Thousand Five Hundred and Fifty nine pounds p^r Anñ and which the present Excises on Excisable Liquors in Scotland being Thirty Three Thousand and Five Hundred pounds p^r Anñ do bear to the Excises on Excisable Liquors in England Computed at Nine Hundred Forty Seven Thousand Six Hundred and Two Pound p Anñ Which summe of Three Hundred Ninty Eight Thousand Eighty five pounds Ten shillings shall be due and payable from the time of the Union, And in regard that after the Union Scotland becoming lyable to the same Customs and Dutys payable on Import and Export, and to the same Excises on all Excisable Liquors as in England, as well upon that account, as upon the account of the Encrease of Trade and People (which will be the happy consequence of the Union) the said Revenues will much Improve beyond the before mentioned annual Values thereof, of which no present Estimate can be made, Yet nevertheless for the reasons aforesaid there ought to be a proportionable Equivalent answered to Scotland, It is agreed That after the Union there shall be an Account kept of the said Dutys arising in Scotland, to the End it may appear what ought to be answer'd to Scotland as an Equivalent for such proportion of the said Encrease as shall be applicable to the payment of the Debts of England, And for the further, and more Effectual answering the several ends hereafter mentioned It is agreed That from and after the Union the whole Encrease of the Revenues of Customs and Dutys on Import and Export and Excise upon Excisable Liquors in Scotland, over and above the annual produce of the said respective Dutys as above stated shall go, and be apply'd for the Term of seven years to the uses hereafter mentioned And that upon the said account there shall be answered to Scotland annually from the end of Seven years after the Union, and Equivalent in Proportion to such part of the said Encrease as shall be applicable to the Debts of England,[7] And whereas from the Expiration of Seven years after the Union, Scotland is to be lyable to the same Dutys for Salt made in Scotland as shall be then payable for Salt made in England It is agreed that when such Dutys take place there an Equivalent shall be answered to Scotland for such part thereof as shall be apply'd towards payment of the Debts of England of which Dutys an Account shall be kept to the end it may appear what is to be answered to Scotland as the said Equivalent, And generally that an Equivalent shall be answered to Scotland for such parts of the English Debts as Scotland may hereafter become lyable to pay by reason of the Union other then such for which Appropriations have been made by Parliament in England, of the

Customs, or other Dutys on Export, or Import Excises on all Excisable Liquors,[8] or Salt, In respect of which Debts, Equivalents are herein before provided And as for the Uses to which the said Summe of Three Hundred Ninty Eight Thousand Eighty five pounds Ten Shillings to be granted as aforesaid, and all other moneys which are to be answered or allowed to Scotland as aforesaid It is agreed[9] That out of the said Sume of Three Hundred Ninty Eight Thousand Eighty five pound Tenn Shillings all the publick Debts of the Kingdom of Scotland, And also the Capital Stock, or Fund of the Affrican and Indian Company of Scotland advanc'd, together with the Interest for the said Capital Stock after the Rate of Five pounds p Cent. P Anñ from the respective times of the Payment thereof shall be paid, upon payment of which Capital Stock and Interest, It is agreed the said Company be disolv'd and cease, and also That from the time of passing the Act of Parliament in England for raising the said Summe of Three Hundred Ninty Eight Thousand Eighty five pounds Tenn Shillings the said Company shall neither Trade, nor Grant Licence to Trade,[10] And as to the Overplus of the said Sume of Three Hundred Ninty Eight Thousand Eighty five pound Ten Shillings, after the payment of[11] the said Debts of the Kingdom of Scotland, and the said Capital Stock and Interest, and also the whole Encrease of the said Revenues of Customs Dutys and Excises, above the present Value which shall arise in Scotland during the said Term of Seven Years Together with the Equivalent which shall become due upon Account of the Improvement thereof in Scotland after the said Term, And also as to all other sums, which according to the agreements aforsaid may become payable to Scotland by way of Equivalent for what that Kingdom shall hereafter become lyable towards payment of the Debts of England, It is agreed That the same be apply'd in manner following viz[t] That[12] out of the same, what Consideration shall be found necessary to be had for any losses which privat persons may sustain by reducing the Coyn of Scotland to the Standard and Value of the Coyn of England may be made good, And afterwards the same shall be wholly applyed towards Encourageing and Promoting the Fisheries and such other Manufacturys and Improvements in Scotland as may most Conduce to the General Good of the United Kingdom, And It is agreed that Her Majesty be Impowred to appoint Commissioners who shall be accountable to the Parliament of Great Britain for disposing the said Summe of Three Hundred, Nynty Eight Thousand Eighty five pounds Ten Shillings and all other moneys which shall arise to Scotland upon the agreements aforsaid, to the purposes before mentioned Which Commissioners shall be Impowred to Call for, Receive and Dispose of the said moneys in manner aforesaid, And to Inspect the Books of the several Collectors of the said Revenues, and of all other Dutys, from whence an Equivalent may arise, And that the Collectors and Mannagers of the said Revenues and Dutys be Obliged to give to the said Commissioners Subscribed Authentick Abbreviats of the Produce of such Revenues and Dutys arising in their respective Districts, And that the said Commissioners shall have their Office within the Limits of Scotland, and shall in such Office Keep Books containing Accounts of the Amount of the Equivalents, and how the same shall have been disposed of from time to time which may be Inspected by any of the Subjects who shall desire the same.

XVI. THAT from and after the Union the Coyn shall be of the same Standard and Value throughout the United Kingdom as now in England, And a Mint shall be Continued in Scotland under the same Rules as the Mint in England[13] Subject to such Regulations as Her Majesty, Her Heires, or Successors, or the Parliament of Great Brittain shall think fit.

XVII. THAT from and after the Union the same Weights and Measures shall be used throughout the United Kingdom, as are now Established in England, and Standards of Weights and Measures shall be Kept by those Burroughs in Scotland to whom the keeping the Standards of Weights and Measures now in use there do's of Special Right belong. All which Standards shall be sent down to such respective Burroughs from the Standards kept in the Exchequer at Westminster Subject nevertheless to such Regulations as the Parliament of Great Brittain shall think fit.

XVIII. THAT the Laws Concerning Regulation of Trade, Customs and such Excises to which Scotland is, by virtue of this Treaty to be lyable, be the same in Scotland, from and after the Union as in England And That all other Laws in use within the Kingdom of Scotland doe after the Union and notwithstanding thereof remain in the same force as before (Except such as are Contrary to, or Inconsistent with the Terms of this Treaty) but alterable, by the Parliament of Great Britain, with this difference betwixt the Laws concerning Publick Right, Pollicy and Civil Government, and those which concern privat Right, That the Laws which concern Publick Right, Policy and Civil Government may be made the same throughout the whole United Kingdom, But that no alteration be made in Laws which Concern Privat Right Except for evident utility of the Subjects within Scotland.

XIX. THAT the Court of Session, or College of Justice do, after the Union and notwithstanding thereof Remain, in all time coming within Scotland, as it is now Constituted by the Laws of that Kingdom, and with the same Authority and Priviledges as before the Union, Subject nevertheless to such Regulations for the better Administration of Justice, as shall be made by the Parliament of Great Brittain[14] And That the Court of Justiciary do also after the Union, and notwithstanding thereof, remain in all time coming within Scotland as it is now Constituted by the Laws of that Kingdom And with the same Authority and Priviledges as before the Union, Subject nevertheless to such Regulations as shall be made by the Parliament of Great Brittain And without prejudice of other Rights of Justiciary, And That all Admiralty Jurisdictions, be under the Lord High Admiral, or Commissioners for the Admiralty of Great Brittain for the time being And that the Court of Admiralty now Established in Scotland Be Continued, And that all Reviews, Reductions, or Suspensions of the Sentences in Maritim Cases Competent to the Jurisdiction of that Court remain in the same manner after the Union, as now in Scotland, untill the Parliament of Great Brittain shall make such Regulations and Alterations as shall be judg'd Expedient for the whole United Kingdom so as there be always Continued in Scotland a Court of Admiralty such as is in England, for determination of all Maritim Cases, relating to Private Rights in Scotland, Competent to the Jurisdiction of the Admiralty Court Subject nevertheless to such Regulations, and Alterations as shall be thought proper to be made by the Parliament of Great Brittain, and that the Heretable Rights of Admiralty and Vice Admiraltys in Scotland be reserved to the respective proprietors, as Rights of property Subject nevertheless as to the manner of Exercising such Heretable Rights, to such Regulations and Alterations as shall be thought proper to be made by the Parliament of Great Brittain And That all other Courts now in being within the Kingdom of Scotland do remain, But subject to Alterations by the Parliament of Great Brittain And That, all Inferior Courts within the said Limits doe Remain subordinat as they are now to the Supreme Courts of Justice within the same in all time coming And that no Causes in Scotland be Cognoscable, by the Courts of Chancery, Queens Bench, Common Pleas, or any other Court in Westminster Hall, And that the said Courts, or any other, of the like nature after the Union shall have no Power to Cognosce, Review, or Alter the Acts, or Sentences of the Judicatures within Scotland, or Stop the Execution of the same, And That there be a Court of Exchequer in Scotland after the Union, for deciding Questions Concerning the Revenues of Customs and Excises there, having the same Power and Authority in such Cases as the Court of Exchequer has in England And That the said Court of Exchequer in Scotland have power of passing Signatures, Gifts, Tutories, and in other things as the Court of Exchequer at present in Scotland hath, And that the Court of Exchequer that now is in Scotland do Remain untill a New Court of Exchequer be settled by the Parliament of Great Brittain in Scotland after the Union, And That after the Union The Queens Majesty and Her Royal Successors, may Continue a Privy Council in Scotland for preserving of Publick Peace and Order, untill the Parliament of Great Brittain shall think fit to alter it, or Establish any other Effectual Methode for that end.

XX. THAT all Heretable Offices[15], Heretable Jurisdictions, Offices for Life, and Jurisdictions for Life be reserved, to the Owners thereof as Rights of Property in the same manner as they are now enjoy'd by the Laws of Scotland notwithstanding of this Treaty.

XXI. THAT the Rights and Priviledges of the Royal Burrowghs in Scotland as they now are doe Remain entire after the Union and notwithstanding thereof.

XXII. THAT by virtue of this Treaty of the Peers of Scotland at the time of the Union Sixteen shall be the Number to Sit and Vote in the House of Lords, and Forty Five the Number of the Representatives of Scotland in the House of Commons of the Parliament of Great Brittain And that when Her Majesty, Her Heires, or Successors shall Declare Her, or their pleasure for holding the first, or any subsequent Parliament of Great Brittain untill the Parliament of Great Brittain shall make further Provision therein A Writ do issue under the Great Seal of the United Kingdom Directed to the Privy Council of Scotland Commanding them to Cause Sixteen Peers who are to Sit in the House of Lords to be summon'd to Parliament and Forty Five Members to be Elected to Sit in the House of Commons of the Parliament of Great Brittain according to the Agreement in this Treaty in such manner as by[16] the Parliament of Scotland shall be Settled before the Union, And that the Names of the Persons so summon'd and Elected shall be Returned by the Privy Council of Scotland into the Court from whence the said Writ did issue, And That if Her Majesty on, or before the first day of May next, on which day the Union is to take place, shall Declare under the Great Seal of England That it is Expedient that the Lords of Parliament of England, and Commons of the present Parliament of England should be the Members of the respective Houses of the First Parliament of Great Brittain, for, and on the part of England, Then the saids Lords of Parliament of England, and Commons of the present Parliament of England shall be the Members of the respective Houses of the first Parliament of Great Brittain, for, and on the part of England And Her Majesty may by Her Royal Proclamation under the Great Seal of Great Brittain, appoint the said first Parliament of Great Brittain to meet, at such time and Place as Her Majesty shall think fit, which time shall not be less than Fifty days after the date of such Proclamation, and the time and place of the meeting of such Parliament being so appointed, a Writ shall be immediatly issued under the Great Seal of Great Brittain Directed to the Privy Council of Scotland for the Summoning the Sixteen Peers and for Electing Forty Five Members by whom Scotland is to be represented in the Parliament of Great Brittain And the Lords of Parliament of England and the Sixteen Peers of Scotland, such Sixteen Peers being summoned and return'd in the manner agreed in this Treaty, And the Members of the House of Commons of the said Parliament of England and the Forty five Members for Scotland, such Forty five Members being Elected and Return'd in the manner agreed in this Treaty, shall assemble and meet respectively in their respective Houses of the Parliament of Great Brittain at such time and place as shall be so appointed by Her Majesty, and shall be the two Houses of the First Parliament of Great Brittain And that Parliament may Continue for such time only as the present Parliament of England might have Continued if the Union of the two Kingdoms had not been made unless sooner disolved by Her Majesty, And That every one of the Lords of Parliament, of Great Brittain, and every member of the

House of Commons of the Parliament of Great Brittain, in the first & all succeeding Parliaments of Great Brittain, untill the Parliament of Great Brittain shall otherwise direct, shall take the respective Oaths appointed to be taken, Instead of the Oaths of Allegiance and Supremacy by an Act of Parliament made in England in the first year of the Reign of the late King William and Queen Mary Intituled an Act for the Abrogating of the Oaths, of Supremacy and Allegiance and appointing other Oaths and make, subscribe and audibly Repeat the Declaration mention'd in an Act of Parliament made in England in the Thirtieth year of the Reign of King Charles the Second Entituled an Act for the more effectwall preserving the King's person and Government by disabling Papists from sitting in either House of Parliament and shall Take & Subscribe the Oath mention'd in an Act of Parliament made in England in the first year of Her Majestys Reign Intituled An Act to Declare the Alterations in the Oath appointed to be taken by the Act Intituled An Act for the further Security of His Majestys Person & the Succession of the Crown in the Protestant Line, and for Extinguishing the hopes of the pretended Prince of Wales and all other Pretenders and their open and secret abbettors and for Declaring the Association to be determin'd, at such time and in such manner as the Members of both Houses of Parliament of England are by the said respective Acts directed to take, make and Subscribe the same upon the Penaltys & Disabilitys in the said respective Acts contain'd And it is declar'd and agreed that these Words, *This Realm, The Crown of this Realm*, and the *Queen of this Realm* mentioned in the Oaths and Declaration contained in the aforesaid Acts, which were Intended to Signify the Crown and Realm of England shall be understood of the Crown & Realm of GREAT BRITTAIN, and that in that Sence the said Oaths, and Declaration be taken & subscrib'd by the Members of both Houses of the Parliament of Great Brittain.

XXIII. THAT the forsaid Sixteen Peers of Scotland mentioned in the last preceeding Article to sit in the House of Lords of the Parliament of Great Brittain shall have all privileges of Parliament which the Peers of England now have, and which they, or any Peers of Great Brittain shall have after the Union, and particularly the Right of Siting upon the Tryalls of Peers, And in Case of the Tryal of any Peer in time of Adjournment, or Prorogation of Parliament the said Sixteen Peers shall be summon'd in the same manner and have the same Powers and Privileges at such Tryal as any other Peers of Great Brittain And that in Case any Tryalls of Peers, shall hereafter happen when there is no Parliament in being, The Sixteen Peers of Scotland who sate in the last preceeding Parliament shall be summon'd in the same manner, and have the same Powers and Privileges at such Tryals as any other Peers of Great Brittain, And That all Peers of Scotland and their Successors to their Honours and Dignitys shall from and after the Union be Peers of Great Britain, and have Rank and Precedency next and Immediatly after the Peers of the like Orders and Degrees in England at the time of the Union, And before all Peers of Great Brittain of the like Orders and Degrees who may be Created after the Union, and shall be Tryed as Peers of Great Brittain, and shall Enjoy all priviledges of Peers as fully as the Peers of England do now, or as they, or any other Peers of Great Britain may hereafter Enjoy the same, Except the Right & Privilege of Sitting in the House of Lords, and the Privileges depending thereon and particularly the Right of Sitting upon the Tryalls of Peers.

XXIV. THAT from and after the Union there be One Great Seal for the United Kingdom of Great Brittain, which shall be different from the Great Seal now us'd in either Kingdom, And that the quartering the Arms[17] as may best suit the Union be left to Her Majesty, And that in the mean time the Great Seal of England be us'd as the Great Seal of the United Kingdom, And that the Great Seal of the United Kingdom be us'd for Sealing Writs to Elect and Summon the Parliament of Great

Brittain, and for Sealing all Treatys with Forreign Princes and States, and all Publick Acts, Instruments and Orders of State which Concern the whole United Kingdom, And in all other matters Relating to England, as the Great Seal of England is now us'd, And that a Seal in Scotland after the Union be always kept and made use of in all things relating to Privat Rights, or Grants, which have usually passed the Great Seal of Scotland, and which only concern Offices, Grants Commissions and Privat Rights within that Kingdom, And that untill such Seal shall be appointed by Her Majesty the present Great Seal of Scotland shall be us'd for such purposes, and that the Privy Seal, Signet, Casset, Signet of the Justiciary Court, Quarter Seal and Seals of Courts now used in Scotland be Continued, but that the said Seals be Altered and Adapted to the State of the Union as Her Majesty shall think fit, And the said Seals and all of them and the Keepers of them shall be subject to such Regulations as the Parliament of Great Brittain shall hereafter make.[18]

XXV. THAT all Laws and Statutes in either Kingdom, so far as they are Contrary to, or Inconsistent with the Terms of these Articles, or any of them, shall from and after the Union Cease and become void and shall be so Declared to be by the respective Parliaments of the said Kingdoms.

The Treaty of Union
2 Amendments (apart from minor adjustments of spelling and punctuation) agreed by the Scottish Parliament between 3 October 1706 and 16 January 1707. (*Acts of the Parliament of Scotland*, Vol. XI, pages 406 to 414).

Art. V

For "signing" in line 2, read "Ratifying".
At (1) insert:
"in haill or in part".

Art. VI

After "Encouragements" in lines 2 and 4 insert "and drawbacks".
At (2) insert:
excepting and reserving the Duties upon Export and Import of such particular Commodities from which any persons the Subjects of either Kingdom are specially Liberated and Exempted by their private Rights which after the Union are to remain safe and entire to them in all respects as before the same And that from and after the Union no Scots Cattle carried into England shall be lyable to any other Duties either on the publick or private Accounts than these Duties to which the Cattle of England are or shall be lyable within the said Kingdom. And seeing by the Laws of England there are Rewards granted upon the Exportation of certain kinds of Grain wherein Oats grinded or ungrinded are not expressed, that from and after the Union when Oats shall be sold at fifteen shillings Sterling per quarter or under there shall be payed two shillings and six pence Sterling for every quarter of the Oat-meal exported in the terms of the Law whereby and so long as Rewards are granted for Exportation of other Grains And that the Bear of Scotland have the same Rewards as Barley. And in respect the Importation of Victual into Scotland from any place beyond Sea would

prove a Discouragement to Tillage, Therefore that the Prohibition as now in force by the Law of Scotland against Importation of Victual from Ireland or any other place beyond Sea into Scotland, do after the Union remain in the same force as now it is until more proper and effectuall ways be provided by the Parliament of Great Britain for discouraging the Importation of the said Victual from beyond Sea.

Art. VII

At (3) insert:

excepting only that the thirty four Gallons English Barrel of Beer or Ale amounting to twelve Gallons Scots present measure sold in Scotland by the Brewer at nine shillings six pence Sterling excluding all Duties and Retailed including Duties and the Retailers profit at two pence the Scots pint or eight part of the Scots Gallon, be not after the Union lyable on account of the present Excise upon Exciseable Liquors in England, to any higher Imposition than two shilling Sterling upon the forsaid thirty four Gallons English barrel, being twelve gallons the present Scots measure

Art. VIII

At (4) insert:

But in regard the Duties of great quantities of foreign Salt Imported may be very heavie on the Merchants Importers; That therefore all forreign Salt imported into Scotland shall be Cellared and Locked up under the custody of the Merchant Importer and the Officers imployed for levying the Duties upon Salt And that the Merchant may have what quantities thereof his occasion may require not under a Weigh or fourtie bushells at a time; Giving security for the duty of what quantity he receives payable in six Months.

At (5) delete from "And that during the said seven years" to end of Article and insert:

with this exception that Scotland shall after the said seven years remain exempted from the Duty of two shillings and four pence a Bushell on home Salt Imposed by ane Act made in England in the Ninth and Tenth of King William the Third of England And if the Parliament of Great Britain shall at or before the expiring of the said seven years substitute any other fund in place of the said two shillings and four pence of Excise on the bushel of Home Salt, Scotland shall after the said seven years, bear a proportion of the said Fund, and have an Equivalent in the Terms of this Treaty, And that during the said seven years there shall be payed in England for all Salt made in Scotland and imported from thence into England the same duties upon the Importation as shall be payable for Salt made in England to be levied and secured in the same manner as the Duties on forreign Salt are to be levied and secured in England. And that after the said seven years how long the said Duty of two shillings four pence a Bushel upon Salt is continued in England the said two shillings four pence a Bushel shall be payable for all Salt made in Scotland and imported into England, to be levied and secured in the same manner And that during the continuance of the Duty of two shillings four pence a Bushel upon Salt made in England no Salt whatsoever be brought from Scotland to England by Land in any manner under the penalty of forfeiting the Salt and the Cattle and Carriages made use of in bringing the same and paying twenty shillings for every Bushel of such Salt, and proportionably for a grater or lesser quantity, for which the Carrier as well as the Owner shall be lyable jointly and severally, And the persons bringing or carrying the same, to be imprisoned by any one Justice of the Peace, by the space of six months without Bail, and until the penalty be payed: And for Establishing an equality in Trade That all Fleshes exported from Scotland to England and put on Board in Scotland to be Exported to parts beyond the Seas and provisions for ships in Scotland and for forreign voyages may be salted with Scots Salt paying the same Dutie for what Salt is so employed as the like quantity of such Salt pays in England and under the same penalties forfeitures and provisions for preventing of frauds as are mentioned in the Laws of England And that from and after the Union the Laws and Acts of Parliament in Scotland for Pineing Curing and Packing of Herrings White Fish and Salmond for Exportation with Forreign Salt only without any mixture of British or Irish Salt and for preventing of frauds in Curing and Packing of Fish be continued in force in Scotland subject to such alterations as shall be made by the Parliament of Great Britain And that all Fish exported from Scotland to parts beyond the Seas which shall be Cured with Forreign Salt only and without mixture of British or Irish Salt, shall have the same Eases Præmiums and Drawbacks as are or shall be allowed to such persons as Export the like Fish from England: And that for Encouragement of the Herring Fishing there shall be allowed and payed to the Subjects Inhabitants of Great Britain during the present allowances for other Fishes ten shillings five pence Sterling for every Barrel of White Herrings which shall be exported from Scotland; And that there shall be allowed five shillings Sterling for every Barrel of Beef or Pork salted with Foreign Salt without mixture of British or Irish Salt and Exported for sale from Scotland to parts beyond Sea alterable by the Parliament of Great Britain. And if any matters of fraud relating to the said Duties on Salt shall hereafter appear which are not sufficiently provided against by this Article the same shall be subject to such further provisions as shall be thought fit by the Parliament of Great Britain.

Art. XIV

At (6) insert:

"With this further provision That any Malt to be made and consumed in that part of the United Kingdom now called Scotland shall not be charged with any Imposition upon Malt during this present War."

Art. XV

At (7) delete from "And whereas from the Expiration" to "as the said Equivalent" (6 lines)

At (8) delete "or salt"

At (9) delete from "That out of the said Sume" to "Kingdom of Scotland" (3 lines) and add:

"That in the first place out of the forsaid Sum what consideration shall be found necessary to be had for any Losses which privat persons may sustain by reducing the Coin of Scotland to the Standard and Value of the Coin of England may be made good. In the next place"

At (10) add:

"Providing that if the said Stock and Interest shall not be paid in twelve months after the Commencement of the Union That then the said Company may from thence forward Trade or give Licence to Trade until the said hail Capital Stock and Interest shall be payed."

At (11) after "payment of" delete: "the said debts of the Kingdom of Scotland"; insert: "of what consideration shall be had for loses in repairing the Coin and paying."

At (12) delete from "out of the Same" to "and afterwards" (3 lines);

insert: "That all the publick Debts of the Kingdom of Scotland as shall be adjusted by this present Parliament shall be payed and that two thousand pounds per annum for the space of seven years shall be applied towards Encouraging and Promoting the Manufacture of coarse Wool within these shires which produce the Wool And that the first two thousand pounds sterling be payed at Martinmas next, and so yearly at Martinmas during the space forsaid."

Art. XVI

At (13) insert: "And the present Officers of the Mint continued".

Insert 'and Alterations' after 'such Regulations'.

Art. XIX

At (14) insert:

And that hereafter none shall be named by Her Majesty or Her Royal Successors to be Ordinary Lords of Session but such who have served in the Colledge of Justice as Advocats or Principal Clerks of Session for the space of five years, or as Writers to the Signet for the space of ten years With this provision That no Writer to the Signet be capable to be admitted a Lord of the Session unless he undergo a private and publick Tryal on the Civil Law before the Faculty of Advocats and be found by then qualified for the said Office two years before he be named to be a Lord of the Session, yet so as the Qualifications made or to be made for capacitating persons to be named Ordinary Lords of Session may be altered by the Parliament of Great Brittain.

Art. XX

At (15) insert "Superiorities".

Art. XXII

At (16) delete: from the "Parliament of Scotland" to "the Union" (2 lines)

Insert: "a subsequent Act of this present Session of the Parliament of Scotland shall be settled; Which Act is hereby Declared to be as valid as if it were a part and ingrossed in this Treaty".

Art. XXIV

At (17) insert: "and the Rank and Precedency of the Lyon King of Arms of the Kingdom of Scotland"

At (18) add:

And that the Crown, Scepter and Sword of State, the Records of Parliament, and all other Records, Rolls and Registers whatsoever, both publick and private generall and particular, and Warrands thereof Continue to be keeped as they are within that part of the United Kingdom now called Scotland, and that they shall so remain in all time coming notwithstanding of the Union.

Appendix D: Note on Names and Titles

I have followed the usual practice of referring to peers by the territorial part of their title. The following table identifies the particular bearer of the title concerned:

Annandale:	William Johnstone, 3rd Earl and 1st Marquis. (?–1721)
Argyll:	John Campbell, 2nd Duke of A. and 1st of Greenwich. (1678–1743)
Atholl	John Murray, 2nd Marquis and 1st Duke. (1660–1724)
Balmerino:	John Elphinstone, 4th Lord B and 3rd Lord Coupar. (1652–1736)
Belhaven:	John Hamilton, 2nd Baron. (1656–1740)
Cromartie:	George Mackenzie, 1st Earl. (1630–1714)
Glasgow:	David Boyle, 1st Earl. (1666–1733)
Godolphin:	Sidney Godolphin, 1st Earl. (1645–1712)
Haddington:	Thomas Hamilton, 6th Earl. (1680–1735)
Hamilton:	James Douglas, 4th Duke. (1658–1712)
Home:	Charles Home, 6th Earl. (?–1706)
Hopetoun:	Charles Hope, 1st Earl. (1681–1742)
Kilmarnock:	William Boyd, 3rd Earl. (1683–1717)
Lauderdale:	John Maitland, 5th Earl. (1650–1710)
Leven:	David Melville, 3rd Earl. (1660–1728)
Lothian:	William Kerr, 2nd Marquis. (1662–1722)
Loudoun:	Hugh Campbell, 3rd Earl. (?–1731)
Marchmont:	Patrick Hume, 1st Earl and Lord Polwarth. (1641–1724)
Marischal:	William Keith, 9th Earl. (?–1712)
Mar:	John Erskine, 6th or 11th Earl. (1675–1732)
Montrose:	James Graham, 4th Marquis and 1st Duke. (?–1742)
Northesk:	David Carnegie, 4th Earl. (1676–1763)
Queensberry:	James Douglas, 2nd Duke of Q. and 1st of Dover. (1662–1711)
Roseberry:	Archibald Primrose, 1st Earl. (1661–1723)
Rothes:	John Leslie, 8th Earl. (1679–1722)
Roxburgh:	John Ker, 5th Earl and 1st Duke. (?–1741)
Seafield:	James Ogilvie, 1st Earl. (1664–1730)

Stair: John Dalrymple, 1st Earl. (1648–1707)
Tweedale: John Hay, 2nd Marquis. (1645–1713)

Lairds are often designated in quotations from contemporary sources by the name of their estate or barony, as Fountainhall for Sir John Lauder of Fountainhall, Jerviswood for George Baillie of Jerviswood, and Saltoun for Andrew Fletcher of Saltoun.

Bibliographical Note

Works by Andrew Fletcher
In Fletcher's life-time a number of his essays and speeches were published as separate pamphlets and all anonymously, as was customary at the time. After his death they were collected by an unknown editor and published in 1732 as *The Political Works of Andrew Fletcher Esq of Saltoun*, with subsequent editions in 1737, 1749 and 1798. Further details of this publishing history can be found in R. A. Scott Macfie's *Bibliography of Andrew Fletcher of Saltoun* in the Publications of the Edinburgh Bibliographical Society, Vol. IV, Pt. II, October 1901.

Apart from the publication of *An Account of a Conversation in 1888* (*see page 224 above*), *there have been no further editions of Fletcher's writings until this century. Fur the Association for Scottish Literary Studies, David Daiches has edited Andrew Fletcher of Saltoun: Selected Political Writings and Speeches* (Edinburgh, 1979). This includes the whole of the original 18th Century edition apart from the *Discourse Concerning the Affairs of Spain* and the *Speech Upon the Affairs of the Nation in April 1701*. In 1982 the Saltire Society published *State of the Controversy Betwixt United and Separate Parliaments*, with an Introduction by the present author. (See Chapter 14 above).

Biographies
Apart from short essays and entries in works of reference, there have been only two previous biographies of Fletcher. G. W. T. Omond's *Fletcher of Saltoun* in the Famous Scots Series (Edinburgh and London, 1897) is a brief but competent sketch. W. C. Mackenzie's *Andrew Fletcher of Saltoun: His Life and Times* (Edinburgh, 1935) is a much more elegant and comprehensive work. It contains fairly full summaries of Fletcher's pamphlets which were justifiable because they were then not otherwise in print. Some of the political judgements are simplistic.

Historical background
Details of the source material are given in the references. For a modern introduction to the historical background, see Michael Lynch's *Scotland: A New History* (London, 1991) which is probably the best single-volume history of Scotland. For a more particular study of the period in question, I recommend two books by William Ferguson: *Scotland: 1689 to the Present*, which is Vol. 4 in the Edinburgh History of Scotland (Edinburgh, 1968) and *Scotland's Relations with England: A Survey to 1707* (Edinburgh, 1977).

Among recent books on the Union are: T. C. Smout, *Scottish Trade on the Eve of the Union* (Edinburgh, 1963); David Daiches, *Scotland and the Union* (London, 1977); P. W. J. Riley, *The Union of England and Scotland* (Manchester, 1978), which gives an English view of the matter, and P. H. Scott, *1707, The Union of Scotland and England* (Edinburgh, 1979).

List of Abbreviations

1. Primary Sources

A.P.S.	*The Acts of the Parliament of Scotland* (Printed 1824)
Argyle	Duke of Argyle (James Douglas Sutherland Campbell) *Intimate Society Letters of the 18th Century* 2 vols. (London, 1910)
Burnet	Bishop Gilbert Burnet, *History of His Own Time* (Oxford 1823) 6 volumes.
Carstares	Edited by Joseph McCormick, *State Papers and Letters Addressed to William Carstares* (Edinburgh 1774)
Clerk	Edited by John M. Gray, *Memoirs of the Life of Sir John Clerk of Penicuik.* (SHS) Edinburgh 1892)
Defoe, *History*,	David Defoe, *The History of the Union of Great Britain.* (Edition of 1768, London)
Defoe, *Letters*,	Edited by G. H. Healey, *The Letters of Daniel Defoe.* (Oxford, 1955)
E.U.L.	Edinburgh University Library.
Fletcher	Edited by David Daiches, *Fletcher of Saltoun, Selected Political Writings and Speeches.* (Edinburgh, 1979) (Unless otherwise stated, all references are to this edition.)
Fountainhall, *Notices*	Sir John Lauder of Fountainhall, *Historical Notices of Scotish* (sic) *Affairs* (Edinburgh, Bannatyne Club, 1848)
Fountainhall, *Observes*,	Sir John Lauder of Fountainhall, *Historical Observes; 1680–1686* (Edinburgh, Bannatyne Club, 1840)
Greg	Letters of William Greg in H.M.C., Fifteenth Report, Appendix Part IV. Manuscripts of the Duke of Portland Vol IV (London, 1897)
H.M.C.	Historical Manuscripts Commission.
Halkett	Manuscript *History of the Fletcher Family* EUL MS. La III 364.
Hume	Sir David Hume of Crossrigg, *Diary of the Proceedings in the Parliament and Privy Council of Scotland, May 21, 1700–March 7, 1707.* (Edinburgh, Bannatyne Club, 1828)
Jerviswoode	*Correspondence of George Baillie of Jerviswoode* (Edinburgh, Bannatyne Club, 1842)

Lockhart   *The Lockhart Papers, containing Memoirs and commentaries upon the Affairs of Scotland from 1702 to 1715 by George Lockhart, Esq. of Carnwath etc. 2 volumes*, (London, 1817)

Mar   *Report on the manuscripts of the Earl of Mar and Kellie* (H.M.C., London, 1904)

NLS   National Library of Scotland.

Ridpath   George Ridpath, *An account of the Proceedings of the Parliament of Scotland which met at Edinburgh, May 6, 1703* (Edinburgh, 1704.)

SHS   Scottish History Society

Seafield   Edited by P. Hume Brown, *Letters Relating to Scotland in the Reign of Queen Anne*, by James Ogilvy, First Earl of Seafield, and others. (SHS, Edinburgh 1915)

2. Secondary Sources

Hume Brown,   P. Hume Brown, *History of Scotland* 3 vols. (Cambridge, Edition of 1909)

Hume Brown,   (1914) P. Hume Brown, *The Legislative Union of England and Scotland.* (Ford Lectures, 1914) (Oxford, 1914)

Dalrymple   Sir John Dalrymple, *Memoirs of Great Britain and Ireland* 3 vols. (London, 1790)

Ferguson (1968)   William Ferguson, *Scotland, 1687 to the Present*, (Edinburgh 1968)

Ferguson (1977)   William Ferguson, *Scotland's Relations with England; a Survey to 1707.* (Edinburgh, 1977)

Macaulay   T. B. Macaulay, *History of England from the Accession of James III* Edited by G. H. Firth (London 1914)

Macfie   R. A. Scott Macfie, *A Bibliography of Andrew Fletcher Of Saltoun*, Publications of the Edinburgh Bibliographical Society, vol IV, Pt II October 1901.

Mackenzie   W. C. Mackenzie, *Andrew Fletcher of Saltoun: His Life and Times* (Edinburgh 1935)

Omond   G. W. T. Omond, *Fletcher of Saltoun* (Famous Scots Series, 1897)

Riley   P. W. J. Riley, *The Union of England and Scotland* (Manchester, 1978)

References

Introduction
1. Hume Brown (1914) p 3.
2. Edited by Leslie A. Marchand, *Byron's Letters and Journals* vol 9 (London (1979) p 156).
3. As 1. pp 4, 5.
4. Sir Walter Scott, *Tales of a Grandfather* Edition of 1889 (Edinburgh) p 770.
5. The full text is in H.M.C. MSS of Duke of Portland. Vol V (London 1899) pp 114–5.
6. Christopher Hill, *History and the Present*, Conway Memorial Lecture (London 1989) p 26.
7. For example, T. C. Smout, "The Road to Union" in *Britain After The Glorious Revolution*, edited by Geoffrey Holmes (London, 1969) p 184 and John Robertson; "Andrew Fletcher's Vision of Union" in *Scotland and England, 1286–1815* edited by Roger A. Mason. (Edinburgh, 1987) pp 203–4.

Chapter 1
1. Robert Burns, "Such a parcel of rogues in a nation." *Poems and Songs edited by James Kinsley. (London 1969) p 511.*
2. *EUL MS LaII 451–2.*
3. *Statistical Account of Scotland* (1791–1799) Reprint of 1975 vol II p 608.
4. Sir Walter Scott, *Tales of a Grandfather*, Edition of 1889 (Edinburgh) p 727.
5. William Anderson *The Scottish Nation* (Edinburgh 1863) vol II p 225.
6. Robert Chambers, *A Biographical Dictionary of Eminent Scotsmen* (Edinburgh, 1835) vol II p 317.
7. David Hume, *History of England*, Edition of 1835 (London) p 761.
8. Tobias Smollett, *History of England* of 1835 (London) p 929.
9. Dalrymple, Vol III, Part III Book VI, p 129.
10. Burnet vol III pp 23–4.
11. Clerk pp 48–9.
12. John Mackay, *Memoirs of the Secret Services of John Mackay* (London, 1733) pp 220–223.
13. Copy of above in British Library.
14. See my article, "The Secret Services of John Mackay" in *Scottish Literary Journal* vol 6 No. 1 (May 1979) pp 72–80.
15. Lockhart vol I p 75–77.
16. Ridpath. pp A4–5.
17. Robert Wodrow, *History of the Sufferings of the Church of Scotland from the Restauration to the Revolution.* Edition of 1830, (Glasgow) vol IV p 227
18. Macfie, p 119.

19. Thomas Hearne, Diary of 17th August, 1731 (cxxx, 126) quoted in Macfie, p 23.
20. James Boswell, *Boswell on the Grand Tour, Germany and Switzerland, 1764* edited by Frederick A Pottle (London 1953) p 43.
21. Ibid p 214.
22. Jean Jacques Rousseau, *Confessions*. Everyman's Library edition (London 1946) vol II p 235.
23. James Boswell, Op Cit. p 218.
24. EUL, MS La III 364.
25. EUL, MS La II 588.
26. J. R. MacDonald, "Andrew Fletcher, The Scottish Patriot" in *The Scottish Review*. July 1893, vol XXII (Paisley and London). p 73.
27. EUL, La III 364 pp 21, 22.
28. NLS, MSS Catalogue XII, MSS 1,6501–1,7880.
29. As 27 f 28.
30. NLS MSS 17,863 and 17,864.
31. EUL MS La II 588.
32. Quoted by Marinel Ash in *The Strange Death of Scottish History*, (Edinburgh 1980) p 37.
33. Hume Brown, *History* vol III pp 88–9.

Chapter 2

1. Ferguson (1977) p 173.
2. *Recollections respecting the Family of the Fletchers of Salton* (Edinburgh, 1803) p 2.
3. Edited by H. C. Foxcroft, *A Supplement to Burnet's History of My Own Time* (Oxford, 1902) pp 85–6.
4. Ibid p 88.
   Op. Cit. pp 19, 20, 39, 49.
   Bannatyne Club, Miscellany vol III, (1855).
7. Ibid p 392.
8. As 3. p 161.
9. Burnet, vol I, pp viii & ix. Vol III p 24.
10. Macaulay, vol II, chapter VII, pp 824–5.
11. *Statistical Account* vol X (Edinburgh 1792) Reprint of 1975 vol II p 608.
12. Burnet, vol V pp 98, 94.
13. Omond, p 12. Mackenzie p 5.
14. D. S. Erskine, Earl of Buchan, *Essay on the Life of Andrew Fletcher* (Edinburgh, 1742).
15. Dugald Stewart, *Collected Works*, ed Sir William Hamilton (Edinburgh 1884) vol I p 551.
16. NLS MSS 17,863 and 17,864.
17. Fletcher p 108
18. NLS MS 17, 861.
19. NLS MS 16,503 ff 57–8.
20. NLS MS 17,863.
21. Halkett f 28.
22. As 11. 1975 Reprint vol II p 600.
23. Miscellany X of the Scottish HIstory Society, (4th Series, Vol 2. Edinburgh, 1965) p 162.
24. NLS MS 17,864.
25. As 23., pp 150–163 and 166.
26. EUL MS La II 588.
27. Edward Gibbon, *Autobiography* (Everyman's Library Edition, London 1932) p 90.
28. As 2.

Chapter 3
1. R. L. Mackie, *King James IV of Scotland*. (Edinburgh, 1958) p 93.
2. Hume Brown, *History* Vol II, p 240.
3. Gordon Donaldson, *Scotland, James V–James VII*. (The Edinburgh History of Scotland, Vol 3.) (Edinburgh, 1965) p 276.
4. As 2. pp 276 and 240.
5. As 3. pp 268–9.
6. Quoted by Ferguson, (1977) p 100.
7. Bruce Galloway, *The Union of England and Scotland, 1603–1608*, (Edinburgh 1986) pp 82 and 71.
8. Ibid p 163.
9. James Anthony Froude, *History of England from the fall of Wolsey to the Defeat of the Spanish Armada*. (London 1873) Vol IV p 5.
10. Alexander Grant, *Independence and Nationhood; Scotland 1306–1469*. (The New History of Scotland. Vol 3) pp 153 and 172. As 3, p 291.
11. George E. Davie, *The Democratic Intellect*. (Edinburgh, 1961).
12. Hume Brown, *History* Vol II p 242.
13. *The Diary of James Melville, 1556–1601*. (Bannatyne Club, Edinburgh 1829) p 245.
14. *The Second Book of Discipline* in *A Source Book of Scottish History*, edited by William Croft Dickinson and Gordon Donaldson. 3 Vols. Vol 3 p 22.
15. As 3. pp 284–5.
16. Hume Brown, *History* Vol II p 240.
17. Hume Brown, *History* Vol II p 284.
18. H. A. L. Fisher. *A History of Europe* (London, 1938) p 650.
19. Hume Brown, *History* Vol II p 304.
20. The National Government. Text in *A Source Book of Scottish History*, edited by W. C. Dickinson and Gordon Donaldson. 3 Vols. Vol 2 p 101.
21. David Stevenson, *The Scottish Revolution, 1637–1644* (Newton Abbot, 1973) p 194 and Ferguson (1977), p 118.
22. The phrase is David Stevenson's in his book mentioned at 21.
23. Quoted by Ferguson. (1977), p 123.
24. As 18, p 658.
25. Hume Brown, *History* Vol II pp 384–5.
26. Hume Brown, *History* Vol II p 409.
27. Henry Cockburn, *Journal, 1831–1854*. 2 Vols (Edinburgh, 1874) Vol II, pp 30–31.
28. Robert Wodrow, *The History of the Sufferings of the Church of Scotland*, 4 Vols. (Glasgow, 1830) Vol IV, p 354.

Chapter 4
1. APS Vol VIII p 214.
2. Hume Brown, *History* Vol II p 401.
3. J. H. Burton, *History of Scotland*. 8 Vols. (Edinburgh, 1876). Vol VII pp 184–5.
4. Hume Brown, *History* Vol II p 390.
5. Ferguson, (1977) p 150.
6. Burnet, Vol II p 135.
7. APS Vol VIII p 216.
8. Fountainhall *Observes* p 277.
9. Hume Brown, *History* Vol II p 403.
10. APS Vol VIII p 219.
11. APS Vol VIII p 230.
12. Burnet Vol II p 139.
13. Fountainhall *Observes* p 280.

14. Fountainhall *Observes* p 270–271.
15. Omond p 16.
16. APS Vol VIII pp 238–9.
17. Fountainhall, *Observes* p 209
18. APS Vol VIII pp 244–5.
19. Burnet Vol II p 303.
20. APS Vol VIII p 245.
21. Hume Brown Vol II p 419.
22. Burnet Vol II p 312.
23. Fountainhall *Notices* Vol I p 270.
24. Fountainhall *Notices* Vol I p 281.
25. *The Register of the Privy Council of Scotland*, edited by P. Hume Brown. Third Series, Vol V (1676–1678) (Edinburgh, 1912). p 380 and Fountainhall *Notices* vol I p 352.
26. Halkett f 23.
27. HMC, 7th Report (London, 1879) Appendix p 343.

Chapter 5
1. Halket f 23.
2. Burnet Vol II pp 345 & 357.
3. Burnet Vol II p 370.
4. Fountainhall *Observes* pp 213–4.
5. Burnet Vol II p 346.
6. Burnet Vol II p 384.
7. Fountainhall *Notices* Vol I, p 572.
8. Macaulay Vol II pp 535–6.
9. Fountainhall *Observes* p 208.
10. Burnet, Vol III pp 23–4.
11. Burnet, Vol III pp 24–5 and foot-note 'P'. Dalrymple Vol II p 137.
12. Burnet, Vol III pp 44–5.
13. Halkett f 25.
14. James Ferguson, *Robert Ferguson, the Plotter* (Edinburgh, 1887) pp 220–221.
15. Halkett ff 28, 29, 30, 77.
16. Fountainhall *Notices* Vol I p 600.
17. Fountainhall *Observes* p 213–4.
18. Fountainhall *Observes* p 208.
19. Fountainhall *Notices* Vol I p 661.
20. Fountainhall *Notices* Vol I p 665.
21. Fountainhall *Notices* Vol I pp 690–1.
22. The Coltness Collection. (Maitland Club, 1842) pp 166–7. *A Journey in England, Holland and the Low Countries by Mrs Calderwood of Polton, 1756.*

Chapter 6
1. Scottish Record Office Misc 260/1 (Fletcher to Russell 8/1/1689). Quoted by T. C. Smout in his essay, "The Road to Union" in *Britain After the Glorious Revolution*, edited by Geoffrey Holmes. (London, 1969) pp 183–4.
2. Op. Cit. pp 183.
3. Ferguson, (1977) p 171.
4. P. H. Scott: *The Union of Scotland and England. (Edinburgh , 1979) p 22.*
5. See for example Bruce Galloway, *The Union of England and Scotland: 1603–1608* (Edinburgh 1986) and Brian P. Levack, *The Formation of the British State* (Oxford 1987).
6. Op. Cit. pp 5 and 6–7.

7. Hume Brown, *History* Vol III, p 24.
8. Burnet, Vol IV, p 1.
9. W. C. Dickinson and Gordon Donaldson, *A Source Book of Scottish History*. (London 1961), Vol 3, pp 200–207. APS Vol 4, pp 38–40.
10. Leven and Melville Papers. (Bannatyne Club, Edinburgh, 1843) p 159.
11. Ibid p 10.
12. As 9. *Source Book* p 207. APS Vol IX p 45.
13. As 9. *Source Book* pp 240–241. APS Vol IX p 113.
14. See Chapter 1 above.
15. Lockhart, Vol I, p 75. See Chapter I above.
16. Robert Wodrow: *Analecta* (Maitland Club, Edinburgh; 1842) Vol II p 46.
17. David Stuart Erskine, Earl of Buchan, *Essays on the Lives and writings of Fletcher of Saltoun and the poet Thomson*, (London 1792). p 45.
18. Dalrymple, Vol III Appendix to Part II, Book VI p 208.

Chapter 7
1. Hume Brown, *History* Vol III, p 24.
2. Fletcher p 31.
3. Ferguson, (1968) pp 78–9.
4. Hume Brown, *History* Vol III pp 25–6.
5. John Prebble, *The Darien Disaster* (London, 1968) pp 12–15.
6. Dalrymple, Vol III, Part III; Book VI. pp 128–9.
7. Hume Brown, *History* Vol III, p 30.
8. John Prebble, Op Cit p 107.
9. Fletcher p 30.
10. James Mackinnon, *The Union of England and Scotland* (London 1876) p 15, quoted in Ferguson p 178.
11. Fletcher p 29.
12. Omond, p 48.
13. Fletcher p 34.
14. Defoe, *History* p 33.

Chapter 8
1. Caroline Robbins, *The Eighteenth-Century Commonwealthman*. (Cambridge, Mass, 1959) pp 20, 89, 11, 9. I am indebted to Bruce Lenman for this reference.
2. Ibid pp 4, 5, 6.
3. Ibid pp 8, 9, 16, 20, 178.
4. J. G. A. Pocock, "Machiavelli, Harrington and English Political Ideologies in the Eighteenth Century" (1965) in *Politics, Language and Time*. (London, 1973) pp 104–147.
5. Ibid pp 110 and 114.
6. Ibid P 139.
7. Dugald Stewart, "Account of the Life and Writings of Adam Smith" (1793) in *Collected Works*, edited by Sir William Hamilton (Edinburgh 1858) Vol X p 34.
8. Lord Kames: *Sketches of the HIstory of Man*. Vol I p 185.
9. Adam Ferguson, *An essay on the History of Civil Society* (1767), (Edinburgh, 1966) p 122.
10. Ibid p 19.
11. Fletcher pp 12, 18.
12. Ibid 12, 3.

13. Ibid 4, 5, 6.
14. J. G. A. Pocock Op Cit pp 139–140.
15. J. G. A. Pocock, *The Machiavellian Moment* (Princeton, 1975) p 428.
16. Ibid p 431.
17. Fletcher p 4.
18. Nicholas Phillipson, "The Scottish Enlightenment" in *The Enlightenment in National Context*, edited by Roy Porter and Mikulaus Teich (Cambridge 1981) pp 19–40, especially 24 & 25. John Robertson, "The Scottish Enlightenment at the limits of the civil tradition", in *Wealth and Virtue*, edited by Istvan Hont and Michael Ignatieff (Cambridge 1983) pp 141–151. John Robertson: *The Scottish Enlightenment and the MIlitia Issue* (Edinburgh 1985) pp 22–59.
19. Fletcher p 31.
20. John Robertson (1985) pp 34 & 33.
21. Fletcher p xi.
22. Fletcher pp 13, 14, 24, 20, 21, 22.
23. J. G. A. Pocock (1965) pp 129, 131.
24. Fletcher p 29.
25. For example, John Robertson (1985) p 33.
26. Fletcher pp 20, 21.
27. Op Cit p 25.
28. Fletcher pp 8–9, 31, 37.
29. Fletcher pp 35, 37, 33, 32–3.
30. Fletcher pp 32, 129–130.
31. Fletcher p 46.
32. Fletcher pp 47–50.
33. Fletcher pp 51, 52, 56.
34. Fletcher pp 56, 65.
35. Hugh Millar – Op Cit, Edition edited by W. F. Laughlan (Hawick, 1983) p 213.
36. Fletcher p 52.
37. Macaulay, Vol II Chapter v, p 535.
38. For example, Tam Dalyell, *Devolution: The End of Britain*. (London, 1977) p 281.
39. *Edinburgh Review* Vol 189, Jan 1879, pp 119–148.
40. Op Cit Vol II, p 201.
41. Ramsay MacDonald in *Scottish Review* Vol XXII no XLIII, July 1893.
42. Fletcher pp 58, 61–2.
43. Macfie, P 128.
44. EUL MS La II 588.
45. John Robertson, "Andrew Fletcher's Version of Union" in *Scotland and England 1286–1815*, edited by Roger A Mason (Edinburgh 1987) pp 216–217.
46. As 43
47. Andrew Fletcher, *Political Works* (Glasgow, 1749) p 179.
48. Fletcher p 8.
49. Dalrymple, Appendix No VIII fn on pp 332–333.
50. See Chapter 1 at fn 11.
51. Edward Topham: *Letters from Edinburgh* (1776) fascimile edition (Edinburgh 1971) p 55.
52. Alexander Carlyle: *Autobiography* (1722–1805), edited by John Hill Burton (London and Edinburgh, 1910) p 453.
53. As 43.
54. John Robertson makes this point in a footnote to his essay, "Andrew Fletcher's Version of Union" (fn 45 above) p 220 fn 2.
55. NLS MS Number 17863, ff 87, 88.

56. Robert Wodrow, *Analecta* (1712), Maitland Club (Edinburgh, 1842) 2 Vols, Vol II, p 46.
57. As 55. f 70.
58. Op Cit pp 19, 54, 55.
59. Ibid p 57.
60. As 43, p 141.
61. EUL MS LA III, 364 ff 37–38.

Chapter 9
1. Burnet Vol V, p 13.
2. William Ferguson, "The Making of the Treaty of Union" in *Scottish Historical Review* Vol 43 (1964) p 91.
3. Fletcher pp 96–7.
4. Ridpath p 2.
5. See Chapter 7 of my *1707: The Union of Scotland and England* (Edinburgh, 1979) and below.
6. Lockhart Vol I pp 45 and 52.
7. Lockhart Vol I pp 55–6.
8. Clerk p 57.
9. Lockhart Vol I pp 71 and 27.
10. Ferguson (1970) p 207.
11. John Robertson, "The Scottish Enlightenment at the limits of the civic tradition". in *Wealth and Virtue*, edited by Istvan Hont and Michael Ignatieff (Cambridge, 1983) p 141.
12. Robertson Op Cit and Nicholas Phillipson, "The Scottish Enlightenment" in *The Enlightenment in National Context*, edited by Roy Porter and Mikulas Teich (Cambridge 1981) p 25.
13. APS Vol XI p 37.
14. Ridpath pp 24–27.
15. APS Vol XI pp 41
16. Ridpath p 35.
17. Fletcher p 69.
18. APS Vol XI p 45; Ridpath p 36.
19. Hume p 100.
20. APS Vol XI p 45; Fletcher pp 69–70; Hume p 102.
21. Ridpath p 47–8 et seg.
22. Hume p 104.
23. Ridpath p 73.
24. Fletcher p 73.
25. APS Vol XI pp 47–67; Hume p 109.
26. Hume pp 105–110; APS Vol XI pp 65–67; Clerk p 49.
27. Ridpath p 132.
28. Fletcher pp 70–72.
29. Hume p 115.
30. APS Vol XI p 68; Fletcher pp 73; 76–80; Hume p 115.
31. Fletcher pp 74–6.
32. Hume p 115; Fletcher pp 81–82.
33. Hume pp 115–6; APS Vol XI p 68.
34. Hume p 117.
35. Hume p 117; APS Vol XI p 69.
36. Hume p 117.
37. Hume pp 118–19; APS Vol XI p 69.
38. APS Vol XI p 69; Hume pp 119–20.

39. Lockhart Vol I p 207.
40. Riley p 58.
41. Ridpath p 193.
42. Ridpath pp 302–3. On this point see my *1707* (fn 5 above).
43. Ridpath p 194; Hume pp 120–121; APS Vol XI p 70.
44. Ridpath pp 242–249.
45. APS Vol XI pp 136–137.
46. Clerk pp 53–4.
47. Ridpath p 219; Hume p 123; APS Vol XI p 73.
48. Fletcher pp 89–90; Hume p 124.
49. APS Vol XI pp 73–74.
50. Fletcher pp 83–4.
51. Fletcher pp 84–5; APS Vol XI p 74.
52. APS Vol XI p 74; Hume p 126; Fletcher p 85.
53. Ridpath p 271; Lockhart Vol I pp 68–9.
54. Hume Brown *History* Vol III p 91; Halkett f 36.
55. Fletcher p 75; APS Vol XI p 75–6.
56. Fletcher p 33.
57. APS Vol XI p 84; Hume p 131; Ridpath pp 322–328.
58. Hume p 131; Ridpath p 328; APS Vol XI p 84.
59. Ridpath p 331.
60. Ridpath p 304.
61. Fletcher p 91.
62. Fletcher p 92.
63. Fletcher pp 90–93; APS Vol XI pp 77, 101, 102.
64. Hume pp 133; Fletcher pp 85–89; APS Vol XI p 101.
65. APS Vol XI p 101.
66. Fletcher p 102; APS Vol XI p 102.
67. Hume p 135; Fletcher pp 94–99.
68. Lockhart Vol I pp 69–70; Hume p 135.
69. APS Vol XI p 112.
70. Riley pp 56 and 59.
71. Burnet Vol V p 98.
72. Ferguson (1977) p 207.
73. Ridpath pp A4–5.

Chapter 10

1. Fletcher p 96.
2. Lockhart Vol I p 77.
3. Mar p 242.
4. Mackenzie p 346 fns 1 and 2; Fletcher p 123.
5. Fletcher pp 106.
6. Fletcher pp 106, 108, 132.
7. Fletcher pp 110–113.
8. Fletcher pp 113–114.
9. Fletcher pp 115–116.
10. Fletcher pp 116–118.
11. Fletcher pp 119.
12. Fletcher pp 119–120.
13. Fletcher p 120.
14. Fletcher pp 121, 122, 123, 126.
15. Fletcher pp 127–128.
16. Fletcher pp 129–130.

17. Fletcher pp 130, 131, 132.
18. Fletcher pp 131–132.
19. Fletcher pp 134–135.
20. Fletcher p 136.
21. Fletcher p 136.
22. Fletcher p 137.
23. Chapter 6 above fn 1.
24. Fletcher p 65.
25. John Robertson, "Andrew Fletcher's Version of Union" in *Scotland and England 1286–1815*. Edited by Roger A. Mason. (Edinburgh) 1987 p 213.
26. Ibid pp 218–219.

Chapter 11
1. John S. Gibson, *Playing the Scottish Card; The Franco-Jacobite Invasion of 1708*. (Edinburgh, 1988), especially chapter 2, Part I.
2. Ferguson (1977) p 214.
3. Lockhart Vol I pp 78–9, 82; Gibson, Op Cit p 26.
4. Burnet Vol I p 133; Ferguson p 216; Hume Brown *History* Vol III p 92.
5. Lockhart Vol I p 97.
6. Fletcher p 70.
7. NLS MS 7102.
8. Ibid ff 13, 14, 15, 16.
9. Ibid ff 18, 19.
10. Burnet Vol V pp 167–9; Lockhart Vol I p 96–7; Mar p 228; Hume p 139.
11. Lockhart Vol I p 98; Mar p 229.
12. Seafield p 14.
13. APS Vol XI p 126.
14. Seafield p 150.
15. Hume p 137.
16. Hume p 138.
17. Lockhart Vol I p 100.
18. Seafield pp 137–8.
19. Lockhart Vol I p 100; Hume p 139.
20. APS Vol XI p 127–8; Seafield p 138; Hume p 140; Lockhart Vol I pp 101–2.
21. Lockhart Vol I p 102.
22. Lockhart Vol I p 102–3.
23. Burnet Vol V p 171.
24. Burnet Vol V p 171–2.
25. NLS MS 7121 f 30.
26. Hume pp 129–148; APS Vol XI pp 128–130.
27. Hume p 148.
28. NLS MS 7121 ff 34, 36, 38.
29. Adam Smith, *The Wealth of Nations*. (Everyman's Library, Edition, London 1971). Vol II p 113.
30. APS Vol XI pp 133–137; Hume p 151; Clark p 53.
31. Hume pp 145, 147–8.
32. Hume pp 139–140, 152; Lockhart Vol I pp 103–104.
33. Hume p 144; Lockhart Vol I p 106.
34. Edited by James Grant: *Correspondence of James, fourth Earl of Findlater and first Earl of Seafield* (Edinburgh, SHS, 1912) pp 378–9.
35. Hume p 158.
36. Mar p 289.
37. Hume p 160.

38. *Letters of George Lockhart of Carnwath*, edited by David Szechi. (Edinburgh, Scottish History Society, 1989) p 15.
39. Mar p 231.
40. Seafield p 139.
41. Hume p 162; APS Vol XI p 204.
42. Fletcher p 71.
43. See my *1707; The Union of Scotland and England* (Edinburgh 1979), especially chapter 7.
44. As 34 above, p 382.
45. N. T. Phillipson in "Culture and Society in the 18th Century Province: The Case of Edinburgh and the Scottish Enlightment" in *The University in Society*. (Princeton, 1975) Vol II p 417.
46. Carstares pp 583–586.
47. For a study of Defoe's activities in Scotland see my essay in *Blackwood's Magazine* No 1944, Vol 322 of October 1977, pp 334–347.
48. Jerviswood p 21.
49. Jerviswood p 22.
50. Jerviswood p 47.

Chapter 12
1. Defoe *History* pp 52–3.
2. Defoe *History* p 50.
3. Defoe *History* p 74.
4. Burnet Vol V pp 174–5.
5. Burnet Vol V p 175.
6. Bruce Lenman, *The Jacobite Risings in Britain, 1687–1746*, (London, 1980 pp 80–81; Burnet Vol V p 277.
7. Bruce Galloway, *The Union of England and Scotland, 1603–1608* (Edinburgh 1986) pp 151–157; Defoe *History* p 86, 54.
8. Hume Brown *History* Vol III p 95.
9. Defoe *History* p 33.
10. Riley, p 127 quoting *Scottish History Review* (1922) p 191.
11. Lockhart Vol I p 114.
12. Burnet Vol V p 181.
13. Lockhart Vol I p 115.
14. Seafield p 49.
15. Argyle Vol I pp 9, 14–15, 18–21, 21–24, 25–26, 29–31.
16. Mar p 270.
17. Lockhart Vol I p 110.
18. As 15. p 9.
19. Seafield p XXV.
20. As 15. p 54.
21. Lockhart Vol I p 52.
22. Seafield p VIII.
23. Fletcher p 71.
24. Lockhart Vol I pp 114–115.
25. Greg. p 199.
26. APS Vol XI, pp 213–4.
27. Burnet Vol V p 221.
28. As 15, pp 35–39.
29. Seafield p 49.
30. Burnet, Vol V, p 221.
31. APS Vol XI p 215.

32. Hume p 162.
33. Mar p 234; Seafield p 58; Greg pp 197, 207.
34. Mar p 234.
35. APS Vol XI p 216.
36. Hume p 165.
37. Seafield p 60.
38. APS Vol XI p 238.
39. APS Vol XI pp 216 & 217.
40. APS Vol XI p 217; Seafield p 64.
41. Lockhart Vol I p 116.
42. Seafield pp 62, 65, 66; Hume p 167; APS Vol XI p 218; Greg p 215.
43. Hume p 167; APS Vol XI p 219.
44. APS Vol XI pp 219, 222; Hume pp 168, 169; Seafield pp 68, 69.
45. APS Vol XI p 221.
46. APS Vol XI p 222; Seafield pp 72–76; Lockhart Vol I pp 120–124; Greg pp 223–5.
47. Seafield p 73.
48. Seafield p 74.
49. Seafield p 75; APS Vol XI p 223.
50. Seafield pp 78.
51. APS Vol XI p 223; Seafield pp 78–80.
52. Seafield pp 76–77.
53. Seafield pp 80, 81; APS Vol XI p 224.
54. Mar p 235.
55. APS Vol XI p 295.
56. APS Vol XI p 224; Hume p 170; Greg p 232.
57. Lockhart Vol I p 127.
58. APS Vol XI p 224; Seafield pp 85, 86.
59. APS Vol XI p 225–235.
60. APS Vol XI p 236; Seafield p 85; Lockhart Vol I pp 127–130.
61. Seafield p 85; Lockhart Vol I p 130.
62. Seafield p 85.
63. Hume p 171; APS Vol XI p 236.
64. APS Vol XI p 236; Hume p 171.
65. APS Vol XI p 236; Hume p 171.
66. Lockhart Vol I p 132.
67. Greg p 239; Joseph Taylor, *A Journey To Edenborough* (Edinburgh, 1903) pp 113, 115–7.
68. Seafield p 87.
69. Lockhart Vol I pp 134–5.
70. Mar p 235.
71. Seafield p 87.
72. Seafield pp 88–9.
73. Lockhart Vol I p 136.
74. Clark p 57.
75. Seafield p 71.
76. G. M. Trevelyan *England Under Queen Anne* (London, 1932) Vol II pp 224–5.
77. Clerk p 57.
78. Jerviswood pp 35–6.
79. Greg p 171.
80. HMC 10th Report App. Pt IV (1885) p 340.
81. Ibid.
82. Clerk p 57.
83. Lockhart Vol I pp 55–6.
84. APS Vol XI pp 237–8.

85. APS Vol XI pp 239, 245; Greg pp 242, 243, 245.
86. APS Vol XI pp 243, 244, 292, 299.
87. Seafield p 90.

Chapter 13
 1. Mar p 243.
 2. Mar pp 250–1.
 3. Riley p 183.
 4. Riley p 183.
 5. Riley pp 177–8.
 6. Burnet Vol V p 240.
 7. Burnet Vol V pp 240–241.
 8. Jerviswood p 28.
 9. Mar p 255.
10. J. Mackinnon *The Union of England and Scotland* (London 1896) p 219.
11. Mar p 289 and p 285.
12. Lockhart Vol I pp 142–3.
13. Clerk p 58.
14. Ferguson (1977) p 234.
15. Burnet Vol V p 255.
16. Clerk p 60.
17. Mar p 267.
18. APS Vol XI p 221.
19. Mar p 267.
20. APS Vol XI p 236; Seafield p 85; Lockhart Vol I pp 127–30. See Chapter 12 above.
21. Mar p 239.
22. Mar pp 242, 243, 254, 258.
23. Carstares pp 743–4.
24. APS Vol XI Appendix p 165.
25. APS Vol XI p 165.
26. Carstares pp 743–4.
27. APS Vol XI Appendix p 166.
28. as 27.
29. Lockhart Vol I pp 152–4.
30. Lockhart Vol I p 128.
31. Ferguson (1977) p 235.
32. APS Vol XI Appendix pp 166–7.
33. Ibid p 169.
34. Ibid p 171.
35. Ibid pp 171, 173–4.
36. Ibid pp 174–5.
37. Ibid pp 176–7; 179–80.
38. Ibid pp 178–180.
39. Burnet Vol V pp 274; 286; Ferguson (1977) p 236.
40. APS Vol XI Appendix pp 180–183.
41. John Hill Burton, *The History of Scotland* (Edinburgh & London 1873) Vol VIII p 131.
42. APS Vol XI Appendix pp 181–2.
43. Ibid pp 184, 186.
44. Ibid p 182.
45. Ibid p 184.
46. Sir Walter Scott, *Tales of a Grandfather*, Edition of 1889 p 769.

47. APS Vol XI Appendix p 185.
48. Bruce Galloway, *The Union of England and Scotland, 1603–1608* (Edinburgh, 1986) p 82.
49. APS Vol XI Appendix p 185–6, 187.
50. Ibid pp 189–90.
51. Ibid pp 190–1.
52. Mar p 271; Clark p 63.
53. Burnet Vol V p 273.
54. Lockhart Vol I pp 156–7.
55. Mar p 271.
56. Daniel Defoe *Review* (London) Vol III, No. 131, 2 Nov 1706.
57. Op Cit (London 1706) p 26.
58. Op Cit pp 66–7.
59. A. V. Dicey and R. S. Rait, *Thoughts on the Union Between England and Scotland* (London, 1920) p 362.
60. This is discussed in my pamphlets, *In Bed with an Elephant*, (Edinburgh, 1985 Saltire Society) and *Cultural Independence* (Scottish Centre for Economic and Social Research, Edinburgh 1989).
61. Daniel Defoe, *A Fourth Essay etc* (1706) pp 8, 26.
62. Burnet Vol V p 284.
63. Edited L. W. Sharp, *Eaely Letters of Robert Woodrow (1698–1709).* (Edinburgh, SHS, 1937) p 291.
64. Robert Burns, NLS MS Acc 8810.
65. Seafield p VIII.
66. Hume Brown (1914) p 128.
67. Mar pp 238, 242, 243, 250–1, 258–9.
68. Jerviswood p 68.
69. Fletcher pp 117–120.
70. Daniel Defoe Op Cit Vol III p 33.
71. Sir Walter Scott as fn 46, p 753.
72. Burnet, Vol V pp 291–2.
73. Op Cit (Edinburgh 1982) p 23.
74. Burnet Vol V pp 292–3.
75. Defoe *History* p 95.
76. Jerviswood p 28.
77. HMC 14th Report. Appendix Part III pp 198–199.
78. Fletcher pp 13, 81, 83–4; Appendices I & II.
79. Fletcher pp 83–4.
80. Op Cit pp 22, 4, 20.
81. Op Cit pp 20, 29.
82. Op Cit p 20.
83. SHS, 4th Series, Vol 2, *Miscellany X* (1965) p 197.
84. T. B. Smith, "The Union of 1707 as Fundamental Law" in *Studies Critical and Comparative* (Edinburgh 1962) p 9.
85. Gordon Donaldson, *Scotland: The Shaping of a Nation* (Newton Abbot and London, 1974) p 57.
86. Riley pp 281, 177–8, 314.

Chapter 14

1. Dalrymple, *Appendix No VII p 332.*
2. McFie pp 133–135.
3. Andrew Fletcher, State of the Controversy Betwixt United and Separate Parliaments. *ed P. H. Scott (Edinburgh, Saltire Society, 1982)* pp 12, 14–15.

 4. Ibid pp 28, 15, 29, 31; Fletcher p 120.
 5. Ibid pp 21, 23, 27.
 6. Ibid pp 22, 23.
 7. Ibid pp 31, 32–33.
 8. Jerviswood p 154.
 9. Mar pp 267–8.
10. Ibid p 272.
11. Ibid p 273.

Chapter 15
 1. Burnet Vol V p 292.
 2. Argyle p 2.
 3. Mar p 270.
 4. Mar p 279.
 5. Mar p 291.
 6. Mar pp 272, 278–9, 280.
 7. Defoe *Letters* pp 132–6.
 8. Defoe *History* pp 33, 64, 246, 229.
 9. Ibid p 229.
10. Ibid p 232.
11. Ibid p 229.
12. Lockhart Vol I pp 171–2.
13. Brian P. Levack, *The Formation of the British State* (Oxford, 1987) p 164.
14. Ibid p 151.
15. Mar p 315.
16. Defoe *Letters* p 226.
17. Levack Op Cit p 20.
18. Lockhart Vol I p 169.
19. Robert Wodrow, quoted in Chapter 13 above fn 63.
20. Defoe *History* Appendix Px pp 630–1.
21. Hume Brown (1914) p 131.
22. Levack Op Cit pp 105, 121.
23. Mar pp 284–5.
24. Seafield p 94.
25. Jerviswoode p 138.
26. Mar p 379.
27. Ibid pp 290, 294.
28. Lockhart Vol I pp 262, 272.
29. B. M. Add ms 34,180.
30. HMC Portland MSS Vol V (London 1899) pp 114–5.
31. Argyle Vol I p 54.
32. Lockhart Vol I p 271.
33. Mar p 286.
34. Lockhart Vol I p 272.
35. Sir Walter Scott Op Cit (Edition of 1889) p 769.
36. Lockhart Vol I p 189.
37. See Chapter 17 below.
38. Mar p 336.
39. Lockhart Vol I pp 264–6.
40. Mar p 353.
41. Argyle pp 49–52.
42. Op Cit Chapter 42.
43. Defoe *History* p 236.

44. Mar p 329.
45. Lockhart Vol I p 159.
46. Defoe *History* p 226.

Chapter 16
1. Hume Brown (1914) p 116.
2. APS Vol XI pp 305–6.
3. APS Vol XI p 307, Hume pp 173–4, Mar p 290.
4. Seafield pp 96–97; Mar p 292.
5. Lockhart Vol I p 162; Mar p 294.
6. Mar p 293; Defoe *Letters* pp 132–136.
7. Hume p 174; Mar p 300.
8. Mar pp 304, 306; Hume p 177.
9. Mar pp 302, 305, 307.
10. Hume p 178.
11. Defoe *History* pp 632–6.
12. Mar pp 308, 309.
13. Lockhart Vol I p 180; Mar p 309.
14. Hume Brown (1914) pp 117–8.
15. Defoe History pp 312 and 313–316.
16. Defoe *History* p 254.
17. APS Vol XI p 312; Lockhart Vol I pp 179; Hume p 179.
18. Lockhart Vol I pp 177–8.
19. Mar p 312; APS Vol XI p 312; Burnet Vol V p 277.
20. APS Vol XI p 312; Lockhart Vol I pp 183–4.
21. APS Vol XI p 312; Hume p 179.
22. APS Vol XI p 316; Hume pp 179–80; Mar p 317.
23. Mar p 318; APS Vol XI p 319.
24. APS Vol XI p 320; Hume p 182.
25. Hume Brown *History* Vol III p 118.
26. APS Vol XI p 320; Hume p 182; Mar p 318.
27. Mar pp 315, 319, 326.
28. APS Vol XI pp 319, 299.
29. APS Vol XI p 322; Hume p 182; Mar pp 321–2.
30. Mar pp 323–5; Lockhart Vol I pp 170–1.
31. Mar pp 320 & 328.
32. Defoe *History* p 387; Hume p 188.
33. Daniel Defoe, *A Fifth Essay at Removing National Prejudices* (1707) p 7.
34. Mar p 325; APS Vol XI p 325; Hume p 182.
35. Defoe Op Cit pp 8, 26; APS Vol XI p 328; Mar pp 326–9; Hume p 183.
36. APS Vol XI p 328; Hume p 183, Mar pp 325, 329.
37. Mar pp 327–8; Defoe History p 231.
38. Lockhart Vol I pp 194–196; Defoe *History* pp 614–514.
39. Mar p 335; APS Vol XI p 340; Hume p 187; Lockhart Vol I pp 196–201.
40. Hume p 184; APS Vol XI pp 331–2; Mar pp 328, 330.
41. Mar pp 331, 328, 330.
42. Mar p 338.
43. Mar p 350; Hume pp 189–190.
44. Mar pp 349, 352; Hume pp 190, 192.
45. Mar p 363; Hume p 190.
46. Hume pp 188, 191; Defoe *History* pp 387, 627–8.
47. George E. Davie, *The Scottish Enlightenment* (London, 1981) p 5.
48. APS Vol XI pp 369–371.

49. Lockhart Vol I pp 201–3.
50. Lockhart Vol I pp 203–5.
51. APS Vol XI pp 369, 372; Lockhart Vol I p 177.
52. Defoe *History* p 441.
53. Defoe *History* p 445.
54. Defoe *History* p 458; APS Vol XI p 383.
55. Defoe *History* p 449.
56. APS Vol XI pp 383, 401, 396, Defoe *History*.
57. Defoe, *History* p 447.
58. Hume-Brown, *History* Vol II p 123.
59. APS Vol XI pp 386–391; Defoe *History* p 462.
60. APS Vol XI pp 386–7.
61. APS Vol XI p 387.
62. APS Vol XI p 386.
63. APS Vol XI p 391.
64. Lockhart Vol I pp 206–214.
65. Lockhart Vol I pp 207–211.
66. Lockhart Vol I p 214.
67. Lockhart Vol I pp 212–214.
68. Edited by Daniel Szechi, *Letters of George Lockhart of Carnwath* (Edinburgh, SHS 1989) p 15.
69. Lockhart Vol I p 211.
70. APS Vol XI pp 396–404; Lockhart Vol I p 223.
71. Burnet Vol V p 284.
72. Defoe *History* pp 475, 484–5.
73. Clerk pp 67–69.
74. Mar p 389.

Chapter 17

1. APS Vol XI pp 427–8.
2. Hume p 197; APS Vol XI p 418.
3. Defoe *History* p 500.
4. APS Vol XI p 491.
5. Omond pp 138–9.
6. NLS MS 16502 ff 208–9.
7. Fletcher pp 25–6; 135.
8. Sir John Gibson, *Playing the Scottish Card* (Edinburgh, 1988).
9. Mar p 435.
10. Mar p 436.
11. Mar p 272.
12. Opt Cit p 24.
13. Mar p 421.
14. Hume Brown *History* Vol III p 145.
15. Mar p 447.
16. Mar p 437.
17. NLS MS 17863.
18. Robert Somerville, *General View of the Agriculture of East Lothian.* (London, 1805) pp 294–6.
19. NLS MS 16503 f 77.
20. Op Cit. (Published by Oliver and Boyd, Edinburgh, 1803) p 2.
21. Edited by Daniel Szechi, *Letters of George Lockhart of Carnwath* (Edinburgh, SHS, 1989) pp 54–6.
22. NLS MS 16503 ff 57–8.

23. As 21 above, p 73.
24. NLS MS 16503 f 120.
25. as 24. above f 92.
26. In *Miscellany* Vol X of the SHS (Edinburgh 1965) pp 145, 147.
27. Ibid p 156.
28. Ibid pp 149, 150, 152, 153–4, 157.
29. NLS MS 16503 ff 90–91; 135–6.
30. As 26. above, pp 165–7.
31. Ibid p 167.
32. Ibid p 168.
33. Ibid pp 169, 170.
34. Ibid p 150.
35. Robert Chambers *Biographical Dictionary of Eminent Scotsmen* (Glasgow, 1835) Vol II pp 39–40.
36. As 26. above, p 171.

Chapter 18
1. Lord Murray: from the typescript of his speech (1982) in Saltire Society archives; Tom Scott in *Chapman* No. 54, Autumn 1988, p 84.
2. John Robertson: "The Scottish Enlightenment at the limits of the civic tradition", in *Wealth and Virtue* edited by Istvan Hont and Michael Ignatieff (Cambridge, 1983) p 141.
3. See Chapter 1 above.
4. Fletcher pp 131–2.
5. Geoffrey Burrow: from typescript of speech (1985) in Saltire Society archives; Andrew Fletcher letter in *Miscellany X* (1965) p 164.
6. *Letters of George Lockhart of Carnwath*, edited by Daniel Szechi (SHS, Edinburgh, 1989) p 15.
7. Lockhart Vol I p 77.
8. As 2 above.
9. Ibid fn 5.
10. Nicholas Phillipson. "The Scottish Enlightenment" in *The Enlightenment in National Context* edited by Roy Porter and Nicholas Teich (Cambridge 1981) p 25.
11. John Robertson in "Andrew Fletcher's Vision of Union" in *Scotland and England, 1286–1815, edited by Roger A Mason (Edinburgh, 1987) pp 215 & 212.*
12. John Robertson: "The Political Intelligence of Andrew Fletcher of Saltoun" in *Chapman* No. 61/62 (September 1990) p 113.
13. I. G. A. Pocock: *The Machiavellian Moment: Florentine Political Thought and the Atlantic Republican Tradition* (Princeton, 1975) p 427 and "Machiavelli, Harrington and English Political Ideologies in the Eighteenth Century" in the *William and Mary Quarterly* 3″ Series Vol XXII No. 4 (October, 1965). Reprinted in *Politics, Language and Time.* (New York 1971, London edition of 1773) p 139.
14. John Robertson, *The Scottish Enlightenment and the Militia Issue* (Edinburgh, 1985) p 37.
15. Roger L. Emerson, "Science and Moral Philosophy in the Scottish Enlightenment" in *Oxford Studies in the History of Philosophy: Vol I, Studies in the Philosophy of the Scottish Enlightenment.* (Oxford, 1990) p 33.
16. *Proposals for carrying on certain Public Works in the City of Edinburgh* (Edinburgh 1752). Attributed to Sir Gilbert Elliott. p 9. Quoted by A. J. Youngson in The Making of Classical Edinburgh. (Edinburgh, 1966) p 6.
    (I am grateful to George Davie for drawing my attention to this reference).
17. David Hume. *History of England*; Edition of 1835 (London) p 761.

18. George Davie *The Scottish Enlightenment*, Historical Association Pamphlet. No. GS 99 (London 1981) pp 21–24.

19. Nicholas Phillipson, "Scottish Public Opinion and the Union in the Age of the Association" in *Scotland in the Age of Improvement*, edited by N. T. Phillipson and Rosalind Mitchison. (Edinburgh 1970) p 126. Bruce Lenman in "Aristocratic Country Whiggery in Scotland and the American Revolution" in *Scotland and America in the Age of the Enlightenment*. Edited by Richard B. Sher and Jeffrey R. Smitten (Edinburgh 1990) p 184.

20. Caroline Robbins *The Eighteenth Century Commonwealthman* (Cambridge, Mass. 1959) pp 20, 178.

21. Bruce Lenman Op Cit p 188.

22. Ibid p 184.

23. Thomas Paine, *Rights of Man* edited by Eric Foner, (Harmondsworth, 1988) pp 143, 156, 83, 176.

24. See Chapter 1 above.

25. Henry W. Meikle: *Scotland and the French Revolution* (Glasgow 1912) p 169.

26. Ibid p 175.

27. Op Cit pp iv, v.

28. James Aikman, *The History of Scotland, Translated from the Latin of George Buchanan (Edinburgh, 1827) pp 527–8, 532–3, 544–5, 556, 534, 527.* (I am indebted to a reference by Bruce Lenman in the work cited at fn 19 above p 184.

29. John Hill Burton, *The History of Scotland* 8 Vols, 2nd Edition (Edinburgh, 1873) Vol 8, pp 5–8.

30. See Chapter 8 at fn 41.

31. Op Cit p 8.

32. A number of these addresses have been published: Gordon Donaldson (1979) in *The Scottish Review* No. 17 pp 21–26 (Feb 1980); Bruce Lemman (1987) and Arnold Kemp (1990) in *Radical Scotland* No. 29 (Oct/Nov 1987) pp 25–27.

33. Op Cit. pp 21–22.

34. Allan Massie, *101 Great Scots*, (Edinburgh, 1987) pp 80–81.

35. Op Cit p 27.

36. Neal Ascherson, "A Step Nearer Utopia", in *Observer, Scotland* 9 July 1989, p 10.

37. John Robertson, "The Political Intelligence of Andrew Fletcher of Saltoun" in *Chapman* No. 61/62. (Sept. 1990) pp 107, 114, 115.

INDEX